ARENA LEGACY

The Western Legacies Series

Published in Cooperation with the
NATIONAL COWBOY & WESTERN HERITAGE MUSEUM

ARENA LEGACY
The Heritage of American Rodeo

Richard C. Rattenbury

Foreword by **Larry Mahan**

Collection Photography by **Ed Muno**

University of Oklahoma Press : Norman

Also by Richard Rattenbury

The Art of American Arms Makers: Marketing Guns, Ammunition and Western Adventure

The Browning Connection: Patent Prototypes in the Winchester Museum

Hunting the American West: The Pursuit of Big Game for Life, Profit, and Sport, 1800–1900

Packing Iron: Gunleather of the Frontier West

Arena Legacy: The Heritage of American Rodeo is Volume 8 in the Western Legacies Series.

LIBRARY OF CONGRESS CATALOGING-IN-PUBLICATION DATA

Rattenbury, Richard.

  Arena legacy : the heritage of American rodeo / Richard C. Rattenbury ; foreword by Larry Mahan ; collection photography by Ed Muno.

      p. cm. — (Western legacies ; v. 8)

  Derived from the rodeo collections of the National Cowboy & Western Heritage Museum.

  Includes bibliographical references and index.

  ISBN 978-0-8061-4084-1 (hardcover : alk. paper)

  1. Rodeos—West (U.S.)—History. 2. Rodeos—West (U.S.)—History—Pictorial works. 3. Material culture—West (U.S.) 4. Material culture—West (U.S.)—Pictorial works. I. Muno, Ed. II. National Cowboy & Western Heritage Museum. III. Title.

  GV1834.55.W47R38 2010

  791.8'40978—dc22

The paper in this book meets the guidelines for permanence and durability of the Committee on Production Guidelines for Book Longevity of the Council on Library Resources, Inc. ∞

1 2 3 4 5 6 7 8 9 10

But to understand, you must look with your own eyes on these things. . . .
It is a spectacle which makes you go away with a bigger, finer feeling
toward life, and a genuine respect and appreciation for the quiet, modest
manhood and womanhood who have "taken chances," have risked limb
and even life at times in their sports of daring and skill.

Charles Wellington Furlong
Let 'Er Buck, 1921

We have just returned from the rodeo and, after watching four or five hours
of horse-play, cow-play, and almost every other kind of play, we have
decided that if this is PLAY we shall just keep on trying to WORK for a living.

Charles W. Collier
The Recorder, 1938

CONTENTS

◀ **E. Pardee, Roping Time 16 ¹/s** *(detail)*
Aurora [Colorado], Fair [Rodeo], circa 1926
Ralph Russell Doubleday, photographer
NCM—Dickinson Research Center
McCarroll Family Trust Collection,
RC2006.076.201

FOREWORD

ONE OF OUR GREATEST master horsemen, the late Jimmy Williams, had a saying: "The important things that we learn in life are the things that we learn after we think we know it all." I take my hat off to Richard Rattenbury and the National Cowboy & Western Heritage Museum—I thought I knew all there was to know about rodeo until I read *Arena Legacy*.

This book covers it all—the history, the personalities, and, just as important, the plain and the extraordinary objects of the sport. And all of it drawn from unequaled collections that can be enjoyed nowhere else. We who have been involved with rodeo should feel proud that our truly American sport has an honored place in one of the United States' most important cultural gems— the National Cowboy & Western Heritage Museum—and in this wonderfully illustrated book.

Arena Legacy is a great ride and a great read! Thanks to the author and the museum for having created such jewels.

God bless ya,
Larry Mahan
aka The Duke of The Chutes

← **Robert Rishell, *Larry Mahan*, 1974** *(detail)*
Oil on canvas
NCM—Gift of R. J. Reynolds Tobacco
Company, 1975.18

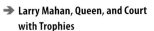

→ **Larry Mahan, Queen, and Court
with Trophies**
Eugene, Oregon, Rodeo, 1968
DeVere Helfrich, photographer
NCM—Dickinson Research Center
DeVere Helfrich Collection, 81.023.29205-01

A HIGH STEPPING STEER, TUCUMC

ACKNOWLEDGMENTS

IN BRINGING THE RODEO COLLECTIONS of the National Cowboy & Western Heritage Museum to publication, the author is particularly indebted to his fellow staff members. Registrar Melissa Owens and assistant registrar Karen Phillips provided essential collection documentation, while exhibit technician Steve Boyd, with the excellent assistance of Jim Cardoni and Tim Shelton, furnished signal aid in accessing hundreds of collection items on exhibition.

At the museum's Donald C. & Elizabeth M. Dickinson Research Center, director Chuck Rand, librarian Karen Spilman, and librarian-archivist Jennifer Wochner proved invaluable in locating crucial research and graphic materials, while imaging technician John Hayes cordially reproduced hundreds of historic photographs and other print imagery from the center's voluminous holdings.

My thanks go to curatorial colleagues Don Reeves and Steve Grafe for their useful perspectives in developing the work, and special appreciation must be extended to long-suffering friend and curator of art Ed Muno, who again outdid himself in producing the fine color reproductions of the collections. As well, gratitude is due information technology director Sharon Kasper and graphic arts director Leslie Fisher for their special talents—and patience—in recording and preparing scores of digital images. Assistant director Mike Leslie ably shepherded the project along, and executive director Chuck Schroeder proved a consistent and fervent supporter of the undertaking throughout.

For their generous and timely assistance with singular imagery, I must express my appreciation to longtime rodeo performer and supporter Mitzi Lucas Riley, journalist Guy Clifton of the *Reno Gazette-Journal*, and media coordinator Jourdan Foran of the Professional Rodeo Cowboys Association.

← **Jim Wilkes on a High Stepping Steer**
(detail)
Tucumcari, New Mexico, Rodeo, 1919
Doubleday-Foster Photo Company, publisher
NCM—Dickinson Research Center
McCarroll Family Trust Collection,
RC2006.076.059

At the University of Oklahoma Press, thanks go to director B. Byron Price and editor-in-chief Charles E. Rankin for their enthusiasm in adopting the project and seeing it to publication. Also at the press, the way was smoothed by assistant director and production manager Emmy Ezzell, by special projects editor Alice Stanton, by graphic designer Julie Rushing, and by "image wrangler" Anna María Rodríguez. And particular thanks to copyeditor Sally Bennett, whose discriminating eyes are manifest throughout the work.

Extraordinary gratitude is extended to six-time all-around-champion cowboy, western-wear entrepreneur, and Rodeo Historical Society supporter Larry Mahan, who magnanimously agreed to author the foreword of this book.

Last, but certainly not least, the author and the National Cowboy & Western Heritage Museum are especially grateful to the directors and members of the Rodeo Historical Society for their generous financial support of this Western Legacies Series volume.

Errors of fact or interpretation are the author's alone.

Richard C. Rattenbury, Curator of History
National Cowboy & Western Heritage Museum
Oklahoma City, Oklahoma

INTRODUCTION

The National Cowboy & Western Heritage Museum preserves and interprets one of the finest and most extensive collections of rodeo memorabilia in the nation, representing the sport from its early development at the beginning of the previous century through its rise to national prominence and acclaim in the 1960s and the 1970s. Encompassing the history, biography, and material culture of this venerable athletic pastime and pageant, the museum's holdings consist of approximately 1,250 significant objects and associated ephemera. The institution's Dickinson Research Center also maintains the original photographic collections of such prominent rodeo documentarians as Ralph Russell Doubleday, DeVere Helfrich, and Bern Gregory, as well as extensive holdings of rodeo day sheets, programs, periodicals, postcards, and biographical files.

In addition to constituting one of the premier public artifact and archival collections covering much of the history of rodeo, this assemblage is distinguished for the number, quality, and rarity of its biographically associated pieces. These encompass the personal materials of great champions such as Bob Crosby, Pete Knight, Everett Bowman, Casey Tibbs, Bill Linderman, Jim Shoulders, Larry Mahan, and Tom Ferguson; cowgirl contenders including Bertha Kaepernik Blancett, Lorena Trickey Peterson, Tad Barnes Lucas, Bonnie Treadwell McCarroll, Florence Hughes Randolph, and Alice Greenough Orr; and several ancillary performers such as trick riders and fancy ropers Leonard Stroud, Chester Byers, Sam Garrett, and Junior Eskew.

America's truly indigenous sport, rodeo developed as a colorful celebration of the riding and roping skills of the working cowboy. From its informal origins in isolated roundup contests more than a century ago to the big-business excitement of today's National Finals competition, the sport personifies the drama, rugged individualism, and competitive spirit of the nineteenth-century American West. Yet rodeo is much more than mere historical spectacle.

⬅ **Rodeo Cowgirls Bessie and Ruby Dickey**
(detail)
Tucumcari, New Mexico, Rodeo, circa 1918
Doubleday-Foster Photo Company, publisher
NCM—Dickinson Research Center
McCarroll Family Trust Collection,
RC2006.076.045

Part I

A RODEO OVERVIEW

American rodeo is the vibrant athletic legacy of the working cowboy. The sport was born in the casual riding and roping contests held at roundups during the 1860s and 1870s. Beginning in the 1880s, various Wild West shows presented colorful "cowboy tournaments" throughout the country, gradually associating the demonstration of western range practices with authentic sport in the public mind. By 1900, formalized rodeo competitions had come to enliven county fairs, Fourth-of-July celebrations, cattlemen's conventions, and old settlers' reunions across much of the West.

Under the management of independent promoters and producers, and through the parallel efforts of an increasing number of civic-minded local committees, rodeo emerged as a legitimate spectator sport during the 1910s. A decade later, championship venues from Salinas, California, to New York, New York, attracted nationwide attention. The formal organization and regulation of rodeo, starting in the 1930s with the Rodeo Association of America (RAA) and the Cowboys Turtle Association (CTA), brought increasing professionalism and prosperity to the sport over succeeding decades. Today, operating under the long-tested leadership of the Professional Rodeo Cowboys Association (PRCA) and enjoying unprecedented commercial sponsorship and media exposure, rodeo and its independent athletes—both male and female—have secured their place in the hallowed halls of American sport.[1]

1 Getting Started

Cowboy Fun from Prairie to Arena

THE CONTEMPORARY SPORT of rodeo (from the Spanish *rodear*, to "surround" or "encircle") has its roots in the work and play of the nineteenth-century American cowboy and his Spanish-Mexican antecedents.[1] The isolation and boredom that characterized vaquero and cowboy life in the West prompted these laborers on horseback to create their own amusements on the ranch, range, and trail. Proud of their chosen trade and the special skills that set them apart from other westerners, cowboys quite naturally indulged in competitions that tested their traditional riding and roping abilities. During seasonal roundups or at the end of long trail drives, the hands from different outfits often challenged one another to matches in working skills such as saddle-bronc riding, steer roping, and calf roping. These spontaneous contests had no arenas, no paying spectators, no entry fees, few (if any) rules, and no prizes—though wagering among the challengers and their respective coworkers might be quite brisk. Winners typically prevailed through a process of elimination or through the exceptional performances of man and beast.

Perhaps the first recorded competition of the kind occurred at Deer Trail, Colorado Territory, on the Fourth of July in 1869. This cowboy tournament, pitting the best bronc riders from the Mill Iron, Campstool, and Hashknife outfits against a fractious remuda of unbroken horses, went to Mill Iron cowhand Emilnie Gardenshire. As subsequently reported in Denver's *Field and Farm* magazine, the youthful Englishman "let it be known that he wanted the worst animal in the pen, and he got it in the shape of a bay, from the Hashknife ranch, known . . . as the Montana Blizzard. . . . For fifteen minutes

← **A Southwestern Round-Up Camp**
Location unknown, circa 1895
Photographer unknown
NCM—Dickinson Research Center
Photographic Study Collection, 2003.241

→ **Cowboys [and Cowgirl] on the Round-Up**
Sterling, Colorado, circa 1905
Photographer unknown
NCM—Dickinson Research Center
Photographic Study Collection, 2005.177

the bay bucked, pawed, and jumped from side to side, then, amid cheers, the mighty Blizzard succumbed, and Gardenshire rode him around the circle at a gentle gallop."[2] In recognition of his performance, the victorious cowboy received a new suit of clothes from the ranch owners, and the quite-unofficial title of "Champion Bronco Buster of the Plains" from his comrades.

Pecos, Texas, today claims to have conducted the first semiformal, community rodeo exhibition with a public audience in 1883—a steer-roping and bronc-riding contest held on the main street and in an open lot next to the county courthouse. But credit is given to Prescott, Arizona Territory, for inaugurating the first annual rodeo (today the Prescott Frontier Days Celebration) on July 4, 1888. Organized by a local "town committee," this patriotic competition entailed the first public advertising and recorded admission charges, establishing the event as a true spectator sport. The *Arizona Journal-Miner* reported that winning steer roper Juan Leivas "made a beautiful throw with his rope, bringing his steer to earth so suddenly that it pulled his horse over, also throwing him to the ground."[3] The Hispanic cowboy brought the animal down from a one-hundred-yard lead in 1 minute, 17.5 seconds. The victory earned him a brand new saddle with an appropriately inscribed, silver "Citizens' Prize" plaque—formal awards that initiated the long-standing tradition of tangible tributes for winning competitors.[4] During subsequent years, the Prescott rodeo committee also formulated some of the first basic contest rules of the sport, including this general regulation: "No cowboy will be entered who is not willing to wear his big hat and boots at all times."[5]

The dress and equipment worn and used by working cowboy-contestants at these early rodeos differed little if any from that employed on the range. The Prescott-mandated Stetson hat and high, western-style boots with underslung heels most likely appeared in conjunction with a collarless cotton shirt and denim trousers, the latter shrouded in straight-legged, "shotgun"-style chaps. Spurs, ranging in quality from cheap, store-bought OK's to custom-made and embellished blacksmith products, appeared on every boot heel. Whether bronc riding or steer roping, the contestant's saddle probably was his own—in the 1880s and 1890s typically a slick-forked, high-cantled pattern rigged and skirted according to regional preference. During this initial period of rodeo's development, the practical clothing and equipment of the working cowhand dominated throughout, varying little except for expressions of individual taste in trim and decoration. Only somewhat later, as "traditional" cowboy culture changed both in fact and in interpretation, and as rodeo contestants refined their practices in the arena, would real

Cowboy Dewitt Gray
Holton, Kansas, circa 1888
W. R. Ireland, photographer
NCM—Dickinson Research Center
Photographic Study Collection, 2002.224

Roping and Tying Contest
Malheur County Fair Rodeo, Ontario, Oregon,
circa 1915
J. B. Burrell, publisher
NCM—Dickinson Research Center
Photographic Study Collection, 2005.115

Wild West Performers May Lillie
and "Pawnee Bill"
York, Pennsylvania, circa 1895
Swords Brothers, photographers
NCM—Dickinson Research Center
Photographic Study Collection, 2005.199

⬆ Wild West Showman
"Buffalo Bill" Cody
Chicago, Illinois, circa 1905
Brisbois, photographer
NCM—Dickinson Research Center
McCarroll Family Trust Collection,
RC2006.076.439

considerations of function and fashion noticeably impact the material culture of the emerging sport.[6] One Wyoming cowboy observed in 1887, "Don't think there was a $60 saddle on the roundup in that neck of the woods. Those kinds of saddles and ten gallon hats came into vogue when the 'Drug store and rodeo' cowboys became popular."[7]

Though the celebration at Prescott may be said to mark the formal beginnings of rodeo, elements of the fledgling athletic presentation actually received their first broad public attention through various traveling Wild West shows. In fact, the public exhibition of several of the cowboy skills and contests that would become the sport of rodeo really began when Colonel William F. "Buffalo Bill" Cody staged his Old Glory Blow Out at North Platte, Nebraska, on the Fourth of July in 1882. This production included roping, riding, and bronc-busting events, with prizes awarded to the winning cowboy performers. The following year, Cody took his Wild West extravaganza on the road. His program and many similar shows, such as Pawnee Bill's Historic Wild West, the Miller Brothers' 101 Ranch Real Wild West, the Tom Mix Circus and Wild West, and Colonel Tim McCoy's Real Wild West and Rough Riders of the World, showcased cowboy recreation and skill throughout the United States—and across much of Europe—for some forty years. And although Wild West cowboys (and cowgirls) were paid performers rather than true contestants, they came to represent in the popular imagination romantic and daring personas whose fearless horsemanship and manifest athletic abilities gradually became identified with sport.[8]

Wild West shows proved important not only in bringing the Anglo American cowboy-athlete to public attention but also in introducing the talents of Hispanic and African American performers in an era when race discrimination was commonplace. For example, Mexican trick and fancy roper Vicente Oropeza and famed black bronc rider and steer wrestler Bill Pickett gained wide recognition with the Buffalo Bill and 101 Ranch shows, respectively.

Born in 1858 in Puebla, Mexico, Oropeza became one of his nation's greatest professional *charro* riders and a pioneer innovator of the *charreada*, Mexico's venerable counterpart to rodeo. He hired on with Buffalo Bill in 1894, and during his sixteen years as one of Cody's stellar attractions, the elegant showman

visited several continents and taught American cowboys a new approach to an old art. In 1900, Oropeza was declared the fancy-roping "Champion of the World" at a contest held in New York City. By the time of his death in 1923, trick and fancy roping had become featured elements of American rodeo.[9]

The originator of rodeo bulldogging, or steer wrestling, African American cowboy Bill Pickett was born in 1870 in Travis County, Texas. With four siblings, he established the Pickett Brothers Bronco Busters and Rough Riders, an outfit that specialized in "catching and taming wild cattle." Pickett's technique for subduing stubborn bovines involved grabbing them by the horns, twisting the head up, biting the tender nose or lower lip to acquire their full attention, and then pulling them to earth. By the early 1900s, he and other bold performers were "bulldogging" steers in this manner as a rodeo exhibition. (The biting method soon gave way to the application of twisting leverage to "throw" the steer, and this refined version of steer wrestling remains a prominent competition in rodeo today.) Probably the first black cowboy to contend in the public arena, Bill Pickett was a featured performer with the Miller Brothers' 101 Ranch Real Wild West show for more than twenty-five years; he also starred in two all-black motion pictures. He died in 1932 of head injuries received from the kick of a rogue horse.[10]

American Indians, of course, played a significant part in virtually every Wild West show, and, although largely confined to reservations in the early twentieth century, they too transferred their experience to the rodeo arena. Major venues such as the Cheyenne Frontier Days rodeo, the Pendleton Round-Up, and the Calgary Stampede regularly highlighted Indian parade contingents and pony races. And a few American Indians won acclaim as outstanding contestants in the arena. Tom Three Persons, for example, came off Canada's Blood Reservation to capture the bronc-riding championship aboard the notorious outlaw Cyclone at the first Calgary Stampede in 1912—the only Canadian to win a major contest at the inaugural event. In the United States, Jackson Sundown, a Nez Perce from the Flathead Reservation, entered the bucking-horse competition at the Pendleton Round-Up in 1914, 1915, and 1916, winning the event in the latter year at the age of fifty-three. Likewise, Lakota cowboy George Defender left the Standing Rock Reservation in the mid-1910s to forge an enviable bronc-riding record extending from Miles City, Montana, to Madison Square Garden in the 1920s. These celebrated contestants established an Indian presence in early rodeo that gradually declined

GOING TO CHEYENNE FOR FRONTIER DAYS (H.F.P.CO)

into the 1930s. Today, the majority of indigenous cowboys contest within the All-Indian Rodeo Cowboys Association (established in 1958) and since 1979 have focused most of their attention on the Indian National Finals Rodeo.[11]

As with racial minorities, female athletes who sought to challenge—or defy—the common gender constraints of the late nineteenth and early twentieth centuries likewise found Wild West shows to be effective social levelers. In the mid-1890s, the Buffalo Bill show advertised a "Bevy of Beautiful Rancheras, genuine and famous frontier girls" proficient in "feats of daring equestrianism."[12] Talented cowgirl competitors, such as Lucille Mulhall and Bertha Kaepernik (later Blancett), benefited immeasurably from participation in the Wild West shows, which furnished them with a natural stepping-stone into the rodeo arena.

Born in 1885 in Saint Louis, Missouri, Mulhall learned to ride and rope in Oklahoma under the tutelage of her father, famed Wild West impresario Colonel Zack Mulhall. In 1904, after roping and tying a steer in the record time of thirty seconds at Dennison, Texas, she was dubbed the "Queen of the Range." For fifteen years, American audiences raved about the beautiful, devil-may-care girl who could out-rope and out-ride the men. President Theodore Roosevelt became one of her ardent fans. By the mid-1910s, in fact, Lucille Mulhall, then widely celebrated as "The Girl Ranger," was herself providing multievent rodeo

LUCILE MULHALL LADY CHAMPION ROPER WALLA-WALLA FRONTIER DAYS 1914

programming (with livestock) to several venues around the West. Her renown had all but faded away, however, by the time a car accident took her life in 1940.[13]

Bertha Kaepernik was born in 1883 in Cleveland, Ohio, but she grew up on a Colorado ranch and began riding at age five. She entered the rodeo arena at the 1904 Cheyenne Frontier Days, accepting the management's challenge for an exhibition lady bronc rider. Her successful performance, over a dangerously muddy field on which the men had refused to compete, clearly broke the gender barrier in rough-stock competition. Over the next decade, while performing with the Pawnee Bill and 101 Ranch Wild West shows and working with Bison Films in Los Angeles, she competed in numerous rodeos as a bronc rider and Roman racer (standing astraddle on a pair of galloping horses). She captured many bucking-horse championships (three at the Pendleton Round-Up, for example, in 1911, 1912, and 1914), won several Roman-riding titles, and served frequently as a "hazer" for her bulldogging husband, Dell Blancett. Widowed during World War I, Bertha Kaepernik Blancett retired from active competition around 1919, but she rode in some California rodeos as a "pickup man" for several decades while also working as a trail guide in Yosemite National Park. She died in California in 1979 at age ninety-six.[14]

The presence of ethnic and gender diversity in Wild West shows carried forward into early-day rodeo. Though discrimination certainly was not unknown, even in the 1910s several prominent rodeo venues, such as the Pendleton Round-Up, hosted and celebrated Indian, African American, Hispanic, and female contenders in the arena. Indeed, rodeo can be considered the first integrated sport in America, preceding the fall of the color barrier in baseball by some thirty years. Minority acceptance would wane and wax over succeeding decades, but rodeo sport always has recognized manifest talent.

In addition to showcasing typical cowboy and cowgirl skills in riding and roping, Wild West shows also introduced two ancillary activities that for many years would have a prominent place in rodeo sport—trick and fancy roping, and trick riding. Trick and fancy roping originated among the charro horsemen of Old Mexico, where it was known as *floreo de reata,* or "making flowers of rope." Vicente Oropeza introduced stylish roping to the United States with Cody's Wild West show, and beloved cowboy-humorist Will Rogers popularized the skill all across the nation as a vaudevillian during the early twentieth century. Rodeo programmers also borrowed trick riding from the extravagant equestrian feats of Cossack performers in Wild West shows. A popular contested event at most prominent rodeos between 1915 and 1930, trick riding attracted both male and female athletes—sometimes in direct competition with one another. Both of these challenging exercises enjoyed the participation of scores of talented contenders—and thrilled and amazed thousands of spectators—into the early 1930s, when both were changed by programmers from contested events to contract performances. Though trick and fancy ropers and trick riders still perform at contemporary venues as contract entertainment, their prevalence has decreased dramatically over the past half century.

Wild West showmanship also brought a flamboyance to cowboy and cowgirl apparel that was rarely seen on the range. The traditional Stetson hat took on a remarkable scale—with up to six-inch brims and seven-inch crowns stylishly rolled and creased—that soon became the standard for arena performers. Fringed and beaded coats, vests, cuffs, gauntlets, and pants suggestive of the "Old Frontier" joined with colorful neckerchiefs and fancily embellished western boots and flashy spurs. Chaps covered with angora goat hair, which provided a sensational flouncing effect on a tossing bronc, soon displaced the long-serving "shotgun" pattern of fringed leather with the occasional concha decoration. Angora, or "woolie," chaps appeared in an array

⬆ **Bertha Blancett on Eagle** *(detail)*
Riding in the bucking contest for championship of the world
Pendleton, Oregon, Round-Up, circa 1913
Walter S. Bowman, photographer
NCM—Dickinson Research Center
Photographic Study Collection, 1988.9.72

⬇ **Bea Kirnan Trick Riding** *(detail)*
Fred Beebe's New York Rodeo, circa 1925
Ralph Russell Doubleday, photographer
NCM—Dickinson Research Center
Tad S. Mizwa Collection, 2005.03.3.12

of colors—from the familiar black, white, or mixed, to brilliant dyed hues of yellow, gold, pink, and red. Most of these extravagant, eye-catching Wild West interpretations of traditional cowboy costume moved quite naturally to the rodeo arena in the first decades of the twentieth century, as many proficient hands made the challenging transition from paid performer to independent athletic competitor. Equestrian gear, too, underwent a decorative transformation within the Wild West milieu. The lavishly tooled and silver-

mounted parade saddles ridden by impresarios such as Buffalo Bill, Zack Mulhall, and the Miller brothers set a standard that would be emulated in the rodeo arena by promoters, managers, producers, and champion contestants down to the present day.[15]

Between 1895 and 1920, rodeo gradually emerged as a recognized public entertainment separate from Wild West shows. *The Wild Bunch* (a special-interest news publication devoted largely to cowboy and cowgirl performers in vaudeville acts, circuses, Wild West shows, and rodeos) reflected this trend from its inception in 1915. Most of its opinion pieces focused on rodeo issues, ranging from the establishment of uniform contest rules and the institution of guaranteed contestant prize monies to outright calls for organization and cooperation among the growing cadres of rodeo contestants, promoters, managers, and committees. In the November 1915 issue, for instance, rodeo promoter-manager Guy Weadick wrote,

> I feel sure that if all interested in this form of amusement will co-operate and work together, it will be the means of better rules, better prizes, and more satisfactory decisions in the judging of the different events for the contestants. It will mean better understanding between contest managers, help to eliminate the conflicting of dates, [and] enable them to offer larger prizes. . . . Taken all in all, it will give the managers more contestants of a desirable kind, give them a much better performance, please their audiences, and contestants will be satisfied. . . .
>
> Personally, I will herein go on record as stating that in my coming contests I am perfectly willing to have contestants pick their own judges, and will do the same as in the past, give good big cash prizes. I will state, however, that . . . each and every event will be strictly competitive, all events open to the world. Those that win take the prizes and those that don't are out of luck.[16]

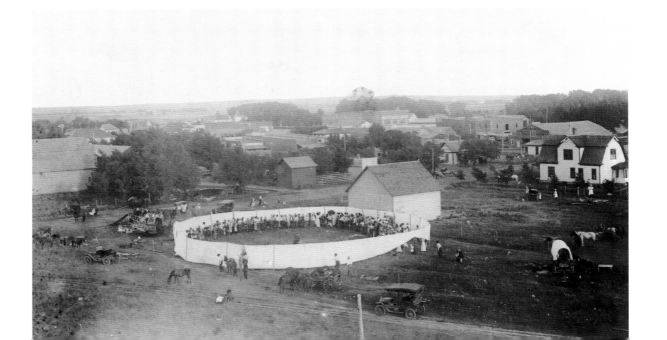

Unfortunately, Weadick's promise of "good big cash prizes" failed to materialize the following year at his Sheepshead Bay, New York, Stampede, which paid out but a fraction of the $50,000 "in real American gold" advertised. Unfortunate as well was that his forward-looking sentiments about rodeo organization would go unrealized for another two decades.

Nevertheless, the early, often-singular contests typically associated with Fourth-of-July celebrations, old-settlers' reunions, and cattlemen's conventions steadily were supplanted by annual venues such as the Cheyenne Frontier Days rodeo (established 1897), the Pendleton Round-Up (established 1910), and the Calgary Stampede (established 1912). Indeed, by 1916, *The Wild Bunch* had begun publishing listings of established rodeos that included these classic venues, as well as soon-to-be-famous western contests at Idaho Falls, Idaho; Miles City and Billings, Montana; Sheridan, Wyoming; Belle Fourche, South Dakota; Garden City, Kansas; Dewey, Oklahoma; Las Vegas, New Mexico; and Prescott, Arizona. As these and other "community" rodeos adjusted their schedules to relieve the favored Fourth-of-July date and better cover the entire year with attractive venues, the sport began to offer contestants a rudimentary circuit on which to compete. Concurrently, through the constant efforts of dedicated civic bodies and visionary promoters, rodeo gained increasing attention and publicity, eventually attracting hundreds of contestants and audiences numbering in the tens of thousands. By 1920, certainly, rodeo had established itself throughout the West and beyond as a legitimate athletic contest and a recognized spectator sport.

The first two decades of the twentieth century witnessed the rise to prominence of the first "name contestants"—individuals including steer roper Clay McGonagill, saddle-bronc rider Harry Brennan, and steer wrestler Mike Hastings. McGonagill, considered by many to be one of the greatest itinerant ropers in early-day rodeo, was born in 1879 at Old Sweet Home, Lavaca County, Texas. By 1910, he had made his reputation in several hundred matched, jerk-down steer-roping contests held around the Southwest and in Mexico. One of the first cowboy-competitors to attempt to earn a living in rodeo before the sport was truly organized, McGonagill met an untimely death in 1921. Upon hearing of the cowboy's demise, practiced

↑ **A County Fairgrounds Rodeo**
Location unknown, circa 1920
Photographer unknown
NCM—Dickinson Research Center
Photographic Study Collection, 1988.9.1514

↑ **Steer and Calf Roper Clay McGonagill with Prize Check**
Match-roping, venue unknown, 1919
Photographer unknown
NCM—Dickinson Research Center
Photographic Study Collection, 2006-026.39.01

← **Grand March [of the] Cowboys and Girls**
Pendleton, Oregon, Round-Up, 1914
Walter S. Bowman, photographer
NCM—Dickinson Research Center
Photographic Study Collection, RC2006.027.2

roper and cowboy-humorist Will Rogers remarked, "They must have needed a top cowhand in heaven."[17]

Harry Brennan, another of the earliest, "regular" contestants in rodeo, was born in 1880 at Sheridan, Wyoming Territory. Often acknowledged as "the father of rodeo bronc riding," his spurring style—toes pointing out and sweeping from the horse's withers to the saddle cantle-board—established the pattern for later contestants. He also helped to formulate the original "Cheyenne Rules," the guidelines from which many later customs and codes evolved. A true rodeo pioneer, Brennan won the Champion Rough Rider of the World title at the 1902 Festival of Mountain and Plain in Denver, took the bronc rider title again at Cheyenne in 1904, and remained a top contender for more than a decade. He passed from the arena in 1934, by then little known for his seminal contributions to the sport.[18]

➜ **Harry Brennan, Champion Rough Rider of the World, with Trophy Saddle**
Cheyenne, Wyoming, Frontier Days, 1904
W. B. Walker, photographer
NCM—Dickinson Research Center
Photographic Study Collection, 1988.9.1513

One of the greatest bulldoggers in early-day rodeo, Mike Hastings was born in 1891 at Casper, Wyoming. He entered his first rodeo in 1910, competing in calf roping, steer wrestling, and bronc riding, but by 1916 he had come to specialize in bulldogging. That year, he set a record at Guy Weadick's New York Stampede, downing a steer in eleven seconds. Tremendously strong and always competitive, during more than twenty years of competition Hastings became known as "The Iron Man of Steer Wrestling." He later worked as stock foreman for the great Colonel W. T. Johnson and Gene Autry rodeos, retiring in the 1940s. A sound judge of livestock, he served as foreman of the Cimarron Dude Ranch near Putman Valley, New York, until his death in 1965.[19]

Not unlike the talented cowboy athletes, a few infamous bucking horses—including Steamboat, Hell-to-Set, Tipperary, Cyclone, and Blue Jay—achieved extensive name recognition in this era because of their ability to consistently unseat the best of riders. Steamboat, purchased by rodeo impresario C. B. Irwin in 1903, allowed only about half a dozen successful regulation rides over an eleven-year career. One of those came at the hands of Clayton Danks at the 1909 Cheyenne Frontier Days rodeo—an event later commemorated in bronze by western artist Harry Jackson.[20] In a 1962 interview with *Frontier Times*,

➜ **Mike Hasting[s], Champion Bulldogger**
Cheyenne, Wyoming, Frontier Days, 1931
Ralph Russell Doubleday, photographer
NCM—Dickinson Research Center
Photographic Study Collection, 2004.026.02

Danks remembered Steamboat as "dynamite," and "a kite that turned inside out and showed the rider the bottoms of four hooves. He was flying mane under you, and a projectile that put you halfway across the arena in four jumps."[21]

Some conception of the notoriety of the great buckers, the distinction of their daring riders, and the general character of the early rodeo cowboy can be gleaned in the report of a dramatic bronc-busting contest held at Lucille Mulhall's Fort Worth Round-Up in 1917.

> Before the eyes of thousands of almost frenzied spectators . . . Rufus Rollens mounted and rode the famous Texas outlaw horse, Blue Jay, at the round-up on Wednesday night, for a side purse of $500. . . . [He performed] with all the confidence of a champion, and then, not content to screw down and merely ride, had to scratch [spur] him, just to show the equine wonder that he was not so wonderful after all. Poor old Blue Jay, after successfully unseating one hundred and one riders or aspirants for riding honors during his brilliant career, finally succumbed to this master of ornery cayuses, but he died game and pulled every trick in his entire repertoire, but there was no time when Rollens was not master of the situation, and he even did it gracefully. And, while W. C. Scott of Anson, Texas, owner of the famous steed, led his defeated champion away, [the hands] lifted "Rufe" to their shoulders and carried him around the arena like a gridiron hero, while the playing of the forty-piece band was drowned by the applause.
>
> Blue Jay entered the arena a three-to-one favorite back in the audience, while Rollens went to the post a five-to-one favorite among the real hands in the arena, and the boys who had forethought enough to get back in the audience were buying wine the next day.[22]

Said to be the most notorious bucking horse since Steamboat, Blue Jay saw an abrupt end to his admirable record with this defeat, and he never recovered his reputation—some reports have him pulling a plow the next year. The victorious Rufus Rollens remained a stellar bronc rider right up to his conviction

and imprisonment for bank robbery in 1921. From its inception, rodeo would provide a haven to scores of outlaw animals and not a few outlaw contestants.

Great riders and ropers—and great horses—could not have achieved widespread notoriety without the devoted exertions of early-day rodeo promoters and contractors such as C. B. Irwin, Tex Austin, and Verne Elliott. Much in the spirit of the Wild West entrepreneurs, these independent operators recognized the opportunity of making the emerging sport into a distinctively American pageant. Between 1900 and 1930, their vision, organizational ability, and sometimes-sacrificial efforts helped to consolidate and popularize rodeo throughout the West and beyond.

→ **Rodeo Promoter and Stock Contractor C. B. Irwin**
Y6 Ranch, Wyoming, circa 1915
Photographer unknown
NCM—Dickinson Research Center
Photographic Study Collection, 1978.7.10

Among the early figures prominently involved in rodeo development, Charles Burton "C. B." Irwin certainly ranked as the largest and most energetic. Born in Chillicothe, Missouri, in 1875, he eventually tipped the scales at more than 350 pounds and, during a lengthy and colorful career, worked as a rancher, blacksmith, livestock agent, Wild West show entrepreneur, horse trainer, rodeo promoter, and stock contractor. From his Y6 Ranch near Cheyenne, Wyoming, Irwin provided administrative ability and fine rough stock that contributed to the early success of the Frontier Days rodeo. (His bucking string at one time included the famous equine outlaws I Be Damn and Steamboat.) After disbanding his own Wild West show in 1917, Irwin continued to contract livestock and conduct rodeos throughout the Great Plains for more than a decade. He died in 1934, by which time his adopted sport had become a proven and popular athletic attraction across the United States.[23]

Often affectionately referred to as "The Daddy of Rodeo," John Van "Tex" Austin ranks as perhaps the first great promoter and showman of the sport. Born in West Texas in 1887, he cowboyed in Mexico and participated in the revolution of 1911. He then purchased the Forked Lightning Ranch near Las Vegas, New Mexico, and began producing cowboy contests. Prior to 1920, he staged rodeos in New

↓ **Rodeo Promoter and Manager**
Tex Austin *(detail)*
Yankee Stadium, New York City, 1923
Ralph Russell Doubleday (?), photographer
NCM—Dickinson Research Center
Photographic Study Collection, 1988.9.22

Mexico, Oklahoma, Indiana, and Illinois. A colorful impresario, Austin founded the Chicago Championship Rodeo at Soldier Field in 1920, but he is better remembered as the original producer, in 1922, of the famed World's Championship Rodeo at New York's Madison Square Garden. Held in late fall, this annual extravaganza declared many champions prior to the establishment in 1929 of the Rodeo Association of America (RAA) point system that determined all-around champions—the basic system now under Professional Rodeo Cowboy Association (PRCA) auspices that culminates with the unrivaled National Finals Rodeo (NFR). Tex Austin's productions introduced pageantry and spectacle, brought individual "star" contestants to public prominence, and made big-money competitions a fundamental element of the sport. Among his many accomplishments, he also orchestrated the first international rodeo pageant, held in London, England, in 1924 and repeated the performance a decade later. Austin continued his ardent promotion of the sport until his death in 1941.[24]

For their arena productions, legitimate rodeo promoters such as Tex Austin sought not only star athletes but also outstanding rough stock. Stock contractors, an integral element of rodeo from

the early twentieth century onward, supplied the horses, steers, calves, and bulls essential to the sport. Outstanding contractors, such as Verne Elliott, had to be excellent judges of livestock as well as sound and energetic businessmen. Born in 1890 on a ranch near Plateville, Colorado, Elliott also possessed a keen sense of showmanship, once riding a buffalo bull at the Cheyenne Frontier Days for the amusement of then president Theodore Roosevelt. In 1917, he and Eddie McCarty joined forces to establish the greatest rodeo-stock-contracting partnership in the sport. (The following year at Fort Worth, Texas, they produced the first rodeo ever held in an indoor arena.) They dominated the business throughout the 1920s and 1930s, furnishing rough stock to such enormous productions as the rodeos at Cheyenne, Denver, Omaha, Pendleton, Fort Worth, Los Angeles, and New York. Their best bucking horses, Midnight and Five Minutes to Midnight, earned high respect among the contestants during the 1930s. Later partnered with Don Nesbitt, Verne Elliott ultimately became one of the most successful and revered rodeo stockmen in the business. He merged his contracting company with Beutler Brothers in 1952 and died a decade later.[25]

Though the exigencies of World War I briefly slowed rodeo's development, the sport stood poised on the threshold of its first golden era. The decade of the 1920s saw rodeo blossom into a nationally recognized athletic competition. The passing of Buffalo Bill Cody in 1917, coupled with the fast-growing attraction of western movies, commenced a gradual decline in the popularity of Wild West shows. Recognizing an opportunity to fill this potential vacuum in western entertainment, dynamic rodeo promoters such as Tex Austin and Fred Beebe established several major venues in metropolitan centers in the East and Midwest. By 1925, New York City, Philadelphia, Chicago, and Saint Louis were hosting some of the most prominent and influential rodeo contests in the country, markedly increasing the audience, publicity, and credibility of the sport. By the late 1920s, New York City's annual Madison Square Garden World's Championship Rodeo had come to eclipse the famous Cheyenne Frontier Days celebration both in duration and in purse awards; as the season's last major venue for several years, it became the unofficial, but widely accepted, arbiter of "world-championship" titles.[26]

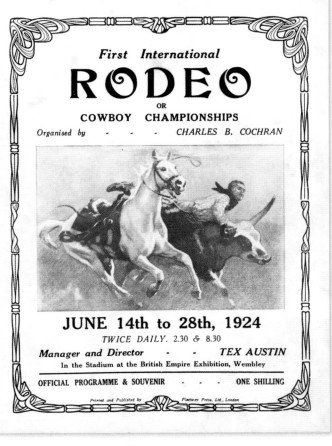

Rodeo's popular "coming-of-age" during the twenties was perhaps best exemplified in its first major presentation overseas. In 1924, promoter and manager Tex Austin introduced the English people to genuine cowboy sport with his First International Rodeo. Staged at Wembley Stadium outside London in tandem with the British Empire Exhibition, the two-week venue headlined many top American contenders and drew tens of thousands of enthusiastic spectators from virtually all levels of British society. Cowboy and cowgirl satin shirts and leather chaps apparently mixed easily with aristocratic tailcoats and gowns at several social soirees. Only the Royal Society for the Prevention of Cruelty to Animals took exception to the spectacle, bringing charges against Austin and several contestants over the violence of the steer-roping competition. Nonetheless, the first London rodeo marked a milestone in international recognition of the sport—so much so that Austin felt compelled to repeat the venture a decade later.[27]

Throughout the 1920s, rodeo companies and committees promoted the burgeoning sport year-round and nationwide, creating full-time occupations for the most dedicated competitors. The increasing establishment of annual venues that organized on a seasonal and regional basis, coupled with the growing prevalence of automobile travel and the adoption of rudimentary horse trailers, produced a viable circuit and prompted competitors to commence "going down the road" on a regular basis. They went not only for money and acclaim but also for a growing panoply of resplendent prizes that marked the sport's increasing commercial sponsorship. The Roaring Twenties also witnessed the rise to prominence of a new cadre of rodeo competitors, several of whom succeeded in making lucrative livelihoods of varying length in the sport. A few displayed such talent and charisma—and garnered sufficient publicity—that they won enthusiastic followings among the expanding legions of rodeo fans. Celebrated among the many outstanding hands in this exciting decade were competitors such as bronc rider Paddy Ryan, all-around roper Chester Byers, and all-around cowgirl Mabel Strickland.

Born in 1896 in Leroy, Minnesota, red-haired, freckle-faced John Francis "Paddy" Ryan moved with his family to a Montana homestead in 1910. There he learned to wrangle horses on a nearby ranch and entered professional rodeo in 1916 at Miles City. An all-around competitor, he specialized in bronc riding and bulldogging, proving a consistent champion from 1924 to 1928. In 1924 he won the prestigious Roosevelt Trophy, awarded to the hand who earned the all-

↑ **Rodeo Program**
First International / Rodeo / or Cowboy Championships
Illustrator unknown
British Empire Exhibition, 1924
NCM—Dickinson Research Center
Rodeo Programs Collection, 2006-126.39.14

↓ **Paddy Ryan on Romeo, Tex Austin's Rodeo** (detail)
Yankee Stadium, New York City, circa 1925
Ralph Russell Doubleday, photographer
NCM—Dickinson Research Center
Howard Tegland Collection, 1991.046.094

around titles at both Pendleton and Cheyenne. Always a colorful character in the arena, Ryan sometimes bulldogged steers from the running board of a car. He often wrestled the brutes while wearing a silk shirt and necktie and frequently dressed in a full suit of clothes to ride rogue saddle broncs. Although he retired to his Montana ranch in 1946, he did not pass from the arena until 1980.[28] "In his heyday," wrote an admirer in 1941, "Paddy Ryan could, when garbed in one of his green silk shirts, merely lope across the arena on a gentle saddle horse and draw more applause than any contesting cowboy ever known."[29]

Certainly the best—and best-known—roper in the world throughout the 1920s and 1930s, Chester Byers was born in 1892 at Knoxville, Illinois. He made his debut as a performing roper at age thirteen with the Pawnee Bill show and toured for a time with Lucille Mulhall's Congress of Rough Riders. In 1911 he entered his first competitive rodeo at Los Angeles, California, and five years later won the trick-roping championship at the Sheepshead Bay Stampede, retaining the title against all comers until 1933. Byers proved an outstanding calf and steer roper as well, competing and winning at Pendleton, Calgary, Cheyenne, Fort Worth, Madison Square Garden, and many other major rodeo venues. Prior to his death in 1945, he twirled his ropes and made "five horse catches" to the delight of thousands in the United States,

Canada, Mexico, South America, and England.[30] Humorist Will Rogers, a talented roper in his own right, wrote in the foreword of Byers' book, *Roping,* "I only have two things that I will always die very proud of, one of them is that I used to teach Chet Byers tricks with a rope."[31]

During a twenty-five-year career, Mabel Strickland probably won as many individual and venue titles as any other rodeo cowgirl of her era. Born Mabel Delong in 1897, she was raised in Walla Walla, Washington, and began relay racing and trick riding while still in high school. In 1917 she married all-around hand Hugh Strickland, and they traveled the circuit throughout the 1920s. Diminutive, lithe, and

very athletic, Mabel proved to be a practiced relay racer, winning the event at Pendleton in 1916, 1920, 1923, 1928, and 1929 and at Cheyenne in 1922 (along with the coveted McAlpin Trophy) and 1923 (along with the women's saddle-bronc-riding title). Also a talented trick rider, she and her white Arabian mare, Buster, captured the title at Madison Square Garden in 1922, 1923, and 1924. She contested in steer riding and steer roping as well, turning in a personal best time of eighteen seconds flat in the latter event at Pendleton in 1927—nearly besting the men's world record at the time. As women's events declined in the 1930s, Strickland turned to Hollywood stunt work and retired from rodeo around 1940. Described by many as the sport's "most beloved cowgirl," she died in 1976 in Buckeye, Arizona.[32]

Even though their distinctive sport remained essentially unorganized through the 1920s, these and scores of other rodeo contenders prospered remarkably during the decade. Challenges and changes lay just ahead, however, and over the following twenty years, rodeo and its growing legion of participants would be tested and transformed in preparation for a second golden era.

➢ **Mabel DeLong [Strickland], Champion Relay Rider** *(detail)*
Missoula, Montana, Stampede, 1916
McKay, photographer
NCM—Dickinson Research Center
Photographic Study Collection, 2005.238

⬆ **Mabel Strickland Roping [a] Steer**
San Antonio, Texas, Rodeo, circa 1923
Ralph Russell Doubleday, photographer
NCM—Dickinson Research Center
Howard Tegland Collection, 1991.046.096

⬅ **Cowboys Hand Picked by Doubleday**
Venue unknown, circa 1925
Ralph Russell Doubleday, photographer
NCM—Dickinson Research Center
Massey Collection, Doubleday 093

2 The Main Events

Laying Loops and Staying Aboard

THE RODEO ARENA—whether set in an open field, a county racetrack, a city stadium, or a metropolitan coliseum—provides the ultimate forum for cowboy and cowgirl athletes. There, they contend in a series of competitions combining the skills of the working cowhand with the spectacle of the Wild West show. From the sport's outset, traditional practices such as saddle-bronc riding and steer roping featured as premiere events, but early rodeos also hosted an abundance of supplementary—sometimes peculiar—contests and exhibitions. The 1915 Frontier Days celebration of Walla Walla, Washington, for example, boasted a program of nearly thirty events. Then-familiar contests included steer roping, saddle-bronc riding, steer wrestling (cowboys only), trick and fancy riding and roping, and a variety of relay and single-heat horse races. As well, spectators thrilled to stagecoach and chariot races, an Indian war dance, and demonstrations of wild burro and bull riding and wild bear and buffalo roping. Special exhibitions included a "Drunken Ride by 'Wild Bill' Donovan," "Roping and Tying of Steers by Ed McCarty . . . Without the Use of a Bridle on Roping Horse," and "Roping and Tying of Wild Buffalo by George Weir." As an extra enticement, the program noted that, "During [the] afternoon of each day there will be a herd of wild elk run around the track, and also a herd of wild buffalo."[1]

Over the decades, various contests and exhibitions have come and gone in the sport of rodeo, but several events have withstood the tests of time and tradition. Three of these—saddle-bronc riding, steer roping, and calf roping—represent the practical range work of the nineteenth-century cowboy. (Steer roping, a familiar rodeo event for several decades in the early twentieth century, is today a rather

← **"Some Stunt"**
Frontier Days Rodeo, Walla Walla,
Washington, 1913
Edward F. Marcell, photographer
NCM—Dickinson Research Center
Photographic Study Collection, RC2006.019

→ **Maverick Race** *(detail)*
Frontier Days Rodeo, Walla Walla,
Washington, circa 1925
Ralph Russell Doubleday, photographer
NCM—Dickinson Research Center
Massey Collection, Doubleday 096

segregated competition practiced in but a few states because of humane considerations.) Three other primary contests—bareback-bronc riding, steer wrestling, and bull riding—appeared as feats of cowboy daring during the first decades of the twentieth century, and they steadily gained in audience approval as rodeo gradually developed its distinctive character. Today, most of the prominent rodeos include cowgirl barrel racing and team steer roping as regular program events as well.

These competitions typically are defined as "judged" or "rough-stock" events (saddle-bronc riding, bareback-bronc riding, and bull riding) and "timed" events (steer wrestling, calf roping, team roping, barrel racing, and steer roping). In the former contests, experienced arena judges observe and score the performance of contestants and critters alike for a potential total tally of one hundred points per ride. In the latter events, competitors race the clock through a series of heats or "go-rounds" for the fastest (lowest) cumulative time.[2] Most contemporary performances sanctioned by the Professional Rodeo Cowboys Association (PRCA) generally follow a specific order: after the entry parade, bareback riding leads off, followed by calf roping, saddle-bronc riding, steer wrestling, team roping, barrel racing, and, as the grand finale, bull riding. For the past several decades, steer-roping competitions usually have been conducted as singular venues.

Bareback-bronc riding developed strictly as a contest within the sport of rodeo. Never practiced by working cowboys, the event appeared at some rodeos in the 1910s as an exhibition, typically performed with only a mane-hold or a loose rope. Around 1920, the adoption of leather surcingles having one or two handholds for the cowboy-contestant, and the introduction of front-delivery, or "shotgun," chutes for the horses, made the bareback event more practical. It gained wider favor throughout the 1930s and 1940s, as rodeo venues installed functional, side-opening chutes and cowboys adopted the standardized Bascom rigging—a shaped leather panel with a single riveted handhold, or "suitcase handle," secured to a surcingle with D-rings. Only since the 1950s, though, has bareback riding been a standard event at the majority of sanctioned rodeos.

← **Bryan Roach in Bareback Contest** *(detail)*
Cheyenne, Wyoming, Frontier Days, 1919
Ralph Russell Doubleday, photographer
NCM—Dickinson Research Center
Edith Jones Waldo Bliss Collection, R.241.190

A rough-stock contest, bareback-bronc riding joins exceptional strength and coordination with dramatic action. The contestant employs only the rigging surcingle, a single rosined leather glove, and a pair of bronc-riding spurs. He must spur the animal over the shoulders as it leaves the chute ("marking out") and not touch himself, the animal, or the rigging with his free hand. All qualifying rides last a violent eight seconds. Scoring is based on a cumulative total of up to fifty points each for the performance of the bronc and the cowboy. Wild bucking by the horse and aggressive spurring by the contestant can markedly improve the overall tally. With vigorous bucking stock and showy contestants, competitive scores usually reach or exceed eighty points.[3]

Eddy Akridge ranks among the best and most consistent bareback-bronc riders ever to compete in the event. Born in 1929 in Pampa, Texas, he began rodeoing in 1946 and joined the Rodeo Cowboys Association (RCA) in 1948. The next year he won the all-around championship at Calgary, contesting in all three riding events, and he repeated the feat at Pendleton in 1953. Always diligent about "going down the road," Akridge accumulated sufficient points to capture the RCA World Champion Bareback Rider title in 1953, 1954, 1955, and 1961. (He beat out his friend Buck Rutherford for the 1954 crown by a mere seven points!) His bareback record tied that of all-around great Jim Shoulders (1950, 1956–58) but ultimately was eclipsed by that of Joe Alexander (1971–75). A talented guitarist and singer, Eddy Akridge took up country-and-western music after leaving the arena. He formed the Gold Buckle Band in Las Vegas, Nevada, in 1982, and the group entertained for the National Finals Rodeo (NFR) World Championship Awards Banquet from 1985 to 1992. In 1995 he was honored by Gist Buckle Company as an "American Rodeo Legend."[4]

↑ **Bill Martinelli on Sun Goose** (detail)
Phoenix, Arizona, Rodeo, 1956
(Note single-hold Bascom rigging.)
DeVere Helfrich, photographer
NCM—Dickinson Research Center
DeVere Helfrich Collection, 81.023.11170

↑ **Bareback Bronc Rigging**
Bascom pattern by Dixon Riggin', circa 1950.
NCM—Gift of Mrs. E. A. Spaulding, R.210.09

Fitted with large D-rings for cinching around the horse just behind the withers, and incorporating a single handhold (likely replaced) for the contestant, this bareback rig served Bill Linderman for several years. He took the bareback championship only in 1943, but consistent performance in the event contributed to his earning all-around champion titles in 1945, 1950, and 1953. This rigging bears the inscription "Mr. President" in recognition of Linderman's service to the Rodeo Cowboys Association (RCA) from 1951 to 1957.

↑ **Bronc Riding Spurs**
Maker unknown, circa 1935.
NCM—Gift of Don Bell, 1983.49.01 A&B

Fabricated of cast aluminum, or "airplane metal," these bronc spurs incorporate hinged, swinging loops for the leathers, stationary loops for tie-down thongs, and slightly angled shanks with small, toothed rowels. They were worn by rough-stock rider Don Bell of Colorado, who competed around the West during the 1930s. The pattern was designed by bronc rider Paul Carney, who won the champion bareback-riding title in 1937 and 1939 and the all-around-champion cowboy title in 1939.

↑ **Bareback Bronc Rigging**
Bascom pattern, maker unknown, circa 1955.
NCM—Loan courtesy Eddy Akridge, L.1985.01.01

This rigging belonged to talented bareback rider Eddy Akridge, who won the
International Rodeo Association and Rodeo Cowboys Association (RCA) event
championships in 1953 and the RCA event title again in 1954, 1955, and 1961.
Fabricated of heavy saddle-skirting leather, the outfit features laced-in D-rings,
a fleece lining, and a single handhold, or "suitcase handle." The rig retains its
latigo leathers and cinch along with the contestant's rosined leather glove.

Calf roping, today usually referred to as **tie-down roping**, evolved directly from the traditional tasks of roundup time on the ranch and range, when calves were roped and subdued for branding and doctoring. Typically, riders simply roped a calf and pulled it to the work area, where a dismounted cowhand grounded the animal by either "flanking" or "legging" it down. In rodeo competition, the contestant carries out these operations and also secures the calf with a tie-rope. By the mid-1920s, some roping horses had been trained not only to brake to a stop as the rope was thrown but also to maintain a taut line and even back up to shorten the cowboy's running distance to the calf. The event also proved influential in the development of functional, low-cantled stock saddles that facilitated the roper's ability to easily and rapidly dismount, and in the adoption of flat, low-heeled cowboy boots that improved the contender's mobility and stability when working on the ground. (Steer wrestlers benefited directly from these modifications as well, and both have been adopted in the broader realm of western saddle and footwear design.)

➡ **Catch Rope**
Plymouth Cordage Company, Plymouth, Massachusetts, circa 1955
NCM—Loan courtesy Mrs. Tom Nesmith, LR.233.05

Made of manila hemp, this "grass" lariat is typical of those used by calf ropers before the appearance of synthetic materials such as nylon. The main line measures three-eighths of an inch in diameter by twenty-two feet in length. At the "home end," a braided-leather knot secures the small loop that slips over the saddlehorn for "hard-and-fast" roping. At the "business end," the catch loop is formed through the knotted honda, which has a stitched-on leather "burner" to reduce wear. Champion calf roper Tom Nesmith used this rope. Of his skill, a friend remarked, "Tom burns loops around calves' necks. He doesn't fish."

➡ **Tie Rope**
Maker unknown, circa 1925
NCM—Gift of Esta Cleo Robinson Noles, R.244.02

Made of manila hemp, this six-foot tie rope, or "piggin' string," is used to make the three-legged wrap and tie-down that completes the calf-roping event. Two such ropes typically are carried coiled in the roper's mouth or tucked in his belt for instant access in the arena. This specimen belonged to Lee Robinson, a great calf roper of the 1920s. At Tex Austin's 1922 World Championship Rodeo, Robinson broke a long-standing challenge by roping six calves in an average time of fifteen seconds.

A timed event, calf roping pits the contestant and his well-trained horse against the clock and a 250- to 350-pound calf. As with all the roping contests, success hinges on the coordinated efforts of horse and rider. With a designated ten- to fifteen-foot head start, the calf bursts from the chute and trips a barrier that signals pursuit by the roper. As his horse overtakes the calf, the contestant must rope it cleanly around the neck (two catches can be attempted if two ropes are carried) and simultaneously bring his mount to an abrupt stop, halting the calf's flight as he dismounts. The horse must maintain a taut rope while the cowboy runs to the calf, throws it on its side, and ties three legs securely (typically two wraps and a half-hitch) with a five- to six-foot "piggin' string." Official time is declared by the arena judge when the cowboy throws up his hands after the tie-down. For an acceptable qualified time, however, the calf must stay tied for six seconds after the contestant has remounted and slackened his catch rope. If the cowboy breaks the start barrier, a ten-second penalty is added to his time. Today, competitive times usually range between seven and ten seconds.[5]

During the 1930s and 1940s, the calf-roping event was dominated by two of the greatest competitors ever to cast a loop—Clyde Burk and Toots Mansfield. Burk, a one-quarter Choctaw Indian, was born near Comanche, Oklahoma, in 1913. Orphaned as a teenager, he supported his younger siblings through rodeo, becoming one of the smartest ropers on the professional circuit. He competed on a pair of famous roping horses named Bartender and Baldy, ultimately taking four calf-roping world championships (1936, 1938, 1942, and 1944). Burk made his last ride in 1945 at Denver, Colorado. Hazing for another contestant in the steer-wrestling event, he was killed when his horse fell and rolled over him. He was only thirty-two years old.[6]

Toots Mansfield, born in Bandera, Texas, in 1914, picked up where Clyde Burk left off, dominating the calf-roping competition for twelve

Bob Ragsdale Calf Roping (detail)
Grover, Colorado, Rodeo, 1966
Bern Gregory, photographer
NCM—Dickinson Research Center
Bern Gregory Collection, 1999.025.0090.24

Clyde Burk on Bartender (detail)
Oklahoma City, Oklahoma, circa 1943
Ralph Russell Doubleday, photographer
NCM—Dickinson Research Center
R. R. Doubleday Collection, 79.026.2135

Toots Mansfield Calf Roping
Phoenix, Arizona, Rodeo, 1947
DeVere Helfrich, photographer
NCM—Dickinson Research Center
DeVere Helfrich Collection, 81.023.02544

Clyde Burk on Baldy
Brownwood, Texas, 1942
John Addison Stryker, photographer
NCM—Dickinson Research Center
Tad S. Mizwa Collection, 2005.003.3.38B.18

Toots Mansfield and Smokey
Location unknown, circa 1950
John Addison Stryker, photographer
NCM—Dickinson Research Center
Mansfield Collection, 1997.013.4

years. He won at Madison Square Garden seven times, Pendleton three times, Cheyenne three times, and Fort Worth four times. He captured the championship an unprecedented seven times (1939–41, 1943, 1945, 1948, and 1950) and placed second three times. (His record remained unchallenged until Dean Oliver bested it with eight calf-roping championships in 1969.) A big man, Mansfield developed a widely imitated style of "flanking down" and then tying a calf. He served as president of the Rodeo Cowboys Association from 1945 to 1951 and opened a popular calf-roping training school in 1954. He died in 1998.[7]

Great ropers rarely achieved outstanding success without great horses—animals mentally attuned to, and thoroughly trained in, the "mechanics" of roping. Horses well schooled in calf-roping technique were (and are) much sought after by champion contenders, and several of them gained not only fame in their own right but also no little fortune for their owners. Horseman L. E. "Ed" Bowman is credited with training one of the first great roping horses, Back-Up Pete, to maintain a taut rope while the rider tossed and tied his calf. (Bowman so appreciated Pete's talents that he fed the horse grain from the large, Hoot Gibson trophy cup he won as "Champion Calf Tier" at the 1924 Prescott Frontier Days rodeo.) Baldy, a bald-faced sorrel foaled in 1932 and trained by famed roper Ike Rude, is remembered even today as one of the greatest calf-roping horses of all time. Rude won on the hard-stopping horse for five years and then sold him to Clyde Burk for the then-unheard-of sum of $2,500. Burk rode Baldy to the world calf-roping title in 1944, and upon his death, the horse was acquired by Troy Fort, who secured calf-roping championships on him in 1947 and 1949. Baldy died in 1961, having won various hands an estimated $300,000 in thirteen years of roping. Likewise, seven-time calf-roping champion Toots Mansfield garnered many victories from the backs of his favored and talented steeds, Old Quaker and Smokey.[8]

Saddle-bronc riding is the classic rough-stock competition of rodeos past and present, having evolved from the traditional horse-breaking tasks of the nineteenth-century cowboy. In early-day contests before the installation of arena chutes, rogue mounts typically were snubbed, blindfolded, and saddled in the open. With the contestant aboard, the bronc was turned out for a bucking spree that might last several

#20 BILL STANTON ON "SANDY" AN "88" THAT'S ALL,
"COPYRIGHT 1916 R.R. DOUBLEDAY";

minutes. Once instituted, qualifying times rapidly declined from thirty to ten and then eight seconds. Like calf roping, this rodeo event had some influence on the design of the western stock saddle. During the first two decades of the twentieth century, the long-serving slick-fork tree was supplanted among bronc riders by wide-swelled patterns known as "bear-traps" or "freaks." These became so exaggerated and dangerous to competitive riders that, in 1919, several rodeo committees convened to formulate a saddle pattern expressly for bronc riding. The so-called Committee, or Association, saddle enjoyed nearly instant and universal acceptance among veteran bronc riders, and the basic—now hornless—design remains in use today at rodeos throughout the country. During the first decades of the twentieth century, bronc

↑ **Bill Stanton on Sandy: An "88" That's All**
Venue unknown, 1916
Ralph Russell Doubleday, photographer
NCM—Dickinson Research Center
Photographic Study Collection, 2003.159.6

Saddling up at the
Missoula Stampede. McKay.

← **Saddling Up for the Bronc Riding**
Missoula, Montana, Stampede, circa 1920
McKay, photographer
NCM—Dickinson Research Center
Photographic Study Collection, RC2006.101

→ **Bill Morrison on Flaxie** (detail)
Billings, Montana, Rodeo, 1956
(Note saddle pommel without horn.)
DeVere Helfrich, photographer
NCM—Dickinson Research Center
DeVere Helfrich Collection, 81.023.11554

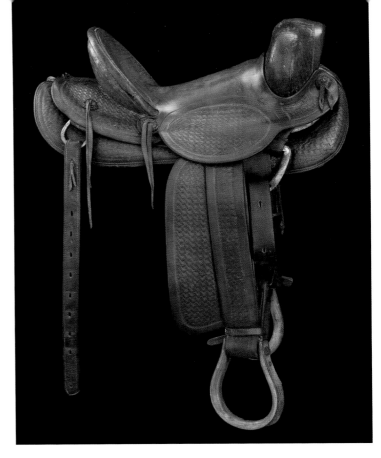

Bronc-Riding Saddle
Hamley Saddlery Company
Pendleton, Oregon, circa 1930
NCM—Gift of Dr. Tommy L. Pike, H.130

Designed in 1919 by the Hamley shop in consultation with the rodeo committees of Walla Walla, Pendleton, Boise, and Cheyenne, the "Committee" or "Association" saddle rapidly became the standard equipment of the bronc-riding event throughout the sport. Fabricated on an Ellensburg tree, the saddle typically incorporated a somewhat undercut, swell-forked pommel and a slightly dished, five-inch cantle. Early specimens came with roping horns, but these often were sawed off, as with this example. Contemporary bronc saddles usually are finished in rough-out rather than smooth leather and come without a horn.

riders also rapidly adopted new, "batwing"-pattern chaps, the lower legs of which widened out into broad, loose flaps. Their dramatic waving and snapping motion on a pitching horse proved useful not only in attracting additional audience attention but also in distracting arena judges from noting a contestant's sometimes-less-than-exemplary spurring technique.[9]

A judged event, saddle-bronc riding demands flamboyant style and superb balance—more than brute strength—on the part of the cowboy contestant, who has to remain atop a 1,200-pound bucking horse for the duration of a bone-jarring qualifying time. The standard riding equipment consists of a hornless Association saddle, a plain halter with a single six-foot braided rein, and a pair of short-shanked bronc spurs with dull rowels. To make an acceptable qualifying score, the contestant must leave the chute with his spurs over the shoulders of the horse ("marking out"), keep his feet in the stirrups, and not let his free hand touch the horse, the saddle, or himself for the eight-second ride. At the sound of the horn, the rider will either leap off dramatically or, far more likely, dismount over the back of the pick-up man's horse. Scoring in this event combines a total of up to fifty points apiece for the performance of horse and rider. Rhythmic spurring in time with the gyrations of the bronc—from the horse's shoulders back along the flanks near the cantle-board of the saddle—will accrue extra points to the contestant. Winning scores typically exceed eighty combined points, while eighty-five or above represents a superior ride.[10]

Saddle-Bronc Rein
Hank Abbie, circa 1970
NCM—Loan courtesy Phil Lyne, L.1985.02.01

Fashioned of loosely braided hemp and nylon, this six-foot bronc rein is relatively soft to the hand yet quite strong. It was used by Phil Lyne, all-around-champion cowboy in 1971 and 1972. Though he retired from full-time, professional competition at the pinnacle of his career in 1972, some rodeo aficionados thought Lyne "the finest all-around hand in history."

Saddle-Bronc Rein
Maker unknown, circa 1940
NCM—Gift of Mrs. George McElhinney, R.211.03

Fitted with a buckled strap to attach to the headstall, this seven-foot bronc rein of loose-braided hemp was used by Doff Aber, the world champion bronc rider in 1941 and 1942. A tuft of horsehair is woven into the rein to mark the contestant's usual handhold.

Bronc-Riding Spurs
Maker unknown, circa 1940
NCM—Anonymous loan, L.1987.01.05 A&B

Worn and battered from many an exciting ride, these bronc spurs incorporate swinging buttons for the leathers, tie-down pins on the heel bands for auxiliary thongs or wires, relatively short shanks with modest chap guards, and dull, eighteen-point rowels. They belonged to Louis Brooks, the Rodeo Association of America (RAA) champion bronc rider and all-around-champion cowboy in 1943 and 1944. He also captured the RAA bareback-riding championship in 1942 and 1944.

Ranking among the best bronc riders in rodeo history, Pete Knight was born in 1903 in Philadelphia, Pennsylvania. While he was still a youth, his family moved to Crossfield in Alberta, Canada, where he learned to break and gentle unruly horses. He began rodeoing around 1918 and won his first major championship in 1924 at the Edmonton Exhibition and Stampede. Again at Winnipeg in 1926, he took the saddle-bronc championship after topping six consecutive mounts. In 1932 at Reno, Nevada, he prevailed in an unusual "Match of Champions," beating Frank Studnick, Earl Thode, and Gene Ross to capture and retire the singular trophy awarded by the event's sponsor, famed boxer Jack Dempsey. The following year, Knight retired the coveted Prince of Wales Challenge Trophy after three victories at Calgary as Canadian Champion Bucking Horse Rider. To prove that these triumphs were no fluke, he won four world titles as saddle-bronc-riding champion in a five-year period (1932, 1933, 1935, and 1936). What more he might have accomplished in the arena can only be speculated, as he was fatally injured by a bronc named Duster at Harry Rowell's Haywood, California, rodeo in 1937.[11] Bronc-riding champion Herman Linder thought his fellow Canadian "the best rider I ever saw because he rode steadier on harder horses." Knight is memorialized in Crossfield, Alberta, as the "finest bronc rider of all time and one of nature's gentlemen."[12]

↑ **Pete Knight on Jack Dempsey** *(detail)*
Sheridan, Wyoming, Rodeo, 1932
Ralph Russell Doubleday, photographer
NCM—Dickinson Research Center
Photographic Study Collection, 88.9.502

Bucking broncs work only about ten minutes per year, but they are the principal symbol of rodeo. Whether bareback broncs or saddle broncs, these horses are "nonconformists" that refuse to tolerate a rider. Rodeo broncs are not trained to buck—they simply have a natural and consistent tendency to do so. The flank strap used in bucking events does not hurt the horse or cause it to buck but provides an annoyance that encourages the animal's natural inclinations. Prior to the 1950s, bucking horses came from the farm, ranch, and range. Famous early buckers included Steamboat, Tipperary, and Blue Jay.

McCarty and Elliott's Midnight and Five Minutes to Midnight, two infamous saddle broncs of the 1920s and 1930s, are laid to rest on the grounds of the National Cowboy & Western Heritage Museum. Hell's Angel was another outlaw horse that consistently unseated aspiring saddle-bronc champions in the 1930s and 1940s. Contemporary rodeo broncs are genetically "bred to buck." The finest are awarded Saddle Bronc and Bareback Bronc of the Year titles. A rogue named Descent received the saddle-bronc title an unrivaled six times between 1966 and 1972, and Sippin' Velvet won the bareback-bronc title five times in the 1980s.[13]

Invariably ranked among the greatest, best-known, and most-respected saddle broncs in the annals of rodeo, Midnight was foaled in 1916 on Jim McNab's Cottonwood Ranch west of Fort

← **Bill Ward on Sea Lion** *(detail)*
San Angelo, Texas, Rodeo, 1956
(Image adopted as the PRCA's brand logo.)
DeVere Helfrich, photographer
NCM—Dickinson Research Center
DeVere Helfrich Collection, 81.023.11042

MacLeod in Alberta, Canada. A Thoroughbred-Percheron-Morgan cross weighing about 1,300 pounds, the big gelding proved to be a natural bucker and, thus, inevitably unserviceable as a working range horse. McNab recalled some attributes of the horse's early bucking behavior—all of it exhibited without the inducement of a flank strap:

> Midnight bucked straight ahead, hit the ground hard on [his] front feet, turned his hind quarters side ways and kicked about the same time as his front feet hit the ground. You got hit in the belly with the front of the saddle and at or about the same time in the seat with the cantle. . . . He would buck just as hard with his head up [as down]. And if you pulled too hard on the halter rope, he would give you his head [and] then jerk it away [and] sometimes throw his head around to the side.[14]

The horse made his debut at the 1924 Calgary Stampede, where he tossed every rider who drew him. In 1926 at Toronto, Canada, the bronc disposed of talented rider Bob Askin and then bucked so violently that the oak stirrups clashed above the saddle, smashing one of them. Although sources vary and debates continue to the present, Midnight appears to have been ridden effectively fewer than 8 times in an estimated 370 outings during his bucking tenure from 1924 to 1934. Pete Knight, one of the greatest bronc riders of the era, for example, successfully rode the horse only once in seven attempts. A great drawing card at Fort Worth, Cheyenne, and other prominent venues with stock contractors McCarty and Elliott from 1929 through 1933, Midnight retired after a farewell performance at Tex Austin's 1934 London rodeo. He passed from the arena in 1936.[15]

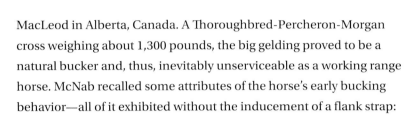

ED WRIGHT BULLDOGGING PENDLETON ROUND-UP

Steer wrestling is strictly a Wild West show and rodeo contest—real working cowboys certainly never practiced it on the range. Long-accepted tradition has African American cowboy Bill Pickett first performing the feat in the early 1900s, and he soon began demonstrating his technique with the Miller Brothers' 101 Ranch Real Wild West for amazed audiences around the country. The style of steer wrestling practiced by Pickett and other early-day performers, usually referred to today as "bulldogging," actually involved biting the animal's tender nose or lower lip to gain control. Today's rodeo contestants—perhaps more mindful of their personal health and hygiene—omit the biting element in favor of the application of leverage and brute strength. Not unlike calf and steer ropers, these contestants appreciate the advantages of the "low-roping" stock saddle and the low-heeled western boots that evolved at least in part in response to rodeo-arena demands.

A timed event, steer wrestling combines good horsemanship, expert timing, and sheer muscle power to bring down a 550- to 650-pound steer from a running steed. As with the roping events, the steer is released with a designated head start, tripping a barrier that

LYNCH BULL DOGGING
© 1917, B.F. PHOTO CO.

allows the steer wrestler and his partner, the "hazer," to pursue at the gallop. The hazer parallels the steer into a straight run while the contestant leans from his horse, launches himself onto the steer's head and neck while grasping its horns, and then goes to the ground, planting his heels forward to brake the run. Once the steer slows down, the bulldogger wrestles it to the ground with a twisting and falling motion. (Rules stipulate that the cowboy must seize the steer only from the moving horse—never while dismounted. If the steer is accidentally knocked down during the catch, it must be allowed up and then thrown.) Time is declared when the steer lands on its side with all four legs extended in the same direction. A penalty of ten seconds is added for breaking the start barrier. Today, contestants usually achieve winning times in the neighborhood of four to six seconds.[16]

Undeniably among the finest steer wrestlers, or bulldoggers, of all time, Homer Pettigrew was born on a Grady, New Mexico, ranch in 1914. He started rodeoing in the Southwest during the early 1930s and dominated the professional circuit throughout the following decade. A fine horseman, Pettigrew made getting down on a hard-running steer look easy. His coordination and strength won him a still-unequaled six world championship titles in steer wrestling (1940, 1942–45, 1948) in eight years. A strong contender as well in

↑ **Homer Pettigrew Steer Wrestling** (detail)
Cheyenne, Wyoming, Frontier Days, 1955
DeVere Helfrich, photographer
NCM—Dickinson Research Center
DeVere Helfrich Collection, 81.023.10314

↑ **Steer Wrestler Homer Pettigrew**
Location unknown, circa 1945
Ralph Russell Doubleday, photographer
NCM—Dickinson Research Center
R. R. Doubleday Collection, 79.026.1945

calf roping, he placed second nationally in 1945 and 1949 and parlayed his arena talents to an all-around cowboy championship in 1941. Pettigrew retired from competitive rodeo during the 1950s and died in 1997.[17] *Rodeo Sports News* observed of him in 1961, "There may never be another cowboy that can take charge of an event the way he did, and keep it in hand so long."[18]

Somewhat akin to calf-roping horses, those used for steer wrestling are specially trained for the requirements of the event. Good bulldogging steeds typically exhibit exceptional physical and "mental" qualities. Usually of Quarter Horse stock, they must be able to provide tremendous acceleration out of the box to overtake the steer quickly. They also must be sufficiently savvy to briefly "rate," or pace, the

steer once alongside so as not to overrun the cowboy's leap, and bold enough to bring the rider within easy grasping distance of his bovine target. Like those employed in roping, the best dogging horses win considerable acclaim on the circuit. During the 1930s, for example, Everett Bowman's horse, Coon Dog, gained wide recognition while carrying its owner to four steer-

← **Bulldogger Missing His Steer**
Venue unknown, circa 1925
Photographer unknown
NCM—Dickinson Research Center
Edith Jones Waldo Bliss Collection, R.241.034

Buff Brady Bulldogging from [an] Automobile
Wichita, Kansas, Rodeo, circa 1935
Ralph Russell Doubleday, photographer
NCM—Dickinson Research Center
R. R. Doubleday Collection, 79.026.0356

Willard Combs with Baby Doll *(detail)*
Cow Palace, San Francisco, California, 1959
DeVere Helfrich, photographer
NCM—Dickinson Research Center
DeVere Helfrich Collection, 81.023.15248

wrestling championships. Among the most celebrated of dogging horses, Willard Combs's mare Baby Doll took him to the 1957 steer-wrestling championship—and in the same year garnered him an additional $75,000 from the winnings of other hands who borrowed the talented animal. Baby Doll is said to have helped make more world champion cowboys than any other steer-wrestling horse in rodeo.[19]

Team roping first appeared as team steer tying among the vaqueros and cowboys of Arizona and California, becoming a regular rodeo competition at the Prescott Frontier Days in 1919. Contemporary team roping came into vogue in the late 1950s, and it is now a standard event at PRCA-sanctioned rodeos. As in the other roping events, the steer is given a predetermined head start, after which the two contestants pursue it at the gallop. The leading roper, or "header," must catch the steer about the horns, dally his rope, and change the direction of the steer's run to benefit the throw of his partner. The second roper, or "heeler," then ropes the steer's back feet, dallies his rope, and stops his horse. Time is marked when the steer is immobilized on taut ropes between the two ropers, their horses both facing the steer, all in a straight line. Penalties of ten seconds and five seconds, respectively, are added to the scored time for breaking the start barrier and for catching only one hind foot. Competitive times usually range from five and one-half to eight seconds under standard arena conditions.[20]

Among the great early team ropers in the sport, Asbury "Raz" Schell competed for more than twenty years from the 1930s into the 1950s. Born in 1903 at Gisela, Arizona, he worked and contested with the best of his time, including

Ben Johnson and Dub Taylor Team Roping
Klamath Falls, Oregon, Rodeo, 1951
DeVere Helfrich, photographer
NCM—Dickinson Research Center
DeVere Helfrich Collection, 81.023.07278

Clay Carr, Buckshot Sorrells, Toots Mansfield, and Jake McClure. Dedication, skill, and well-trained and talented horses brought Schell three world titles in team roping in 1937, 1939, and again in 1952. He, along with John Rhodes, Joe Bassett, and Olan Sims, brought team roping to a new level by heeling from the right, instead of the usual left, or "California," side. He also was known for his string of great roping horses that included Cowboy and Cherokee Jake—both half brothers of famous calf-roping horse Poker Chip, who is honored on the grounds of the National Cowboy & Western Heritage Museum. Remembered as one of Arizona's great ropers, in his heyday Schell was recognized as always having "three aces" in the arena—"good horses, good partners [and] good attitude." He died at Cottonwood, Arizona, in 1980.[21]

Barrel racing is the only women's event regularly featured at contemporary PRCA-sanctioned rodeos. The contest came to prominence in the early 1950s through the Girls Rodeo Association (GRA), now the Women's Professional Rodeo Association (WPRA). Often ranked second only to bull riding in popularity among today's rodeo fans, this fast-paced, timed event combines superb horsemanship with breakneck speed. Contestants are allowed a running start, tripping the time clock and entering the arena at the gallop. There, they must negotiate a cloverleaf pattern of three barrels and then ride all-out to exit where they entered. The cowgirl contenders employ skillful timing and reining technique to maneuver their well-trained mounts around the barrels. After turning the third barrel, horse and rider charge the length of the arena to stop the clock. Riders may use

spurs and crop to urge the horse to greater speed, but finesse in turning the barrels is equally important in this colorful and exciting competition—oftentimes referred to as "can chasing" among seasoned fans. Tipping over a barrel adds a five-second penalty to the time, while running an incorrect pattern disqualifies the rider. With good ground conditions, winning times in a standard cloverleaf-pattern arena typically range from thirteen to fifteen seconds.[22]

Charmayne James, the greatest barrel racer ever, was born in 1970 in Amarillo, Texas. She exploded on the rodeo scene in 1984, winning the WPRA Rookie of the Year title and her first world barrel-racing championship at age fourteen. A full decade later, she still dominated the cloverleaf event, having taken an unprecedented ten consecutive world champion titles—an accomplishment unequaled by any other female athlete in professional sport. Along the way, Charmayne became the first woman in rodeo history to earn more than a million dollars. In 1986 she won more prize money than any other rodeo contestant during the regular season and thus became the first woman ever to wear the coveted *No. 1* back-number at the National Finals Rodeo (NFR). In 1988 she captured a gold medal at the Calgary Olympics Rodeo. She gives much of the credit for these records to Scamper, her five-time Barrel Racing Horse of the Year. Charmayne James retired in 2003 following her eleventh barrel-racing championship, having won nearly two million dollars in a twenty-year rodeo career. She now conducts barrel-racing clinics and breeds, raises, and trains promising horses, including a 2007 clone of Scamper.[23]

⬆ **Charmayne James Barrel Racing** (detail)
Sikeston, Missouri, Bootheel Rodeo, 1984
Bern Gregory, photographer
NCM—Dickinson Research Center
Bern Gregory Collection, 1999.025.2427.23

⬅ **Charmayne James Barrel Racing** (detail)
Memphis, Tennessee, Rodeo, 1984
Bern Gregory, photographer
NCM—Dickinson Research Center
Bern Gregory Collection, 1999.025.2439.29

➡ **Howard Tegland Steer Riding** (detail)
Miles City, Montana, Round-up, circa 1920
Doubleday-Foster Photo Company, publisher
NCM—Dickinson Research Center
Photographic Study Collection, 2003.159.7

Bull riding presents the most dramatic and dangerous spectacle in contemporary rodeo. The practice began in the early 1900s as open-arena steer riding and typically was performed as a paid exhibition. Not until the late 1920s and early 1930s, when arena bucking chutes came into common use, did the larger bulls (Brahma and crossbreds) make an appearance. Because these tremendously powerful animals spin and twist as well as buck and will readily attack a downed contestant, many consider this event the ultimate in rough-stock riding. For contemporary rodeo fans, certainly, no event surpasses bull riding in popularity. To stay aboard the animal, the rider utilizes only a loose, flat-plaited rope with a braided-in handhold and an attached bell. The rope passes around the bull behind his shoulders and wraps snugly about the cowboy's gloved hand. Besides its attendant clanking, the bell—purportedly popularized by Jim Shoulders—serves to pull the rope from the bull when the contestant lets go. In addition to their spurs, most contemporary bull riders now also wear Kevlar vests for protection, and some don protective helmets with face masks as well.[24]

⬅ **Bull Rope and Bell**
Hank Abbie, circa 1965
Bell maker unknown, circa 1960
NCM—Loan courtesy Phil Lyne,
L.1985.02.02.A&B

Made of tightly woven manila hemp, this bull-riding rigging is intended to barely hold man and beast together. The round portion goes around the bull behind the shoulders and is pulled tight through the looped end. The flat braided segment, beyond the double-layered handhold, wraps tightly over the cowboy's gloved palm. Only the contestant's tenacious grip holds the rope secure for an eight-second ride. Attached to the bull rope, the bull bell serves two purposes: its clanking incites the beast to buck harder, while its weight helps to drag the rope off the bull when the cowboy releases his grip, thus demonstrating that the rope was not illegally secured. This bull rope and bell belonged to Phil Lyne, calf roper, bull rider, and all-around-champion cowboy in 1971 and 1972.

⬇ **Bull-Riding Spur**
Crockett Bit and Spur Company
Boulder, Colorado, circa 1948.
NCM—Loan courtesy Harry Tompkins,
L.1987.07.06

Designed by bull and bronc rider Jerry Ambler, this bull-riding spur differs somewhat from those used by typical working and arena cowboys. For added stability, the inside heel band is slightly longer than the outer, and tie-down bars are mounted on both the heel band and the shank. To get a good "purchase" on the bull's flank, the shank is canted inward, and the five-point, toothed rowel is locked in place with a rivet through the slot. This spur was used by five-time champion bull rider and two-time all-around-champion cowboy Harry Tompkins.

A judged event, bull riding pits the determined competitor against a cantankerous bull weighing from 1,700 to 2,000 pounds. For a qualified ride, the contestant must stay aboard the animal for eight seconds out of the chute and cannot touch the bull with his free hand. (If the cowboy is entirely in the air—but still holding the rope—at the horn, he makes a qualified ride.) Success requires tremendous arm and shoulder strength and good coordination in time with the animal's extravagant gyrations. As in other rough-stock events, the competitor's final score is a combined tally of up to fifty points each for the performance of man and beast. Spurring the bull, though not required, can garner extra points from the arena judges, and bulls that buck and spin aggressively also receive higher marks. At PRCA-sanctioned rodeos, competitive scores usually range above eighty combined points, with ninety or better representing an exceptional ride.[25]

One of the smallest—but greatest—bull riders in rodeo, Albert Edward "Smokey" Snyder was born in 1908 at Cripple Creek, Colorado. Raised on ranches in western Canada, he entered his first tournament at Hussar, Alberta, in 1923 and soon was competing in all three rough-stock events. He hit his stride during the Great Depression, capturing the World Champion Bull Rider title five times (1931, 1932, and 1935–37), the World Champion Bareback Bronc Rider title twice (1932 and 1936), and the Canadian All-Around Champion title in 1932. In addition to his many North American championships, Snyder captured the bareback crown at the 1934 Royal Easter Show in Sidney, Australia, and both the bull-riding and bareback-riding titles at the Tex Austin London rodeo that same year. Always a leader in his chosen sport, he served with the initial directors of the Cowboys Turtle Association (CTA). Smokey Snyder made his last rough-stock ride in 1946 at San Diego, California. A rogue bronc named Miss Newhall crashed over a fence with him, breaking his back. He never rodeoed again, and he died in an auto accident in 1965.[26]

↑ **These Brahma Bulls of Homer Todd Will Have Their Little Joke** *(detail)*
Muskogee, Oklahoma, Free State Fair Rodeo, circa 1945
Ralph Russell Doubleday, photographer
NCM—Dickinson Research Center
R. R. Doubleday Collection, 79.026.3528

← **Smokey Snyder on # 87** *(detail)*
Phoenix, Arizona, Rodeo, 1944
DeVere Helfrich, photographer
NCM—Dickinson Research Center
DeVere Helfrich Collection, 81.023.00839

Sometimes referred to as "a ton of unleashed fury," the rodeo bucking bull provides the most dangerous—and certainly the most popular—action in the sport. Unlike the bucking broncs, which are not naturally aggressive toward man, bucking bulls will deliberately attack a downed rider with deadly hooves and horns. Today, most rodeo bulls represent crossbred Shorthorn and Brahma strains that combine amazing agility and brute power in a belligerent package weighing up to 2,000 pounds. Known by their temperament, the most famous rodeo bulls of the 1930s and 1940s carried such well-deserved names as Double Trouble, Cyclone, and Bad Dreams. During the 1960s, Tornado lived up to his moniker, blowing away every cowboy who climbed aboard for eight consecutive years. Today's rodeo bulls are "bred to buck" especially for the arena, and the most successful earn the title of Bucking Bull of the Year. Red Rock, probably the greatest ever, retired in 1987 after going unridden 312 times during his competitive career.[27]

Tornado, a crossbred Brahma-Hereford sired in the salt-grass marshlands of South Texas, rose from his obscure origins to become the most respected bucking bull of 1960s rodeo. Owned by sixteen-time-world-champion-cowboy Jim Shoulders, the 1,800-pound critter eliminated 220 successive riders during his first eight years on the circuit and was acclaimed the National Finals Rodeo Bull of the Year from 1962 through 1966. At the 1967 NFR, however, arena history and legend joined when a diminutive but dauntless Freckles Brown rode Tornado to the buzzer for the first time. "The minute I got on his back," Brown recalled, "I could feel his muscles harden and his skin tighten up. He came out spinning to the

Freckles Brown on # 461 Tornado (Shoulders)
Oklahoma City, Oklahoma, NFR, 1967
Ferrell Butler, photographer
NCM—Dickinson Research Center
PRCA Rodeo Sports News Collection,
98.008.2580

right. He was not only big and powerful, but fast. He kept hooking his head back at me. Somehow I kept my balance as he spun and pitched. . . . Then suddenly, I was off, standing in the middle of the arena holding my hat up . . . the crowd was giving me one of them ovations. . . . I had rode Tornado."[28] (The eight-second drama is remembered even today as "The Ride.") Once considered an "impossible" bull by the best riders of the period, the athletic bovine continued to toss both raw and seasoned hands until Shoulders retired him with a record of 306 victories in 311 rides. On his death in 1972, Tornado was interred on the grounds of the National Cowboy & Western Heritage Museum.[29]

The introduction of powerful and often-aggressive bulls to the arena necessitated some means of protecting contestants from attack once they "left" the animal. Rodeo clowns, who since the early 1910s had provided light entertainment for audiences in the idle time between events, took up the challenge. By the 1930s, bullfighting clowns had begun to distract the enraged animals head-to-head, relying on their quickness and athletic ability to elude injury while the rider scrambled to safety. Clowning bullfighters soon were joined by clowning barrelmen, who employed heavy, reinforced, open-ended barrels to distract the bull and protect themselves if charged. Today some clowns specialize around the bull-riding event, either as bullfighters or barrelmen, while many others continue to enliven the rodeo program with humorous dialogue, slapstick routines, and acts that include everything from educated mules to exploding cars.[30]

Most rodeo clowns began as regular contenders who ultimately found more satisfaction—and steadier money—in arena entertainment. Both Homer Holcomb and Ralph "Jasbo" Fulkerson followed this route and came to rank among the best known of the early "fearless funnymen" in the sport. Born in 1896 in Sioux City, Iowa, Holcomb moved to Idaho, learned to cowboy in his youth, and entered his first rodeo in 1919, riding bareback broncs and saddle broncs. A natural comic and mimic, he soon switched from riding to entertaining. His most famous specialty acts featured the educated mules Orphan Annie, Parkyacarcass, and Mortimer Snerd. As his career coincided with the introduction

↑ **Homer Holcomb and Jasbo Fulkerson**
(detail)
Phoenix, Arizona, Rodeo, 1942
DeVere Helfrich, photographer
NCM—Dickinson Research Center
DeVere Helfrich Collection, 81.023.00369

of Brahma bulls in rough-stock competition, Holcomb carefully studied the animals and originated bullfighting tactics still in use today. From 1923 to 1945, he traveled the circuit, protecting hundreds of cowboys and making thousands of spectators laugh. Severely injured by a Brahma bull that broke his back and shattered one leg in twelve places at San Francisco in 1945, he thereafter retired to Lewiston, Idaho, where he died in 1971.[31]

Holcomb's sometime clowning partner, Ralph "Jasbo" Fulkerson, was born in 1904 in Midlothian, Texas, grew up

← **Homer Holcomb Bullfighting** *(detail)*
Hayward, California, Rodeo, 1943
DeVere Helfrich, photographer
NCM—Dickinson Research Center
DeVere Helfrich Collection, 81.023.00634

around the Fort Worth Stock Yards, and entered his first rodeo in 1923 as a bronc and bull rider. He rode at the first London rodeo in 1924 and won the bull-riding title at Fort Worth in 1926. In 1927, Fulkerson bought and trained a small mule named Elko, and the two began a rodeo-clown act that lasted many years. "Jasbo" performed at the great Madison Square Garden Rodeo for twenty-one consecutive years and clowned in Australia in 1938, 1939, and 1940. Because of his small stature, he needed some protection when bullfighting, and it was he who introduced the reinforced bull barrel to the rodeo arena. He nevertheless suffered several serious injuries from bulls that managed to get a hoof or a horn into his barrel. Besides Homer Holcomb, Fulkerson's arena partners included such great clowns as Hoyt Hefner, George Mills, and Jimmy Nesbitt. He and Mills formed perhaps the best-known team of comedy bullfighters in rodeo history. "Jasbo" Fulkerson met an untimely death in a truck accident in 1949.[32]

Steer roping, though a segregated and rather limited event today, was a time-honored practice among working cowboys. Often out on the range alone, a hand frequently had to catch and immobilize a 400- to 600-pound animal single-handedly. The technique required a fine coordination between the rider and his horse to trip the steer with sufficient impact to keep it down until its legs could be tied. Often referred to at early-day rodeos as "jerk down" roping, or "fairgrounding," such competitions now are held at only a limited number of venues because of occasional—sometimes fatal—stock injuries.

A timed event, steer roping resembles calf roping except that the animal is considerably larger and heavier, and after the catch, it is thrown in a tripping maneuver. Once the steer frees the start barrier, the cowboy contestant must pursue, rope, trip, and tie down the critter in a race against the clock. He must

rope the steer's horns cleanly—two throws are permitted if two ropes are carried. He then lays slack rope along the animal's outside flank and spurs his horse off at an oblique angle, upsetting and jerking the steer to the ground, then briefly dragging it on its side. The well-trained horse maintains a taut rope as the cowboy dismounts, runs to the steer, and secures any three legs with a heavy "piggin' string" for the tie-down. Time is called

when the contestant throws his hands in the air, but the steer must remain tied for six seconds after the cowboy remounts and slackens the catch rope. As in other timed events, a ten-second penalty is added if the cowboy breaks the start barrier. Winning times generally fall in the twelve- to fifteen-second range.[33]

⬆ Clark McIntyre Steer Roping
Cheyenne, Wyoming, Frontier Days, 1954
DeVere Helfrich, photographer
NCM—Dickinson Research Center
DeVere Helfrich Collection, 81.023.09343

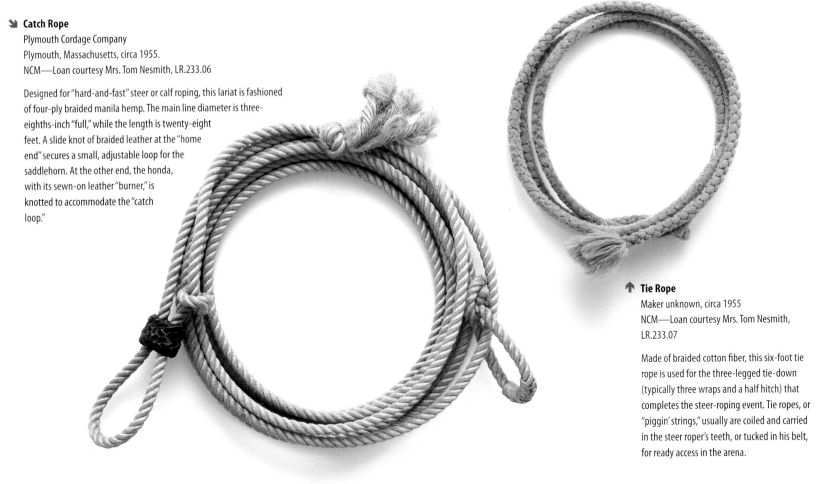

⬃ Catch Rope
Plymouth Cordage Company
Plymouth, Massachusetts, circa 1955.
NCM—Loan courtesy Mrs. Tom Nesmith, LR.233.06

Designed for "hard-and-fast" steer or calf roping, this lariat is fashioned of four-ply braided manila hemp. The main line diameter is three-eighths-inch "full," while the length is twenty-eight feet. A slide knot of braided leather at the "home end" secures a small, adjustable loop for the saddlehorn. At the other end, the honda, with its sewn-on leather "burner," is knotted to accommodate the "catch loop."

⬆ Tie Rope
Maker unknown, circa 1955
NCM—Loan courtesy Mrs. Tom Nesmith, LR.233.07

Made of braided cotton fiber, this six-foot tie rope is used for the three-legged tie-down (typically three wraps and a half hitch) that completes the steer-roping event. Tie ropes, or "piggin' strings," usually are coiled and carried in the steer roper's teeth, or tucked in his belt, for ready access in the arena.

Ikua Purdy of Hawaii, Tying his first Steer,
Cheyenne Frontier Park.

Photograph only Copyrighted by J. E. Stimson, Cheyenne, Wyo.

← **Ikua Purdy of Hawaii, Tying His
First Steer**
Cheyenne, Wyoming, Frontier Park, 1908
J. E. Stimson, publisher
NCM—Dickinson Research Center
Photographic Study Collection, 2003.276

↓ **Catch Rope**
Maker unknown, circa 1925
NCM—Gift of Johnie Schneider, R.218.02

Similar to the *reatas* used by steer-roping
vaqueros nearly a century earlier, this catch
rope is fashioned from four strands of tightly
braided rawhide. Intended for "dally" roping,
the main line is one-quarter inch in diameter
and thirty-four feet in length. The "catch
loop" is formed by drawing some of the main
line through the heavy, knotted and braided
honda at the business end of the rope.

An intriguing manifestation of the Hispanic influence in steer-roping practice can be seen in the contest held at the Cheyenne Frontier Days rodeo in 1908. Since its inception in 1897, the Frontier Days event had been dominated by Wyoming cowboys from area ranches. One of these hands, Angus McPhee, returned in 1908 from the Parker Ranch in Hawaii, and he brought along four seasoned *paniolos* (Hawaiian cowboys) named Archie Ka'aua, Ikua Purdy, Eban "Rawhide Ben" Low, and Jack Low. All were steeped in the Hispanic ranching practices introduced to the islands by Mexican vaqueros in the 1830s, and all entered the Frontier Days steer-roping contest with their lariats at the ready. To both the chagrin and the delight of the Wyoming spectators, Ikua Purdy rode off with the championship, having roped and tied two steers from a sixty-foot scoring line in a cumulative time of one hundred seconds.[34]

Among the best and most colorful steer ropers in the sport, Bob Crosby was born in 1897 at Midland, Texas, and raised around Kenna, New Mexico. He was a seasoned cowhand prior to his debut as a rodeo contestant in 1923 at New York's Yankee Stadium. Known as "Wild Horse Bob"

← **Bob Crosby Steer Roping** (detail)
Pendleton, Oregon, Round-Up, 1944
DeVere Helfrich, photographer
NCM—Dickinson Research Center
Gene Lamb Collection, 1990.016.059

on the circuit, he always competed aggressively. In 1925, in 1927, and again in 1928, Crosby captured the combined, "all-around" titles at both the Pendleton Round-Up and the Cheyenne Frontier Days, thus winning—and finally retiring—the coveted Roosevelt Trophy. These exploits—racking up the most cumulative points among the bronc-riding, steer-roping, bulldogging, and wild-horse-racing events at both venues—essentially equaled three world-championship titles for that era. In later years, Bob Crosby participated in numerous matched-roping contests around the Southwest, many of which he won. Once called "The King of the Cowboys" by *Life* magazine, he was killed in a jeep accident near his New Mexico ranch in 1947. He is remembered for his "lucky" black hat, for a string of exceptional roping horses that included Powder Horn and Jelly Bean, and for his endurance and tenacity in competing and winning with serious injuries.[35]

As earlier noted, rodeos for many years featured various competitive events that are no longer a regular part of venue programming. Most prominent among these were trick and fancy roping, trick riding, and relay racing. Based on Wild West show antecedents, trick ropers and riders thrilled crowds at major rodeos for twenty years, then dwindled from prominence as their skills were relegated to the status of contract performances in the early 1930s. Relay racing remained prominent only as long as rodeos utilized available fairgrounds and racetracks—once they built their own arenas or adopted indoor accommodations, the event disappeared almost entirely.

Trick roping involves the capture of from one to as many as ten running horses—and their riders—using various horizontal or vertical loops. Catches are made by "casting" the loop onto the target and drawing the slack, or by "setting" the loop and allowing the target to run into it. Traditional catch

↑ **Bob Crosby on Nickel** *(detail)*
Winner of Steer Roping and Roosevelt Trophy
Pendleton, Oregon, Round-Up, 1928
Ralph Russell Doubleday, photographer
NCM—Dickinson Research Center
R. R. Doubleday Collection, 79.026.2407

← **Chet Byers Doing a Five Man Catch** *(detail)*
Venue unknown, circa 1935
Photographer unknown
NCM—Dickinson Research Center
Tad S. Mizwa Collection, 2001.036.148

ropes for trick demonstrations usually are fashioned of maguey, a stiff plant fiber that allows control in forming and throwing large loops such as the Ocean Wave and the Figure Eight. Evolved from Mexican *charro* traditions, **fancy roping** consists of spinning or twirling a loop at different speeds and in various horizontal and vertical combinations. Expert fancy ropers can create a variety of loop shapes, movements, and positions using forward and backward twirling motions—either on foot or on horseback. Spinning ropes are fashioned of soft, braided cotton fiber (often referred to as "clothesline rope" or "spotted rope") for smooth motion in creating intricate movements and patterns such as the Spanish Flat, Butterfly, Lift-Over, Roll-Over, and Zig-Zag.[36]

During the era when trick and fancy roping qualified as a competitive event, one of its leading practitioners was Sam Garrett. Born in 1892 at Mulhall, Oklahoma Territory, he grew up among the

↗ **Catch or Trick Rope**
Maker unknown, circa 1920
NCM—Gift of Sam Garrett, 1986.11.16

Fashioned of hard-woven and relatively stiff maguey fiber, this type of rope was made to throw accurately and "hold" a large loop in trick-roping performances. The sixty-five-foot specimen was used by Sam Garrett for many years in making spectacular four- and five-horse catches at rodeo venues across the country.

performing cowboys of the famed Mulhall Congress of Rough Riders and, like Chet Byers, learned fancy roping from Will Rogers. He started touring at age fourteen—billed as "The Boy Wonder of Roping"—with the Miller Brothers' 101 Ranch show and also performed with Buffalo Bill's Wild West, Pawnee Bill's Far East, and the Barnum and Bailey Circus. Garrett began competitive, trick and fancy roping at major rodeos in 1912 and eventually captured the World's Champion Trick Roper title an unprecedented seven times at the Cheyenne Frontier Days. During the 1930s and 1940s, he worked as a riding and roping instructor and as a stunt double in Hollywood, appearing in such films as *Dodge City, Santa Fe Trail,* and *Gone with the Wind.* Famous in later life as the "poet lariat," Garrett and his performing Palomino, Yellow Hammer, delighted audiences around the nation for a generation prior to his death in 1989.[37]

↑ **Spinning Rope**
Plymouth Cordage Company
Plymouth, Massachusetts, circa 1920
NCM—Gift of Edith Jones and W. A. Bliss,
R.241.89

Used by Leonard Stroud in his demonstrations of fancy roping, this twenty-foot line of "spotted cord" incorporates a brass-lined honda for easy passage of the main line when changing the loop's size or position. Made of comparatively pliable cotton fiber, ropes like this proved ideal for spinning loops in various fast-moving patterns.

↑ **Sam Garrett Trick Roping**
Sheridan, Wyoming, Rodeo, circa 1935
Ralph Russell Doubleday, photographer
NCM—Dickinson Research Center
R. R. Doubleday Collection, 79.026.2810

➜ **Sam Garrett with Movie Star Debbie Reynolds**
Los Angeles, California, circa 1955
Rothschild, photographer
NCM—Dickinson Research Center
Sam Garrett Collection, 1986.011.20

Trick riding, adopted from the equestrian stunts of Cossack performers in Wild West shows, combines excellent horsemanship with daring acrobatic maneuvers. A popular contested event at most prominent rodeos between 1915 and 1930, the practice drew both male and female competitors— sometimes in direct competition with one another. Whatever the particular exercise or drill performed, trick riding requires a well-trained, calm, and steady-gaited horse tolerant of a rider's movements around its neck, belly, and hindquarters. The contestants must combine daring, strength, gymnastic skill, superb timing, and real showmanship to successfully perform dangerous maneuvers such as crupper somersaults and handstands while moving around the arena on a loping— sometimes galloping—steed. In addition to relying on dependably trained mounts, trick riders employ saddles uniquely designed for acrobatics on horseback. The extended horn allows a central point to hook a knee around in lay-over stunts, as well as a firm handhold for moving into and recovering from maneuvers

↑ **Trick Rider Mabel Strickland** (detail)
Location unknown, circa 1925
Robert Burns, photographer
NCM—Dickinson Research Center
Howard Tegland Collection, 1991.046.119

← **Barbara Huntington Fender Trick Riding**
(detail)
Klamath Falls, Oregon, Rodeo, 1953
DeVere Helfrich, photographer
NCM—Dickinson Research Center
DeVere Helfrich Collection 81.023.08626

such as the pass-under and the Russian drag. Handholds behind the saddle cantle assist in crupper tricks such as roll-ups and vaults over the rear of the horse. And various support straps allow stability and control in dramatic lay-over and standing stunts.

Certainly among the greatest trick riders of all time, Leonard Stroud was born in 1893 at Monkstown, Texas. He joined the circus at age sixteen and for a time contracted with Ringling Brothers World's Greatest Shows, performing "Wild West trick riding . . . and general Wild West arena work" at $25 per week. Having developed as an all-around hand, he regularly competed in saddle- and bareback-bronc riding, steer roping, and bulldogging—as well as taking command of the trick-riding event—during his prime as a rodeo contestant between 1914 and 1924. In 1918 at Sheepshead Bay, New York, for example, he swept the saddle-bronc, bareback-bronc, and trick-riding contests. He was the first rodeo trick rider to pass under the belly of a galloping horse, and he originated the "Stroud Stand Out," among the most physically challenging and dangerous of trick-riding maneuvers. An adventurous, multitalented, and colorful contender, perhaps the first to make a paying business of contesting in the arena, Stroud died in 1961.[38]

⬆ **Leonard Stroud Going under His Horse while at Full Speed**
Tucumcari, New Mexico, Rodeo, 1919
Ralph Russell Doubleday, photographer
NCM—Dickinson Research Center
Tad S. Mizwa Collection, 2001.036.088

310. Pikes Peak Rodeo.

⬅ **Leonard Stroud Trick Riding and Roping**
Pikes Peak, Colorado, Rodeo, circa 1924
Photographer unknown
NCM—Dickinson Research Center
Edith Jones Waldo Bliss Collection, R.241.121

CONGIRL RACE ROUND UP PENDLETON "LET 'ER BUCK"

Relay racing, a cowgirl contest that had its origins in Montana and Wyoming, became a regular rodeo event in the first decades of the twentieth century. Most early rodeo arenas, such as those at Cheyenne, Pendleton, and Calgary, incorporated half- or one-mile tracks where cowgirl contestants vied for honors in grueling and sometimes-dangerous relay races conducted over two or three days. During each heat, the ladies had to change horses, dismounting and remounting or making "flying mounts" from saddle to saddle, at designated intervals. In early relays, they had to unsaddle and resaddle their steeds at every exchange as well, and such gear swaps and mount changes proved the cause of many accidents. After her first relay race, in which she lost a tooth in a dramatic mishap, Vera McGinnis recalled, "I was the most exhausted girl in the whole world. . . . My lungs ached, my knees buckled under me, and I wished wholeheartedly that my long corset was in Hades."[39] Typically, the rider with the fastest average time over the two- or three-heat contest took home the trophy. Particularly in the West, ladies' relay racing enjoyed great popularity for several decades, but it gradually declined as many venues relocated to smaller, trackless, or indoor arenas.

BONNIE GREY   DONNA GLOVER
MABLE STRICKLAND LORENA TRICKEY
LADY RELAY RIDERS CHEYENNE, WYO.
(DOUBLEDAY)

Among the many extraordinary lady trick riders and relay racers of the 1920s and early 1930s, Vera McGinnis (Farra) proved to be one of the most adventurous and tenacious. Born in 1892 in Missouri, she resided for a time on a Cimarron, New Mexico, ranch, where riding burros and horses captured her heart. Following a fleeting interlude as a movie extra in Hollywood, she started rodeoing in 1913, taking a second in trick riding at the Winnipeg Stampede. She won the relay-race event at Calgary in 1919 and earned the title of World Champion Cowgirl with her twin victories in the trick-riding and relay-riding contests at Tex Austin's 1924 showcase rodeo in London, England. Thereafter, she performed and competed briefly in Europe, participated in an arduous tour through the Orient, and appeared around the United States, occasionally adding bronc riding to her repertoire. An often-difficult and injury-laden career ended abruptly in 1934 when McGinnis went down with a galloping horse, breaking her back in five places, fracturing a hip, and collapsing a lung. Once recovered, she resided for many years in North Fork, California, where she died in 1990, aged ninety-eight.[40]

⬆ **Miss Vera McGinnis Roman Riding** *(detail)*
Klamath Falls, Oregon, Elks Rodeo, circa 1922
Photographer unknown
NCM—Dickinson Research Center
Photographic Study Collection [Vera.04]

⬆ **Vera McGinnis** *(center)* **as "Cossack" Trick Rider**
Touring Rodeo, Yokohama, Japan, 1925
Photographer unknown
NCM—Dickinson Research Center
Photographic Study Collection [Vera.03]

⬅ **Rodeo Cowgirl Vera McGinnis**
Location unknown, circa 1930
Photographer unknown
NCM—Dickinson Research Center
Photographic Study Collection [Vera.01]

The Cowgirl Contenders

Combining Grace and Grit

RODEO COWGIRLS WERE AMONG the first women in the United States to achieve recognition as professional athletes. Combining Wild West showmanship with real athletic skill, they defied conventional gender roles by competing in a traditionally male sport. By the early 1920s, women had achieved a prominent place in rodeo as trick riders, relay racers, and rough-stock contenders. Commencing in the 1930s, however, competitive cowgirls declined in number and prominence. Male-dominated rodeo organizations ignored women as serious participants, opting instead for glamorous but hardly athletic "Ranch Girls." With Gene Autry's virtual monopoly of big-time, East Coast rodeo in the 1940s, the role of female contestants all but disappeared. Yet self-reliant western women did not give up. In 1948 they founded the Girls Rodeo Association (GRA) to ensure their future participation in legitimate rodeo sport. All-girl rodeos gained some standing in the 1950s and 1960s but have never achieved real prominence. Today, under the auspices of the Women's Professional Rodeo Association (WPRA), the majority of female rodeo athletes focus on barrel racing, a timed event at most PRCA-sanctioned rodeos that currently pays out some three million dollars in annual prize money.[1]

Between 1900 and 1920, virtually all the women competing in rodeo grew up on western ranches. All shared superior equestrian skills, and all demonstrated a willingness to challenge the accepted

← Iris Hart on Burnt Feaver [*sic*]
Pendleton, Oregon, Round-Up, 1925
Ralph Russell Doubleday, photographer
NCM—Dickinson Research Center
Photographic Study Collection, 2005.281

→ Olive Lindsey on Sun Fish Molly
Weiser, Idaho, Round-Up, circa 1918
Doubleday-Foster Photo Company, publisher
NCM—Dickinson Research Center
McCarroll Family Trust Collection,
RC2006.076.007

OLIVE LINDSEY ON 'SUN FISH MOLLY' WEISER, ROUND-UP,
(P.F.P. CO, INC.)

stereotypes of the time regarding female fragility and "proper decorum." Although the majority of these early cowgirl contestants actually made much of their livelihood as Wild West show performers, they had few professional peers in American sport at that time. In 1907, May Lillie, the wife of Wild West impresario Pawnee Bill and a talented equestrian performer in her own right, advised others of the fair sex to consider life in the arena. "Let any normally healthy woman who is ordinarily strong screw up her courage and tackle a bucking bronco," Mrs. Lillie proclaimed, "and she will find the most fascinating pastime in the field of feminine athletic endeavor. There is nothing to compare, to increase the joy of living, and once accomplished, she'll have more real fun than any pink tea or theater party or ballroom ever yielded."[2] Within a decade, a bevy of bold cowgirls had taken her advice.

Early-day rodeo women frequently competed in rough-stock events such as saddle-bronc riding, steer roping, and steer wrestling. Bertha Kaepernik (Blancett) and Fannie Sperry (Steele), both of whom rode "slick" (that is, without "hobbled" stirrups tied beneath the horse for increased stability), achieved fame as bronc riders prior to World War I. At the 1913 Winnipeg Stampede, Lucille Mulhall contested head-to-head with the men in the steer-roping competition, taking two go-rounds and receiving the title of

Champion Lady Steer Roper of the World. A determined Tillie Baldwin defeated an otherwise all-male field in Roman racing at the same venue and, that same year, put on a daring steer-wrestling exhibition at the Pendleton Round-Up—a feat no other woman then performed. In addition to Winnipeg and Pendleton, the Cheyenne and Calgary venues also played significant roles in establishing women's place in rodeo sport and creating the first cowgirl superstars. Cheyenne introduced bronc riding and relay racing as customary cowgirl events in 1906, while Calgary's 1912 inaugural rodeo featured these contests as well as fancy roping and trick riding. By 1916, more than twenty rodeos around the West had come to include women's competitions, and perhaps as many as one hundred females pursued the sport with varying intensity. Though World War I slowed arena competition for a time, pioneer cowgirls already had proven their athletic ability, showmanship, and personal determination to excel in a conspicuously masculine and often-dangerous sport.[3]

Women such as Blancett, Steele, Mulhall, and Baldwin were not Amazons on horseback but adventurous and dedicated contestants whose femininity remained unrepressed by their drive for athletic excellence. Nearly all rodeo cowgirls married, and most pursued what domesticity their itinerant lives allowed. Many, for example, became adept seamstresses, creating innovative costumes for the arena. Perhaps with a little embroidery, the *New York World* in 1900 portrayed America's then-leading cowgirl in all her varied dimensions and character: "Little Miss Mulhall, who weighs only 90 pounds, can break a bronco, lasso and brand a steer, and shoot a coyote at 500 yards. She can also play Chopin, quote Browning, construe Virgil, and make mayonnaise dressing."[4] Though Mulhall, her peers, and their many successors obviously demonstrated their daring, determination, athletic skill, and toughness in the arena,

↑ **Mildred Douglas Riding a Steer** *(detail)*
Venue unknown, circa 1920
Doubleday-Foster Photo Company, publisher
NCM—Dickinson Research Center
Photographic Study Collection, 2003.159.04

→ **Dorothy Morrell and Her Prize Saddle**
Cheyenne, Wyoming, Frontier Days, 1914
Photographer unknown
NCM—Dickinson Research Center
McCarroll Family Trust Collection,
RC2006.076.450

most of them also retained their womanly virtues. Bertha Blancett remembered her years in the arena: "I was always a lady. They (the cowboys) treated me as such."[5] The public—and the press—proved nearly unanimous in lauding both the grit and the grace of female contenders in and out of the arena.[6]

Typical of the early rodeo cowgirls, Fannie Sperry (Steele) was born in 1887 and raised on a small ranch in the Bear Tooth Mountains north of Helena, Montana. A lover of horses, she broke them in her youth, made good money in relay and flat racing as a teenager, and came quite naturally to rodeo competition around 1905. Among the finest and most competitive lady bronc riders of the early twentieth century, she won Canada's major stampede two years in a row (first at Calgary in 1912 and then at Winnipeg in 1913), capturing the title of Woman Saddle-Bronc Riding Champion of the World and taking home more than $2,000 in cumulative prize money and trophies. She was noted for never using hobbled stirrups or other "cheat straps" in the arena, a practice common among some women contestants of the era. In 1913, Fannie married W. S. (Bill) Steele, a bronc rider and arena clown. The pair rodeoed sporadically and rode for the C. B. Irwin and Miller Brothers' Wild West shows until about 1930. When her husband died in 1939, she retired to her Montana ranch and worked as a backcountry guide and outfitter. In later life she told an interviewer, "I've never seen one rodeo too many nor ridden one ride too long in my life."[7] Fannie Sperry Steele died in 1983.[8]

Tillie Baldwin, a major rival of both Bertha Kaepernik Blancett and Fannie Sperry Steele during the 1910s, shared none of the western, ranching, or equestrian background typical of early cowgirl competitors. Born Anna Matilda Winger in Avendale, Norway, in 1888, she immigrated to the United States in 1902 with aspirations of becoming a hairdresser. She shortly decided that horses would provide a more interesting life, and in 1909 she joined the Miller Brothers' 101 Ranch Wild West show as a cowgirl trick and bronc rider. Baldwin probably adopted her stage name in 1909–10, when she spent the off-season in Hollywood working with Bison Films. She entered her first real rodeo in Los Angeles in 1912, winning the

ladies' bronc title riding "slick." Later in the year she captured the trick-riding and all-around cowgirl titles at the Pendleton Round-Up. In 1913 she won the cowgirls' trick-riding and relay-race events at Los Angeles, captured the trick-riding and Roman-riding honors at the Winnipeg Stampede, and repeated her trick-riding victory at Pendleton—along with putting on the first demonstration of ladies' steer wrestling. She earned another bronc-riding title at Guy Weadick's New York Stampede in 1916. Though Baldwin was a phenomenal athlete, she forsook contest rodeo for the more lucrative exhibition circuit in the East during the 1920s. She retired from the arena altogether in 1941 and managed the Fred Stone Ranch in Lyme, Connecticut, until her death in 1958 at age eighty.[9]

At about the time Sperry Steele and Baldwin began diminishing their competitive rodeo appearances in the late 1910s and early 1920s, other female contenders, such as Lorena Trickey (Peterson) and Ruth Scantlin (Roach), were ascending to prominence in many of the same events. Born in 1893 near Palmer, Oregon, Trickey grew up in ranching country and joined the Clarence Adams Wild West Show in 1917 as a trick and Roman rider. On the recommendation of Wild West impresario and rodeo stockman C. B. Irwin, she entered competitive rodeo during 1918, specializing in ladies' relay racing and saddle-bronc riding.

As was common at the time, Irwin initially backed her, paying her $25 a week and expenses in exchange for half of any purse she won. The arrangement was short-lived, however, as Lorena began a meteoric career, capturing the saddle-bronc-riding title at Pendleton in 1919; winning the coveted Hotel McAlpin Trophy for the Cowgirl's Relay Race at Cheyenne in 1920 and again as Champion Woman Rider of the Year in 1921; taking the famed *Denver Post* Ladies' Relay Race cup at Cheyenne three times, in 1921, 1924, and 1926; winning the girl's relay race at Pendleton in 1923; and seizing the bronc-riding title at Chicago in 1925. Trickey's reputation as a skilled equestrienne took her briefly to Hollywood, where in 1921 she doubled for Mary Pickford in *Through the Back Door* and rode Roman style with Tom Mix in *The Queen of Sheba*. Her once-stellar rodeo career disintegrated, however, following a first-degree-murder charge in 1927. Though sustained by her arena friends and ultimately exonerated, she dropped from the circuit, married cowboy-prospector Magnus Peterson in 1928, and worked quicksilver claims with him around Tonopah, Nevada, for many years. Today little remembered in rodeo circles, Lorena Trickey Peterson died in 1961, just a few months after making a memorial appearance at the Tonopah Lions Club Horse Show.[10]

Frequently proclaimed "The World's Most Beautiful Cowgirl," Ruth Roach encountered her own picture on the front page of some of the nation's biggest newspapers during the 1920s and 1930s. Of rather humbler origins, she was born Ruth Scantlin in 1896 at Excelsior Springs, Missouri, where as a child she gained some riding experience on her uncle's donkeys. She left home at sixteen for the

⬇ **Ruth Roach on Tony**
Location unknown, circa 1925
Ralph Russell Doubleday, photographer
NCM—Dickinson Research Center
Tad S. Mizwa Collection, 2001.036.174

⬆ **Rodeo Cowgirl Ruth Roach**
Location unknown, circa 1925
Ralph Russell Doubleday, photographer
NCM—Dickinson Research Center
R. R. Doubleday Collection, 79.026.1953

Miller Brothers' 101 Ranch Wild West show, married fellow performer Buck Roach in 1914, and entered competitive rodeo at Lucille Mulhall's 1917 Fort Worth rodeo. There, in her bronc-riding debut, she triumphed on an animal that had bucked off several male contestants. She captured the ladies' bronc-riding title at Cheyenne in 1919, and thereafter, her natural athletic ability kept her in championship contention at the major venues for two decades. Roach competed unfailingly at the great Madison Square Garden rodeo from 1922 through 1936, taking the bronc-riding title in 1932. Additionally, with her horse, Tony, she ranked as one of the era's outstanding trick and fancy riders, winning the championship at both Cheyenne and Pendleton in 1919. Between venues, Roach often posed for rodeo advertisements, and she made appearances in silent movies with Tom Mix and other stars. After remarrying in 1938, she retired from active competition, but she came back in 1942 to participate as a bronc rider in Vaughn Krieg's Flying V All Cow-Girl Rodeo, a patriotic production staged in support of the nation's participation in World War II. Ruth Roach died in 1986.[11]

"West Meets East"
(Rodeo Program Cartoon Art)
Fay King, illustrator
Great Western Rodeo
Harrisburg, Pennsylvania, 1936
NCM—Dickinson Research Center,
06-126.39.01

The 1920s marked a golden decade for sportswomen in America, and this was nowhere more true than in the rodeo arena. New metropolitan venues in Saint Louis, Chicago, New York, and Philadelphia introduced dauntless and glamorous cowgirl athletes to enthusiastic eastern and midwestern crowds, while forward-thinking promoter-producers such as Tex Austin featured ladies' events and highlighted rising female contestants including Florence Hughes (Randolph), "Tad" Barnes (Lucas), and Bonnie Treadwell (McCarroll). Monetary awards increased remarkably throughout the decade, allowing many of these cowgirls to pursue rodeo on a full-time basis. The most talented and energetic of them often accrued annual earnings four to five times the average per-capita income of the decade. And their growing public recognition and popularity encouraged commercial concerns to sponsor special trophies for champion female competitors. For example, the McAlpin Hotel and *Ranch Romances* magazine, both of New York City, and the Juergens and Anderson jewelry company of Chicago inaugurated annual ladies' awards at the Cheyenne Frontier Days, Madison Square Garden, and Tex Austin Chicago competitions, respectively, during the Roaring Twenties. They joined the already dedicated *Denver Post* newspaper, whose silver trophy cups—inaugurated in 1904 at the Cheyenne Frontier Days rodeo—would become the longest-lived prizes reserved especially for female equestrian contestants. The ultimate cowgirl trophy, underwritten by Hollywood's Metro Goldwyn Mayer (MGM) Studio, first appeared in 1927. This prestigious, $10,000, solid-silver art piece—created by Lambert Brothers Jewelers of New York City—went to the annual All-Around Champion Cowgirl at the celebrated Madison Square Garden rodeo until retired by a consecutive three-time winner.[12]

Florence Hughes (Randolph) certainly ranked among the leading cowgirl beneficiaries of the popular acclaim and commercial largesse of 1920s and 1930s rodeo sport. Born in Augusta, Georgia, in 1898, she got her first riding experience on plow mules. After an "apprenticeship" in trick and Roman riding with Colonel King's IXL Ranch Wild West show, she organized Princess Mohawk's Wild West Hippodrome in 1916 and showcased her skills with traveling carnivals. In 1919 at the Calgary

Stampede, Florence made international headlines when she defeated thirteen male contenders in Roman-race riding over a grueling three-mile course, capturing the Prince of Wales Trophy. At the height of her career in the 1920s, she often starred in the trick- and fancy-riding arena on a steady Paint horse named Boy. She married rodeo cowboy and saddlemaker Floyd Randolph in 1925. The following year, Florence earned $6,000 as the bronc-riding, trick-riding, and all-around-champion cowgirl at Philadelphia's Sesquicentennial Rodeo.

In 1927 she rode off with the first MGM Trophy awarded to the All-Around Champion Cowgirl at the big Madison Square Garden rodeo. When not pursuing her favored sport, Florence sometimes raced motorcycles and doubled in challenging equestrian stunts for the movie industry. Retired from active competition in 1939, she and her husband for many years managed and produced the annual Ardmore, Oklahoma, rodeo. Florence Randolph died in 1971.[13]

During the 1920s and 1930s, Tad Barnes (Lucas) ranked as the only female contender to rival and surpass Florence Randolph in cumulative rodeo victories. Born Barbara Barnes in 1902, she was raised around Cody, Nebraska, and started racing horses in her youth. She entered her first rodeo in 1917 at Gordon, Nebraska, getting bucked off a saddle bronc but taking first place in steer riding. Though Tad began rodeoing as a rough-stock contestant and rode saddle broncs all through her career, she realized her greatest triumphs as a relay racer and trick rider. Married to Buck Lucas in 1924, she honeymooned at Tex Austin's London rodeo but rode with only modest success. Thereafter, however, Tad Lucas truly hit her stride in the arena. She won the trick-riding title at Cheyenne in 1925 and 1927 and took relay-race championships in

1930, 1931, and 1932. Between 1925 and 1929, her record at Chicago numbered three trick-riding titles, two relay titles, and two all-around cowgirl championships. At Fort Worth between 1926 and 1933, she captured the trick-riding event four times. And at the much-acclaimed Madison Square Garden rodeo, Tad won the trick-riding title seven times—and the all-around cowgirl championship six times—in the eight years between 1925 and 1932. In achieving the latter feat, she took permanent possession of the coveted Metro Goldwyn Mayer Trophy in 1930 after three consecutive all-around cowgirl victories—thereby retiring the most impressive and costly rodeo prize ever awarded to a female rodeo athlete. In 1940 Lucas joined the U.S. Rodeo Team, competing in the Royal Easter Show at Sidney, Australia. During the early 1940s, she participated in several all-girl rodeos, and after World War II, she actively supported the nascent Girls Rodeo Association. With her husband, Buck, she produced rodeos for a number of years

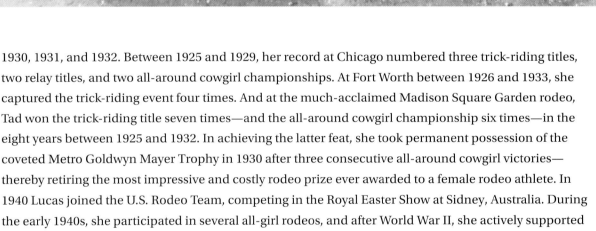

and performed in the arena in some capacity for four decades.[14] Tad Barnes Lucas died in 1990 in Fort Worth, Texas. Rodeo-cowgirl historian Mary Lou LeCompte characterized her as "truly the quintessential cowgirl of the twenties."[15]

The dauntless arena cowgirls of the 1910s, 1920s, and 1930s became the pacesetters of rodeo dress both in function and in flamboyance. Initially

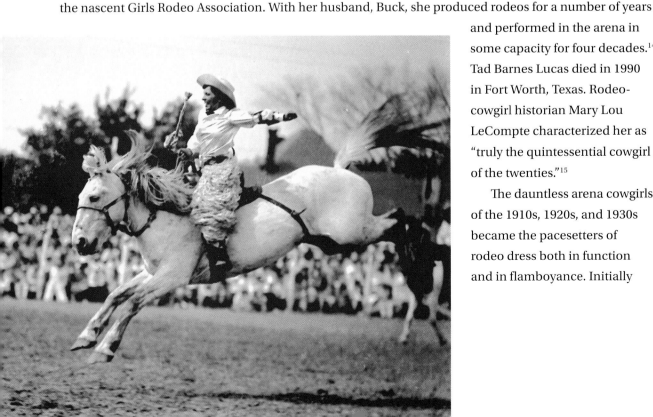

influenced by Wild West costume, most early contestants favored shirtwaists with embroidered vests and divided riding skirts of supple leather adorned with fringe. Enormous, ten-gallon hats; fancy gauntlets; wide, contoured bronc or kidney belts adorned with spots; and finely decorated, custom-made boots were standard dress elements, and many would remain in vogue into the 1940s. Prior to World War I, however, some cowgirls—led by Norwegian-emigrant Tillie Baldwin—began adopting more-athletic ensembles comprising a middy blouse worn with knee-length bloomers. These early "gym suits" allowed greater freedom of movement and found special favor among the trick riders and relay racers. In addition, trick riders sometimes replaced their boots with gum-soled swimming or tennis shoes to maintain better "purchase" in maneuvering around their loping steeds. Virtually all female rodeo competitors designed and sewed their own costumes, and a few of them, such as irrepressible Prairie Rose Henderson, went to outlandish lengths to express their individualism.[16] "Prairie Rose was the queen of fashion," wrote Vera McGinnis, who described one of Henderson's garish outfits as "bloomers with a long matching overblouse trimmed in chiffon, sequins, and a wide band of marabou feathers. With this of course she wore matching stockings, a wide brimmed [and] tall crowned western hat, boots, and spurs."[17]

↑ Rene Hafley Shelton, Fox Hastings,
 Rose Smith, Ruth Roach, Mabel
 Strickland, Prairie Rose [Henderson],
 and Dorothy Morrell
Location unknown, circa 1920
Doubleday-Foster Photo Company, publisher
NCM—Dickinson Research Center
Howard Tegland Collection, 1991.046.083

McGinnis found split riding skirts a nuisance, so in the early 1920s she donned a pair of boys' pants and initiated lasting changes in women's rodeo fashion. Elements of her later outfits—particularly her bell-bottomed trousers, styled bolero vests and jackets, and flamboyant scarves and colorful sashes—established the standard around the ladies' circuit for a decade. At the 1922 Madison Square Garden rodeo, functionalism came to the fore when several female contestants appeared wearing jodhpurs. Within but a few years, various patterns of knee-length and ankle-length riding pants had completely supplanted divided skirts and bloomers among cowgirl bronc and trick riders. Then, in 1924, Tad Lucas donned chaps for the bronc-riding event, and they, too, became de rigueur among the lady rough-stock riders almost overnight.[18] Around 1930, a *Fort Worth Star-Telegram* article on rodeo women observed that cowgirl outfits usually were fairly feminine and form-fit, as well as being—for the most part—functional. "That's quite a trick of tailoring," the paper digressed tongue in cheek, "considering the way the clothes fit. You may have noticed what happened to the breeches of [that] cowgirl trick rider Monday afternoon. She was very embarrassed."[19] Embarrassments aside, these elements of arena dress remained fairly uniform among female rodeo performers into the late 1930s. Thereafter, "western wear" began to appear as a distinct commercial fashion—and the demonstration of genuine riding skill dwindled in the face of other commercial considerations.

→ [Rodeo] Cowgirls
Colorado Springs, Colorado, Round-Up,
circa 1925
Ralph Russell Doubleday, photographer
NCM—Dickinson Research Center
McCarroll Family Trust Collection,
RC2006.076.264-01

↓ Cowgirls at Tex Austin's Rodeo
Chicago, Illinois, 1927
Ralph Russell Doubleday, photographer
NCM—Dickinson Research Center
McCarroll Family Trust Collection,
RC2006.076.279-01

COWGIRLS AT THE ARK-OKLA RODEO, (DOUBLEDAY)

↑ **Cowgirls at the Ark-Okla Rodeo**
Fort Smith, Arkansas, circa 1935
Ralph Russell Doubleday, photographer
NCM—Dickinson Research Center
Photographic Study Collection, Doubleday 106

← **Cowgirl Arena Western Wear**
Location unknown, circa 1952
Levi Strauss marketing photograph
NCM—Dickinson Research Center
Photographic Study Collection, 06-190.39.02

The participation of women in arena competition commenced a steady decline beginning in 1929. The signal event that seemingly precipitated this change occurred when a bucking horse named Black Cat fatally trampled popular bronc rider Bonnie McCarroll in front of thousands of spectators at the Pendleton Round-Up. Born Mary Ellen Treadwell in 1897 on a ranch outside of Boise, Idaho, she entered her first rodeo at Vancouver, Washington, in 1915 and married steer wrestler Frank McCarroll that same year. Throughout the 1920s, she competed and won against the best of her time, including greats such as Vera McGinnis, Mabel Strickland, and Tad Lucas. She captured the saddle-bronc-riding title at Pendleton in 1921 and 1922 and was the first to take the event at Madison Square Garden in the latter year. At Tex Austin's First International Rodeo in London in 1924, McCarroll won the Lord Selfridge Trophy as the Champion Lady Saddle-Bronc Rider.[20] Her tragic death stunned rodeo fans and generated reams of negative publicity. Within months, cowgirl rough-stock events were canceled at Pendleton and many other venues around the West. (At the larger, independent rodeos in the East, however, ladies' bronc riding continued for another decade.) In perspective, Bonnie McCarroll's fatal ride endures as a dramatic portent amidst larger currents and developments that would diminish the position of cowgirl contenders in succeeding decades.

In society at large, the exuberant freedom of the Roaring Twenties, in which the cowgirl athlete had flourished, succumbed to the economic and social constraints of the Great Depression, which dominated life throughout the 1930s. Although the finest and most energetic rodeo cowgirls, such as Tad Lucas and Florence Randolph, continued to find an adequate—or better—living going down the road, many of those who had formerly thrived on western venues alone found the going difficult. Within the sport, contrary influences arose with the formation of the Rodeo Association of America (RAA) in 1929. This rather patriarchal organization of managers and committees, founded in an effort to standardize rodeo productions and events, evinced little enthusiasm for female contestants and refused to sanction cowgirl rough-stock events. The place of women diminished further starting in 1931, when trick riding was changed from a contested event to a contract act, once again decreasing the paying venues open to female competitors. The organization in 1936 of the

Bonnie McCarroll Horseback *(detail)*
Location unknown, circa 1924
Photographer unknown
NCM—Dickinson Research Center
McCarroll Family Trust Collection,
RC2006.076.422

Bonnie McCarroll on Morning Glory *(detail)*
Tex Austin's Rodeo, Yankee Stadium, New York, 1923
Ralph Russell Doubleday, photographer
NCM—Dickinson Research Center
McCarroll Family Trust Collection,
RC2006.076.104-02

Cowboys Turtle Association (CTA) further marginalized the distaff contenders. Much like the male-dominated RAA, this fledgling union of rodeo athletes provided arena cowgirls with little meaningful voice or representation.[21]

Though aspiring rodeo cowgirls found fewer opportunities to contest in the 1930s, some nonetheless rose to prominence. One of these was Alice Greenough, whose victories in the arena brought her much commercial success as well. Born in 1902 on the Red Lodge, Montana, ranch of "Packsaddle Ben" Greenough, she, like her siblings, grew up as a working hand. Answering an ad in *Billboard Magazine* for lady bronc riders, in 1929 she and her sister, Marjorie, entered the arena for a "high-ridin', high-kickin' career." Rather indelicately nicknamed "She-Boss," Alice captured the ladies' bronc-riding title at Boston Garden in 1933, 1935, and 1936 and at Madison Square Garden in 1940. In 1935 and 1939, she won the "buckjumping" championship at the Royal Easter Show and Rodeo held in Sydney, Australia. Her acclaim "down under" and at home led to lucrative commercial endorsements for a variety of products ranging from saddles to cigarettes. In 1942, Alice retired from the arena and teamed with her longtime friend Joe Orr to produce the Greenough-Orr Rodeo in the Northwest. In 1967 they sold out and got married. Alice Greenough Orr died in 1995, having lived by a simple creed: "I never smoked. I never drank. I never swore. I was always taught by my father that you ought to conduct yourself like a lady."[22]

↑ **Tad Lucas and Florence Randolph** (detail)
Location unknown, circa 1935
Ralph Russell Doubleday, photographer
NCM—Dickinson Research Center
R. R. Doubleday Collection, 79.026.1661

← **Marge [and] Alice Greenough**
Location unknown, circa 1935
Ralph Russell Doubleday, photographer
NCM—Dickinson Research Center
Thompson/Doubleday Collection,
2001.014.1.017

↓ **Alice Greenough Saddle Bronc Riding**
(detail)
Great Falls, Montana, Rodeo, circa 1940
Ralph Russell Doubleday, photographer
NCM—Dickinson Research Center
R. R. Doubleday Collection, 79.026.3865

MARGE + ALICE GREENOUGH
(DOUBLEDAY)

➜ **A Rodeo Sponsor Contestant, or "Ranch Girl"**
Location unknown, circa 1945
Photographer unknown
NCM—Dickinson Research Center
Photographic Study Collection,
1979.025.1765

The emergence of so-called sponsor contests during the early 1930s marked another setback for competitive cowgirl athletes. First held at the Stamford, Texas, Cowboy Reunion in 1931, these events featured attractive but largely nonathletic "Ranch Girls" whose participation was intended to "add a little charm and glamor to the previously masculine rodeo."[23] The young women were judged not on their riding or roping prowess but on their looks, outfit, mount, and rudimentary horsemanship. Within a decade, sponsor contests spread from the Southwest to the big eastern rodeos, gradually marginalizing true female competitors. The impact of America's entry into World War II and the monopoly of big-time, East Coast rodeo by Gene Autry and Everett Colborn in the early 1940s further altered the character and status of the arena cowgirl, as she was transformed from a skilled athlete into a patriotic cheerleader or a largely passive ornament for the cowboy star. In 1942, Autry eliminated ladies' bronc riding at the prestigious Boston and New York rodeos. Within a year, female rough-stock contestants virtually vanished from the sport, to be replaced by fetching lady riders proficient at little more than entry parade spectacles and exhibition barrel running.[24]

➜ **Everett Colborn and Gene Autry** *(detail)*
Venue unknown, circa 1945
Ralph Russell Doubleday, photographer
NCM—Dickinson Research Center
R. R. Doubleday Collection, 79.026.3120

Reporting on the Madison Square Garden World's Championship Rodeo in 1945, well-known announcer Foghorn Clancy inadvertently pointed up the much-diminished and altered status of rodeo cowgirls in his description of the opening ceremonies. "Instead of breaking right into the grand entry," Clancy observed, "the house was darkened and the spotlight thrown upon the beautiful ranch or sponsor girls as they were introduced one by one. . . . All were mounted on snow white horses and made a gorgeous picture as they galloped to the end of the arena and took up position in front of the chutes from which they reviewed the grand entry."[25] The six sponsor girls—all Texans—were named in Clancy's article along with their hometowns, but when his reportage came to the champions and runners-up in each of the venue's competitive events, no women's event or woman's name appeared.

➜ **Rodeo Program**
Rodeo Souvenir Annual/ 1947
Southwestern Exposition and Fat Stock
Show/ Fort Worth, Texas
P. Belew, illustrator
Fort Worth Rodeo Committee, 1947
NCM—Dickinson Research Center
Willard Porter Collection, 2001.049.05

As style supplanted real athleticism, rodeo Ranch Girls (and many male contestants as well) donned the flamboyant western apparel popular among B-western cowboy crooners. Made by prominent custom outfitters such as Rodeo Ben of Philadelphia, Nudie Cohn of Hollywood, Fay Ward of New York, and regional tailors such as Maude McMorries of Doole, Texas, these eye-catching outfits centered on finely crafted shirts with shaped yokes, "smile" pockets, pearl snap fasteners, contrasting piping, and fancy figural embroidery. Between 1935 and 1950, these and other stylistic elements came to personify "western wear," which rapidly evolved into a garment industry standard with companies including Miller Stockman (now Miller Western Wear), Rockmount Ranch Wear, Trego's Westwear, and H-Bar-C Ranchwear. By the early 1950s, this often-colorful apparel had become commonplace among arena cowgirls and cowboys alike, and it continues in vogue with all types of westerners.[26] Today, rodeo cowgirls—and their male counterparts—usually compete in Wrangler jeans and fancy, western-cut shirts that are further adorned with the names and brand logos of the sport's leading commercial sponsors.

Though banished from big-time rodeo, the truly athletic and competitive cowgirl did not disappear altogether. During the early 1940s, Texans Fay Kirkwood and Vaughn Krieg organized several all-

girl rodeos in their state that included bronc riding, calf roping, bulldogging, and steer riding. In 1948 a group of working cowgirls established the Girls Rodeo Association (GRA)—the first organization of professional female athletes in the country—to perpetuate ladies' events and reestablish women's participation in the sport. Though the group made only modest progress in reviving women's rough-stock competition through all-girl rodeos, it did succeed in establishing ladies' barrel racing as a standard contest event on the professional circuit. In 1954 barrel racing appeared at the Madison Square Garden rodeo, and in 1967, the event was officially sanctioned at the National Finals Rodeo (NFR), then in Oklahoma City. Cowgirls finally were back in the big-time.

Today, the successor to the GRA, the Women's Professional Rodeo Association (WPRA), boasts over two thousand members who compete for some three million dollars in prize money at more than six hundred sanctioned rodeos across the country.[27]

Cowboys and Cowgirls at the
15th Annual Worlds Championship Rodeo
Madison Square Garden - N.Y. City - Oct. 9-17 1940.
#4951-C-1

4 Coming of Age

Organization, Professionalism, Big Business

THOUGH RODEO AS A SPECTATOR SPORT grew and flourished throughout the 1920s, it nonetheless remained fundamentally unorganized at the managerial and contestant levels alike. Promoter Guy Weadick's 1915 appeal for organization (quoted in chapter 1) was forcefully reiterated the following year by rodeo-manager Tex Austin, who pointed up the need, as well, for increased cooperation and understanding among venue organizers and arena contestants.

I have seen the game from both sides, and in my opinion there are some things left unsaid that need saying. I am now helping to ramrod the Cowboys' Reunion at Las Vegas [New Mexico], which we hope to make one of

← **Cowboys and Cowgirls at the 15th Annual World's Championship Rodeo**
Madison Square Garden, New York City, New York, October 9–17, 1940
DeVere Helfrich, photographer
NCM—Dickinson Research Center
DeVere Helfrich Collection, 1981.023.00058A

→ **Tex Austin, Everlastingly of Rodeo Fame** (detail)
Chicago, Illinois, 1926
Ralph Russell Doubleday, photographer
NCM—Dickinson Research Center
McCarroll Family Trust Collection,
RC2006.076.291

the greatest shows ever produced. . . . Some things we are not doing[:] We are not advertising the cost of producing this show, as that much prize money. We are not advertising any prize saddle or trophies, as prize money. We are not advertising any money that we can't or won't pay in gold, 100 cents on the dollar. We are not crowing any "so-called" World's Champion in any line, to create more arguments, of which we are all so damned tired. We are not guaranteeing any contestant any money in any competitive event. . . . The contestants will elect their own judges and we will endeavor to see that they get all they earn. Now about the contestants. There are lots of A#1 good people in the game, and a few sorry ones, who are hurting this class of show business worse than anything the managers can do. There are a few who have a bad case of the swelled head and a great many others who show too much . . . professional jealousy that is the worst possible thing for the game. If there were no crooked contestants there would be fewer crooked contests. I have on my desk now numerous requests for guarantees in competitive events. In my opinion most of the people who ask such guarantees are unable to go to a square contest

CdW BOYS WAITING FOR THEIR TURN IN THE BUCKING CONTEST. THE ROUND PENDLETON

and win any money. . . . If the contestants will consider these things and realize that they themselves can do a whole lot for the game[,] with their help we will make this . . . the squarest and best show ever produced, and one worthy of the name "contest."[1]

The problems and issues identified by Austin unfortunately would continue to plague the sport for another twenty years and more. Even among the major venues, little uniformity or unanimity existed in regard to standard rodeo events and their rules, judging, and scoring.

The issue of multiple "world champion" titles, declared in various events and at venues all over the country, caused unending confusion and no little rancor even prior to World War I. In 1915, *Wild Bunch* editor Homer Wilson observed that the constant talk about champions and near champions "sounds like war and rumors of war." He lamented the pervasive awarding of "world titles" and characterized the many side-contests between supposed champions as superfluous:

Published challenges coming from Tom, Dick and Harry bring the game into the limelight of ridicule. . . . It is true that there are a number of round-ups and contests, rodeos and frontier day celebrations, and various contestants win first honors in these various events, perhaps producing many champions for one single title; this shows a lack of organization on the part of the general interest. . . . A general round-up could be inaugurated where all successful contestants could meet and decide the matter of championship in the various lines. This contest should be under the supervision of all the interests in the game, and take place at the close of the contest season. . . . No contestant should be allowed to enter this final that has not won his spurs during the season at the regular round-ups.[2]

The championship-establishing scenario envisioned by Wilson would be realized in its basic details some forty years later with the creation of the National Finals Rodeo (NFR). But this occurred only after a long pull "on the part of the general interest" to bring organization and professionalism to the game.

Not until 1929, when local committees around the West formed the Rodeo Association of America (RAA), were uniform rules and regulations introduced into the sport in a relatively coherent manner. According to its constitution, the organization was formed to ensure "harmony among them [the member rodeos] and to perpetuate traditions connected with the livestock industry and the cowboy sports incident thereto; to standardize the same and adopt rules looking forward towards the holding of contests upon [a] uniform basis; to minimize so far as practicable conflict in dates of contests; and to place such sports so nearly as may be possible on a par with amateur athletic events."[3] The RAA stipulated that to be sanctioned, its member rodeos would have to present a program including the standard events of saddle-bronc riding, steer or bull riding, steer wrestling, steer roping, and calf roping. To eliminate the confusion and controversy arising from the declaration of "world champions" at several venues every year, the RAA instituted a point system based on the total contestant dollars won in any of the recognized events at any recognized venue. At year's end, world event titles went to the competitor with the highest number of points in each contest, while the all-around cowboy championship went to the contestant with the greatest cumulative points in two or more events. Champions are declared under much the same point system today by the Professional Rodeo Cowboys Association.[4]

Bronc rider Earl Thode was the first undisputed all-around-champion cowboy declared under the RAA scoring process, in 1929. Born on a ranch near Belvedere, South Dakota, in 1900, he became a talented bronc rider and entered the rodeo arena around 1918. During twenty years of active competition, he rode successfully in England and Mexico, as well as at premier venues such as Calgary, Cheyenne, Denver, Chicago, and New York. He captured the coveted Ken Maynard trophy as the World's Champion Cowboy at Madison Square Garden in 1928, and he proved that the victory was no accident by winning the first RAA bronc-riding and all-around titles the next year. Topping such tough horses as Pancho Villa, Five Minutes to Midnight, Goodbye Dan, and the Crying Jew, Thode secured the RAA saddle-bronc championship a second time in 1931. His last significant victories came at Cheyenne and Calgary, where he won the bronc-riding laurels in 1934 and 1937, respectively. After departing the arena, he ran a ranching operation near Casa Grande, Arizona, for several years. Remembered as the first "recognized"

⬇ **Earl Thode, 1st Prize**
Cheyenne, Wyoming, Frontier Days, 1927
Ralph Russell Doubleday, photographer
NCM—Dickinson Research Center
R. R. Doubleday Collection, 79.026.1970

↘ **Earl Thode on 5 Till Mid-Nite** [sic]
Cheyenne, Wyoming, Frontier Days, 1936
Out West Photo, publisher
NCM—Dickinson Research Center
Photographic Study Collection, 2005.074.2

all-around-champion cowboy in rodeo annals, Thode drowned in a boating accident near his Arizona home in 1964.[5]

The RAA also attempted to address two long-standing problems of particular concern to the individual and still-independent contestants: dependable purse awards both as advertised and as ultimately paid, and even-handed judging at all venues. For decades, unscrupulous managers and fly-by-night shows had advertised large purse awards to attract the best contestants—only to fail to pay off the winners because of poor attendance, gross mismanagement, or outright chicanery. The organization proved incapable of entirely resolving this problem because many rodeos and shows remained autonomous. Likewise, the issue of fair judging took years to resolve because of favoritism, incompetence, or outright prejudice. Local judges often preferred local cowboys over itinerant contestants—no matter the superiority of the latter. Inept judging also proved common in early rodeo. It especially infuriated seasoned contenders, one of whom commented, "Have Bronc riders to judge Bronc riding, not sheep herders or men that know nothing about it."[6] The manifestation of overt prejudice in judging typically reflected the race discrimination prevalent during the Jim Crow era. Though African American and Hispanic cowboys were not universally barred from competition, they rarely experienced even-handed treatment once in the arena.

Prejudicial judging founded on race was epitomized in the careers of black bronc riders George Fletcher and Jesse Stahl. Born in 1890 at Saint Mary's, Kansas, Fletcher is remembered for his fine riding at the 1911 Pendleton Round-Up, where he unquestionably made a superior showing against top competitors Jackson Sundown and John Spain. The arena judges, however, awarded first place to Spain (even though he probably "pulled leather" on his last ride) and gave second place to Fletcher and third to Sundown. The black cowboy was not allowed into many large rodeos thereafter because the whites did not want to compete against him—owing to both his evident skill and his color. Fletcher died in 1971, two years after the Pendleton Round-Up Hall of Fame honored him among its first ten inductees.[7]

Jesse Stahl, born in 1883 in Tennessee, moved as a young man to California, where he became one of the state's greatest rodeo hands. He began competing at leading venues in 1913 and ultimately made memorable appearances at major competitions such as Salinas, Reno, Pendleton, and New York. Quick, coordinated, and strong, he rode some of the toughest broncs of the day, yet because of his race, he rarely received scores indicative of his performance. "He was a great bronc rider," one white contemporary later quipped, "but he is most remembered for winning first, but getting third."[8] At a John Day, Oregon, rodeo during the 1920s, the judges actually gave Stahl a second place in bronc riding. Perhaps in mockery of their largesse, he then performed an exhibition for the crowd, riding a bronc to a standstill while seated backwards with a suitcase in one hand! (This contrary riding style became an occasional paid performance in subsequent years.) A true champion who earned the respect of other arena cowboys, if not the judges, Stahl rodeoed where admitted until 1936 and died two years later.[9]

Though the RAA fostered improvements during the early 1930s in rodeo programming, procedures, scoring, and payoffs among its affiliate rodeos, the individual contestant remained independent and essentially unprotected. As with venue management, calls for the organization of rodeo contestants dated from the 1910s. Fay Ward, a rodeo hand and later western fashion designer and cowboy author, editorialized in *The Wild Bunch* in 1916 for an "order" of cowboy contestants with a headquarters "camp" in each state that would host an annual convention and rodeo, the proceeds going to the order for "a greater future for the game." Significant among his suggestions was the establishment of a benefit fund to pay the medical and funeral expenses of indigent contestants. A major failing of Ward's prospective "order" stemmed from his insistence that it be restricted to genuine "cowpunchers."[10] As traditional individualists, the majority of the working cowboy contenders of that era held fast to personal self-reliance, shunning the idea of a unifying organization that might direct their activities and behavior. It would take another two decades of hard experience before these men joined together to assert their rights in the arena.

The catalyst that ultimately transformed contestant attitudes emerged at the 1936 Boston Garden Rodeo, which manager Colonel W. T. Johnson had promoted with the declaration "It's goin' to be tougher than hell; if a cowboy claims to be a champion, let him come to Boston and prove it."[11] The best contenders did come, only to find that Johnson offered a paltry total purse of $6,400 for the ten-day show—so little money that even the event winners might fail to cover their expenses. (In contrast, at the eighteen-day Madison Square

→ **Colonel W. T. Johnson**
Location unknown, circa 1940
Clay Dahlberg, photographer
NCM—Dickinson Research Center
Tad S. Mizwa Collection, 2005.003.3.38A.24

October 30, 1936.

For the Boston Show, we the undersigned demand that the Purses be doubled and the Entrance Fees added in each and every event. Any Contestant failing to sign this Petition will not be permitted to contest, by order of the undersigned.

← **Rodeo Cowboys' Strike Document**
Drawn up at Boston, Massachusetts, 1936
NCM—Loan courtesy Frances Fletcher, LR.215.09

Among the most significant documents in rodeo history, this strike petition led directly to the organization of the Cowboys Turtle Association, the first sports union representing the interests of contesting athletes. Dated October 30, 1936, and signed by sixty-one discontented cowboys, it demanded "that the Purses be doubled and the Entrance Fees added in each and every event. Any Contestant failing to sign this Petition will not be permitted to contest, by order of the undersigned." The original document is displayed in the museum's American Rodeo Gallery.

Garden Championship Rodeo that had closed just days earlier, the purse was $45,000.) A few days before the Boston opening, sixty-one cowboys presented Johnson with a petition demanding that the total purse be doubled and entrance fees added to each event. With no satisfactory reply, the cowboy contestants went on strike, watching from the stands as stable boys, former jockeys, and chute hands sought to master rank horses while the band played "Empty Saddles in the Old Corral." Colonel Johnson and the Boston Garden management raised the purse to $14,000 the next day, and the cowboys, recognizing that their unified action had won the confrontation, moved immediately to formalize their newfound power in a union—the United Cowboys Turtle Association (CTA).[12]

The unusual name was adopted in recognition of their tardiness (and perhaps their unwillingness "to stick their necks out") in organizing for the purpose of mutual protection and benefits. In formulating its governing document, the fledgling cowboy coalition declared that its principal objective was "to raise the standard of rodeos as a whole and to give them undisputed place in the foremost rank of American sports. This is to be done by classing as 'unfair' [i.e., striking against] those shows which use rules unfair to the contestants and those which offer purses so small as to make it impossible for contestants to make expenses. The Association asks a fair deal for contestants as well as rodeo organizations and hopes to work harmoniously with them."[13] The CTA adopted rules regarding strikes and individual member conduct that demonstrated its intention to exercise unified action in controversies with management and unified authority over the rank and file. Strikes, whether to demand adequate monies or competent judges, could be called only with the consent of the entire membership. Strikebreakers would be fined $500, while "disgraceful conduct" on the part of any member merited a fine of $100. Fines and annual dues went into a trust fund to underwrite negotiations with rodeo management and to cover the bills of indigent and deadbeat contenders—the latter a clear effort to foster a more positive public image of the cowboy.[14]

⬇ **Original Officers of the Cowboys Turtle Association**
Photographer unknown
NCM—Dickinson Research Center
Photographic Study Collection,
2006-190.39.09

Standing, left to right: Richard Merchant, Jimmy Minoto, Earl Thode, Doff Aber, and first president Everett Bowman. *Seated, left to right:* Harry Knight, Bob Crosby, Eddie Woods, Jake McClure, Shorty Hill, Smokey Snyder, and Johny Bowman. Dallas, Texas (?), 1937.

Rather intoxicated with the newfound power of collective bargaining, the CTA proved unnecessarily contentious over the next few years, battling with RAA and venue managements through the threat of boycotts and outright strikes. Cowboy demands and strong-arm ultimatums brought defiance from several rodeos; the 1937 Pendleton Round-Up, for example, reverted to amateur contestants, advising that "No Turtles Need Apply." Seemingly arbitrary decisions by CTA leadership also brought dissension to the organization's ranks for a time. Gradually, however, the Turtles, whose slogan was "slow but sure," sought and won larger purse awards, competent judges, and the application of uniform rules throughout the sport. By 1940 the body had curbed its zeal for confrontation, seeking improved collaboration with

rodeo management and engendering a greater sense of sportsmanship within the arena. With CTA guidelines and support, the individual cowboy also underwent a positive transformation in demeanor and appearance, foreshadowing the beginnings of true professionalism.[15]

Among the CTA's early leadership, longtime spokesman and president Everett Bowman certainly stood out both for his athletic prowess and his confrontational management style. Born in Hope, New Mexico, in 1899, he grew up on Texas and Arizona ranches and became a skilled cowboy as a youth. He entered his first rodeo at Salt Lake City in 1924 and hit his championship stride five years later. In total, Bowman captured three world event championships in calf roping (1929, 1935, and 1937), one in steer roping (1937), and four in bulldogging (1930, 1933, 1935, and 1938). These triumphs won him all-around cowboy titles in 1935 and 1937, and he was the runner-up for the all-around title as well in 1936, 1938, and 1939—a record of remarkable ability, consistency, and endurance. Elected CTA president in 1937, Bowman, though often shortsighted and arbitrary as a leader, did more to organize and support contesting cowboys during his seven-year tenure than any

↑ Everett Bowman as Calf-Roping Contestant
Location unknown, circa 1926
Photographer unknown
NCM—Dickinson Research Center
Photographic Study Collection, 1988.9.90

president since. Called by some "the George Washington of Rodeo," he retired from active service in 1945 but remained a prominent spokesman for his favored sport until his death in a plane crash in 1971.[16] Rodeo historian Kristine Fredriksson credits Bowman "with the leadership that laid the foundation for organized professional rodeo."[17]

Just as the sport began moving toward greater organization and a more united purpose, it was confronted with the challenges of World War II. Early government-mandated restrictions on public gatherings and travel along the East and West Coasts, coupled with the ongoing rationing of gas and tires, resulted in many venue cancellations in 1942 and curtailed contestant travel for the duration of the conflict. In addition, volunteer and draftee inductions into the military reduced the ranks of rodeo contenders. In the summer of 1943, some 130 CTA members were scattered around the globe in the service of their country, and more would follow as U.S. participation in the war expanded. The sport and its people, however, refused to be retarded by these limitations. By the early 1940s, rodeo had come to enjoy broad appreciation as a distinctly American pastime and, thus, as a patriotic avocation and potential morale builder as well. By the close of 1943, the RAA and various western stock contractors had formed an alliance with the armed services for the presentation of rodeos at military camps around the country. These popular performances exposed hundreds of thousands of soldiers to the sport, creating thousands of new fans and not a few new contenders.[18]

Far Away in the Fox Holes

United We Stand

Yesterday and Today

As the troops dispersed to the various theaters of war, they took their enthusiasm for rodeo with them. By the conflict's cessation, improvised rodeos had been staged in India, China, Australia, Great Britain, North Africa, Italy, France, and Germany, encouraging a worldwide recognition of, and appreciation for, America's cowboy sport. In January 1945, for example, Corporal A. J. Greening wrote to *Hoofs and Horns* magazine of a recent contest in England: "All of us old cowhands got together and put on a rodeo directed under the U.S.A.A.F. [U.S. Army Air Force]. It was a big success with about 18,000 fans and these English people sure did enjoy it. . . . There was no prize money," Greening lamented, "but plenty to drink."[19] Toward the end of World War II, *Hoofs and Horns* editor Ethel "Ma" Hopkins sketched something of the character of the rodeo cowboy at war: "When I get letters from the boys overseas and hear about the rodeos they put on in the various lands, working like beavers to make the most of what they have to do with, it convinces me more than ever that there's no way to take the cowboy out of them. Good fighters they are, in whatever branch of service they are, for they are ingenious, quick-thinking, resourceful, courageous, and have no such word in their dictionary as 'quit,' but first, last and always, they are COWBOYS."[20]

Among the many rodeo hands who served their country and advanced their sport during the war, perhaps none was more emblematic of this characterization than the exuberant Fritz Truan. Born in 1916 at Seeley, California, he joined the circuit in

↑ **Fritz Truan with Brigadier General LeRoy P. Hunt, U.S.M.C.**
Kaneoha Bay, Hawaii, Marine Air Station Rodeo, 1944
Photographer unknown
NCM—Dickinson Research Center
Photographic Study Collection, 1988.9.866

1935, rapidly establishing a reputation as a superb bronc rider and capable bulldogger. He had his greatest ride aboard Hell's Angel in 1939 at Madison Square Garden and ultimately won the saddle-bronc championship for the year. He took the title again in 1940 and added the all-around cowboy championship. Truan joined the U.S. Marine Corps in 1942, fought in the Pacific theater, and flew from his posting in May 1944 to contest at a rodeo in Honolulu, Hawaii, where the calf ropers and bulldoggers competed from Jeeps. Well known for his determination and competitive spirit, he died in action during the battle for Iwo Jima in February 1945. The rodeo arena at Kaneoha Bay Marine Air Station in the Hawaiian Islands later was named in his honor.[21]

Perhaps to its own surprise, rodeo actually found itself stronger at the end of World War II. Venue, contestant, and audience numbers had all increased between 1942 and 1946. And the patriotic fervor of the war had infused the sport with a sense of purpose that ultimately translated to a greater feeling of professionalism. Adopting a progressive attitude, the CTA reorganized as the Rodeo Cowboys Association (RCA) in 1945 with a view to engendering greater cooperation with all rodeo venues and to improving its own public relations. The following year, the RAA reorganized as the International Rodeo Association (IRA). By then representing the majority of rodeos around the nation, it sought to increase contestant prize monies through new advertising sponsorships. Though the RCA and the IRA then maintained dual point-award systems for the determination of annual event and all-around champions (thus causing a decade of controversy over legitimate titles), the two groups otherwise operated with increasing harmony.[22]

In the early 1950s, rodeo entered its second golden era—as manifested by remarkable increases in venues, monetary rewards, spectator attendance, and national publicity. The sport began to enjoy increasing coverage in magazines such as *Time, Life, Saturday Evening Post,* and *Sports Illustrated,* while special features appeared in periodicals as diverse as *Business Weekly* and *Ladies' Home Journal.* (An article in the July 1956 *Town Journal,* for example, noted that the RCA then counted some 3,200 members, sanctioned nearly six hundred rodeos paying out almost $3 million, and drew 13

→ **"Bronc Rider Casey Tibbs"**
Life magazine, October 22, 1951
Photographer unknown
NCM—Dickinson Research Center
Photographic Study Collection, unaccessioned

↑ **Rodeo Conducted in a "Natural" Arena**
Believed to be in Iowa, circa 1950
Ralph Russell Doubleday, photographer
NCM—Dickinson Research Center
R. R. Doubleday Collection, 79.026.

million to 14 million spectators to its performances.)[23] Improved transportation and larger purse awards motivated many rodeo hands to pursue the sport as a full-time livelihood for the first time, and there soon arose a new cadre of competitors who would become well-known sports personalities during the 1950s and into the 1960s. These contestants exhibited a greater sense of responsibility, respectability, and professionalism than those of previous generations, and they found a broadening acceptance in the American public at large. Also, by the mid-1950s, their ranks began to be augmented with a growing tide of serious and well-educated competitors already seasoned by their spirited participation in the National Intercollegiate Rodeo Association (NIRA), which had formed in 1948 and within a decade was functioning at some fifty institutions of higher learning.[24] Today, collegiate rodeo athletes—as opposed to ranch-trained contenders—represent the primary source of professional arena talent.

Among the great athletes of rodeo's second golden era, perhaps none better epitomized—and worked for—the sport's growing professionalism than Bill Linderman. One of the best all-around cowboys ever, he was born at Bridger, Montana, in 1920 and entered his first big-time rodeo at Denver in 1942. He competed consistently in bareback riding, saddle-bronc riding, and steer wrestling, taking seven world championship titles in nine years. His fierce determination, strength, and uncompromising competitiveness brought him the bareback-bronc crown in 1943, saddle-bronc laurels in 1945 and 1950, steer-wrestling honors in 1950, and the all-around title in 1945, 1950, and 1953. Called "The King" by his fellow contenders, Linderman worked tirelessly to

→ **Bill Linderman on Dual [sic] in the Sun**
(detail)
Salinas, California, Rodeo, 1950
DeVere Helfrich, photographer
NCM—Dickinson Research Center
DeVere Helfrich Collection, 81.023.06314

further the prominence and professionalism of the sport. During his tenure as president of the RCA from 1951 to 1957, purse awards, spectator and media attention, and full-time participation increased markedly. Of equal importance is that he instilled something of his personal professionalism and pride as a rodeo competitor in the larger RCA membership. Bill Linderman was on business as RCA secretary-treasurer when he died in a fiery plane crash in 1965. During his fifteen years of ardent leadership, rodeo experienced professional and commercial development that few could have envisioned in the 1930s and 1940s.[25]

Among the galaxy of rodeo champions that appeared in rodeo's second golden era, none shone brighter than the incomparable Jim Shoulders.

Bill Linderman with Bronc Saddle (detail)
Phoenix, Arizona, Rodeo, 1943
DeVere Helfrich, photographer
NCM—Dickinson Research Center
DeVere Helfrich Collection, 81.023.00582

Probably the finest rough-stock contestant ever to compete in the arena, he was born in 1928 in Tulsa, Oklahoma, and entered competition in 1943, winning an evidently inspiring eighteen dollars. In less than twenty years, he would have no peer in the sport, having captured more championships—sixteen—than any cowboy athlete before him (a record since surpassed in total—but not in diversity—by steer roper Guy Allen's eighteen event titles). Shoulders ruled the arena throughout the 1950s, winning five all-around championships (1949, 1956–59). His strength, coolness, and flamboyant spurring style also brought him four bareback-riding championships (1950, 1956–58) and an unprecedented seven bull-riding titles (1951, 1954–59—since exceeded by Don Gay with eight). His cumulative standing, though challenged for nearly fifty years, has never been surpassed by a multievent contender. Professional in business as well as sport, Shoulders achieved a great deal in promoting the future of rodeo. His many media promotions, product endorsements, and spokesmanship for rodeo sponsors such as Justin, Wrangler, Miller, and Dodge made him a national and international figure in rodeo lore. In addition, he maintained great contract bucking stock, inaugurated a rodeo training school for aspiring contestants, and invented the first mechanical bucking machine. Over a period of several decades, Jim Shoulders also gave back to society through his support of programs for sick and disadvantaged children. Rodeo's greatest champion passed from the arena in 2007.[26]

Jim Shoulders on Calamity Jim (detail)
Salinas, California, Rodeo, 1958
DeVere Helfrich, photographer
NCM—Dickinson Research Center
DeVere Helfrich Collection, 81.023.13592

Prodding Shoulders in the bull-riding competition throughout the 1950s, Harry Tompkins might have seemed an unlikely candidate as a rodeo champion. Born in 1927 at Furnace Woods, New York, he worked horses on an eastern dude ranch in his youth, however, and found he had a talent for staying aboard. He entered competition at Madison Square Garden in 1946. Tompkins shared the bull-riding honors with Jim Shoulders over a thirteen-year period. During that time, he won five bull-riding championships (1948–50, 1952, 1960), captured a single title in bareback-bronc riding (1952), and took two world all-around-cowboy crowns (1952, 1960). Endowed with exceptional balance and coordination, he is remembered for riding with a slack rope and looking off into the crowd while in action. Always a consistent performer, Tompkins placed among the top ten money winners for eleven consecutive years. Retired from the professional rodeo circuit, he has continued to compete in occasional old-timers' events around his Dublin, Texas, home.[27]

Casey Tibbs, arguably the greatest saddle-bronc rider of all time, also ranks as one of the most prominent arena "personalities" during rodeo's second golden era. Born near Pierre, South Dakota, in 1929, he learned horsemanship on twenty-mile, round-trip rides to school and started professional rodeo competition in 1943. Though relatively slight of stature, he exhibited superb balance and rhythm—rather than brute strength—as he "floated" on many a rank horse. "When a bronc starts mixing up his tricks," he once quipped, "you gotta know your business. If you don't, you'll either pop your gizzard or eat

→ **Casey Tibbs, World's Champ Cowboy**
Venue unknown, circa 1954
Ralph Russell Doubleday, photographer
NCM—Dickinson Research Center
R. R. Doubleday Collection, 79.026.1971

Casey Tibbs on Easy Money
Nemo, South Dakota, Rodeo, 1959
DeVere Helfrich, photographer
NCM—Dickinson Research Center
DeVere Helfrich Collection, 81.023.14933

dirt."[28] His athletic ability brought Tibbs an unprecedented six saddle-bronc championships (1949, 1951–54, 1959—since equaled by Dan Mortensen), one bareback title (1951), and two all-around-cowboy crowns (1951 and 1955) in only eleven years. He remains one of only two rodeo contestants ever to win the saddle-bronc, bareback-bronc, and all-around championship titles in the same year (1951)—the other was Leonard Ward in 1934. A stylish figure in the western wear of the period and something of a clotheshorse, he was the only rodeo athlete ever to appear on the cover of *Life* magazine. He retired from active competition during the 1960s with a tally of thirty-nine broken bones, but he never left the sport. Casey Tibbs remained quite active with celebrity and benefit performances, wild horse drives, film consulting, and old-timers' reunions and rodeos until his death in 1990.[29]

Among the steer wrestlers of the 1950s and 1960s, James Bynum and Harley May held sway over the competition. Born in 1924 in Danville, Alabama, Bynum entered his first rodeo at Stamford, Texas, at age sixteen. Left-handedness, coupled with a six-foot-four-inch, 210-pound frame, gave him a considerable edge over other bulldoggers. At a rodeo in Marietta, Oklahoma, in 1955, "Big Jim" tossed a steer in 2.4 seconds—a record that still stands. He won the world steer-wrestling championship four times in nine years (1954, 1958, 1961, and 1963) and did not retire from competition until 1969, following a knee injury. Bynum died in Maypearl, Texas, in 1999.[30]

Harley May, who was born in California in 1926 and raised in Deming, New Mexico, traded bulldogging honors with Bynum throughout rodeo's second golden era. He captured the steer-wrestling championship in 1952, 1956, and 1965 and for thirteen years placed among the event's top fifteen contenders. Perhaps as important, May epitomized the new professionalism at work in the sport. The first undergraduate student to enroll in the National Intercollegiate Rodeo Association program at Sul Ross State College in Alpine, Texas, he also became the first college rodeo athlete to turn professional. A serious contender and an excellent representative of the first generation of college-trained rodeo cowboys, he retired from the arena in the late 1960s and died in 2008.[31]

Calf roping, too, produced two outstanding competitors during rodeo's second golden era in the 1950s and 1960s. Born in 1927, Don McLaughlin first headlined as one-half of the famed "McLaughlin Brothers— Champion Juvenile Trick Ropers of the World" at major venues around the country during the 1940s. In their matching western suits, he and his brother, Gene, dazzled audiences with their roping skills. With maturity, Don turned his talent to the serious business of making a living in competition. He captured the calf-roping championship five times during the 1950s (1951–54, 1957) and took the steer-roping championship in 1960, 1963, and 1970. He maintained his position among the nation's top fifteen calf ropers through the early 1960s and was a top-ranked steer roper through the early 1970s. After retiring from the professional arena, McLaughlin continued to rope on the Senior Tour for several years prior to his death in 1994 in Colorado.[32]

⬆ **James Bynum Steer Wrestling** *(detail)*
Cheyenne, Wyoming, Frontier Days, 1954
DeVere Helfrich, photographer
NCM—Dickinson Research Center
DeVere Helfrich Collection, 81.023.09333

⬅ **Harley May Steer Wrestling** *(detail)*
Nemo, South Dakota, Rodeo, 1957
DeVere Helfrich, photographer
NCM—Dickinson Research Center
DeVere Helfrich Collection, 81.023.12577

➡ **Don McLaughlin Calf Roping** *(detail)*
Tucson, Arizona, La Fiesta de los Vaqueros, 1954
DeVere Helfrich, photographer
NCM—Dickinson Research Center
DeVere Helfrich Collection, 81.023.08877

Doubtless among the greatest calf ropers in the history of professional rodeo, Dean Oliver picked up in the midst of McLaughlin's run and ultimately overshadowed him. Born in 1929 in Dodge City, Kansas, Oliver grew up on a farm near Nampa, Idaho, and as a youth often practiced his roping skills on the local dairy calves—a habit that honed his talents prior to entering rodeo competition in 1948. Oliver combined size, speed, and "chocolate smooth" coordination to become one of the sport's finest athletes. He captured the world calf-roping championship an unprecedented, and unequaled, eight times, (1955, 1958, 1960–64, 1969), and he might well have won a ninth title except for two broken catch ropes at the 1966 National Finals Rodeo. He also won a string of three all-around championships (1963–65) through skilled bulldogging. Considered the "speed roper" of the 1960s, Oliver competed well into his forties and was quite active in RCA administration for many years. Now residing near Boise, Idaho, he retired from the arena as one of the biggest rodeo money winners of the 1950s and 1960s.[33]

This catch rope, with its frayed and raveled end, remains notorious for denying Dean Oliver an eighth world champion calf-roping title in 1966. It broke on his last calf at the National Finals Rodeo (NFR) in Oklahoma City. Oliver ultimately won that eighth title in 1969—it might well have been his ninth but for this infamous rope.

With the inauguration of the annual National Finals Rodeo (NFR) in 1959, the cowboy sport took on a new measure of challenge and significance for its full-time competitors—and an increased fascination and drama for its growing legions of ardent followers. Theretofore, annual event and all-around champions—based on their cumulative winnings/points—had been declared at season's end with little fanfare or national attention. At the NFR, not unlike professional baseball's World Series, rodeo's top fifteen money winners in each of the principal events would square off in a prominent championship forum to determine the year's best. The establishment of the NFR marked rodeo's gradual move into the realm of big business in American sport. Over succeeding decades, greatly increased monies from corporate sponsorships and television rights transformed the sport from its essentially regional and traditional character into an athletic spectacle whose superstars commanded national publicity and thousands of devoted fans.[34]

→ **Myrtis Dightman on # 461 Tornado (Shoulders)** *(detail)*
Oklahoma City, Oklahoma, NFR, 1967
Ferrell Butler, photographer
NCM—Dickinson Research Center
Photographic Study Collection,
2006-190.39.01

Another indication of the changing character of rodeo—and society at large—during this era was manifested in the increasing participation and success of African American contestants. In the decade following World War II, black contenders had been restricted to all-black contests or to exhibition rides during the slack in RCA performances, but the color barrier came down in the late 1950s and early 1960s. Among the first African Americans to break into the professional ranks, Myrtis Dightman was born in 1935 in Crockett, Texas. He entered the arena in 1961 as a bullfighting clown, soon progressed into competition, and ultimately focused on bull riding. He is remembered as the first black cowboy to compete in the NFR, and he finished among the top fifteen bull riders four times (1968, 1969, 1970, and 1972). Dightman's accomplishments were surpassed a decade later by another African American bull rider, named Charles Sampson. Born in 1957 in Los Angeles, California, Sampson qualified for the NFR eight times in ten years (1981–86, 1989, and 1990). More important, he won the bull-riding championship in 1982, thus entering the record books as the first black contestant to capture a world-event title.[35]

That African American contestants could consistently compete and triumph in the arena has since been demonstrated by calf roper Fred Whitfield. Born in Houston, Texas, in 1967, he grew up in the small town of Cypress, Texas, with an abiding desire to cowboy. He commenced his rodeo career in 1990, capturing both the calf-roping and the overall Rookie of the Year titles. In 1991 he won his first professional calf-roping championship, becoming the first black world-champion calf roper in the sport. At the time of this victory, Whitfield observed, "I'd like to do it again—time and time again."[36] Since then he has taken the calf-roping championship six more times through 2005, and he continues as a serious challenger in the standings to date. Far more significant is that Fred Whitfield made rodeo history at the 1999 NFR, winning both his fourth calf-roping title and the all-around title, thus becoming the first African American world-champion cowboy ever.[37]

↓ **Champion Calf Roper Fred Whitfield**
Venue unknown, circa 1999
Mike Copeman, photographer
NCM—Dickinson Research Center
Photographic Study Collection, unaccessioned

From the 1960s into the 1980s, improved rodeo management, greater attention from the sports media and television, ever-escalating commercial sponsorship, and consistent increases in scheduled venues, purses, and attendance joined to propel rodeo into the realm of big business. Responding to these changes, the RCA reorganized in 1975 as the Professional Rodeo Cowboys Association (PRCA)—the body largely responsible for the thriving condition of the sport today. The PRCA instituted media and sponsorship programs that elevated both the cowboy-athlete's public image and his potential income. (For example, in 1953 total prize money approached $2.5 million, while thirty years later it exceeded $13 million.)[38] The infusion of big money at the contestant level did not go unnoticed, as champion Jim Shoulders—perhaps ruefully—observed in the late 1970s: "When I was a kid, everybody played baseball. That's where the hundred thousand dollars was. . . . Now there's money in other sports. There's much more in rodeo, though only a small percentage get their hands on it. Tom Ferguson got his hands on a hundred thousand dollars in one year [1976]."[39] Rodeo historian Kristine Fredriksson has credited the dramatic increase in rodeo winnings during this era with the rise of what she termed the "cowboy plutocrat."

Real athletic prowess within the arena also increased—not only through intercollegiate rodeo but also through participation in roping and rough-stock training clinics managed by veteran champions such as Toots Mansfield and Jim Shoulders. The traditional, often-undisciplined, range-trained cowboy contestant of an earlier generation rapidly gave way to a new cadre of very disciplined, arena-trained cowboy-athletes dedicated to excellence in their chosen sport. All these factors encouraged the emergence of a "new breed" of rodeo cowboys—contestants who were better educated, better conditioned, better skilled, and thoroughly enterprising.[40]

Among this new breed of modern rodeo athletes, none proved more dedicated—or more entrepreneurial—than the talented and flamboyant Larry Mahan. Known as "Super Saddle" on the circuit, he was born in 1943 on a farm outside Salem, Oregon, and learned rodeoing not on the range but in junior competitions. At age twelve, he made his arena debut, winning six dollars in a calf-riding contest.

← **Grand Opening Flag Ceremony**
Oklahoma City, Oklahoma, NFR, 1977
Photographer unknown
NCM—Dickinson Research Center
Photographic Study Collection, 2006-190.39.04

→ **Larry Mahan Saddle Bronc Riding**
Venue unknown, circa 1966
Ferrell Butler, photographer
NCM—Dickinson Research Center
Photographic Study Collection, 1988.9.1029

To that modest beginning he added more than a half-million dollars over a professional career spanning sixteen years. A focused rough-stock rider, Mahan studied—and took detailed notes on—the behavior of hundreds of rodeo bulls and broncs that he encountered on the circuit. "Bulls scare you a little," he once observed, "leave you with that little empty feeling you have to conquer. You look forward to riding a good [bucking] horse but you don't always feel that way about a bull. You can't go out on a bull and be real aggressive. . . . Just grit your teeth and go."[41]

⬇ **Larry Mahan on # 53 Kelsey**
Oklahoma City, Oklahoma, NFR, 1966
Ferrell Butler, photographer
NCM—Dickinson Research Center
Photographic Study Collection, 1988.9.1031

Mahan also worked out regularly in the gym and piloted his own plane to as many as 150 competitions a year. Although he never truly dominated a single event in the way Casey Tibbs or Dean Oliver did, his commitment and consistent performances garnered him six all-around-champion cowboy titles (1966–70 and 1973), as well as two bull-riding championships, in 1965 and 1967. Referred to as the "cowboy in the gray flannel suit" by *Time* magazine, Mahan thrived in the big-business atmosphere of 1970s rodeo, actually handing out business cards on the circuit. With his retirement from the arena in 1977, he began an extremely successful business career, conducting rodeo training schools and launching his well-regarded "Larry Mahan" brand of western clothing and boots, which made him a trendsetter in cowboy fashion that continues to this day. Few in rodeo before or since have demonstrated his blend of athletic dedication, competitiveness, showmanship, style, and business acumen.[42]

Bull rider Don Gay proved to be another of the new breed of dedicated—and competitive—rodeo athletes. The son of RCA and PRCA stock contractor Neal Gay, Don grew up in a rodeo environment, commenced riding steers at age six, and held an Association permit in high school. Like Mahan, he reflected the aggressive spirit of big-business rodeo. "I make from thirty to sixty thousand dollars a year," he remarked when only twenty-two, "and I don't know many others my age who make that kind of money. . . . I always knew exactly what I wanted to do and did it. Now I want to make as much money as I can as quickly as I can."[43] Ultimately, like Mahan, Gay flew a personal plane from venue to venue and accumulated eight world-championship bull-riding titles between 1974 and 1984. Among his records is the second-highest-marked ride in rodeo, earning ninety-seven points on the famous bull Oscar at the San Francisco Cow Palace in 1977. Upon retirement from the arena, Gay, too, conducted rough-stock riding clinics and for years has provided the color commentary for the Mesquite Championship Rodeo on the TNN network.[44]

↑ **Don Gay on # 430 Dairy King** *(detail)*
Oklahoma City, Oklahoma, NFR, 1972
Ferrell Butler, photographer
NCM—Dickinson Research Center
Ferrell Butler Collection, 2001.013.4.30

Under the organizational guidance of the PRCA, rodeo has experienced amazing growth during the past quarter century. Throughout that time, increasing television coverage on regular, specialty, and cable networks including CBS, ESPN, and FSN has created an explosion in corporate sponsorship and financial incentives. Today, among rodeo's prominent corporate sponsors, one finds the Justin Boot Company, Blue Bell–Wrangler Western Wear, the Jack Daniel's Distilling Company, the U.S. Smokeless Tobacco Company, the Adolph Coors Company, Dodge Trucks, Montana Silversmiths, the Resistol Hat Company, Coca-Cola, Pace Picante, and the U.S. Army. During 2005, commercial support of rodeo amounted to some $35 million—with more than $4 million in direct, contestant prize money. Over the past twenty years, such monetary largess has created a growing cadre of "million-dollar" contestants, among them great names such as ropers Roy Cooper, Joe Beaver, Fred Whitfield, and Guy Allen; roper and bulldogger Tom Ferguson; rough-stock contenders Ty Murray and Dan Mortensen; and eleven-time barrel-racing champion Charmayne James.[45] (As of this writing, in fact, there are nine "$2 million–dollar" cowboy plutocrats topping the career earnings list.) For all concerned, rodeo is now big business indeed.

Today, in excess of 650 PRCA-sanctioned rodeos are held during the year in some forty states and four Canadian provinces. These venues draw a total audience estimated at 24 million paying spectators—with several million additional fans catching the action on television. The sport's top-ranking contenders typically compete in more than 100 rodeos a year, all striving for qualification at the National Finals Rodeo (NFR), which in 2008 offered a total purse of some $4.5 million.[46]

To all outward appearances, rodeo is certainly thriving. But the marketing glitz, booming sound, and dazzling pyrotechnic displays now prevalent at the contemporary NFR in Las Vegas, Nevada, coupled with the recent appearance and popularity of breakaway affiliations such as the Professional Bull Riders (PBR), also have had the effect of eroding some of rodeo's traditional character. Many of today's finest rodeo competitors are specialist athletes whose experience and world view are far removed from the typical cowboy contenders of eighty, or even fifty, years ago. Unlike Harry Tompkins or Jim Shoulders in

Arena Light Show at the Wrangler National Finals Rodeo
Thomas and Mack Center, Las Vegas, Nevada, 2006
Steven Griffin, PRCA photographer
Image courtesy Professional Rodeo Cowboys Association
PRCA Archive, SGP2667

the 1950s, for example, many of today's professional bull riders would have little or no use for a trophy saddle were they awarded one, because they do not ride—or even own—a horse.[47]

Yet, though it may be argued that today's big-business commercialization of rodeo has somewhat removed the cowboy contender from his traditional western roots, the sport remains perhaps the most authentic—and most colorful—of American athletic competitions. "The way I look at it," three-time saddle-bronc champion Monty Henson observed in the late 1970s, "we're the kind of guys other guys want to be. I don't mean just in the rodeo sense but in the general sense that we're doing what we want to do and nobody gave us anything."[48]

Indeed, the persistence of folk-based authenticity in rodeo is manifested in the Working Ranch Cowboys Association (WRCA), an organization formed in the 1990s that today conducts more than twenty traditional, cowboy ranch rodeos annually around the western states. In addition, many PRCA rodeos still boast much authentic character derived from their venerable histories and colorful traditions. Among such prominent outdoor venues are the Calgary Stampede, the Pendleton Round-Up, the California Rodeo at Salinas, and the Cheyenne and Prescott Frontier Days events. Though smaller in scale, several Fourth-of-July rodeos also retain traditions that rival the great venues; notable among these are the Black Hills Roundup at Belle Fourche, South Dakota, and the Cody Stampede in Wyoming. Opposing all the monetary and postmodernist influences of contemporary, big-business rodeo, much of the "cowboy way" still prevails in the arena—just as it did a century ago.[49]

← **Smoky Branch on Glass Eye**
Monte Vista, Colorado, Ski-Hi Stampede, 1921
Ralph Russell Doubleday, photographer
NCM—Dickinson Research Center
McCarroll Family Trust Collection,
RC2006.076.070

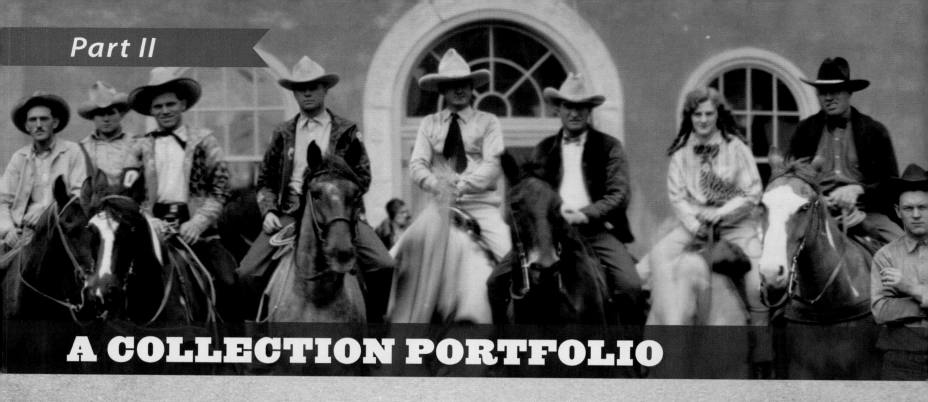

Part II

A COLLECTION PORTFOLIO

S WITH ALL MATERIAL CULTURE (those things created by humanity), the tangible legacy of rodeo is manifested in many forms and materials, most of which derive from various sources in the larger culture. First among these sources for rodeo "things" is the equestrian and ranching heritage of the nineteenth-century West. This is particularly so as regards the cowboy clothing and horse-gear still familiar in cattle country today.

Upon this utilitarian, core material, an evolving veneer of flamboyance was overlaid with rodeo's emergence as public entertainment and athletic spectacle. As a competitive sport, rodeo also adopted both familiar and distinctive kinds of trophies into its material culture as a means of recognizing excellence among its contestants. And as with all cultures, or subcultures, rodeo has generated its own artistic expression—however derivative and aesthetically limited it might be considered by the art connoisseur.

The utilitarian and aesthetic character of rodeo material culture presents a continuum of tradition and innovation that is marked, for the most part, by an attention to quality and artistry. This appears particularly true of cowboy equipment and personal effects that have passed from range to arena and evolved from simple working tools to trophy awards laden with symbolism. Thus, for example, while rodeo sport has spawned specialized, functional saddlery in its bronc-riding, low-roping, and trick-riding patterns, it also has lavished a century of embellishment on the traditional western stock saddle in its continuing creation of championship trophies. This dynamic interplay of evolving needs and established tastes appears as well in the development of arena chaps, competition and trophy spurs, and the aesthetic progression of trophy buckles or belt plates.

Contemplation of the form, function, and ornament of these and other rodeo artifacts

→ **Jim Shoulders and Everything** (detail)
Denver, Colorado, 1958
DeVere Helfrich, photographer
NCM—Dickinson Research Center
DeVere Helfrich Collection, 81.023.12991

over the decades uncovers a colorful, sporting subculture firmly rooted in a romantic, pastoral past. As one perceptive observer noted after attending a rodeo in 1938, "And then there is the brilliant spectacle of the riders with their colored silk shirts, ten-gallon hats, and doggy chaps. And the saddles and bridles are a sight worth seeing. . . . Many are gorgeous creations of hand-tooled leather mounted with silver and gold."[1]

Beyond the functional and aesthetic aspects of rodeo material culture, the artifacts of the sport also carry and convey something of its character and heritage. The very things used, worn, or won by rodeo athletes—particularly those things associated with outstanding champions—are today imbued with no little romance, reverence, and worth. For general sports enthusiasts and collectors, and for rodeo devotees in particular, the artifacts of rodeo sport present the tangible evidence—the proof—of personal and group dedication, achievement, character, and tradition.

The objects and artworks that follow present a broad spectrum of the sport's material culture from the unrivaled collections of the National Cowboy & Western Heritage Museum. All represent in varying degree American rodeo's rich tangible and aesthetic legacy, and many are also distinguished by important biographical associations with the prominent champions of the sport's first century.

EARL THODE
CHEYENNE
1ST PRIZE WYO
(DOUBLEDAY)
1927

WALTER
HEACOCK
1ST PRIZE
BELLE
FOURCHE
S.D.

5 Rodeo Saddlery

Stock, Bronc, Trick, Parade, and Trophy

JUST AS THE WESTERN stock saddle proved essential to the work of the range cowboy, so too did it become a central element in the material culture of the rodeo cowboy. For the riders and ropers of early-day rodeo, the range saddle was the primary requisite object of their competitive sport, even as it also served as a paramount parade and trophy element. Though the saddles of arena competitors underwent several important modifications over the first half of the twentieth century, those utilized for rodeo parades and trophy awards changed only as the working stock saddle changed (sometimes under rodeo's influence) and as styles in ornamentation evolved.

When rodeo emerged as a competitive sport around the turn of the previous century, the architecture of the working saddle was evolving from the slick- or narrow-forked, high-cantled pattern of the 1880s and 1890s to a swell-forked, lower-cantled design. Partly in response to the rise of bronc-riding competitions, some of these rigs featured extremely wide, undercut forks or pommels and deep seats intended to provide the contestant with a more secure ride. During the 1910s, some variations, known as "bear-traps" or "freaks," were so exaggerated in pommel width and seat depth that they proved dangerous to riders. In response to this potential hazard—and to introduce uniform equipment to the sport—the rodeo committees of Cheyenne, Pendleton, Boise, and Walla Walla conferred in 1919 with the Hamley Saddlery Company of Pendleton to create a standardized bronc-riding rig. Built on a modified Ellensburg tree, this "Committee" saddle had a slightly undercut, fourteen-inch fork and a dished, five-inch cantle, with stirrup leathers hung—and angled—forward. Early examples still featured roping horns, but because the cowboys frequently cut these off, manufacturers ultimately omitted them. When the Cowboys Turtle Association (CTA) approved the pattern in the latter 1930s, it became the "Association" saddle, and the basic design has remained in use among professional bronc riders ever since.[1]

As competitive calf roping (and steer wrestling) grew in popularity and prominence in the 1920s, serious ropers (and doggers) sought various means of trimming their time on every go-round—including speeding the dismount. Reducing the western stock saddle's cantle height—so that the contestant's leg could clear the rig with increased ease and speed—proved one ready solution. During the 1920s and 1930s, the familiar stock saddle having a relatively short seat and a steep, four- to five-inch cantle gradually was replaced in the arena by the "low-roping" pattern, featuring a longer and broader seat with a dramatically sloped cantle only two to three inches in height. Often designed and promoted with the aid of famed ropers such as Bob Crosby, Fred Lowry, and Toots Mansfield, by the 1950s the low-roping saddle of rodeo also had become the standard western ranch and pleasure saddle—the basic pattern still popular throughout the West today.[2]

Also by the 1920s, the rodeo trick-riding saddle had achieved its basic form. American stunt and

↑ **Performers Jack Hoxie,**
Mrs. Jack Brown (?), and Jack Brown
Miller Brothers' 101 Ranch Real
Wild West Show
Location unknown, circa 1920
Photographer unknown
NCM—Dickinson Research Center
Photographic Study Collection, 2001.036.018

acrobatic riders in the Wild West shows and early rodeos eschewed the relatively light, padded saddle introduced by performing Cossack horsemen, opting instead for a much heavier western saddle outfitted with all the necessary appurtenances. Typically constructed on a fairly robust tree with large, square skirts and substantial double rigging, these uniquely appointed rigs incorporated several features intended only for acrobatics on horseback. The extended horn at the pommel provided a substantial handhold for moving into and recovering from maneuvers such as the pass-under and the Russian drag, while slots cut in the jockeys behind the cantle served the same purpose in crupper tricks such as roll-ups and vaults over the rump of the horse. The various auxiliary straps and slings fixed over, around, or along one or both sides of the saddle provided stability or recovery in dramatic standing, lay-over, drag, and under-the-belly stunts.[3]

Lavishly embellished rodeo parade and trophy saddles found their origin in the Spanish and Mexican rigs favored by gentleman rancheros in early-nineteenth-century California. Their traditions of fine leather carving and sumptuous silver work set a standard emulated by Anglo American saddlers in the West from the 1850s onward—initially for exhibition and presentation pieces and ultimately for the eye-catching saddles ridden by Wild West impresarios and rodeo showmen including Buffalo Bill Cody, Colonel Zack Mulhall, the several Miller brothers, and Tex Austin. Most of these, though built on common stock trees of the time, represented the very best in materials, workmanship, and custom artisanry. Figural leather carving, precision leather stamping, richly engraved and gold-overlaid silver work, and even precious stones, often costing thousands of dollars, put these fabulous pieces into the realm of high folk art. The generations of rodeo trophy saddles that followed also exhibited splendid leather and silver decoration—albeit on a level somewhat less grand. Early on, venue trophy saddles, such as those made by the Hamley saddlery for the initial Pendleton Round-Up competitions, presented singular detail and decoration. As contestants and awards increased over the succeeding decades, however, most venues provided a "standard" prize saddle to each event champion that differed little except for the citation engraved or carved on the piece.[4]

➜ **Colonel Jim Eskew with Horse** (detail)
Location unknown, circa 1935
Ralph Russell Doubleday, photographer
NCM—Dickinson Research Center
Tad S. Mizwa Collection, 2001.036.054.1

↑ Western Stock Saddle
Miles City Saddlery Company
Miles City, Montana, circa 1910
NCM—Permanent Collection, 1983.05.05

This stock saddle belonged to African American cowboy and Wild West and rodeo performer Bill Pickett. A long-time hand with the Miller Brothers' 101 Ranch, Pickett introduced the "bite-'em-down" method of bulldogging around 1900—a feat of skill and daring that ultimately became rodeo steer wrestling. The well-worn saddle has a moderate swell fork, or pommel; a relatively steep, dished cantle; Texas-style square skirts and double rigging; and floral-and-foliate tooling.

← Western Stock Saddle
Maker unknown, circa 1895
NCM—Gift of Mrs. J. Frank Dobie, H.127.01

A working cowboy's most important piece of equipment, the horned western stock saddle provided a secure seat for riding and a strong platform for roping. "Slick-forked," or narrow-pommeled, examples such as this one—with its high, steep cantle—served in rodeo bronc-riding and steer-roping contests during the late nineteenth and early twentieth centuries. Attached to the saddle fork is a pair of homemade "bucking rolls" (Grandee Collection, 1991.1.1720), which shortened the seat and provided a buttress for the rider's thighs. Some early-day rodeo contestants favored these attachments, but their use declined when the "swell-forked" saddle came into vogue between 1905 and 1915. This stock saddle also incorporates "monkey-nose" *tapaderos,* or stirrup covers—appurtenances rarely seen in later formal rodeo competitions.

⬆ **Western Stock Saddle**

Edelbrock and Son Saddlery
Fort Worth, Texas, circa 1930
NCM—Gift of Mary Byers Fowler, R.260.16

This stock saddle was the property of renowned steer roper and trick-and-fancy-roper Chester Byers. It is ornamented with floral tooling and decorative, sterling silver hearts—those on the skirts are engraved with the initials "C" and "B" for the owner. The rig has a moderate, swell-fork pommel and incorporates an early example of the short, sloping, "low-roping" cantle with "Cheyenne roll" that would become the standard for competitive ropers in later decades. The venerable saddle was acquired by trick roper Jim Eskew, Jr., following Byers's death in 1945.

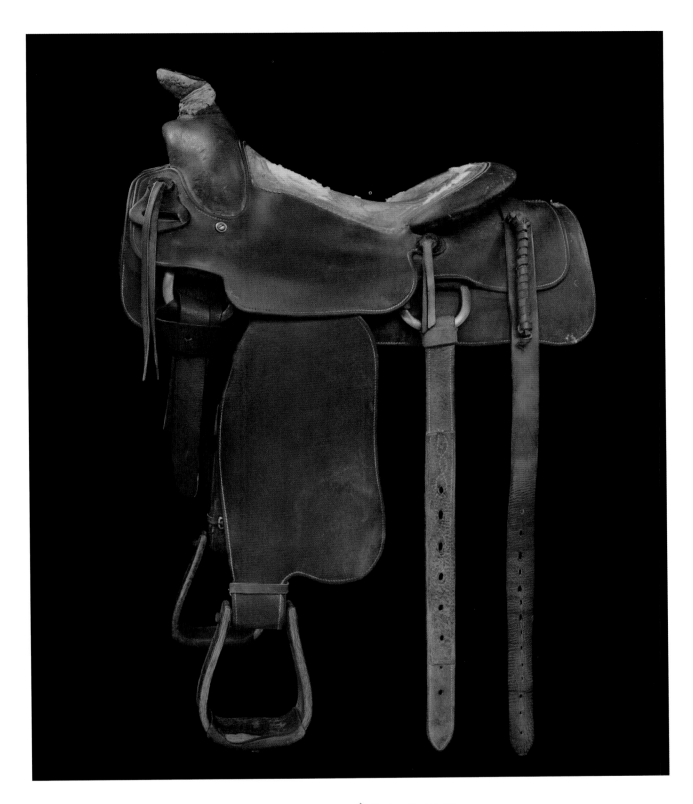

↑ **Western Stock Saddle**
Rowell Saddlery Company
Hayward, California, circa 1950
NCM—Gift of Dean Oliver, R.234.01

Of "low-roping" design, this double-rigged saddle has a low, slightly swelled pommel and a short-capped horn for "hard-and-fast" catches. The even lower, sloping cantle with "Cheyenne roll" allows for unimpeded dismounts in roping competitions. The saddle's padded and quilted seat exhibits the wear of many hundreds—perhaps thousands—of rapid dismounts by eight-time world champion calf roper Dean Oliver.

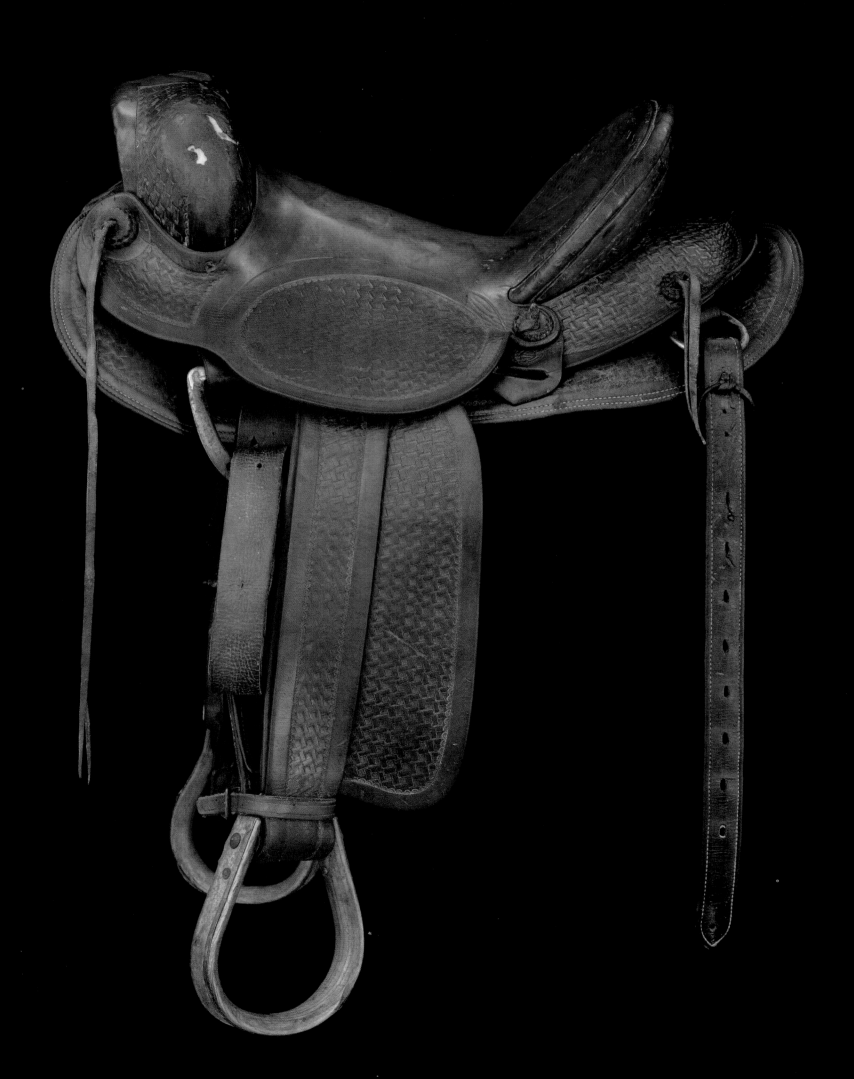

➜ **Bronc Riding Saddle**

O. J. Snyder Saddlery Company
Denver, Colorado, circa 1920
NCM—Permanent Collection, 1983.05.04

Designed especially for female bronc riders, this saddle features a short, deep-dish seat with a high cantle and a wide-swell fork for stability. The outfit incorporates large, ring-pattern stirrups to avoid entanglements. Finished in "rough-out" leather, the rig belonged to champion bronc rider Bonnie McCarroll, who recalled her first rough-stock ride at age fourteen: "I mounted, the boys let go, and the broncho began to behave like a wild cat. I held for about five seconds and then all at once I seemed to grow wings. Up I soared, and turned a sumersault [*sic*], and the earth seemed about ten miles below." Riding with hobbled stirrups (i.e., tied beneath the horse) at the 1929 Pendleton Round-Up, McCarroll was fatally injured near the height of her career, a tragedy that foreshadowed—if it did not precipitate—the decline of women's participation in the sport.

⬅ **Bronc Riding Saddle**

Hamley Saddlery Company
Pendleton, Oregon, circa 1930
NCM—Gift of Dr. Tommy L. Pike, H.130

Developed in 1919 by the Pendleton, Cheyenne, Walla Walla, and Boise rodeo committees in consultation with Hamley Saddlery, the "Committee" or "Association" saddle became standard equipment in the bronc-riding event in little more than a decade. Built on the Ellensburg tree, the saddle typically appeared without a roping horn and incorporated a somewhat undercut, swell-fork pommel and a slightly dished, five-inch cantle. This rather fancy basket-stamped specimen belonged to famed Canadian bronc rider Harry Knight, who rode some of rodeo's rankest horses between 1925 and 1940. In 1941 Knight went into rodeo production and ultimately became a widely respected stock contractor.

⬆ **Florence Randolph, Lady Champion Trick Rider** *(detail)*
Venue unknown, circa 1935
Ralph Russell Doubleday, photographer
NCM—Dickinson Research Center
R. R. Doubleday Collection, 79.026.2726

⬆ **Cossack Trick Riding Saddle**
Right, or off-side, view
Maker unknown, circa 1900
NCM—Permanent Collection, 1986.03

Embellished with scores of nickeled spots and fitted with a heavy auxiliary strap at the side and with knotted leather handholds at the front and rear of the tree, this Russian Cossack saddle was used by a horseman of the steppes for trick-riding performances in Wild West show programs around the United States and abroad. Highly acrobatic Cossack horsemen proved influential in establishing trick riding as a contested event at early rodeo venues.

➡ **Trick Riding Saddle**
Maker unknown, circa 1925
NCM—Gift of Florence H. Randolph, R.237.01

Ornamented with extensive floral tooling, rampant eagles on the seat jockeys, and engraved silver disks on the skirts and jockeys, this trick-riding saddle served Florence Hughes Randolph in her acrobatic and equestrian routines. The saddle incorporates the extended horn, auxiliary straps, and crupper handholds typical of the pattern.

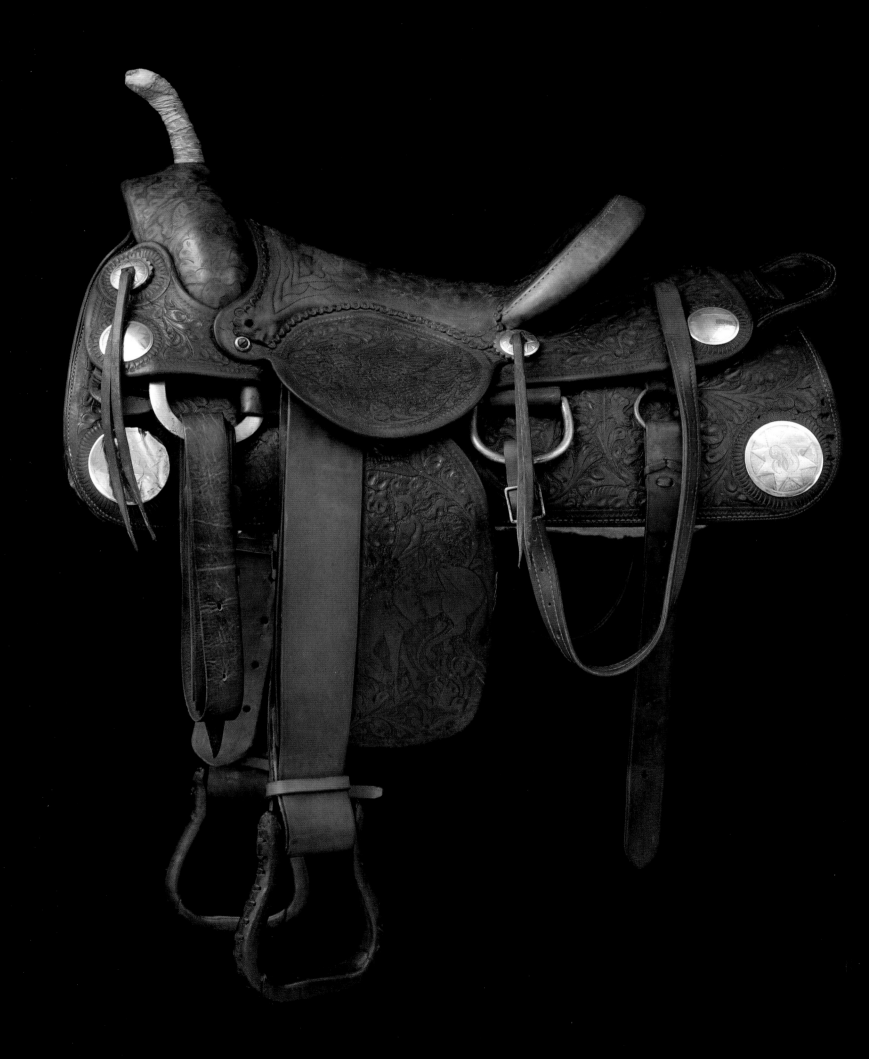

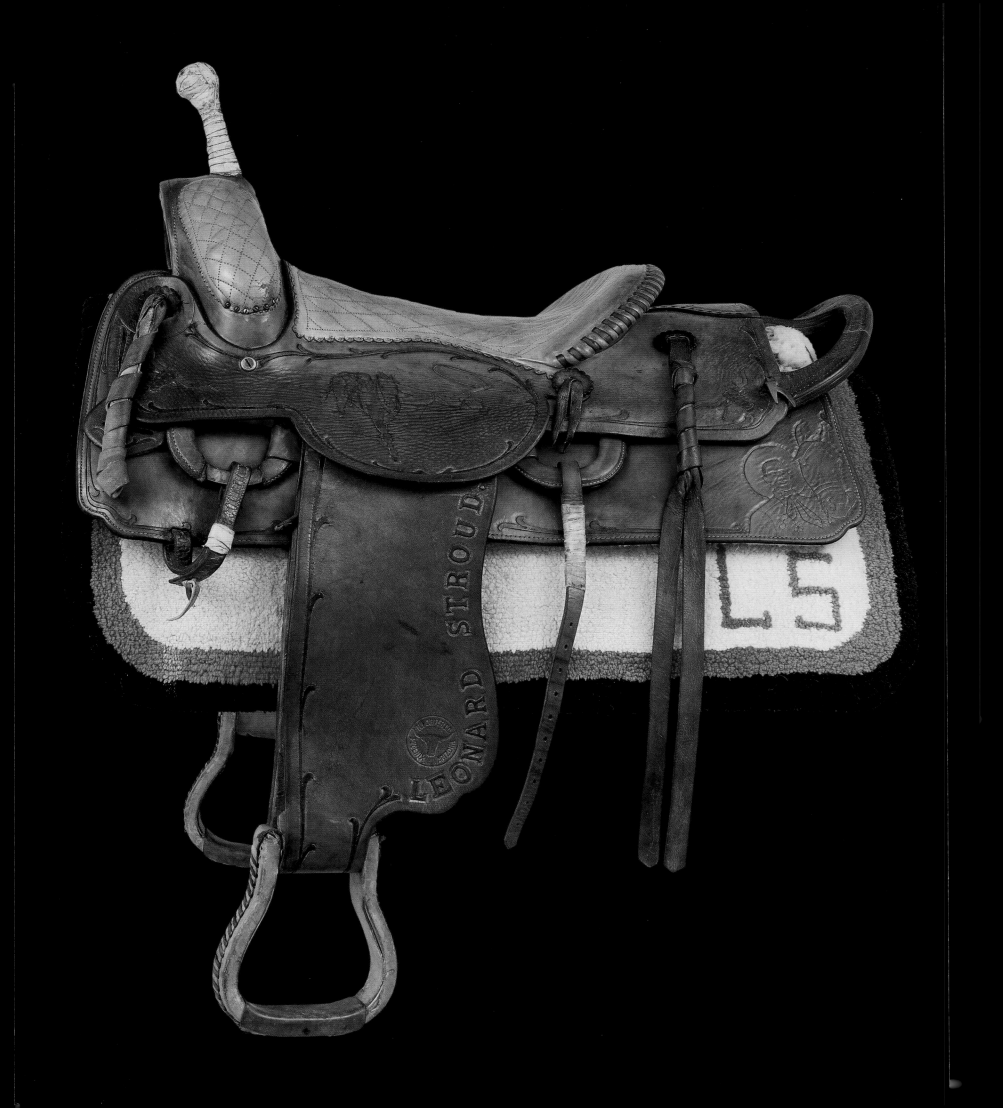

Leonard Stroud on Indian Tom Wins Championship at Cheyenne, Wyo.
(© 1918. D.F.P. CO.INC.)

↑ **Leonard Stroud on Indian Tom Wins Championship at Cheyenne, Wyo.**
Bronco Busting Contest, Cheyenne, Wyoming, Frontier Days, 1918
Doubleday-Foster Photo Company, publisher
NCM—Dickinson Research Center
McCarroll Family Trust Collection, RC2006.076.019-09

← **Trick Riding Saddle**
N. Porter Saddlery Company
Phoenix, Arizona, circa 1925
NCM—Gift of Edith Jones and W. A. Bliss, R.241.01

This special saddle, with its extended horn, auxiliary straps, and crupper handholds, was used extensively by the great trick rider Leonard Stroud. The back of the cantle is stamped "Porter Trick Saddle / Designed Especially For Leonard Stroud," and his name appears along the edge of the fenders. The seat jockeys carry likenesses of the champion performing his signature "Stroud Standout," as illustrated on page 49. The carpeted pad beneath the saddle also carries Stroud's initials.

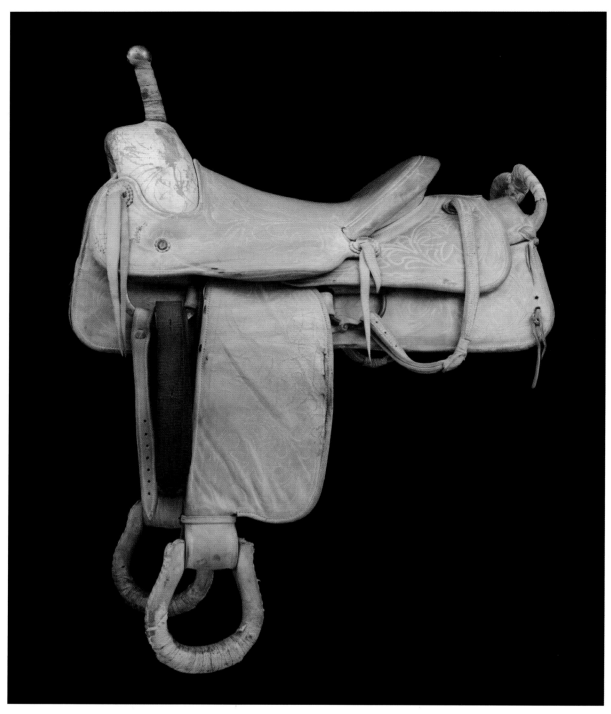

↑ Trick Riding Saddle
Atkins-Ryon Saddlery Company
Fort Worth, Texas, 1924
NCM—Gift of Tad Lucas, R.238.01

Dyed white for greater visibility in the arena, this trick saddle was used by equestrian star Tad Lucas from 1924 to 1958. Probably the greatest female trick rider during the heyday of the event (1920–35), Lucas captured the title once each at Boston and Philadelphia, twice at Cheyenne, three times at Chicago, four times at Fort Worth, and an unprecedented seven times at Madison Square Garden in New York City.

➜ Wild West Parade Saddle
F. A. Meanea Saddlery Company
Cheyenne, Wyoming, circa 1905
NCM—Gift of John M. Lough, 1970.19.01

Ranchman, livestock agent, Wild West impresario, and showman Colonel Zack Mulhall rode this nicely tooled and ornamented saddle at entry parades and presentations across the United States and in Europe. Typical of the period, the square-skirted, double-rigged piece incorporates a slightly swelled fork, or pommel, and a relatively steep and high-backed cantle. Mulhall's Wild West show provided a start for a number of famed western entertainers, among them Will Rogers and Tom Mix. The colonel's daughter, Lucille, was a renowned horsewoman and the best lady steer roper of the early twentieth century.

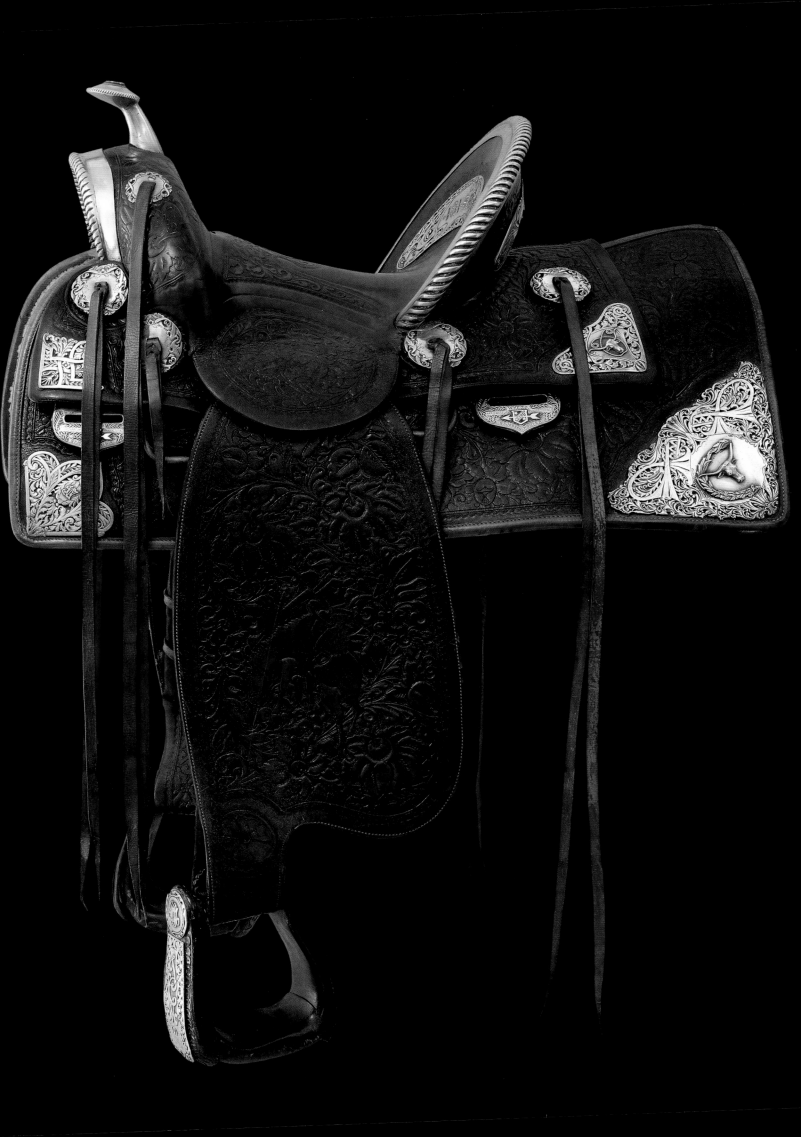

← ↑ ↗
Wild West Parade Saddle
Wyeth Hardware and Saddlery Company
Saint Joseph, Missouri, 1913
NCM—Museum purchase, 2001.11.01

The ultimate in Wild West show opulence, this specially commissioned parade saddle was made for impresario Joseph C. Miller of the Miller Brothers' 101 Ranch Real Wild West at a cost of $5,800. Advertised as the "finest saddle in the world," the rig carried eighteen pounds of pierced and filigreed sterling silver with extensive figural overlay in gold, and it was lavishly inset with 61 rubies, 204 diamonds, and 29 sapphires for a patriotic red-white-and-blue effect. A second, equally extravagant parade saddle was made up for Zack Miller by the S. D. Myres Saddlery Company of Sweetwater, Texas, and the brothers rode them with no little pride at the 101 Ranch near Ponca City, Oklahoma, and at Wild West venues across the United States.

➜ **Colonel Joe Miller Horseback** (detail)
Miller Brothers' 101 Ranch Real Wild West,
circa 1920
Photographer unknown
NCM—Dickinson Research Center
Tad S. Mizwa Collection, 2001.036.030

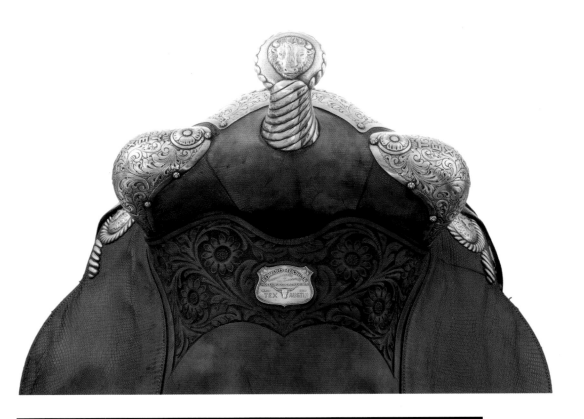

→ → Rodeo Parade Saddle
Bohlin Saddlery and Silversmiths
Hollywood, California, circa 1925
NCM—Museum purchase, 1985.31

Custom manufactured by Hollywood "Saddler to the Stars"
Edward H. Bohlin, this extravagant saddle reflects Tex Austin's
personal showmanship as rodeo promoter and manager. The
rig has a nicely floral-tooled seat, while the jockeys, skirts, and
fenders are finished in exotic lizard skin. These elements boast
distinctive rope-pattern borders of silver, as do the pommel
gullet, horn, and cantle bead. The throat and shoulders of the
pommel are capped in engraved sterling silver with "Tex Austin"
in gold overlay. Sterling silver conchas, each overlaid with a gold
steer head or rearing horse, grace the corners of the jockeys,
skirts, fenders, and stirrups.

→ Rodeo Promoter and Manager Tex Austin
Location unknown, circa 1925
Bronx *Home News* photograph
NCM—Dickinson Research Center
Photographic Study Collection, 1988.9.24

Rodeo Parade and Arena Saddle
Edward Gilmore Saddlery Company
Studio City, California, circa 1950
NCM—Gift of Gene Autry, 1997.21

Tooled in a bold oak-leaf pattern and displaying "Gene Autry Rodeo" on the seat jockeys, this saddle was one of dozens commissioned for the latter-day impresario's arena productions in the 1940s and 1950s. Autry's entertainment formula joined athletic excellence—for male contenders, at least—with personal name recognition and considerable spectacle. The saddle's "low-roping" design confirms the established prominence and popularity of this pattern among western horsemen in the immediate post–World War II era.

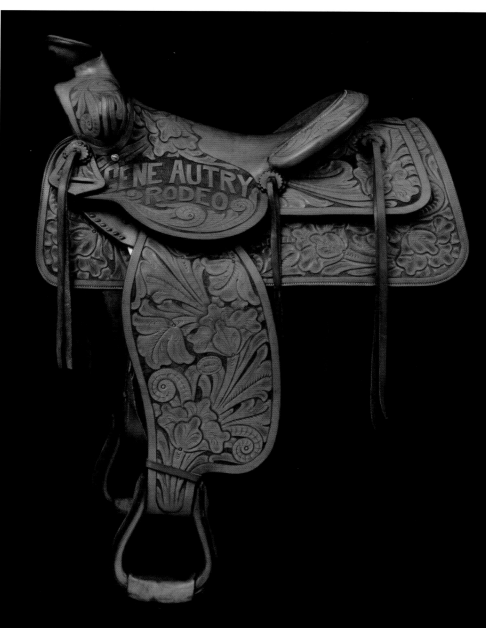

Rodeo Trophy Saddle
Hamley Saddlery Company
Pendleton, Oregon, 1912
NCM—Gift of Dorothy Gibson, 1979.01.01

Awarded at Oregon's famed Pendleton Round-Up, this superbly decorated trophy saddle was captured by rodeo cowboy and later western film star Hoot Gibson. The saddle is embellished with extensive leather tooling in a floral motif and features eight intricately pierced and finely engraved silver corner plates on the skirts and jockeys. Decorative conchas and plates also adorn the contrasting assembly strings and the sides of the stirrups, while the large silver plaque on the back of the cantle is inscribed with Gibson's name as the winner of the 1912 Pendleton all-around cowboy title *(see detail above)*.

Born at Tekamah, Nebraska, in 1892, Edmund Richard "Hoot" Gibson was an expert horseman at an early age, riding with the Miller Brothers' 101 Ranch Real Wild West show in 1906. Gibson went to Hollywood around 1914 and during the 1920s starred in numerous feature-length westerns with Universal Studios, including *Calgary Stampede* (1925), *Chip of the Flying U* (1926), and *King of the Rodeo* (1929). Remaining interested in rodeo, he sponsored a number of trophy cups at various venues during the 1920s (see, for example, page 161).

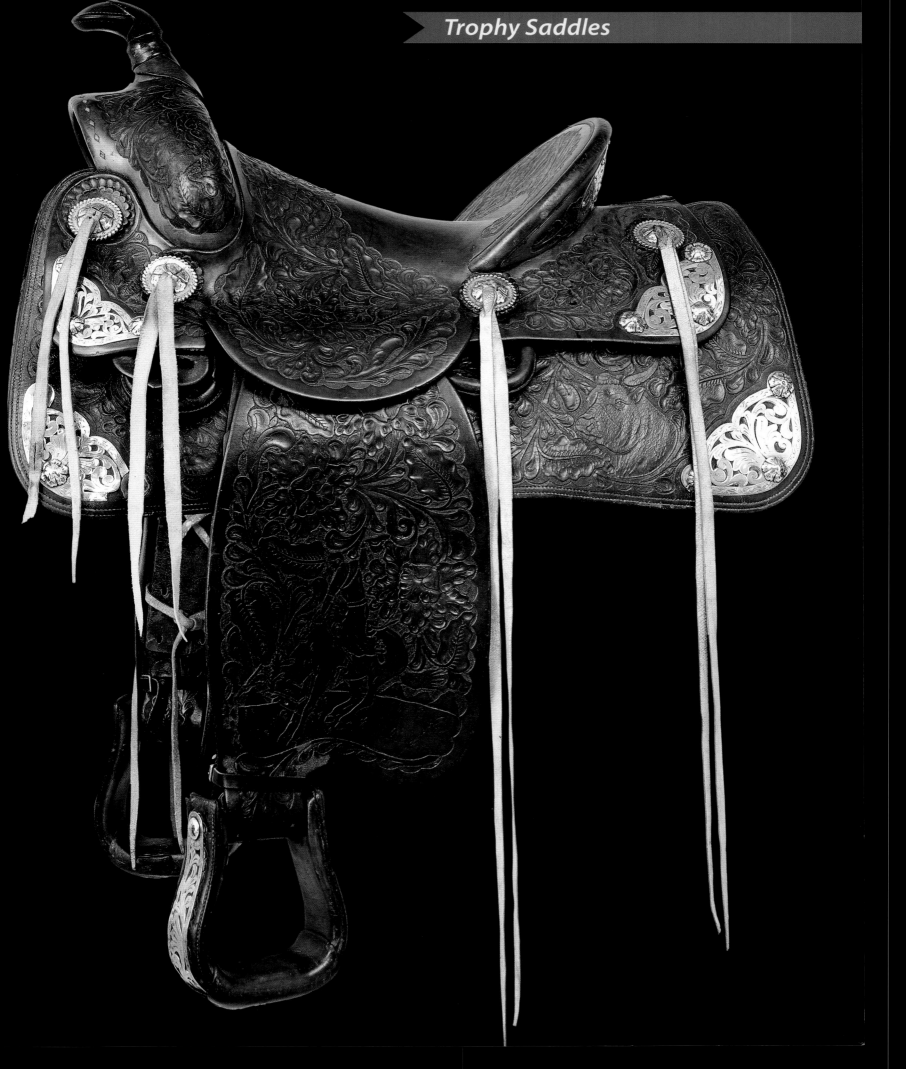

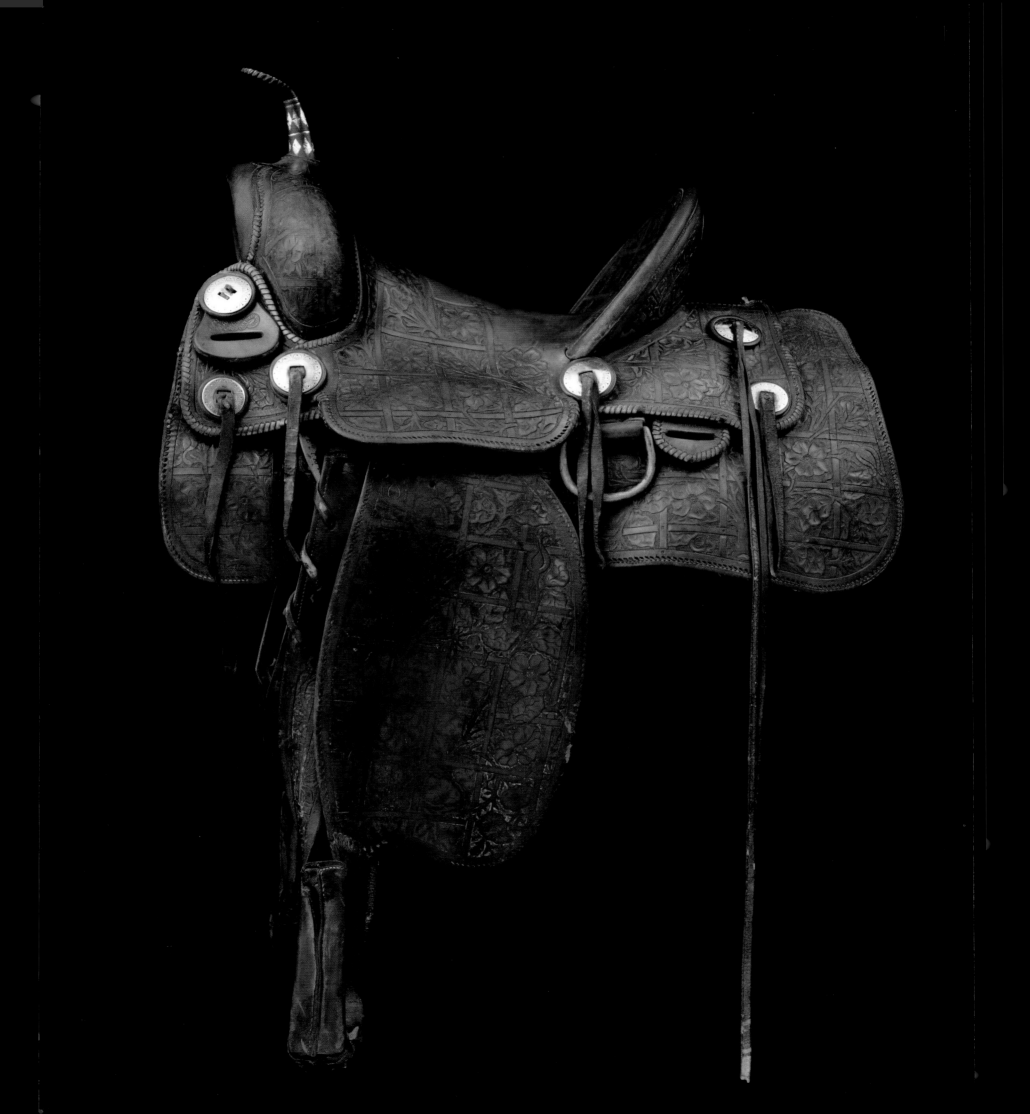

Bertha Blancett, Champion Lady Rider of the World
Pendleton, Oregon, Round-Up, circa 1912
Walter S. Bowman, photographer
NCM—Dickinson Research Center
Photographic Study Collection, 1988.9.74

← **Rodeo Trophy Saddle**
Hamley Saddlery Company
Pendleton, Oregon, 1914
NCM—Permanent Collection, 1983.05.07

This heavy, square-skirted trophy saddle features unusual rose-and-lattice floral tooling over its leather surfaces, while its horn boasts silver inlay with diamond motifs on the neck and Hamley's stylized "H" logo on the cap. The saddle was awarded to Bertha Kaepernik Blancett for her third "Champion Lady Bronc Rider" title at the Pendleton Roundup in 1914. An outstanding pioneer cowgirl saddle-bronc rider, relay racer, and Roman rider, in 1904 at the Cheyenne Frontier Days rodeo Blancett was the first woman to make an exhibition ride on a bronc.

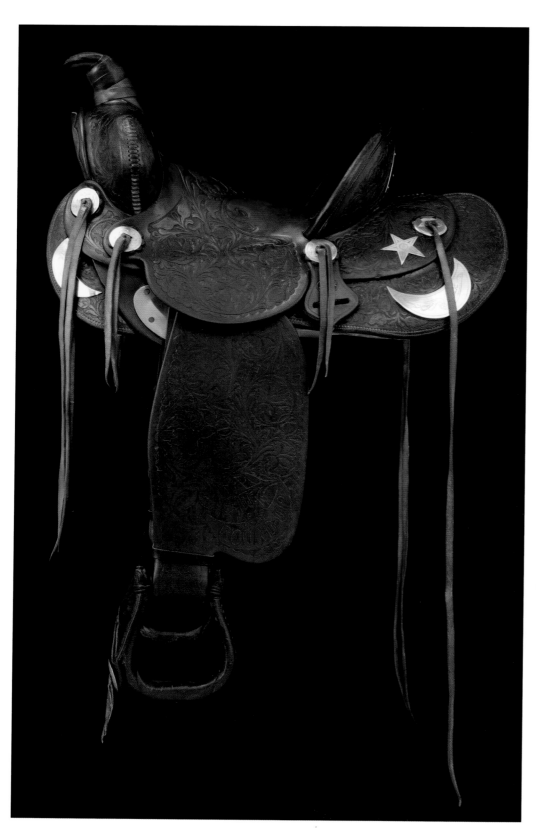

← Rodeo Trophy Saddle
Hamley Saddlery Company
Pendleton, Oregon, 1919
NCM—Gift of M. F. Peterson, R.256.01

Won at the 1919 Pendleton Round-Up by "Champion Lady Bronc Rider" Lorena Trickey, this diminutive, round-skirted trophy saddle is adorned with floral tooling and mountings of fine silver in star and crescent moon motifs. Trickey's Pendleton victory marked her debut as a top competitor. She would enjoy a succession of triumphs at Cheyenne as a bronc rider and relay racer, winning the Hotel McAlpin Trophy and the *Denver Post* Ladies' Relay Race Cup five times in eight years.

→ Rodeo Trophy Saddle
Hamley Saddlery Company
Pendleton, Oregon, 1923
NCM—Gift of M. F. Peterson, R.256.02

Sponsored by the Al Cadre Temple Shrine, this handsome trophy saddle was awarded to Lorena Trickey for the "First Prize, Girl's Relay Race" at the Pendleton Round-Up in 1923. The saddle is elegantly carved in an acorn-and-oak-leaf motif and embellished with eight silver corner plates of acorn pattern having engraved shrine emblems. This was the last of the ladies' trophy saddles awarded at Pendleton—after 1923, women's events became noncompetitive exhibitions.

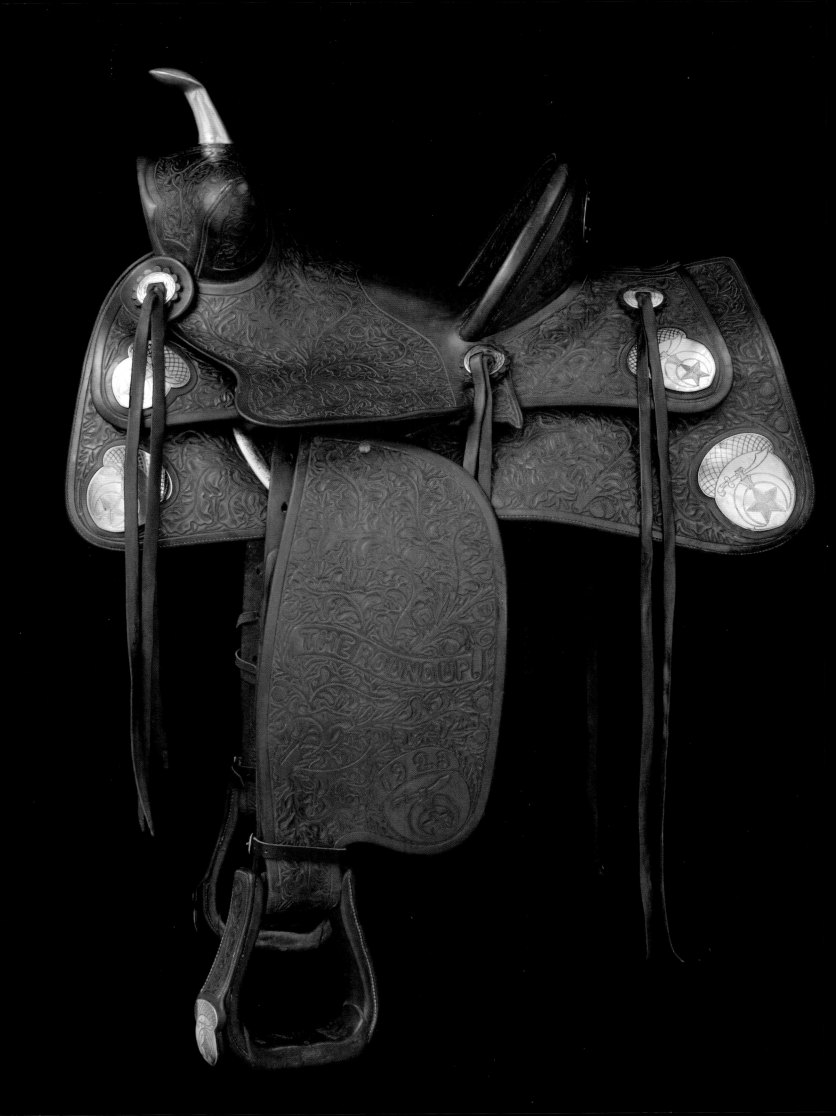

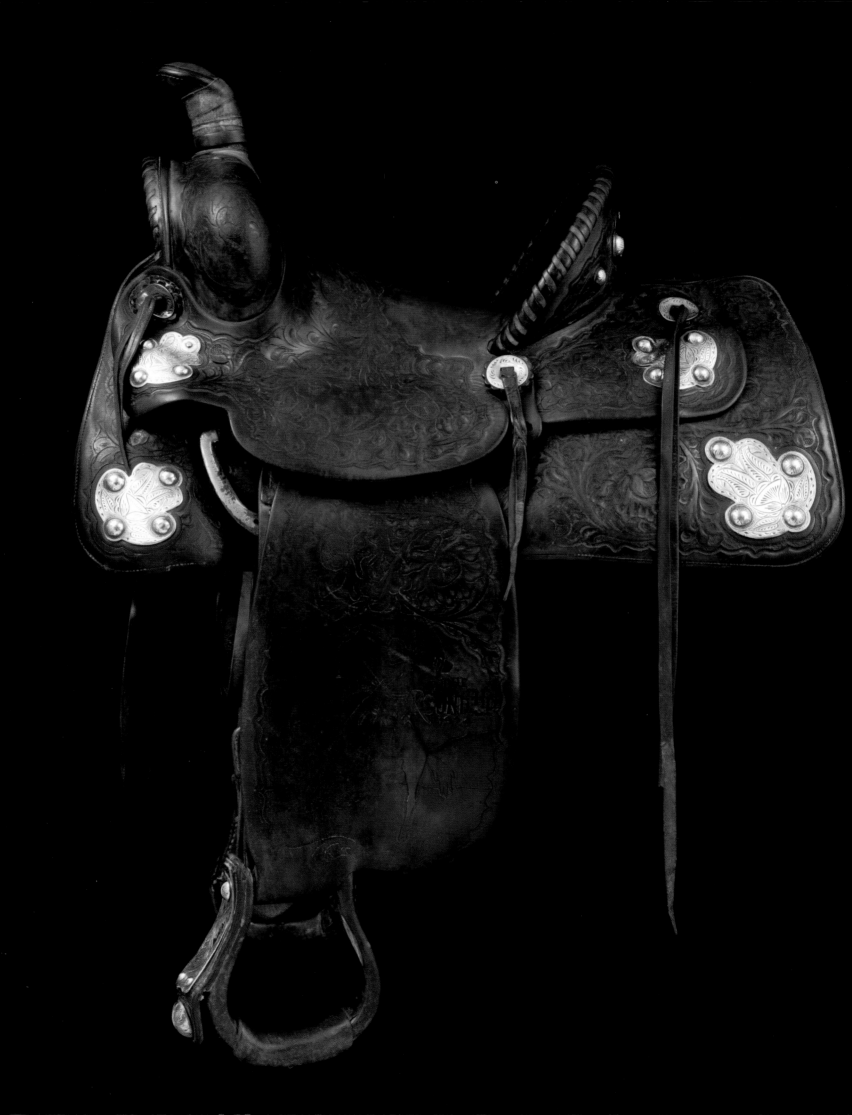

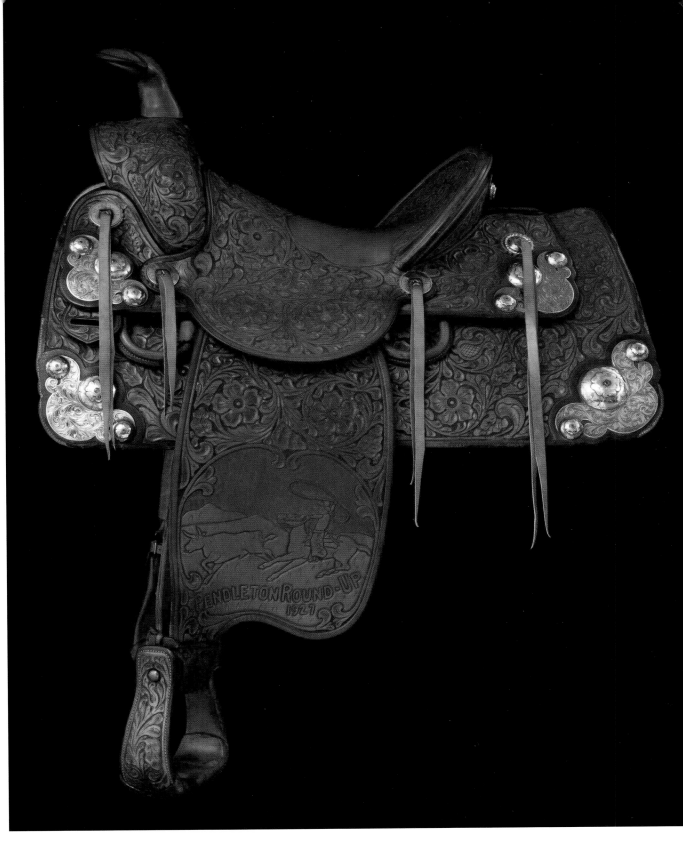

⬅ Rodeo Trophy Saddle

Hamley Saddlery Company
Pendleton, Oregon, 1924
NCM—Gift of Cynthia Olms, 1981.05.01

This trophy saddle was won by famed rodeo cowboy Paddy Ryan. The silver cantle plaque reads "World Champion Bronc Rider / 1924 Pendleton Round-Up." The saddle features a modified bronc-riding-pattern tree with engraved silver corner plates on the skirts and jockeys and floral tooling with the figure of a bronc rider and "Pendleton Round-Up" tooled on the fenders. Given its wear, Ryan evidently put the piece to some arena or range use subsequent to its presentation.

⬆ Rodeo Trophy Saddle

Hamley Saddlery Company
Pendleton, Oregon, 1927
NCM—Loan courtesy Holly D. Crosby, LR.214.51

Made and presented by Hamley's, this trophy saddle was awarded to Bob Crosby, winner of the "World's Championship Roping Contest" at the 1927 Pendleton Round-Up. Floral-and-foliate-carved in semirelief, the saddle features foliate-scroll-engraved silver corner plates accented with gold clover leaves and rubies and an inscribed silver presentation plaque on the back of the cantle. Among the best and most-competitive steer ropers in the sport, "Wild Horse Bob" won the event at Pendleton in 1927, 1928, 1933, and 1934.

↑ **Rodeo Trophy Saddle**

S. D. Myres Saddlery Company, El Paso, Texas, 1929
NCM—Gift of Katheryn M. Howard, 1985.54.01

Virtually identical in design and embellishment with the following
specimen, this prize piece manifests the Myres Saddlery's exclusive
contract for trophy horse-gear at the 1929 Madison Square Garden World
Series Rodeo. The saddle was captured by "World Champion Calf Roper"
Jake McClure. Known as "the gentleman roper," McClure invariably wore a
necktie in the arena. His innovative roping style—throwing a small, hard
"wedding-ring" loop—was quickly adopted by most of his competitors.

→ **Rodeo Trophy Saddle**

S. D. Myres Saddlery Company, El Paso, Texas, 1929
NCM—Gift of the Pete Knight Estate, 2003.289.01

This finely crafted trophy saddle was won by Pete Knight, "World
Champion Bronc Rider" at the 1929 World Series Rodeo held at Madison
Square Garden in New York City. The saddle is fully embellished with
exquisite floral carving, while the seat jockeys carry the hand-tooled
inscription "World Series Rodeo / 1929 / New York." Before his untimely
death in 1937, Knight would capture the world saddle-bronc-riding
championship again in 1932, 1933, 1935, and 1936.

Rodeo Trophy Saddle

Hamley Saddlery Company
Pendleton, Oregon, 1932
NCM—Gift of Everett Bowman, R.221.02

Won by "Champion Steer Roper" Everett Bowman at the 1932 Pendleton Round-Up, this saddle is embellished with floral and figural tooling and corner mountings of engraved silver. Though best remembered today as the first president of the Cowboys Turtle Association (CTA), Bowman also ranked among the greatest all-around contenders in the sport, taking ten championship titles in as many years. He retired from competition in 1943 but remained a prominent spokesman for organized rodeo sport until his death in 1971.

Rodeo Trophy Saddle

Hamley Saddlery Company
Pendleton, Oregon, 1935
NCM—Loan courtesy Virginia Hayes Merritt, LR.263.02

Awarded at Oregon's famous Pendleton Round-Up, this saddle went to King Merritt, "Champion Steer Roper" for 1935. The trophy piece is embellished with extensive, semi-relief-carved floral-and-foliate tooling and incorporates pierced and foliate-scroll-engraved silver corner plates on skirts and jockeys. A competitor and friend of Bob Crosby's, Merritt won the steer-jerking title at Pendleton in 1925 and 1935 and won the event world championship in 1942. He founded the Laramie Plains Steer Roping in 1948, a venue that did much to keep the venerable event alive.

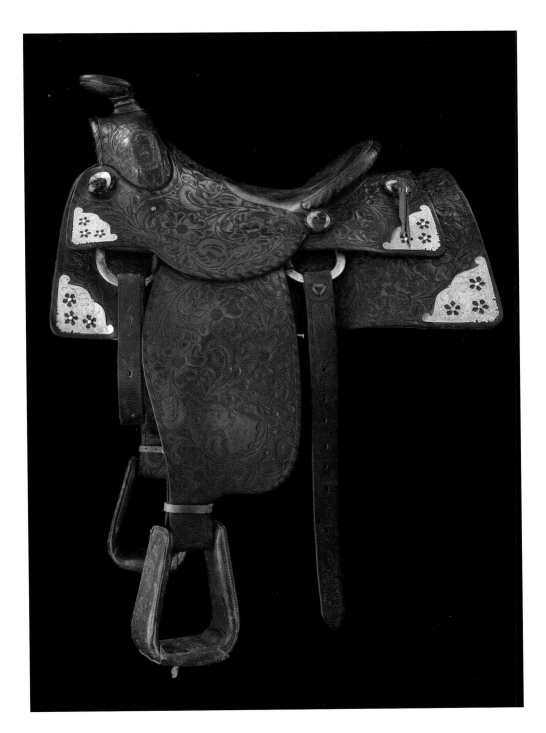

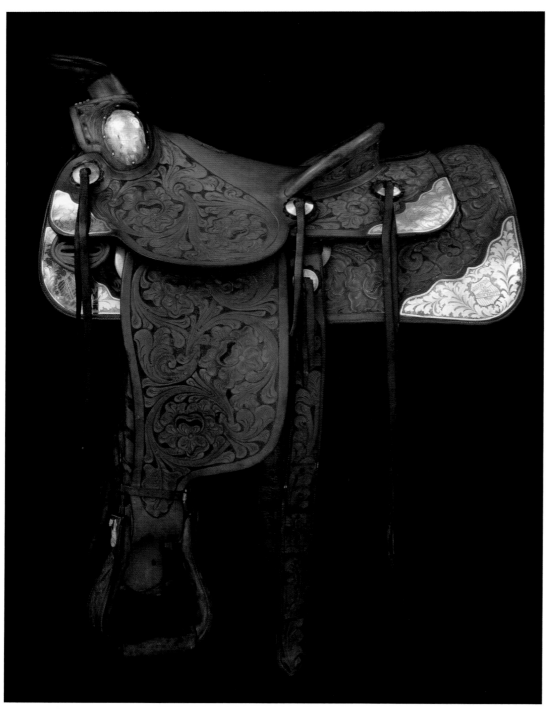

↑ **Rodeo Trophy Saddle**
Powder River Saddlery (Denver Dry Goods Company)
Denver, Colorado, 1936
NCM—Museum purchase, 1980.14

Sponsored by the Union Pacific Railroad, this saddle went to rodeo cowboy
Turk Greenough, "World Champion [Saddle] Bronc Rider" at the 1936
Cheyenne Frontier Days rodeo. The saddle boasts fine floral tooling and
silver corner plates engraved with the Union Pacific logo. Greenough also
won the saddle-bronc championship at Cheyenne in 1933 and 1935.
With his 1936 victory he would ultimately become the first competitor
to capture the so-called Triple Crown of rodeo, winning the event at
Cheyenne, Calgary, and Pendleton in one season.

→ **Rodeo Trophy Saddle**
G. S. Garcia Saddlery Company
Elko, Nevada, and Salinas, California, 1937
NCM—Gift of Everett Bowman, R.221.01

Manufactured and presented by the famed Garcia Saddlery Company, this
trophy saddle was awarded to "World's Champion All-Around Cowboy"
Everett Bowman at the 1937 Salinas, California, rodeo. The piece features
full rose-motif tooling accented with sterling silver corner plates and
bindings over the gullet and cantle, as well as a novel border trim of silver
butterflies and blossoms. In addition to his dedicated leadership in rodeo,
Bowman ranked among the greatest all-around contenders in the sport
throughout the 1930s.

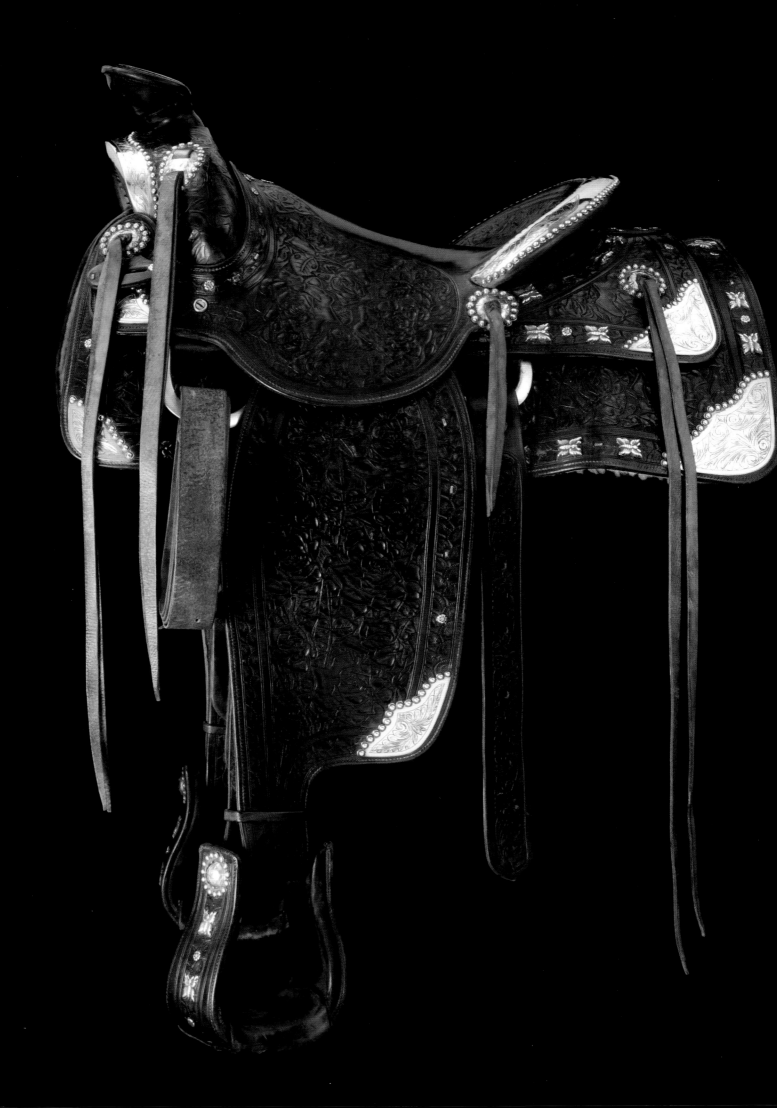

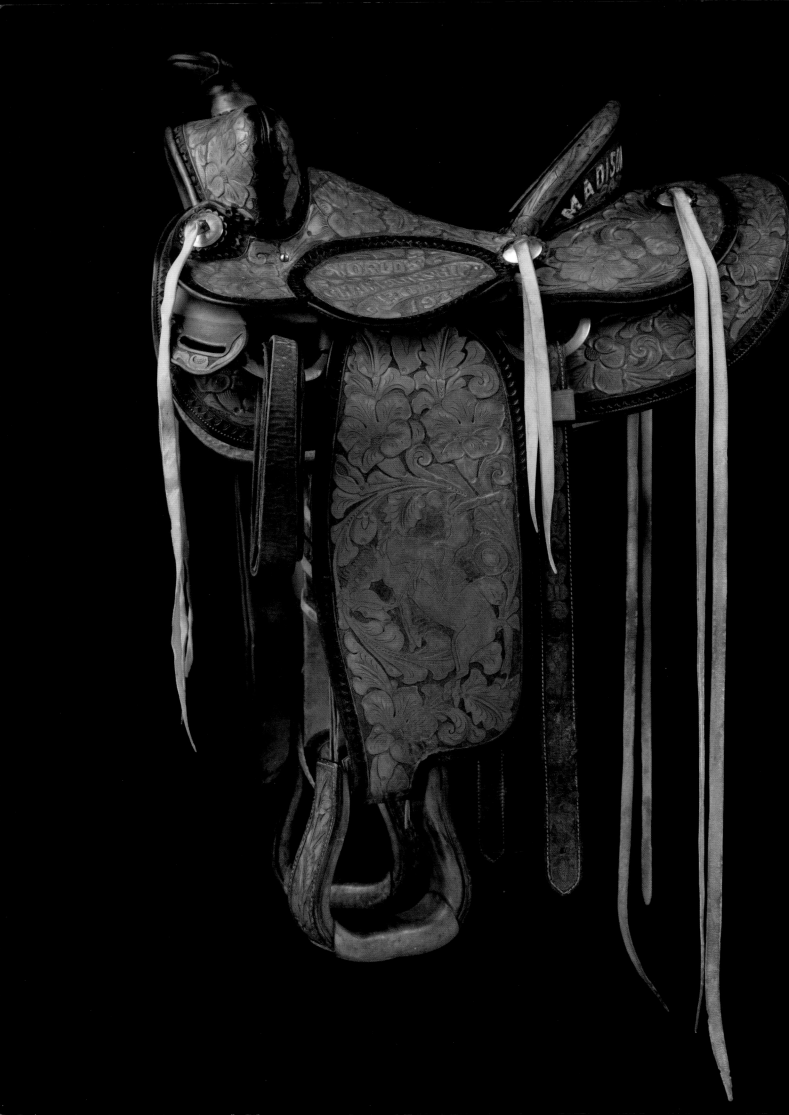

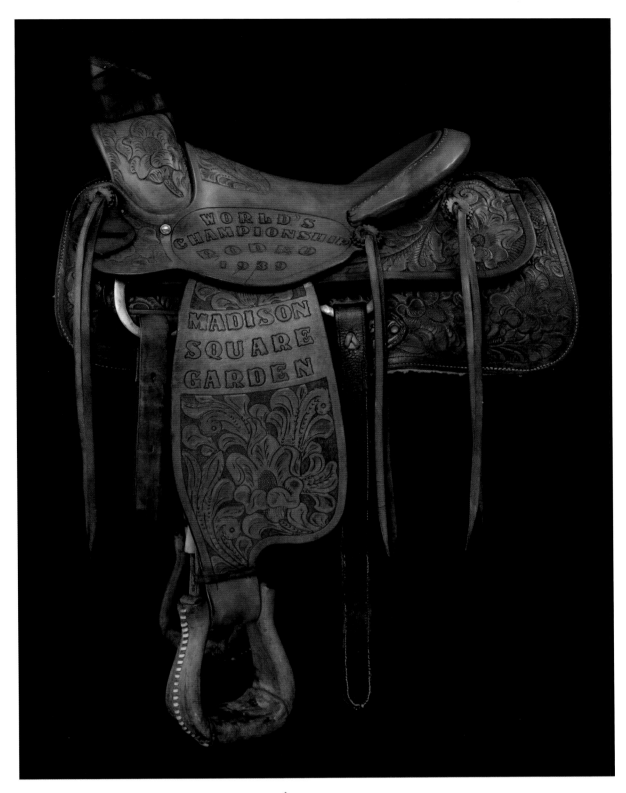

← Rodeo Trophy Saddle

S. D. Myres Saddlery Company
El Paso, Texas, 1937
NCM—Loan courtesy Frances Fletcher, LR.215.01

Embellished with fine floral and figural tooling, this trophy saddle went
to Kid Fletcher, "Champion Bareback Bronc Rider" at the 1937 Madison
Square Garden rodeo. Born in Competition, Missouri, in 1914, Fletcher
personified the name of his birthplace during two decades of rodeoing.
He captured the bull-riding championship in 1938 and remains the only
contestant of record to make a qualified ride on a rank Montana mare
named Dizzy Bertha.

↑ Rodeo Trophy Saddle

Edelbrock and Son Saddlery Company
Fort Worth, Texas, 1939
NCM—Gift of Mrs. Vera M. Herder, R.204.05

Tooled and stamped in a floral-and-foliate motif, this trophy saddle went
to Fritz Truan, declared the "World Champion Bronc Rider" after topping
Hell's Angel at the Madison Square Garden World's Championship Rodeo
in 1939. Truan would capture the event again in 1940, as well as garnering
the Garden's prestigious all-around-champion cowboy title.

Rodeo Trophy Saddle
Powder River Saddlery (Denver Dry Goods Company)
Denver, Colorado, 1942
NCM—Gift of Mrs. George McElhinney, R.211.02

Awarded to "Champion Saddle Bronc Rider" Doff Aber at the 1942 Cheyenne Frontier Days rodeo, this trophy saddle was sponsored by the Union Pacific Railroad. It features extensive semi-relief-carved floral-and-foliate tooling on a stippled ground and has engraved corner plates of sterling silver bearing the UPRR logo. In the late 1930s and early 1940s, Aber won on great bucking horses such as Five Minutes to Midnight, The Crying Jew, Goodbye Dan, and Hell's Angel. His slashing spurring style brought him the world champion saddle-bronc title in 1941 and 1942.

Rodeo Trophy Saddle
Edelbrock and Son Saddlery Company
Fort Worth, Texas, 1940
NCM—Gift of Alice Greenough, 1992.08.01

Hand-carved in an acanthus-leaf motif over a stippled ground, this trophy saddle was awarded to cowgirl-contender Alice Greenough when she captured the ladies' bronc-riding title at the 1940 Madison Square Garden World's Championship Rodeo. Greenough was the next-to-the-last woman to win the title, as all ladies' competitive events were eliminated at New York in 1942.

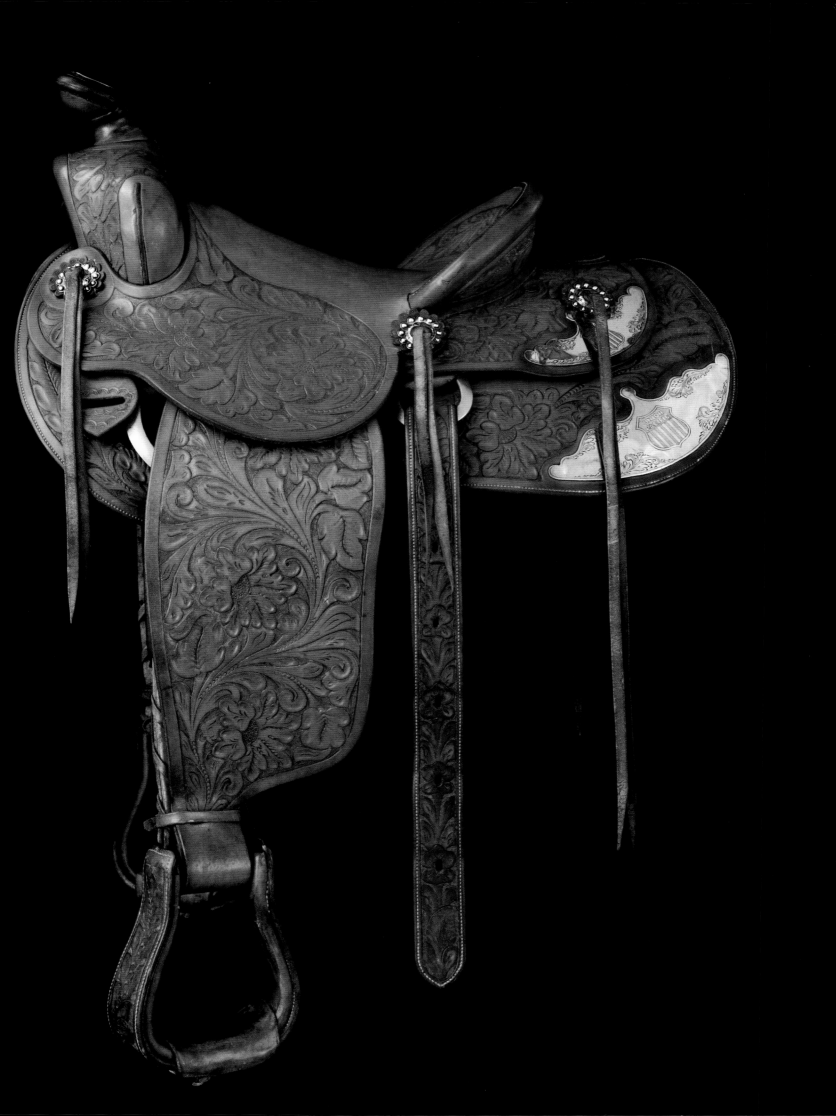

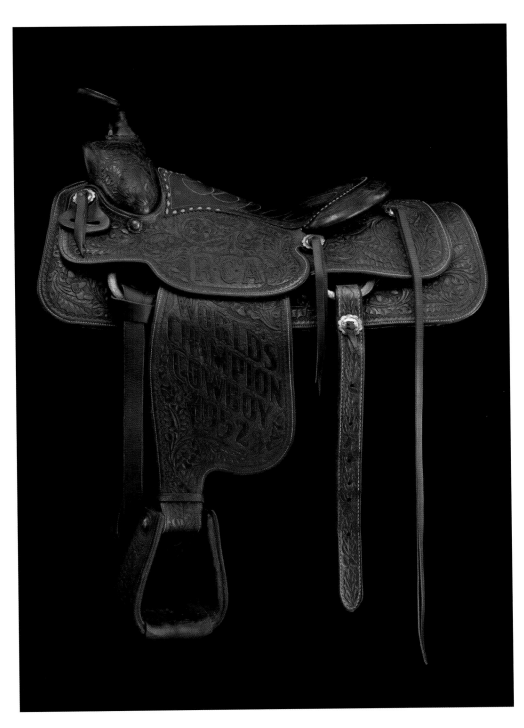

← **Rodeo Trophy Saddle**
Rowell Saddlery Company
Hayward, California, 1952
NCM—Gift of Harry and Melba Tompkins, 1998.05.01

The Rodeo Cowboys Association (RCA) awarded this trophy saddle to
Harry Tompkins for his first "World's Champion All-Around Cowboy" title in
1952. The saddle has a silver horn cap carrying a presentation inscription
and is fully tooled in an attractive acorn-and-oak-leaf motif. The saddle's
architecture exemplifies the widespread popularity of the "low-roping"
pattern by the early 1950s. A tenacious and tough competitor, Tompkins
ranked among the top five bull riders in twelve of the thirteen years from
1948 to 1960.

← **Rodeo Trophy Saddle**
Edelbrock and Son Saddlery Company
Fort Worth, Texas, 1944
NCM—Loan courtesy Mrs. Clyde Burk, LR.212.01

This round-skirted, double-rigged trophy saddle was won by Oklahoma
rodeo cowboy Clyde Burk, "World's Champion Calf Roper" at the 1944
Madison Square Garden World's Championship Rodeo in New York
City. The saddle is a "low-roping" pattern and features extensive floral
tooling on a striated and black-dyed ground. Burk also won the title at
Madison Square Garden in 1936, 1938, and 1942. This presentation piece
represents his last major victory before his untimely death in the arena
in 1945.

↑ Rodeo Trophy Saddle

Rowell Saddlery Company

Hayward, California, 1953

NCM—Gift of Mrs. E. A. Spaulding, R.210.01

This trophy saddle was awarded to Bill Linderman by the Rodeo Cowboys Association (RCA) for his third "World's Champion Cowboy" title in 1953. Of "low-roping" design with a padded, sueded-leather seat and Cheyenne-roll cantle, the piece is tooled in a flowing acorn-and-oak-leaf motif and has an inscribed silver horn cap in lieu of a cantle plaque. Always a tough competitor, Linderman won the world's champion cowboy title in 1945, 1950, and 1953; the saddle-bronc title in 1945 and 1950; the bareback title in 1943; and the steer-wrestling title in 1950.

→ Rodeo Trophy Saddle

R. D. Barnes Saddlery Company

Denver, Colorado, 1954

NCM—Gift of Troy Fort, 1988.19.01

Won by Troy Fort, the "Champion Calf Roper" at the 1954 Cheyenne Frontier Days rodeo, this trophy saddle features extensive floral-and-foliate tooling. A dedicated roper, Fort captured two Rodeo Cowboys Association (RCA) World Champion Calf Roping titles in 1947 and 1949, and he repeated his calf-roping victory at Cheyenne in 1956.

→ Rodeo Trophy Saddle

N. Porter Saddlery Company

Phoenix, Arizona, 1958

NCM—Loan courtesy Jim Shoulders, LR.228.32

This trophy saddle was awarded to Jim Shoulders, "RCA World's Champion Bareback Rider" in 1958. A "Genuine Toots Mansfield," "low-roping" model, the saddle is carved in a floral-and-vine motif on a stippled ground and features silver corner plates engraved in a bright-cut floral pattern. Among the greatest bareback-bronc riders in rodeo sport, Shoulders secured the RCA world bareback title four times—and the International Rodeo Association world bareback title three times—in a single decade.

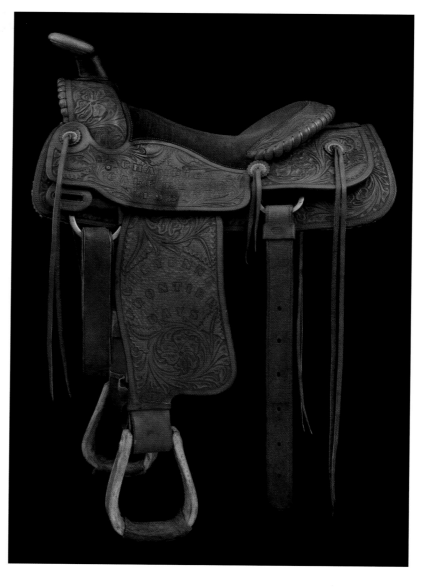

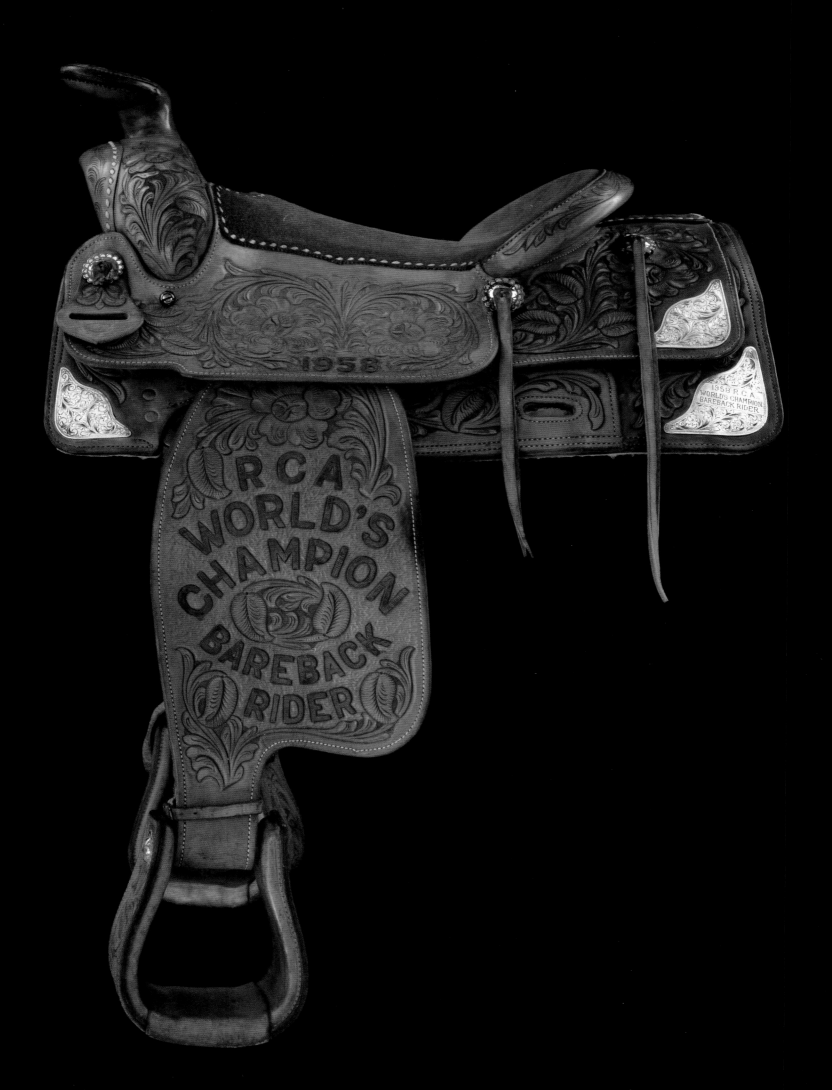

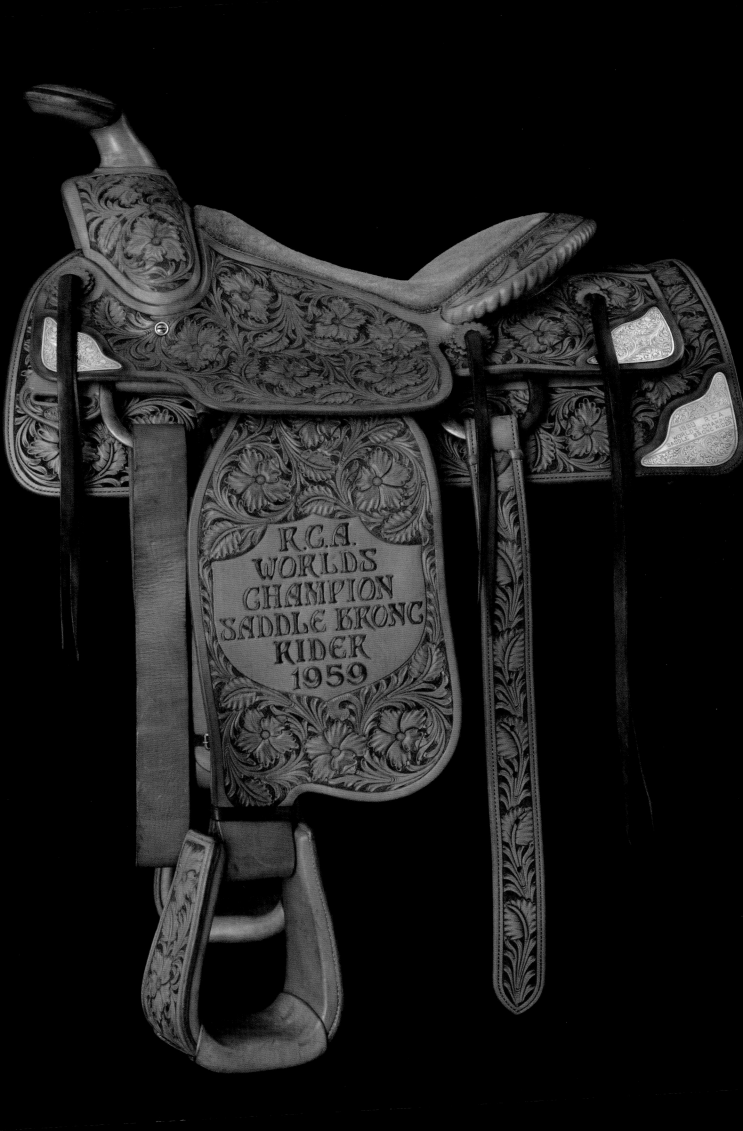

↑ **Casey Tibbs Waving from Saddle Bronc**
(detail)
Pendleton, Oregon, Round-Up, 1958
DeVere Helfrich, photographer
NCM—Dickinson Research Center
DeVere Helfrich Collection, 81.023.14108

← **Rodeo Trophy Saddle**
King's Saddlery Company
Sheridan, Wyoming, 1959
NCM—Museum purchase, R.229.01

Presented by the Rodeo Cowboys Association (RCA), this trophy saddle
went to Casey Tibbs, the "World's Champion Saddle Bronc Rider" in 1959.
The saddle is exquisitely relief carved in the bold foliate-and-floral pattern
over a stippled ground for which King's Saddlery became justly famed.
It also features a sueded-leather seat with Cheyenne-roll cantle and
engraved corner plates of sterling silver. Perhaps the greatest saddle-
bronc rider ever, Tibbs won the world's championship in the event six
times from 1949 through 1959.

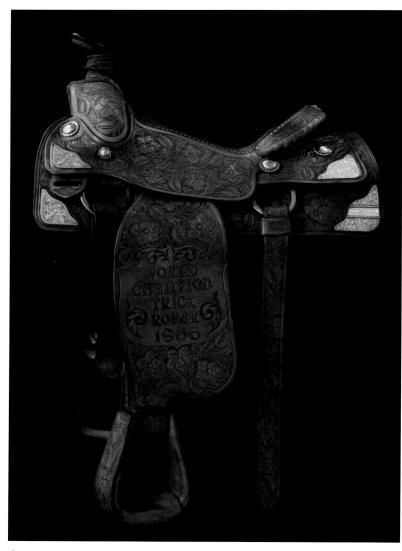

↑ Contest Trophy Saddle
King's Saddlery Company
Sheridan, Wyoming, 1966
NCM—Gift of Mary Louise Eskew Hale, 1981.33.01

Ornamented with floral tooling and engraved silver corner plates, this trophy saddle was awarded to Jim Eskew, Jr., "World Champion Trick Roper" at the 1966 National Cowboy Hall of Fame invitational. The son of rodeo impresario and manager Colonel Jim Eskew, "Junior" Eskew was the last of the prominent trick-roping contestants to practice the event before it became a contract act. The Don King Saddlery produced scores of similar trophy rigs for presentation by the Rodeo Cowboys Association throughout the later 1950s and 1960s.

➔ Rodeo Trophy Saddle
Don Atkinson Saddlery Company
Pawhuska, Oklahoma, 1967
NCM—Gift of Larry Mahan, R.235.01

Reflecting the decline of the design aesthetic that became pervasive in American culture during the later 1960s, this rather garish trophy saddle went to Larry Mahan, winner of the Rodeo Cowboys Association (RCA) "Todd Whatley Memorial/Top Hand Award" at the National Finals Rodeo (NFR) held in Oklahoma City in 1967. Among the best rough-stock riders in rodeo, Mahan captured the all-around-champion cowboy title six times in the eight-year period between 1966 and 1973.

➔ Rodeo Trophy Saddle
W. C. Hape Saddlery
Wyarno, Wyoming, 1977
NCM—Rodeo Historical Society Purchase, 2009.21

Adorned with presentation medallions from the Rodeo Historical Society, this trophy saddle was sponsored by the National Cowboy Hall of Fame and Western Heritage Center (today's National Cowboy & Western Heritage Museum), which worked closely with both the Professional Rodeo Cowboys Association (PRCA) and the National Finals Rodeo (NFR) during the latter's tenure in Oklahoma City, Oklahoma. The saddle is embellished with continuous floral-and-vine carving in the flowing, Sheridan, Wyoming (Don King), style and features engraved silver corner plates and finely braided strings. The trophy rig went to Tom Ferguson, the "PRCA Champion All Around Cowboy" at the 1977 NFR.

Born in 1950 at Tahlequah, Oklahoma, Ferguson erupted onto the professional rodeo scene in 1974, taking the all-around cowboy crown as a calf roper and steer wrestler. Always a tough competitor, and known on the circuit as "rodeo's bionic man," he kept the all-around title for five more years and remained in the top fifteen in his events into the mid-1980s. One of rodeo's "new breed" of contenders, Ferguson retired to his Oklahoma ranch in the late 1980s after having earned nearly a million dollars in the arena.

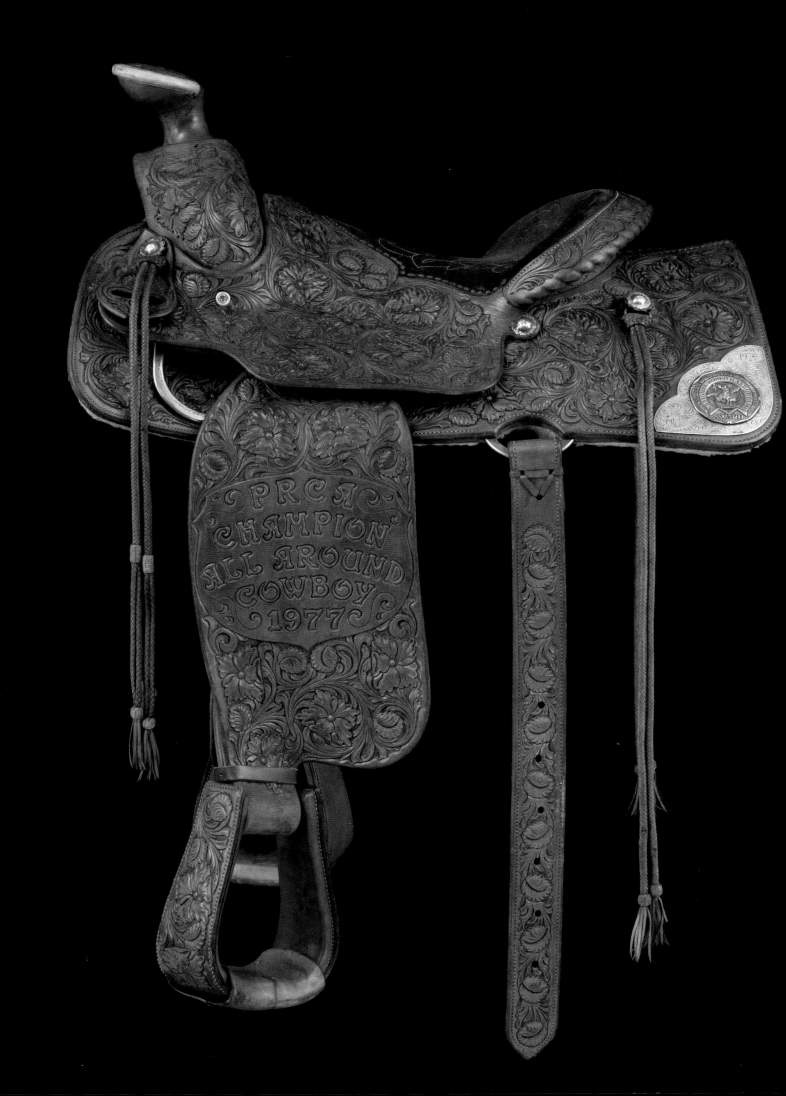

↑ **Charmayne James Barrel Racing** *(detail)*
Tulsa, Oklahoma, Rodeo, 1984
Bern Gregory, photographer
NCM—Dickinson Research Center
Bern Gregory Collection, 1999.025.2367.20

← **Rodeo Trophy Saddle**
J. R. Henry, Jr., Saddlery
Bryan, Texas, 1984
NCM—Gift of Charmayne James, 1995.21.07

Sponsored by the Oklahoma City Chamber of Commerce, this trophy
saddle is embellished with bold floral tooling and engraved silver
corner plates and features a hoof-pick case on the flank strap. It
was presented to Charmayne James, the "Champion Barrel Racer" at
the 1984 National Finals Rodeo (NFR) held in Oklahoma City. With
this victory, James also captured the Women's Professional Rodeo
Association rookie of the year title and the first of ten consecutive world
barrel-racing titles. Consistent performance by Charmayne and her
horse, Scamper, over the next decade made her the first "million-dollar"
cowgirl in rodeo history.

HOOT GIBSON   PADDY RYAN
WITH THE ROSEVELT TROPHY
(DOUBLE PAY)

6 Rodeo Honors

Trophy Plaques, Cups, Sculptures, Buckles, and Spurs

SINCE RODEO'S INCEPTION, tangible prizes recognizing the triumph of skill and daring in the arena have been an integral element of the sport. As related in chapter 1, for instance, victorious steer roper Juan Leivas captured a brand-new saddle with an appropriately engraved presentation plaque at the first competition held in Prescott, Arizona Territory, in 1888. In the first decades of the twentieth century, when the fledgling sport remained more a part-time pursuit than a full-time profession, such trophy prizes often proved more sought after—and more valuable—than prize money. One editorialist wrote in 1915, "Prizes other than cash are beautiful and appropriate, and their value both from the standpoint of their intrinsic worth, as well as the sentiment that attaches to them, goes without saying." The following year, Guy Weadick advertised that his New York Stampede would award "Cups, Medals, Belts, Saddles, Boots, Spurs and other Valuable Trophies" as well as $50,000 in cash purses—most of the latter of which failed to materialize.[1]

Even in the 1930s and 1940s, when the rodeo contestant's monetary winnings markedly increased and his accumulated dollars/points determined annual champions, tangible symbols of excellence remained important to many top competitors. In March 1942, for instance, 1941 champion bulldogger Hub Whiteman wrote to the Rodeo Association of America (RAA) about feeling slighted at not receiving a trophy buckle for his accomplishment. "Of course, I think the money is fine," he allowed, ". . . [but] I didn't receive anything to keep as a reminder of winning the championship." (The N. Porter Saddlery awarded trophy buckles to contestants placing in second through sixth place in the all-around standings that year; Whiteman placed seventh, just missing a buckle and receiving only a $100 cash award from the Stetson Hat Company for his event championship.)[2]

In addition to the trophy saddles discussed earlier, tangible awards customarily took the form of pictorially engraved and oftentimes gold-overlaid belt buckles (technically, belt plates) and handsomely inscribed silver loving cups in a plethora of designs. Other valuable tokens of excellence—such as silver plaques and cigarette cases, gold watches, embellished spurs, and event sculptures—filled out the range of rodeo trophies. Talented silversmiths and jewelers created the most exquisite of these prizes in the decades between 1910 and 1940. By the late 1930s, trophy watches were fast disappearing and trophy cups of sterling silver or fine silver plate dwindled in both number and quality, to be replaced by gold-electroplated pieces of less appealing design and execution. Unusual among tangible awards, trophy sculptures first appeared around 1940, and those created as event awards by artist C. A. Beil for the Calgary Stampede proved popular well into the 1960s. Throughout the twentieth century and beyond, however, the ubiquitous and richly embellished trophy belt buckle (or belt plate) reigned supreme as the common currency of rodeo champions.

← **Hoot Gibson, Paddy Ryan, and the Rosevelt [sic] Trophy**
Pendleton, Oregon, Round-Up, 1924
Ralph Russell Doubleday, photographer
NCM—Dickinson Research Center
Edith Jones Waldo Bliss Collection, R.241.180

⬆ **Victorious Contestants with
Trophy Belt Plates**
Venue unknown, circa 1960
James Cathey, photographer
NCM—Dickinson Research Center
Photographic Study Collection, 1988.9.1542

Commercial enterprises with particular interests in the West, such as the Union Pacific Railroad, the *Denver Post* newspaper, and *Ranch Romances* magazine, began sponsoring rodeo trophies as early as the 1910s. Businesses with more-direct rodeo associations such as the Plymouth Cordage Company (ropes), the Levi Strauss Company (jeans), the Stetson Hat Company, and various western saddleries became regular trophy supporters at particular venues in the 1920s and 1930s. Notable among rodeo's signature and one-of-a-kind trophies were those sponsored by New York City's McAlpin and Roosevelt hotels, by Hollywood western stars Hoot Gibson and Ken Maynard and the dynamic Metro Goldwyn Mayer Studio, by famed pugilist Jack Dempsey, and by rodeo enthusiast and historian Clifford Westermeier. These and many other rare prizes highlight the museum's collections, which, as part of a comprehensive assemblage, constitute an important resource revealing continuums of design development and aesthetic expression.

Trophy belt buckles, or plates, certainly rank as the most common prizes bestowed in the recognition of arena prowess. The earliest of these were fashioned either of sterling silver or of gold in square or rectangular pattern, were relatively smaller in comparison to later specimens, and typically featured only rudimentary figural engraving. The now-familiar, oval-pattern belt plate emerged during the 1920s, along with the increasing utilization of figural gold overlay and more refined, "bright-cut" engraving. (Oval buckles, however, did not become ubiquitous until the mid-1950s.) During succeeding decades, artisans brought greater complexity, refinement, and scale to trophy-buckle design and embellishment, culminating during the 1950s and 1960s with the huge Levi Strauss–RCA plates by R. Schaezlein and Son that rivaled a prizefighter's belt plate in size. Today, oval-pattern buckles of moderate size, their sterling silver bodies lavished with engraved or gold-overlaid event motifs and finished with rope or beaded-and-faceted borders, dominate in rodeo arenas around the nation.[3]

⬆ **Rodeo Trophy Plaques**
Maker unknown, 1913
NCM—Gift of D. N. Humphrey, R.247.02 A&B

These sterling silver trophy plaques or shields—no doubt intended to garnish the backs of saddle cantles—were awarded to cowboy Jack Fretz of Newalla, Oklahoma, for the "1st Prize / Worlds Championship / Bucking Contest" held in 1913 at Dayton, Ohio.

➡ **Rodeo Trophy Plaque**
Maker unknown, 1917
NCM—Gift of Estelle Gilbert, R.272.05

This unusual trophy plaque of embossed, silver-plated copper was awarded to Mike Hastings for "Best Bucking With Saddle" at Canada's Southern Alberta Stampede in 1917. Though he started as an all-around contender, Hastings made his reputation in succeeding years as an accomplished steer wrestler.

SOUTHERN
ALBERTA
STAMPEDE
1917

BEST BUCKING
WITH SADDLE

McALPIN TROPHY
WORLDS CHAMPIONSHIP
COWGIRLS RELAY RACE

WON BY
LORENA TRICKEY

FRONTIER DAYS
CHEYENNE WYO
1920

Hotel McAlpin Trophy
FOR THE
CHAMPION WOMAN RIDER
FRONTIER
DAYS
OF THE
WORLD
CHEYENNE
WYOMING
1921

WON BY
LORENA TRICKEY

The American Brewing Company Trophy Plaque
Maker unknown, 1930
NCM—Gift of Mrs. Oral Zumwalt, R.207.12

Oral Zumwalt captured this saddle plaque of engraved silver as "Champion All-Round Cowboy" at the 1930 Moose Jaw Rodeo in Saskatchewan, Canada. Zumwalt rodeoed in the United States, Canada, Mexico, and Australia (where he once roped and tied a kangaroo). In 1939 at a rodeo in Palm Springs, California, he won a steer wrestling go-round with an official time of 2.4 seconds—still the fastest toss ever recorded from behind a barrier.

The Hotel McAlpin Trophy Plaques
Lambert Brothers Jewelers
New York City, 1920 and 1921
NCM—Gift of M. F. Peterson, R.256.10 A&B

Awarded by the McAlpin Hotel of New York City at the Cheyenne Frontier Days rodeo, these prestigious women's trophies came with an all-expense-paid trip to the Big Apple. The relief-cast bronze plaques, finished in nickel, gold wash, and enamel, feature appealing likenesses of intrepid western womanhood. Captured in successive years by Lorena Trickey, at the top is the 1920 "Worlds Championship Cowgirls Relay Race" trophy, while below is the 1921 McAlpin prize for the "Champion Woman Rider of the World." In all, Trickey won the ladies' relay race title at the Cheyenne Frontier Days four times between 1920 and 1926.

The Sam Jackson Trophy Plaque
Maker unknown, 1931
NCM—Loan courtesy Mrs. Ike Rude, LR.258.02

Carrying a facsimile image of the permanent Sam Jackson Trophy, this "year" plaque was won by Ike Rude, "World's Champion Cowboy" at the 1931 Pendleton Round-Up. Something of a successor to the Roosevelt Trophy, the $5,000 Sam Jackson silver trophy ultimately was retired at Pendleton in 1951 by Choate Webster of Lenapah, Oklahoma, after three successive victories in steer roping, calf roping, and bulldogging. An inveterate calf and steer roper for sixty years, Ike Rude entered his first rodeo in 1910 and contended for the last time at the Cheyenne Frontier Days in 1970. He captured the world steer-roping championship in 1941, 1947, and 1953.

To
VERNE ELLIOTT
IN APPRECIATION OF HIS KINDNESS
AND GOOD FRIENDSHIP
— FROM —
HIS COWBOY AND COWGIRL FRIENDS

Chester Byers
Tom Kirnan
Bob Calen
Cleve Kelley
Joe Welch
Roy Matthews
Dick Shelton
Buck Lucas
Rube Roberts
Buck Stuart
Don Nesbitt
Dick Griffith
Bob McLaughlin
Louis Kubitz
James Irwin
Mamie Francis

Vaughn Krieg
Ruth Roach
Mabel Strickland
Lucyle Richards
Cleone Holcomb
California Frank
Reine Shelton
Bea Kirnan
Chuck Wilson
Chuck Williams
Waid Watkins
Lynn Huskey
Rosin McIntosh
Hub Whitman
Paul Carney
C. O. Leuschner

← **Verne Elliott Memorial Plaque**

Haltom's Jewelers

Fort Worth, Texas, circa 1950

NCM—Gift of the Gretchen Elliott Estate, R.271.05

A tribute to one of the greatest stock contractors and administrators in rodeo, this silver plaque was presented to Verne Elliott in recognition of his many contributions to the sport over more than thirty years. Inscribed "In appreciation of his kindness and good friendship from his cowboy and cowgirl friends," the plaque carries the facsimile signatures of many notable contestants, among them Chester Byers, Paul Carney, Tommy Kirnan, Buck Lucas, Don Nesbitt, Bea Kirnan, Lucyle Richards, and Ruth Roach.

↑ **Rodeo Trophy Watches**

Various domestic watchmakers, 1926–36

Left to right by row, starting from top: Mike Hastings, Bulldogging Champion, Philadelphia, 1926; Everett Bowman, Steer Decorating Champion, Calgary, 1929; Oral Zumwalt, Wild Steer Decorating Champion, Calgary, 1931; Everett Bowman, Calf Roping Champion, Calgary, 1931; Pete Knight, Bronc Riding Champion, Fort Worth, 1933; Herman Linder, Steer Riding Champion, Lethbridge, 1935; Everett Bowman, Calf Roping Champion, Fort Worth, 1935; Bob Crosby, Steer Roping Champion, Cheyenne, 1936.

NCM accession numbers, in order above: R.272.01, R.221.24, R.207.09, R.221.25, 2003.289.12, 1980.37.05, R.221.27, LR.214.49

Rodeo Trophy Watch
Eterna Watch Company
Grenchen, Switzerland, 1927
NCM—Gift of the McCarroll Family Trust,
2006.08.07

This gold-cased, open-faced pocket watch
was captured by Frank McCarroll, who was
proclaimed the "World Champion Steer
Wrestler" at Fred Beebe's 1927 World Series
Rodeo held at Madison Square Garden in New
York City.

Trophy Cups and Sculptures

The *Denver Post* Trophy Cup
Derby Silver Company
Shelton, Connecticut, 1905
NCM—Gift of Betty Steele, 1978.07.05

Presented to Mrs. Bill Irwin, winner of the
"Cowgirls Race" at the Cheyenne Frontier
Days rodeo in 1905, this silver loving cup was
the first award sponsored by the *Denver Post*
newspaper. For the following forty years, the
newspaper underwrote the *Denver Post* Ladies'
Relay Race, one of the most popular and long-
lived events at the Cheyenne celebration.

Frontier Days Trophy Cup
Pairpoint Manufacturing Company
New Bedford, Massachusetts, 1909
NCM—Gift of Betty Steele, 1978.07.02

Mounted with stag-horn handles, this silver loving cup went to C. B. Irwin, the "Winner [of the] Gentlemans Driving" competition at the Cheyenne Frontier Days rodeo in 1909. In addition to his prominence as a rodeo organizer and promoter, Irwin was a noted trainer and competitive driver of fine harness horses during the early twentieth century.

The Albany Hotel Trophy Cup
Reed and Barton Silver Company
Taunton, Massachusetts, 1911
NCM—Gift of Betty Steele, 1978.07.04

Presented by the Albany Hotel Company of Denver, Colorado, this silver-plated trophy cup was awarded at the Cheyenne "Frontier Celebration" to the "Winner of [the] Men's Relay Race." A part of the C. B. Irwin estate, the cup probably was won by his son, Floyd Leslie Irwin, but was never inscribed with the recipient's name.

→ **The *Billboard* Trophy Urn**
Maker unknown, 1916
NCM—Gift of Mary Byers Fowler, R.260.08

The Billboard Publishing Company of
Cincinnati, Ohio, presented this attractive,
silver-plated lidded urn to Chester Byers,
"World Champion Cowboy Fancy Roper" at the
1916 New York Stampede. Founded in 1894,
Billboard magazine served as a trade paper for
the bill-posting industry that presented the
news of outdoor amusements. By the mid-
1910s, it had become the paper of record for
various circuses, carnivals, amusement parks,
vaudeville shows, and a growing number of
rodeo venues.

→ **The *Denver Post* Trophy Cup**

In its continuing support of women's competition at Cheyenne, the *Denver Post* newspaper presented this interestingly embellished trophy cup to Lorena Trickey, "Champion Ladies Relay Racer" at the Frontier Days rodeo of 1921. The piece juxtaposes delicate silver trim in an acorn-and-oak-leaf motif with imposing boar's-tusk handles of mellowed ivory.

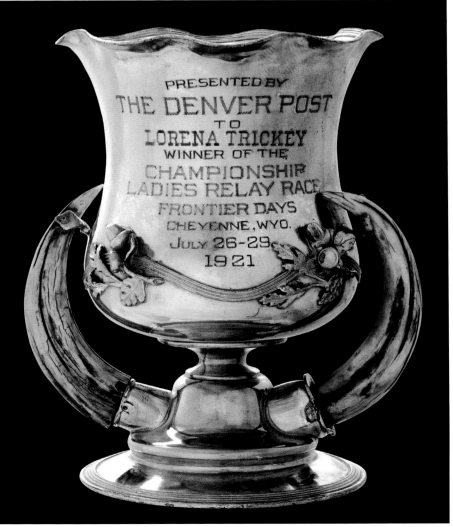

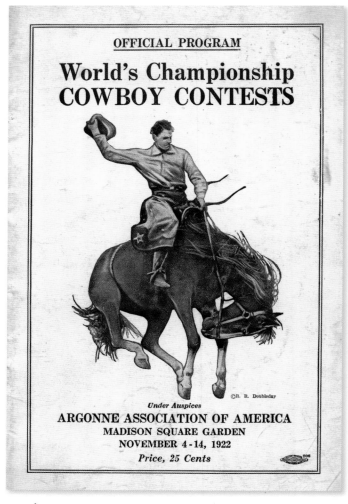

⬆ **Rodeo Program**
World's Championship Cowboy Contests /
November 4–14, 1922 / under auspices
[of the] Argonne Association
(This was the first Madison Square Garden rodeo.)
Cover image by Ralph Russell Doubleday
Argonne Association of America Committee
NCM—Dickinson Research Center
Rodeo Programs Collection, 2005.171.11

⬆ **The Argonne Association Trophy Cup**
William B. Durgin Division / Gorham Silver Corporation
Concord, New Hampshire, and Providence, Rhode Island, 1922
NCM—Gift of the McCarroll Family Trust, 2006.08.03

Captured by Bonnie McCarroll for the "World's Cowgirl Championship" at
Tex Austin's first Madison Square Garden Championship Rodeo in 1922, this
handsome piece was sponsored by the Argonne Association, a group of
Manhattan socialites that raised money for the support of French children
orphaned in World War I. The reverse *(inset)* presents a finely engraved, evocative
likeness of "The Argonne Boy" over the caption "You've been my friend."

↑ **Bonnie McCarroll Posed with Horse**
Location unknown, circa 1924
Photographer unknown
NCM—Dickinson Research Center
McCarroll Family Trust Collection,
RC2006.076.421

↑ **The Lord Selfridge Trophy Cup**
Martin Hall and Company
Shrewsbury Works, Sheffield, England, 1922/1924
NCM—Gift of the McCarroll Family Trust, 2006.08.04

This exquisite sterling silver cup, or lidded urn, was captured by bronc-riding champion cowgirl Bonnie McCarroll at Tex Austin's first International Rodeo, held at Wembley Stadium outside London, England, during the 1924 British Empire Exhibition. The piece was sponsored, and probably presented, by well-known retail magnate Harry Gordon Selfridge, who opened the world's first department store (Selfridge's) in London in 1909.

↑ **The Lord Ebury Trophy Cup**
Maker unknown, circa 1924
NCM—Gift of Harley and Edith Miller, 1998.61.01

Commissioned and presented by the Right Honorable Lord Ebury of Great Britain, this embossed and silver-plated trophy cup was awarded at Tex Austin's First International Rodeo, held in London, England, during the summer of 1924. Saddle-bronc rider Howard Tegland of South Dakota captured the cup in the rodeo's premier event. A reckless and brilliant rider, in 1922 Tegland entered nineteen rodeos and won in eighteen, including the major venues at Pendleton, Cheyenne, Chicago, and New York.

➜ **Howard Tegland, Winner of Bronc Riding [Title], 1922, Cheyenne, Wyo., Bozeman, Mont., Casper, Wyo., Pendleton, Ore.** *(detail)*
Image location unknown
Ralph Russell Doubleday, photographer
NCM—Dickinson Research Center
Photographic Study Collection, 2005.146.2

⬆ **The Hoot Gibson Trophy Cup**
Maker unknown, 1924
NCM—Gift of the Ed Bowman Estate, R.206.13

Sponsored by one-time rodeo champion and Hollywood western star Hoot
Gibson, this large, silver-plated loving cup was awarded to L. E. "Ed" Bowman,
"Champion Calf Tier" at the Prescott Frontier Days Rodeo in 1924. Bowman
roped and tied three calves in 65 and 11/15 seconds to win the trophy. For a
time, he used the cup to feed grain to one of his favorite and most-talented
roping horses, Back-Up Pete, who constituted the other half of the well-honed
winning team.

➡ **Back-Up Pete Eating Grain from the Hoot
Gibson Trophy** (detail)
Edward Bowman's Arizona Ranch, circa 1925
Photographer unknown
NCM—Dickinson Research Center
Photographic Study Collection, 1988.10.3

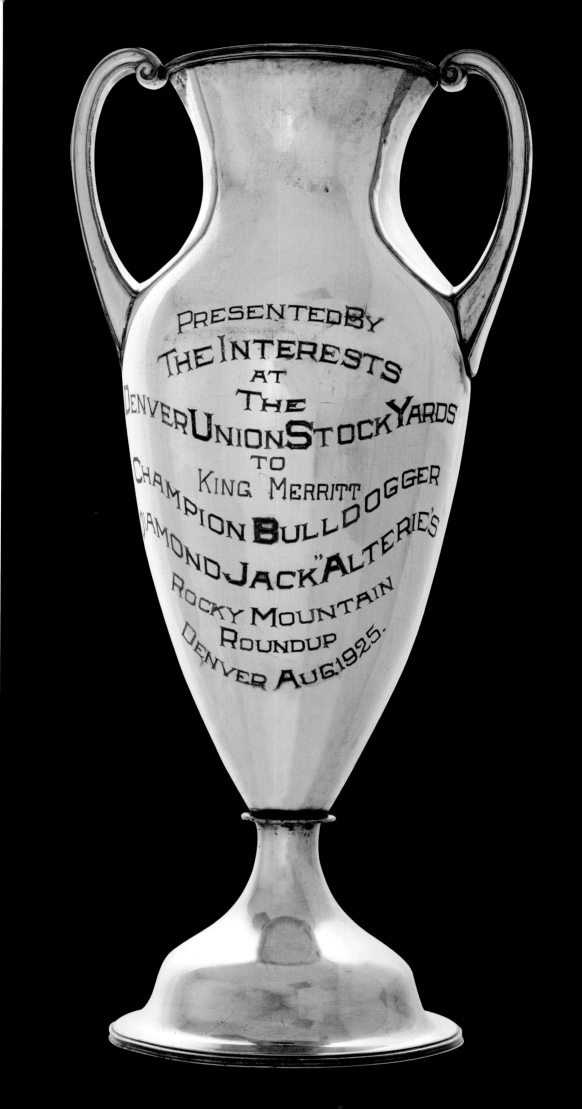

➜ **The Denver Union Stock Yards Trophy Cup**
K. S. Jewelry Company, circa 1925
NCM—Loan courtesy Virginia Hayes Merritt,
LR.263.03

Presented by "The Interests at The Denver
Union Stock Yards," this graceful silver-plated
cup went to "Champion Bulldogger" King
Merritt at the 1925 Rocky Mountain Roundup,
held in Denver, Colorado. Merritt specialized
in steer roping, taking the title at Pendleton
in 1925 and 1935 and winning the world
championship in 1942. Rodeo sponsor Louis
"Diamond Jack" Alterie was a Wild West and
rodeo enthusiast—and a notorious gangster
with Chicago's North Side Mob—who
attended many competitions and often
sported a pair of Colt six-shooters in public.

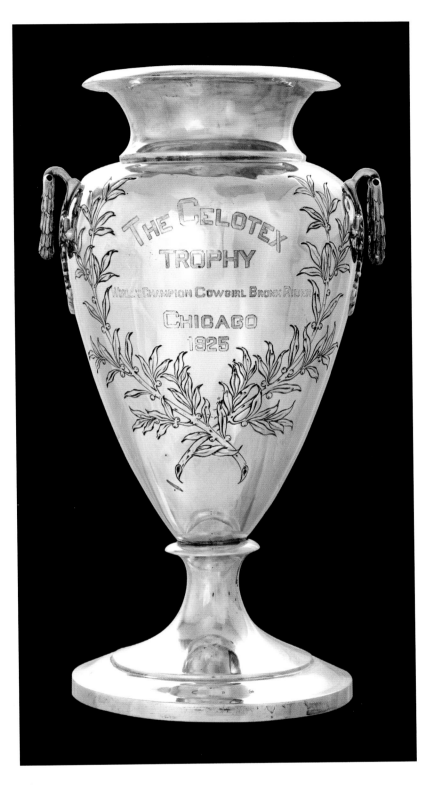

⬆ The Celotex Trophy Cup

International Sterling Company

Meriden, Connecticut, 1925

NCM—Gift of M. F. Peterson, R.256.06

This foliate-engraved, silver-plated trophy cup, or urn, was awarded to Lorena Trickey, the "World's Champion Cowgirl Bronk [*sic*] Rider" at Tex Austin's 1925 Chicago Rodeo. Though she specialized in relay racing and Roman riding, Trickey also proved a very competitive bronc rider, taking her first rough-stock title at the Pendleton Round-Up in 1919.

⬆ Rodeo Trophy Cup

J. E. Caldwell Silver Company

Philadelphia, Pennsylvania, 1914/1926

NCM—Gift of Florence H. Randolph, R.237.13

This silver-plated loving cup was presented to Florence Hughes (Randolph), the winner of the "Ladies Championship Bucking Horse Contest" at the 1926 Sesquicentennial Rodeo held in Philadelphia, Pennsylvania. Florence rode away from the venue with $6,000 in prize money, having also won the trick-riding event and the cowgirl's all-around championship.

The Stetson Trophy Cup
Essex Silver / Wallingford Company
Wallingford, Connecticut, 1927
NCM—Gift of Everett Bowman, R.221.38

Presented by the famed Stetson Hat Company of Philadelphia, Pennsylvania, this silver-plated loving cup went to Everett Bowman, winner of the "Calf-Roping Contest" at the 1927 Cheyenne Frontier Days rodeo. Bowman would take the Rodeo Association of America champion calf-roping title in 1929, 1935, and 1937.

➜ **Everett Bowman with Stetson Trophy**
(detail)
Cheyenne, Wyoming, Frontier Days, 1927
Ralph Russell Doubleday, photographer
NCM—Dickinson Research Center
Photographic Study Collection, 1988.9.1511

The Mescal Ike Trophy Cup
International Sterling Company
Meriden, Connecticut, 1927
NCM—Gift of Mary Byers Fowler, R.260.07

For his second consecutive "World's Champion Trick Roper" title at Chicago in 1927, Chester Byers won this silver loving cup sponsored by the *Chicago Daily News*. The newspaper named the trophy after its popular "Mescal Ike" cartoon strip, which portrayed the humorous adventures of "the cowboy hero of Cactus Corner" from 1926 to circa 1940.

The Studebaker Trophy Cup
Oxford Silver Plate / W. A. Rogers
New York, 1927
NCM—Gift of Cynthia Olms, 1981.05.04

Sponsored by the Studebaker Motor Service
Company of Calgary, Alberta, this silver-plated
cup went to Paddy Ryan, "Steer Decorating"
Champion at the 1927 Calgary Stampede. A
talented and colorful all-around cowboy, Ryan
specialized in bronc riding but won in various
events during his peak years between 1924
and 1928. In 1924, for example, he won the
multievent, multivenue Roosevelt Trophy, and
while working for Leonard Stroud's Congress of
Cowboys, Ryan sometimes bulldogged steers
from the runningboard of a car.

➔ **The Edward F. Albee Trophy Cup**
Maker unknown, 1927
NCM—Gift of the Knight Estate, 2003.289.04

Awarded at the Calgary Stampede, this large and impressive trophy for the "North American Bucking Horse Riding Championship," sponsored by vaudeville theater impresario Edward F. Albee II, was won by famed Canadian bronc rider Pete Knight. Albee's sponsorship probably stemmed from rodeo's early, tangential association with vaudeville and the wider milieu of live entertainment in America during the first decades of the twentieth century.

⬆ **Pete Knight Saddle-Bronc Riding** (detail)
Mount and venue unknown, circa 1930
Ralph Russell Doubleday (?), photographer
NCM—Dickinson Research Center
Photographic Study Collection, 88.9.503

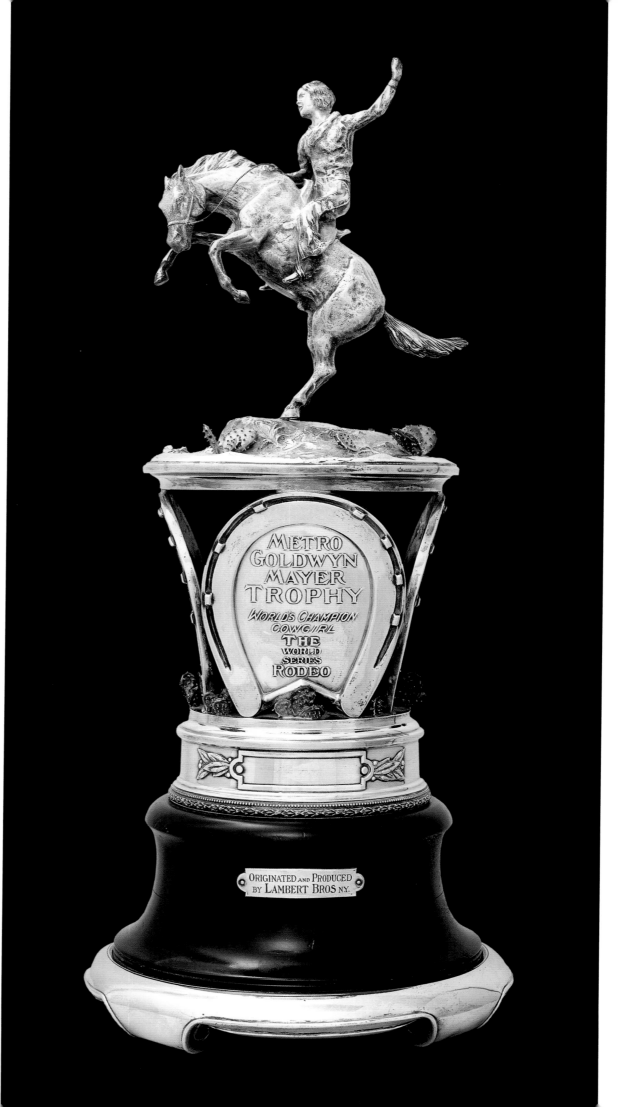

→ The Metro Goldwyn Mayer Trophy
Lambert Brothers Jewelers
New York City, 1927/1934
NCM—Gift of Tad Barnes Lucas, R.238.18

Certainly the most prestigious and valuable trophy ever awarded to female rodeo contenders, this extravagant silver piece, with its appealing sculpture of a cowgirl on the back of a tossing bronc, was commissioned by Metro Goldwyn Mayer Studio in 1927 for $10,000 as "a tribute to the charm and courage of western womanhood." Presented to the "World's Champion Cowgirl" declared at the Madison Square Garden World Series Rodeo, the MGM trophy first went to Florence Hughes Randolph in 1927 and then was retired under the sponsor's rules by Tad Barnes Lucas after three consecutive victories in 1928, 1929, and 1930. Lucas first captured the All-Around Champion Cowgirl title at the Garden in 1926, and she took it again in 1931 and 1932.

This is actually the second rendition of the MGM trophy; the original melted when Tad's Fort Worth, Texas, home burned around 1932. Through the good offices of rodeo manager Colonel W. T. Johnson, Lambert Brothers Jewelers agreed to fashion a second version of the trophy from blobs of melted silver salvaged by Lucas. As documented in the adjacent photographs, the jewelers achieved a quite faithful reiteration—except for the omission of the hat in the cowgirl's outstretched hand.

↑ **Tad Lucas with the MGM Trophy**
Madison Square Garden, 1929
Photographer unknown
Image courtesy Mitzi Lucas Riley

↑ **Tad Lucas with the MGM Trophy**
Fort Worth, Texas, circa 1940
Photographer unknown
Image courtesy Mitzi Lucas Riley

↗ **The Juergens and Andersen Trophy Pitcher**
Towle Silver Company
Newburyport, Massachusetts, 1928
NCM—Gift of Florence H. Randolph, R.237.18

This silver pitcher, or ewer, was won by Florence Hughes Randolph,
"World's Champion Cowgirl Trick Rider" at Tex Austin's 1928 Chicago
Championship Rodeo. The previous year she had captured the first MGM
Trophy, awarded to the champion all-around cowgirl at the Madison
Square Garden rodeo.

→ **Bonnie McCarroll [Saddle Bronc] Riding**
(detail)
Tex Austin's Chicago, Illinois, Rodeo, circa 1925
Ralph Russell Doubleday, photographer
NCM—Dickinson Research Center
McCarroll Family Trust Collection,
RC2006.076.102-07

← **The Burlington Route Trophy Pitcher**
Towle Silver Company
Newburyport, Massachusetts, 1928
NCM—Gift of the McCarroll Family Trust,
2006.08.02

While Florence Randolph rode off with the
trick-riding championship at Tex Austin's
1928 Chicago rodeo, Bonnie McCarroll took
this silver pitcher, or ewer, as the "World's
Champion Cowgirl Bronk [*sic*] Rider" at the
same venue. McCarroll's outstanding arena
career would end the following year in a
tragic bronc-riding accident at the Pendleton
Round-Up.

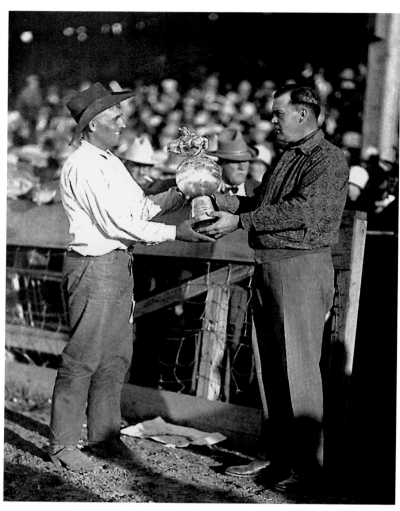

↑ **George Baer Presenting the Roosevelt Trophy to Bob Crosby** (detail)
Pendleton, Oregon, Round-Up, 1928
Ralph Russell Doubleday, photographer
NCM—Dickinson Research Center
R. R. Doubleday Collection, 79.026.2412

 ↑ →

The Permanent Roosevelt Trophy
Lambert Brothers Jewelers
New York City, 1923/1928
NCM—Loan courtesy Mrs. Roberta Crosby Burkstaller, LR.214.40

Sponsored by New York's Hotel Roosevelt (United Hotels Company) in honor of "Cowboy President" Theodore Roosevelt, this rare and much-coveted $5,000 trophy was permanently retired by Bob Crosby after he captured "World's Champion Cowboy" titles at both Cheyenne and Pendleton in 1925, 1927, and 1928—a record equivalent to three all-around championships in that era. Previous winners, recognized on the reverse base plaque (above), were Yakima Canutt in 1923, Paddy Ryan in 1924, and Norman Cowan in 1926. Following his three-time triumph, Crosby enjoyed a complimentary room at the Roosevelt Hotel whenever he was in New York City for the equally prestigious Madison Square Garden contest.

← **The Ken Maynard Trophy**
Lambert Brothers Jewelers
New York City, 1928
NCM—Gift of Earl Thode, R.216.02

Sponsored by onetime rodeo contestant and
Hollywood western movie star Ken Maynard,
this substantial trophy of cast bronze and silver
was presented to Earl Thode, "World's Champion
Cowboy" at the Madison Square Garden World
Series Rodeo in 1928. The next year, under Rodeo
Association of America (RAA) scoring rules,
Thode became the first recognized "All-Around
World Champion Cowboy" in the sport. He won
the RAA saddle-bronc riding title in 1929 as well
and repeated that victory in 1931.

← Tad Lucas with a Sampling
of Her Trophies
Fort Worth, Texas, circa 1935
Photographer unknown
NCM—Dickinson Research Center
Photographic Study Collection, 1988.9.998

↗ **The Harry Gordon Selfridge Trophy**
Adie Brothers Silversmiths
Birmingham, England, 1852/1929
NCM—Gift of Tad Lucas, R.238.14

Sponsored by retail magnate Harry Gordon Selfridge, this sterling silver
trophy cup went to Tad Lucas for the "All-Round Cowgirls Championship" at
Tex Austin's fifth Chicago World's Championship Rodeo in 1929. The founder
of the first department store in London, England, Selfridge evidently
had a special affinity for rodeo cowgirls, as he also sponsored the ladies'
championship bronc-riding trophy at Tex Austin's London rodeo in 1924.
(Interestingly, though Adie Brothers are listed as working only in the early
twentieth century, this trophy's date mark indicates manufacture in 1852.)

↑ **The Juergens and Andersen Trophy Pitcher**
Towle Manufacturing Company
Newburyport, Massachusetts, 1929
NCM—Gift of Tad Lucas, R.238.13

A regular sponsor of trophies at Tex Austin's Chicago rodeo during the late
1920s, the Juergens and Andersen jewelry house of Chicago presented
this nicely engraved and silver-plated trophy pitcher, or ewer, to "Worlds
Champion Cow Girl Trick & Fancy Rider" Tad Lucas. At the time, Lucas was
performing at the peak of her arena prowess, and she captured the all-
around cowgirl championship at this venue as well (see adjacent trophy).

The RAA First Prize Trophy Cup
Maker unknown, 1930
NCM—Gift of Everett Bowman, R.221.35

The Rodeo Association of America awarded
this handsome silver cup (topped with a
likeness of Winged Victory) to Everett Bowman
for the "Cowboy First Prize" (all-around
champion) at the 1930 Oregon City Frontier
Days Rodeo. On the national scene, Bowman
would take the RAA all-around-champion
cowboy title in 1935 and 1937.

↑ **Boxer Jack Dempsey with the Dempsey Trophy**
Reno, Nevada, 1932
Photographer unknown
Image courtesy Guy Clifton, *Reno Gazette-Journal*

◤ **The Jack Dempsey Trophy Urn**
Maker unknown, 1932
NCM—Gift of the Pete Knight Estate, 2003.289.03

Adorned with the figure of a boxer, this large, silver-plated trophy urn was commissioned and awarded by the famed pugilist Jack Dempsey for a special "Match of Champions" held at the 1932 Reno Pony Express Days rodeo. Top bronc riders Gene Ross, Earl Thode, Frank Studnick, and Pete Knight competed on two horses each. Knight emerged the victor, winning the title of "Champion Bronc Rider of the Year."

PRESENTED TO
FLORENCE RANDOLPH
CHAMPION COWGIRL
TRICK AND FANCY RIDER
AT THE
WORLD'S FAIR
RODEO
1933
BY
RANCH ROMANCES
A MAGAZINE
DEVOTED TO THE LIFE AND EXPLOITS
OF
THE COWBOY and COWGIRL

The *Ranch Romances* Trophy Cup
Maker unknown, 1933
NCM—Gift of Florence H. Randolph, R.237.12

Graced with an applied band of laurel leaves for the victor, this substantial trophy cup was sponsored by Clayton Magazines and presented to Florence Hughes Randolph, the "Champion Cowgirl Trick and Fancy Rider" at the Chicago World's Fair Rodeo in 1933. As stated on the prize, *Ranch Romances* magazine was "devoted to the life and exploits of the cowboy and cowgirl."

Florence Hughes Randolph
Location unknown, circa 1928
Ralph Russell Doubleday, photographer
NCM—Dickinson Research Center
R. R. Doubleday Collection, 79.026.1947

↑ **Alice Greenough Saddle Bronc Riding**
(detail)
Salt Lake City, Utah, Rodeo, 1947
DeVere Helfrich, photographer
NCM—Dickinson Research Center
DeVere Helfrich Collection, 81.023.02950

← **Rodeo Trophy Urn**
Wallace Silver Company
Wallingford, Connecticut, 1933
NCM—Gift of Alice Greenough, 1992.08.02

This large and attractive silver-plated trophy urn was awarded to Alice
Greenough, winner of the "Champion Cow Girl Saddle Bronk [*sic*] Riding"
title at the Boston Garden Rodeo in 1933. The trophy is nicely engraved
with the appealing image of a cowgirl, hat in hand, on the back of a
tossing mustang. Greenough also won the saddle-bronc title at Boston
in 1936.

← **Rodeo Trophy Cup**
Dodge Trophy Company
Los Angeles, California, 1935
NCM—Gift of the McCarroll Family Trust,
2006.08.06

Reflecting the decline in trophy quality that
came with the Great Depression, this gold-
electroplated cup was presented by Ray E.
Dodge to Frank McCarroll, winner of the "Steer
Bulldogging" contest at the 1935 Hoot Gibson
Rodeo, believed to have been held that year at
the Kezar Stadium in San Francisco, California.

➔ **Rodeo Trophy Cup**

Haltom's Jewelers
Fort Worth, Texas, 1936
NCM—Gift of Florence H. Randolph, R.237.19

Won by Florence Hughes Randolph, the
"Cowgirls Trick Riding" champion at the 1936
Southwestern Exposition and Fat Stock Show
rodeo, this silver-plated loving cup with its
attached plaque was the standard pattern
for award cups at the celebrated Fort Worth,
Texas, venue for more than a decade.

The Ardath Specials Trophy Urn
Maker unknown, 1939
NCM—Gift of Alice Greenough, 1992.08.04

Sponsored by the makers of Ardath Specials cigarettes, this silver-plated trophy urn went to Alice Greenough, the winner of the "Cowgirl Buckjumping Contest" at the 1939 Royal Easter Show and Rodeo in Sydney, Australia. Greenough was a regular saddle-bronc competitor at Australian rodeos until World War II put an end to American participation.

➜ **Rodeo Trophy Cup**
Maker unknown, circa 1940
NCM—Gift of Homer Pettigrew, R.224.01

This gold-electroplated, Art Deco–style
trophy was awarded around 1940 to Homer
Pettigrew by the Boulder, Colorado, Pow-Wow
Committee "For loyalty to the Boulder Pow-
Wow Rodeo, and an outstanding record in
the sport of rodeo." At that time, the six-time
world champion steer wrestler and 1941
all-around-champion cowboy still had many
victories ahead of him.

➜ **The Major Monte Stone Perpetual Trophy**
Maker unknown, circa 1942/1944
NCM—Anonymous loan, LR.1987.01.02

Sponsored by Major Monte Stone and the
Hollywood Saddlery Company, this substantial
trophy went to the year's "Champion All
Around Cowboy," but it hardly proved to be
"perpetual." It was retired under the stipulated
rules by Louis Brooks, who took the all-around
championship successively in 1943 and 1944.
Brooks's career in rodeo was as meteoric as
it was impressive, lasting only from 1940
to 1945. During that six-year span, he won
two all-around titles and four event titles in
bareback- and saddle-bronc riding. He remains
a classic example of a contestant who used
rodeo earnings to improve his life as a working
cowboy.

↑ **Bill Linderman Horseback** *(detail)*
Denver, Colorado, 1958
DeVere Helfrich, photographer
NCM—Dickinson Research Center
DeVere Helfrich Collection, 81.023.12913

← **Rodeo Trophy Urn**
Maker unknown, 1948
NCM—Gift of Mrs. E. A. Spaulding, R.210.08

Crowned with the figure of a bronc rider atop
the world, this gold-plated trophy urn and
base was captured by Bill Linderman, the
"All Around Champion Cowboy" at the 1948
Phoenix, Arizona, World's Championship
Rodeo. A regular competitor in both bronc-
riding events, as well as a steer wrestler and
calf roper, Linderman captured five consecutive
all-around-champion cowboy titles at the
Calgary Stampede from 1944 to 1948

The Doff Aber Memorial Trophy
Maker unknown, 1948
NCM—Gift of Mrs. George McElhinney,
R.211.02

Among the last great silver pieces produced as a rodeo prize, this large and imposing trophy was established in 1948 by rodeo historian Clifford P. Westermeier, author of the rodeo classic *Man, Beast, Dust,* in honor of two-time world champion bronc rider Doff Aber, who met an untimely death in 1946. Awarded at the Boulder, Colorado, Pow Wow rodeo, the piece was never retired by a stipulated three-time winner. Westermeier took the trophy out of competition after twenty-five years and presented it to the National Cowboy Hall of Fame & Western Heritage Center's rodeo program in 1972.

← **The Cromdale Hotel Trophy**
Maker unknown, 1958
NCM—Loan courtesy Jim Shoulders, LR.228.06

By the late 1950s and early 1960s, trophy cups and urns such as this were rapidly fading from the scene as rodeo prizes. Surmounted by a western boot, this gold-washed specimen was awarded by the Cromdale Hotel of Edmonton, Alberta, to Jim Shoulders, the "Champion Bareback Rider" at the Edmonton Stampede in 1958.

← **The Prince of Wales Challenge Trophy Sculpture**

Mappin and Webb, Cutlers and Silversmiths
Sheffield, England, circa 1920/1933
NCM—Gift of the Pete Knight Estate,
2003.289.05

Sponsored and presented by His Royal
Highness Edward Prince of Wales (later
King Edward VIII of Great Britain), this
sterling silver equestrian trophy went to
the incomparable Pete Knight, "Canadian
Champion Bucking Horse Rider" at the Calgary
Exhibition and Stampede of 1933. Joined with
Knight's previous victories in the prestigious
competition in 1927 and 1930, this win
brought him permanent possession of the
coveted royal trophy. The talented rider took
the world saddle-bronc laurels in 1932, 1933,
1935, and 1936.

➜ **Rodeo Trophy Sculpture**
Maker unknown, 1940
NCM—Permanent Collection, R.257.01

Awarded at the 1940 Southwestern Exposition and Fat Stock Show
rodeo in Fort Worth, Texas, this sterling silver casting of a bronc rider
went to Albert "Smokey" Snyder for the "Champion Cowboys Brahma Bull
Riding" title. One of the smallest—but best—bull riders in rodeo, he took
the event championship in 1931, 1932, 1935, 1936, and 1937. Somewhat
ironically, this sculptural prize foreshadowed Snyder's last rough-stock
ride, made in 1946 in San Diego, California, where a bronc crashed over a
fence with him, breaking his back.

The G. A. Gaherty Trophy Sculpture

C. A. Beil, circa 1942

NCM—Loan courtesy Mike Linderman, L.1983.06

Cast in bronze, this dramatic piece depicts a fallen cowboy beneath the hooves of a rampaging bronc. The trophy was awarded to Doff Aber, the "North American Champion Bucking Horse Rider" at the Calgary Exhibition and Stampede in 1942. During that same year, Aber won the saddle-bronc title at Cheyenne and the "World's Saddle Bronc Riding Championship" at Madison Square Garden. He was the last man to ride the famed bucking bronc Hell's Angel.

← **The Canada Safeway Trophy Sculpture**
C. A. Beil, circa 1959
NCM—Loan courtesy Jim Shoulders, LR.228.07

Jim Shoulders won this trophy sculpture as "Champion Brahma Bull Rider" at the 1959 Calgary Exhibition and Stampede, marking his fifth bull-riding victory at the famed Canadian venue. An indication of changing times, today the Stampede is no longer sanctioned by any professional rodeo association (PRCA or CPRA) but is an invitation-only rodeo for the top competitors from the NFR, CFR, and PBR. Nonetheless, attendance in 2007 topped 1.25 million.

➜ **Rodeo Trophy Sculpture**
C. A. Beil, circa 1966
NCM—Loan courtesy Harry Tompkins, LR.1987.07.04

Portraying a cowboy and his horse at rest, this trophy bronze was awarded to Harry Tompkins for the "Bare Back Bucking Horse Riding Championship" at the 1966 Calgary Exhibition and Stampede. Among the best of bull riders, Tompkins also was a superb bareback-bronc rider, winning the Rodeo Cowboys Association "World's Bareback Bronc Riding Championship" in 1952.

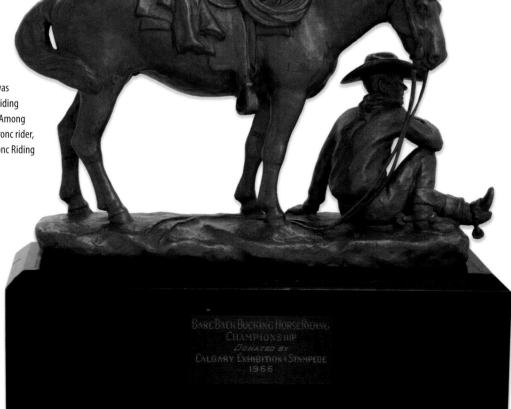

⬆ **National Finals Rodeo Trophy Sculpture**
Jack Riley, Yukon, Oklahoma, circa 1983
NCM—Gift of Reserve National Insurance Company, 2005.121

Sponsored by the Reserve National Insurance Company of Oklahoma City, this bronze sculpture of a contestant and his roping horse was created for the 1984 Professional Rodeo Cowboys Association (PRCA) National Finals Rodeo—the last NFR held in Oklahoma. Identical trophies went to each PRCA event champion and to the All-Around World Champion Cowboy. Reserve National Insurance Company retained this unawarded trophy for two decades, presenting it to the National Cowboy & Western Heritage Museum in 2005.

Rodeo Trophy Belt
Deitsch Brothers Jewelers
Denver, Colorado, 1902
NCM—Gift of Mr. and Mrs. DeMar Robison, 1982.46

This early and extremely rare rodeo trophy belt was captured by bronc rider Harry Brennan, the "Champion Rough Rider of the World" at the 1902 Festival of Mountain and Plain in Denver, Colorado. Sponsored by the Denver Horse Show Association and costing $500, the solid sterling silver belt consists of nine linked plates, eight of which feature relief-embossed and chased western vignettes. The ninth and central plate (*right*) carries the award inscription. The trophy was subject to challenge each year; permanent possession would go to the first three-time winner. The contest moved to Cheyenne, Wyoming, in 1904, where Brennan ultimately retired the belt.

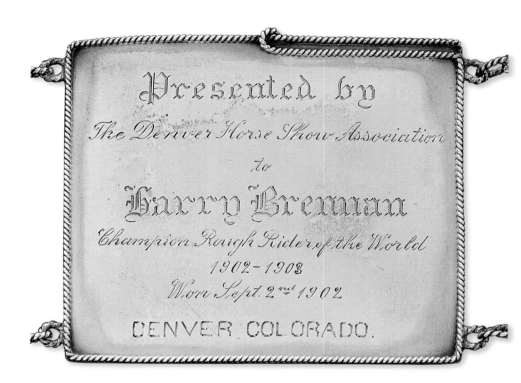

↑ **Harry Brennan** *(right)* **Wearing Silver Trophy Belt**
Denver, Colorado, Mountain and Plain Festival, 1902
Photographer unknown
NCM—Dickinson Research Center
Photographic Study Collection, 2006-026.39.02

⬆ **Rodeo Trophy Buckle and Belt**
Makers unknown, 1913.
NCM—Gift of D. N. Humphrey, R.247.01 A&B

Inscribed "Champion," this hand-tooled leather belt accommodates a
gold-washed belt buckle, or plate, awarded to Jack Fretz of Newalla,
Oklahoma, the winner at the World's Championship Bucking Contest held
at Dayton, Ohio, in 1913. See also trophy plaques won by Fretz at the same
venue, page 148.

⬆ **Rodeo Trophy Buckle and Belt**
Makers unknown, 1915
NCM—Gift of Sam Garrett, 1986.11.09 A&B

Inscribed "Passing of the West," this tooled belt accommodates a solid gold
buckle, or plate, graced with a ruby-eyed steer head. The prize was won
by Sam Garrett, the "World's All Round Champion Cowboy" at the 1915
Billings Roundup in Billings, Montana.

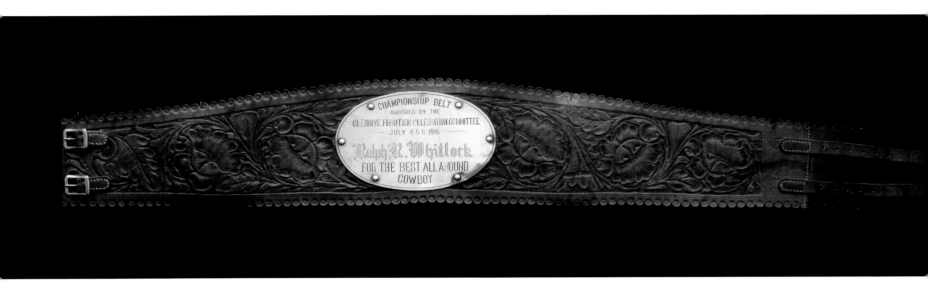

Rodeo Trophy Bronc, or Kidney, Belt
Possibly Miles City Saddlery Company
Miles City, Montana, 1916
NCM—Gift of Dan Whitlock, 1982.47.01

Finely floral carved and mounted with a silver presentation plaque, this prize "kidney," or bronc-riding, belt went to Ralph Whitlock, "Best All Around Cowboy" at the Glendive, Montana, Frontier Celebration on the Fourth of July, 1916.

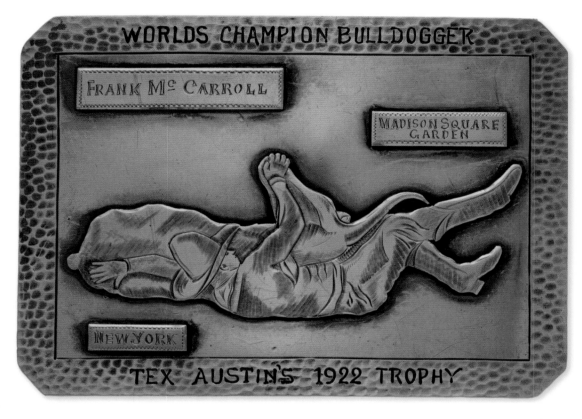

Rodeo Trophy Buckle
Maker unknown, 1922
NCM—Gift of the McCarroll Family Trust, 2006.08.08

Fashioned of pink and yellow gold, this rare trophy belt buckle, or plate, was won by "Worlds Champion Bulldogger" Frank McCarroll at the very first Madison Square Garden Championship Rodeo, held in 1922 under the direction of famed impresario Tex Austin.

Frank McCarroll, Champion Bulldogger
(detail)
Venue unknown, circa 1923
Ralph Russell Doubleday, photographer
NCM—Dickinson Research Center
McCarroll Family Trust Collection,
RC2006.076.664

Rodeo Trophy Buckle and Belt

Lambert Brothers Jewelers
New York City, 1923
N. Porter Saddlery Company
Phoenix, Arizona, 1923
NCM—Gift of Harold Porter, 1983.18.02 A&B

This tooled belt with engraved gold buckle was awarded to Richard
Merchant, the "World Champion Calf-Roper" at Tex Austin's 1923 Yankee
Stadium Rodeo. Merchant went on to win the calf-roping title at Calgary,
Alberta, in 1927, 1928, and 1930, and at Prescott, Arizona, in 1926 and
1933. During a relatively brief career, he took the world calf-roping
championship in 1932 and world steer-roping championship in 1935.

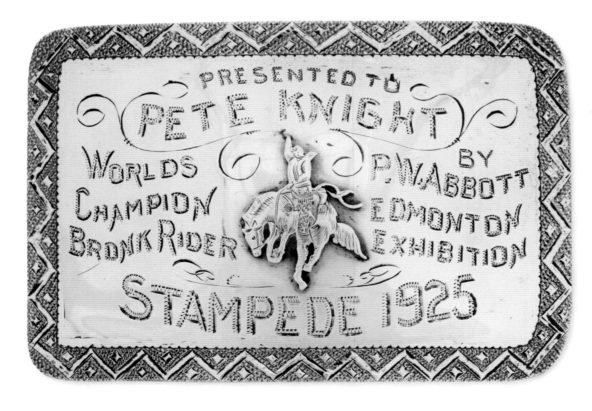

Rodeo Trophy Buckle

Jackson Brothers, Silversmiths
Edmonton, Alberta, Canada, 1925
NCM—Gift of the Knight Estate, 2003.289.11

Graced with the engraved figure of a bronc
buster in action, this sterling silver belt plate
went to Canadian competitor Pete Knight,
who was declared the "Worlds Champion
Bronk [sic] Rider" at the Edmonton, Alberta,
Exhibition and Stampede in 1925. He had
captured the same title in 1924, and he would
do so again at Winnipeg in 1926.

Rodeo Trophy Buckle
Juergens and Anderson Company
Chicago, Illinois, 1926
NCM—Gift of the McCarroll Family Trust,
2006.08.09

Donated by Edward F. Carry and captured by
Frank McCarroll at Tex Austin's 1926 Chicago
Rodeo, held at Soldier Field, this "Worlds
Champion Steer Wrestler" belt buckle, or plate,
is composed of multitone gold and German
silver with the overlaid likeness of a steer
wrestler in pink gold.

Rodeo Trophy Buckle
Juergens and Anderson Company
Chicago, Illinois, 1926
NCM—Gift of Everett Bowman, R.221.12

Presented to "Worlds Champion Calf Roper"
Everett Bowman at Tex Austin's 1926 Chicago
Rodeo, this rare belt plate closely resembles
that captured by steer-wrestling champion
Frank McCarroll at the same venue. It, too,
features a composition of multitone gold and
German silver with the event motif presented
in pink gold on a cloud of silver dust.

Rodeo Trophy Buckle
Allen and Marks Jewelers
Location unknown, 1926
NCM—Gift of Estelle Gilbert, R.272.06

Mike Hastings captured this gold-plated belt buckle, or belt plate, and the "World's Champion Steer Wrestler" title at Fred Beebe's 1926 Madison Square Garden rodeo in New York City. It was during the 1920s that Hastings gained his reputation as the "Iron Man" among competitive bulldoggers.

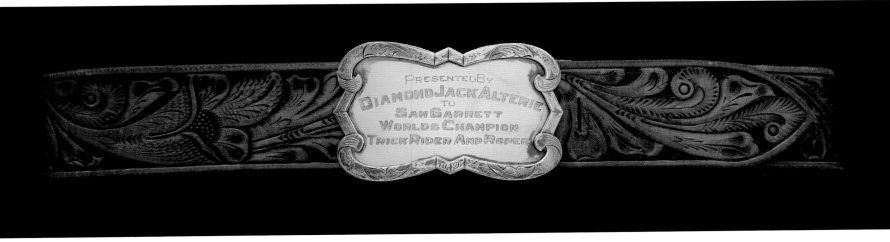

↑ →
Rodeo Presentation Buckle and Belt
Makers unknown, 1926
NCM—Gift of Sam Garrett, 1986.11.08 A&B

Fashioned of engraved and gold-plated silver, this showy belt plate was presented by rodeo enthusiast and gangland personality Diamond Jack Alterie to Sam Garrett in recognition of his amazing trick-riding and trick-roping talents. In 1916, Garrett took the first of his seven World Champion Trick Roping titles at the Cheyenne Frontier Days rodeo in Wyoming.

Rodeo Trophy Buckle
Oval Manufacturing Company
Location unknown, 1927
NCM—Gift of Estelle Gilbert, R.272.03

Naively hand-engraved with a charming steer-wrestling motif, this trophy belt plate, or buckle, went to Mike Hastings, the "Champion Bull Dogger" at the 1927 Southwestern Exposition and Fat Stock Show rodeo held in Fort Worth, Texas. This buckle, like a few other specimens in the museum's collections, was never inscribed with the victor's name.

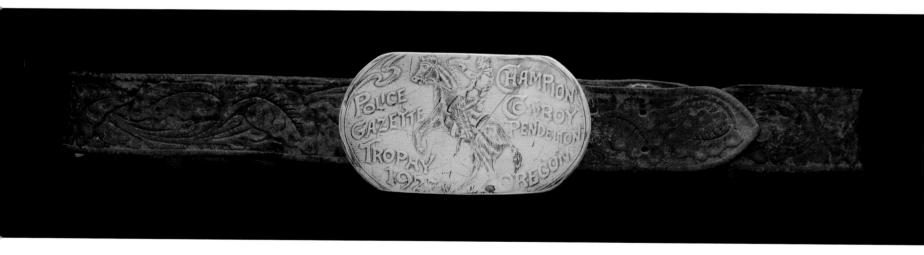

Rodeo Trophy Buckle and Belt
Makers unknown, 1927
NCM—Loan courtesy Mrs. Roberta Crosby Burkstaller, LR.214.30 A&B

The *Police Gazette* newspaper awarded this tooled belt and embossed silver buckle, or belt plate, to Bob Crosby, "Champion Cowboy" at the 1927 Pendleton Round-Up in Oregon. This was the capstone victory (along with that won earlier at the Cheyenne Frontier Days) that contributed to Crosby's taking the coveted Roosevelt Trophy that year.

Rodeo Trophy Buckle and Belt
Makers unknown, 1928
NCM—Loan courtesy Mrs. Roberta Crosby Burkstaller, LR.214.55 A&B

Sponsored by E. W. Beatty of the Canadian Pacific Railroad, this foliate-tooled belt and engraved gold-plated and gold-overlaid belt buckle were awarded to Bob Crosby, the "North American Champion Wild Steer Decorator" at the 1928 Calgary Stampede.

Rodeo Trophy Buckle
John McCabe Silversmiths
Hollywood, California, 1930
NCM—Permanent Collection, R.274.03

Won by Hugh Bennett, the "Champion Calf Roper" at the 1930 Phoenix Rodeo, this engraved and overlaid silver belt plate, or buckle, was presented under the longtime rodeo sponsorship of the N. Porter Saddle and Harness Company of Phoenix, Arizona. A versatile hand, Bennett took the steer-wrestling championship in 1932 and the steer-roping championship in 1938.

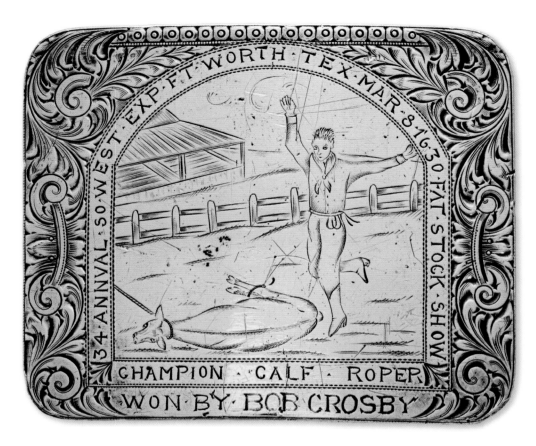

Rodeo Trophy Buckle
Oval Manufacturing Company
Location unknown, 1930
NCM—Loan courtesy Mrs. Roberta Crosby
Burkstaller, LR.214.32

Featuring an engraved panel scene framed
with floral scrollwork, this sterling silver
belt plate was awarded to Bob Crosby, the
"Champion Calf Roper" at Fort Worth's thirty-
fourth annual Southwestern Exposition and
Fat Stock Show rodeo in 1930.

Rodeo Trophy Buckle
R. Schaezlein and Son Silversmiths
San Francisco, California, 1930
NCM—Gift of Everett Bowman, R.221.10

Presented by the Rodeo Association of America (RAA), this sterling silver
and gold-washed buckle, or belt plate, went to all-around cowboy Everett
Bowman, "World's Champion Steer Decorator" in 1930. A benign variation
of the bulldogging event, the steer decorator acquired and slowed the
animal in the usual manner and then, instead of throwing it, placed a
colored band or ribbon about the beast's muzzle or horn.

Rodeo Trophy Buckle
Edward H. Bohlin Silversmiths
Hollywood, California, 1931
NCM—Gift of Everett Bowman, R.221.04

This engraved, sterling silver and gold-overlaid belt plate was won by Everett Bowman for "First Prize Bulldogging" at the 1931 Hoot Gibson Ranch Rodeo in Saugus, California. Hollywood star Hoot Gibson, who captured the saddle-bronc championship at Pendleton in 1912, remained an enthusiastic rodeo fan and trophy supporter for several decades.

Rodeo Trophy Buckle
R. Schaezlein and Son Silversmiths
San Francisco, California, 1931
NCM—Gift of Johnie Schneider, R.218.03

This gold-overlaid, sterling silver belt plate was awarded by the Rodeo Association of America (RAA) to Johnnie [sic] Schneider, "World's Champion Cowboy" in 1931. A talented bull rider, Schneider captured the event championship in 1929, 1930, and 1932. The RAA, an organization of rodeo producers, declared the annual event and world champions from its founding in 1929 until 1954. In 1946, the organization became the International Rodeo Association.

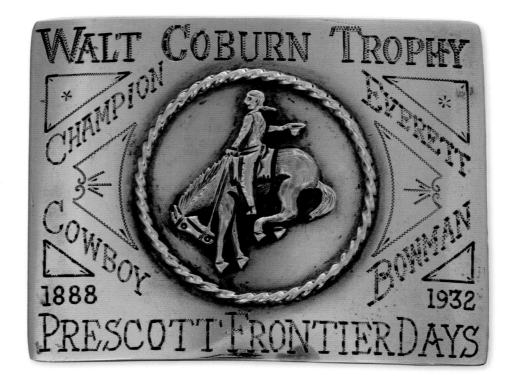

Rodeo Trophy Buckle
Maker unknown, 1932
NCM—Gift of Everett Bowman, R.221.08

Sponsored by western fiction writer Walt
Coburn, this diminutive sterling silver
buckle, or belt plate, features a bronc-rider
motif within a rope border of 10-karat gold.
The trophy was taken by Everett Bowman,
"Champion Cowboy" at the 1932 Prescott,
Arizona, Frontier Days rodeo.

Rodeo Trophy Buckle
Maker unknown, 1932
NCM—Gift of Everett Bowman, R.221.17

This Plymouth Lariat Trophy was captured by
Everett Bowman, "Winner of [the] Champion
Roping Contest" at the Pendleton Round-Up
of 1932. Like the following specimen (*above,
right*), this buckle, or belt plate, features
10-karat gold overlays on an engraved western
landscape of sterling silver. The same artisan,
though unidentified, must have made both
these buckles for the round-up.

Rodeo Trophy Buckle
Maker unknown, 1932
NCM—Gift of Everett Bowman, R.221.06

Incorporating 10-karat gold overlays on an engraved western landscape of sterling silver, this oval belt plate was sponsored by the Hamley Saddlery Company of Pendleton, Oregon, and won by "Champion All Round Cow Boy" Everett Bowman at the 1932 Pendleton Round-Up. In its quality, design, and execution, this piece indicates manufacture by the same artisan or shop that created the preceding specimen, also won by Bowman at Pendleton in 1932.

Rodeo Trophy Buckle and Belt
John McCabe Silversmiths
Los Angeles, California, 1934
Hamley Saddlery Company
Pendleton, Oregon, 1934
NCM—Loan courtesy Mrs. Roberta Crosby Burkstaller, LR.214.29 A&B

Sponsored and awarded by the Plymouth Cordage Company, rope manufacturer of Plymouth, Massachusetts, this foliate-tooled belt and sterling silver buckle with engraved panel scene and 10-karat gold overlay went to "World's Champion Steer Roper" Bob Crosby at the 1934 Pendleton Round-Up.

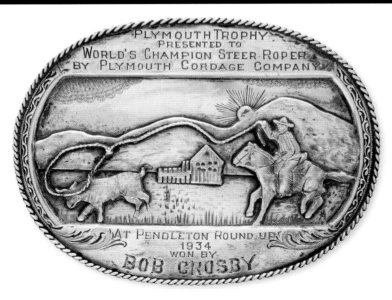

Rodeo Trophy Buckle and Belt
Makers unknown, 1935
NCM—Gift of Herman Linder, 1980.37.04

Sponsored by the Ontario Laundry Company of Ontario, Canada, this tooled leather belt and gold plate were won by Herman Linder, the "North American Champion All-Round Cowboy" at the 1935 Calgary Stampede. Probably the greatest contender ever to represent Canada, Linder was Canadian All-Around Champion Cowboy from 1931 through 1936 and again in 1938.

Rodeo Trophy Buckle
John McCabe Silversmiths
Los Angeles, California, 1935
NCM—Gift of Everett Bowman, R.221.05

Sponsored by the Hamley Saddlery Company, this gold-overlaid, sterling silver belt buckle, or belt plate, went to Everett Bowman, "Champion All-Around Cowboy" at the 1935 Pendleton Round-Up.

Rodeo Trophy Buckle
Al Ray Silversmiths
Location unknown, 1935
NCM—Gift of Everett Bowman, R.221.11

Featuring fine floral engraving and pink gold overlay with a
ruby inset, this diminutive trophy belt plate proclaims the Rodeo
Association of America's (RAA) recognition of Everett Bowman as
"Champion All Around Cowboy" for 1935. Bowman also took the
calf-roping and steer-wrestling titles that year and captured the
all-around cowboy title again in 1937.

Rodeo Trophy Buckle
Al Ray Silversmiths
Location unknown, 1937
NCM—Gift of Everett Bowman, R.221.07

Featuring an extravagant longhorn steer in 10-karat gold with
ruby eyes, this silver buckle, or belt plate, was sponsored by
rodeo's *Hoofs and Horns* magazine and awarded to Everett
Bowman, the "Champion Calf Roper" at the 1937 La Fiesta de Los
Vaqueros rodeo in Tucson, Arizona.

Rodeo Trophy Buckle and Belt
Makers unknown, 1938
NCM—Gift of Mrs. Vera M. Herder, R.204.09 A&B

Harry Rowell awarded this tooled belt and foliate-and-floral-engraved sterling silver belt plate to Fritz Truan, "Winner [of the] Bucking Contest" at the 1938 Elko Rodeo, held at Elko, Nevada. Known as "The Rodeo King of the West," stock contractor Harry Rowell produced the Rowell Ranch Rodeo from the 1920s into the 1970s at Hayward, California. His personal and financial generosity was legendary among the cowboy and cowgirl contenders on the western circuit.

← **Fritz Truan Saddle-Bronc Riding** (detail)
Reno, Nevada, Pony Express Days Rodeo, 1939
Ralph Russell Doubleday (?), photographer
NCM—Dickinson Research Center
Photographic Study Collection, 06-190.39.06

Rodeo Trophy Buckle
Maker unknown, 1938
NCM—Gift of Everett Bowman, R.221.18

Awarded at the Sun Valley, Idaho, Rodeo in 1938, this trophy belt buckle went to "Champion Bulldogger" Everett Bowman. The plate features a finely engraved tableau of the Sun Valley region on sterling silver, with a nicely rendered steer-wrestling motif overlaid in 14-karat gold.

Rodeo Trophy Buckle
Maker unknown, 1939
NCM—Gift of Homer Pettigrew, R.224.11

Graced with a longhorn steer in 10-karat gold, this lightly engraved buckle of sterling silver was presented to Homer Pettigrew, the "Cowboys Steer Wrestling" champion at the 1939 Southwestern Exposition and Fat Stock Show rodeo, held in Fort Worth, Texas.

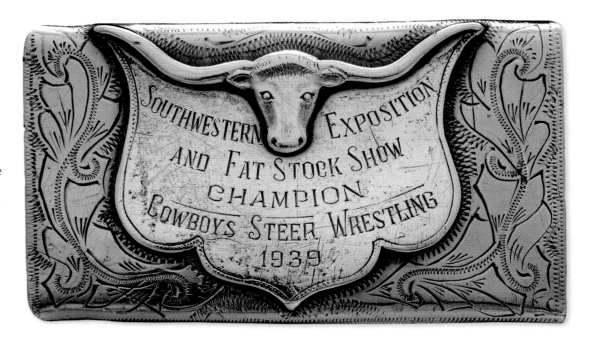

Rodeo Trophy Buckle
R. Schaezlein and Son Silversmiths
San Francisco, California, 1940
NCM—Gift of Mrs. Vera M. Herder, R.204.11

Sponsored by Levi Strauss, this gold-and-silver belt buckle was awarded to Fritz Truan, the 1940 Rodeo Association of America (RAA) "World's Grand Champion Cowboy." This buckle, or plate, pattern provided the design prototype for the enormous Levi's–Rodeo Cowboys Association (RCA) plates produced by Schaezlein in the 1950s and 1960s.

Saddle-Bronc Champion Fritz Truan
(detail)
Red Bluff, California, 1941
DeVere Helfrich, photographer
NCM—Dickinson Research Center
DeVere Helfrich Collection, 81.023.00091

Rodeo Trophy Buckle and Belt
Makers unknown, 1941
NCM—Gift of Mrs. Vera M. Herder, R.204.10 A&B

Sponsored and presented by Bigham's Rodeo Buffet, this finely floral-tooled belt and engraved and gold-overlaid sterling silver belt buckle, or plate, went to Fritz Truan, the "Winner [of the] Bareback Contest" at the 1941 California Rodeo held at Salinas.

➜ **Rodeo Trophy Buckle**
John McCabe Silversmiths
Los Angeles, California, 1941
NCM—Gift of Mrs. Vera M. Herder, R.204.15

The Hamley Saddlery Company sponsored this John Hamley Trophy belt buckle, which was captured by Fritz Truan, the "Champion All-Around Cowboy" at the 1941 Pendleton Round-Up. The sterling silver plate features fine floral-scroll engraving and a superbly rendered vignette of a saddle-bronc rider in overlaid 14-karat gold.

Rodeo Trophy Buckle
John McCabe Silversmiths
Los Angeles, California, 1942
NCM—Loan courtesy Mrs. Clyde Burk,
LR.212.04

"Champion Calf Roper" Clyde Burk captured
this rather long, rectangular silver-and-gold
belt plate, which was sponsored by the
Plymouth Cordage Company at the 1942
Cheyenne Frontier Days rodeo. As exemplified
in the following buckle, Burk was having a
very productive year.

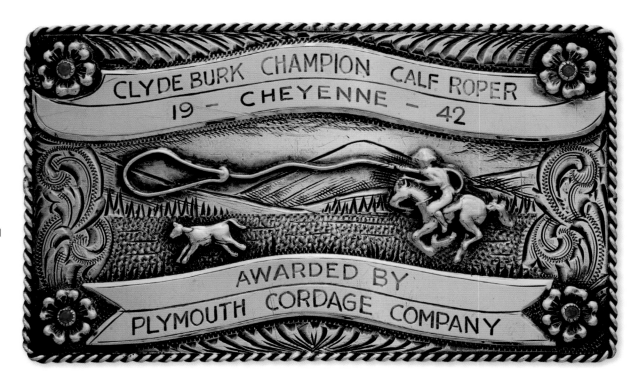

Rodeo Trophy Buckle
Maker unknown, 1942.
NCM—Loan courtesy Mrs. Clyde Burk,
LR.212.02

This sterling silver plate with its rather naive
calf-roping vignette in 10-karat gold was
presented by Everett Colborn's Lightning C
Ranch and the Rodeo Association of America
(RAA) to Clyde Burk, "World's Champion Calf
Roper" for 1942. This marked his third of four
such titles before his untimely death.

Rodeo Trophy Buckle

Maker unknown, 1944
NCM—Loan courtesy Mrs. Clyde Burk,
LR.212.03

This Plymouth Trophy buckle, or belt plate, was underwritten by the Plymouth Cordage Company and presented by the National Rodeo Association (NRA; formerly the Southwest Rodeo Association) to 1944 "Champion Calf Roper" Clyde Burk. The piece incorporates a finely detailed calf-roping tableau in 10-karat gold with matching rope border and flowers with ruby insets. Burk was killed in an arena accident the following year.

Rodeo Trophy Buckle

Maker unknown, 1947
NCM—Loan courtesy Troy Fort, L.1991.53.03

Engraved, gold-overlaid, and inset with rubies, this sterling silver belt plate was won by Troy Fort, "Champion Calf Roper" at the Madison Square Garden World's Championship Rodeo. The plate back is engraved: "Record Time—13 Seconds / Oct. 1947." A string of victories at Tucson, Houston, Salt Lake City, Las Vegas, Madison Square Garden, and elsewhere brought Fort the calf-roping championship in 1947, a feat he repeated in 1949.

Rodeo Trophy Buckle

Nelson Bringolf Jewelers
Houston, Texas, 1947
NCM—Loan courtesy Todd Whatley, LR.227.04

Donated by the Levi Strauss Company, this
gold-and-silver belt buckle, or plate, was
awarded to Todd Whatley, Rodeo Cowboys
Association (RCA) saddle-bronc riding
champion in 1947. He also was declared the
RCA's first all-around-champion cowboy in that
year. From the mid-1940s into the mid-1950s,
Whatley consistently placed in the top five in
bulldogging and bull riding. He took the bull-
riding championship in 1953.

Rodeo Trophy Buckle

Nelson Bringolf Jewelers
Houston, Texas, 1948
NCM—Gift of Homer Pettigrew, R.224.06

Fashioned of sterling silver with overlays of
10-karat gold, this buckle was awarded by the
Rodeo Cowboys Association to 1948 champion
steer wrestler Homer Pettigrew. The buckle,
or belt plate, celebrated the last of Pettigrew's
unprecedented six event titles.

Rodeo Trophy Buckle
Maker unknown, 1948
NCM—Gift of Nell and Bud Kemp, 1995.32.01

Highlighted with 10-karat gold and rubies, this sterling silver belt plate was presented to veteran rodeo clown John Lindsey at the Olathe, Kansas, rodeo in 1948. After riding broncs and bulls for several years, Lindsey began clowning in the early 1930s with a performing mule named Hoover. He took up bullfighting during the late 1930s and retired from the arena in 1963.

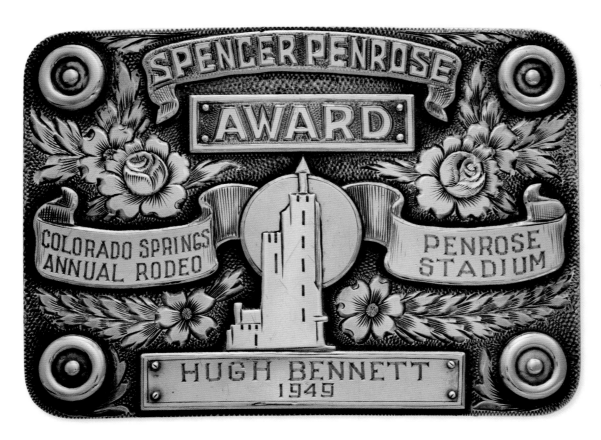

Rodeo Trophy Buckle
Western Silversmiths
Canoga Park, California, 1949
NCM—Permanent Collection, R.274.02

Featuring gold overlay and floral chiseling, this Spencer Penrose trophy belt plate was awarded to Hugh Bennett at the 1949 Colorado Springs Annual Rodeo. Born in Knox City, Texas, in 1905, Bennett captured the steer-wrestling title in 1932 and added the steer-roping championship in 1938. He was revered for his leadership during the 1936 rodeo strike at the Boston Garden, and his insistence on diplomatic negotiations with rodeo administrators proved a stabilizing influence during the cowboy union's early years.

◄ Rodeo Trophy Buckle
William A. Nelson Company
Houston, Texas, 1949
NCM—Museum purchase, R.229.17

Celebrating the first of Casey Tibbs's six saddle-bronc-riding titles under the auspices of the Rodeo Cowboys Association, this rectangular trophy buckle, or belt plate, incorporates a body of engraved sterling silver with 10-karat gold overlays, including a finely rendered saddle-bronc-riding vignette at the center. Tibbs also won five saddle-bronc-riding titles under the International Rodeo Association's scoring program.

➜ Rodeo Trophy Buckle
Western Silversmiths
Canoga Park, California, 1950
NCM—Museum purchase, R.229.11

Mounted with motifs of the Ancient Arabic Order of Nobles of the Mystic Shrine and a well-rendered bronc-riding vignette in 10-karat gold, this curvaceous, rope-bordered buckle of sterling silver features graceful acanthus-leaf-pattern engraving. Casey Tibbs won the piece as the "Champion Saddle Bronc Rider" at the second annual Shrine rodeo held in Portland, Oregon, in 1950.

→ **Rodeo Trophy Buckle**
John McCabe Silversmiths
Hollywood, California, 1951
NCM—Museum purchase, R.229.16

Awarded by the International Rodeo
Association (IRA) to Casey Tibbs as the
"Champion Bareback Rider" of 1951, this rope-
bordered belt buckle, or plate, of sterling silver
features a bronc-riding motif in 10-karat gold
over an engraved western landscape. Tibbs
also captured the saddle-bronc riding and
all-around cowboy titles in 1951.

→ **Rodeo Trophy Buckle**
William A. Nelson Company
Houston, Texas, 1951
NCM—Museum purchase, R.229.10

This rectangular trophy buckle, or belt
plate, of sterling silver with 10-karat-gold
overlays was awarded by the Rodeo Cowboys
Association (RCA) to Casey Tibbs, "Champion
Saddle Bronc Rider" of 1951. Tibbs won the
bareback-riding championship that year
as well, with both the International Rodeo
Association (*above*) and the RCA.

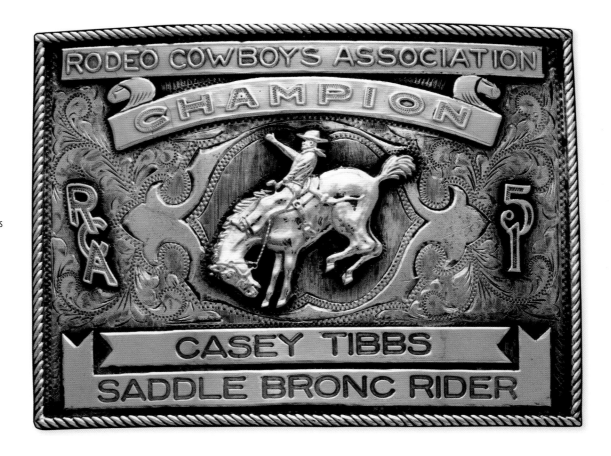

Rodeo Trophy Buckle
Maker unknown, 1952
NCM—Gift of Homer Pettigrew, R.224.10

Four years after his last national Rodeo Cowboys Association steer-wrestling title, the resilient Homer Pettigrew captured this sterling silver and 10-karat-gold buckle as the "World Champion Steer Wrestler" at the 1952 Phoenix rodeo.

Rodeo Trophy Buckle
Don Ellis Silversmiths
Seattle, Washington, 1953
NCM—Museum purchase, R.229.15

Set off with a faceted beaded border and embellished with two-tone gold overlay, this oval trophy buckle was presented by the Rodeo Cowboys Association to Casey Tibbs, the "Champion [Saddle] Bronc Rider" of 1953. He would take two more such titles in 1954 and 1959 for an unprecedented total of six.

Rodeo Trophy Buckle
R. Schaezlein and Son Silversmiths
San Francisco, California, 1953
NCM—Museum purchase, R.229.07

Sponsored by Levi Strauss and Company, this comparatively small trophy buckle went to the colorful Casey Tibbs, recognized by the International Rodeo Association (IRA) as the "World's Grand Champion Cowboy" in 1953. The plate incorporates a body of foliate-engraved sterling silver with overlaid rope border, corner rosettes, horse heads, bronc-riding motif with the IRA monogram, and ribands, all in 14-karat gold with six inset rubies. This buckle provided the basic design for the much larger, grand-champion-cowboy plates bestowed on multiple all-around champions through the IRA and the Rodeo Cowboys Association.

Rodeo Trophy Buckle
Maker unknown, 1954
NCM—Museum purchase, R.229.13

Incorporating rudimentary engraving with bold lettering in 10-karat gold, this rectangular trophy buckle, or belt plate, was captured by Casey Tibbs, who was declared the "Worlds Champion Bronc Rider" at Bridger, Montana's, 1954 rodeo. The victory contributed in some measure to both Casey's Rodeo Cowboys Association and International Rodeo Association world-saddle-bronc-riding championships in 1954.

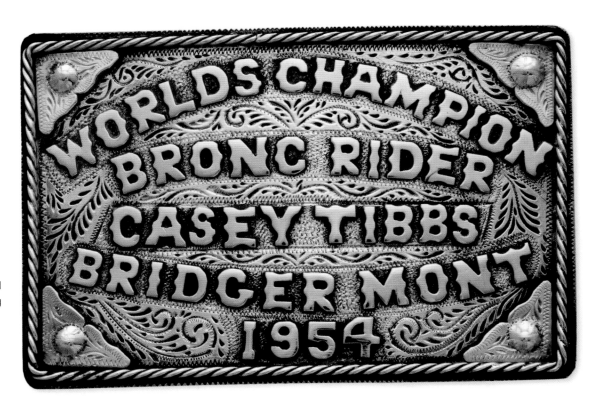

← **Rodeo Trophy Buckle**
Don Ellis Silversmiths
Seattle, Washington, 1954
NCM—Loan courtesy Jim Shoulders,
LR.228.17

The Rodeo Cowboys Association awarded this two-tone gold and sterling silver belt plate to Jim Shoulders for capturing the second of his seven "Worlds Champion Bull Rider" titles in 1954. He would take the bull-riding title five more times in succession, culminating in 1959.

➜ **Rodeo Trophy Buckle**
Don Ellis Silversmiths
Seattle, Washington, 1954
NCM—Gift of Buck Rutherford, 1987.32.01

Though slowed by numerous arena injuries, Buck Rutherford established a creditable record as a bull rider, bareback-bronc rider, and bulldogger. After barely missing the world title in 1952, he took it in 1954, receiving this gold-and-silver belt plate as the year's "Worlds Champion All Around Cowboy" under the auspices of the Rodeo Cowboys Association.

Rodeo Trophy Buckle
R. Schaezlein and Son Silversmiths
San Francisco, California, 1954
NCM—Museum purchase, R.229.06

Sponsored by Levi Strauss and Company of San Francisco, this enormous belt plate was awarded by the International Rodeo Association (IRA) to Casey Tibbs upon his winning a third "World's Grand Champion Cowboy" title. Finished with fine foliate-scroll engraving, the solid-silver piece incorporates many gold-overlaid embellishments accented with rubies. Tibbs won this IRA title in 1951, 1953, and 1954. He won the IRA saddle-bronc title in 1949, 1950, 1952, 1953, and 1954.

Rodeo Trophy Buckle
Maker unknown, 1956
NCM—Gift of Dean Oliver, R.234.06

Sponsored by the Knights of Ak-Sar-Ben, this silver-and-gold trophy buckle, or belt plate, went to Dean Oliver, "Champion Calf Roper" at the 1956 Ak-Sar-Ben Rodeo in Omaha, Nebraska. Oliver must have been in a hurry to get to the next venue, as the buckle was not inscribed with the winner's name.

Rodeo Trophy Buckle and Belt
Western Silversmiths
Canoga Park, California, 1956
Belt maker unknown, circa 1956.
NCM—Gift of Mrs. Oral Zumwalt, R.207.08 A&B

Oral Zumwalt won this tooled belt and engraved silver belt buckle as the "Champion Calf Roper" at the KO Ranch Rodeo held in Missoula, Montana, in 1956. At one time or another, Zumwalt contested in every event, rodeoing in the United States, Canada, Mexico, and Australia.

Rodeo Trophy Buckle
Don Ellis Silversmiths
Seattle, Washington, 1956
NCM—Loan courtesy Jim Shoulders,
LR.228.19

Highlighted with faceted beading around its oval border, this sterling silver trophy buckle boasts finely rendered overlays of pink and yellow gold. The plate was awarded to Jim Shoulders, the 1956 Rodeo Cowboys Association "Worlds Champion Bareback Rider." Shoulders had taken the bareback-bronc title first in 1950, and he would repeat the feat again in 1957 and 1958.

Rodeo Trophy Buckle
Don Ellis Silversmiths
Seattle, Washington, 1958
NCM—Loan courtesy Jim Shoulders,
LR.228.20

Jim Shoulders captured this attractive two-tone-gold and sterling silver trophy buckle in 1958, commemorating his fourth Rodeo Cowboys Association "Worlds Champion Bareback Rider" title. Note that the faceted beads highlighting the plate's oval border are inset with rubies.

Rodeo Trophy Buckle
Don Ellis Silversmiths
Seattle, Washington, 1958
NCM—Loan courtesy Jim Shoulders,
LR.228.15

Embellished with ruby-inset-faceted beading around its border, this oval buckle, or belt plate, incorporates a body of sterling silver with overlays of pink and yellow gold. The trophy went to the indomitable Jim Shoulders, 1958 Rodeo Cowboys Association "Worlds Champion All Around Cowboy." Shoulders took five all-around champion titles commencing in 1949 and concluding in 1959.

⬆ **Rodeo Trophy Buckle**
R. Schaezlein and Son Silversmiths
San Francisco, California, 1958
NCM—Loan courtesy Jim Shoulders, LR.228.12

This oversized belt plate was awarded to Jim Shoulders in recognition of his fourth "World's Grand Champion Cowboy" title in 1958. Sponsored and presented by Levi Strauss and Company of San Francisco, the solid-silver piece is embellished with fine foliate-scroll engraving and a variety of gold-overlaid elements accented with rubies. Shoulders captured the Rodeo Cowboys Association (RCA) world's champion cowboy title in 1949, 1956, 1957, 1958, and 1959.

➜ **Jim Shoulders with Levi's
Big Trophy Buckle**
Denver, Colorado, 1958
DeVere Helfrich, photographer
NCM—Dickinson Research Center
DeVere Helfrich Collection, 81.023.12888

Rodeo Trophy Buckle
Don Ellis Silversmiths
Seattle, Washington, 1960
NCM—Gift of Dean Oliver, R.234.05

Under the auspices of the Rodeo Cowboys Association, this sterling silver belt plate, highlighted with pink and yellow gold, was awarded to "Worlds Champion Calf Roper" Dean Oliver in 1960. This marked his third national calf-roping victory and initiated a string of four more consecutive titles.

Dean Oliver Calf Roping (detail)
Lebanon, Oregon, Rodeo, 1958
DeVere Helfrich, photographer
NCM—Dickinson Research Center
DeVere Helfrich Collection, 81.023.13543

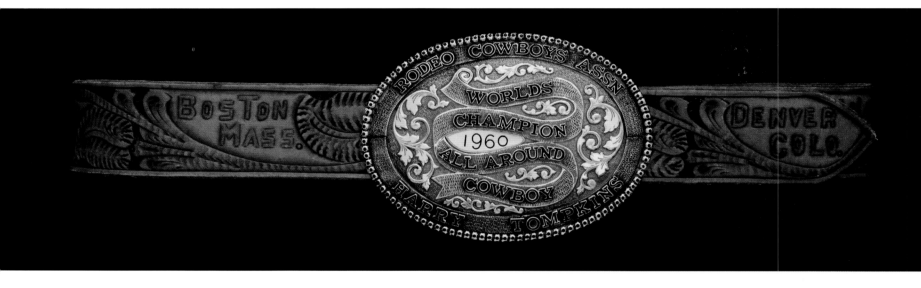

←↑
Rodeo Trophy Buckle and Belt
Don Ellis Silversmiths
Seattle, Washington, 1960
Belt maker unknown, 1948
NCM—Loan courtesy Harry Tompkins, L.1987.07.02 and L.1987.02.03

This gold-and-silver belt plate was awarded to Harry Tompkins by the Rodeo Cowboys Association for his "Worlds Champion All Around Cowboy" title in 1960. The tooled belt commemorates Harry Tompkins's first bull-riding championship, in 1948. The five-time world champion bull rider parlayed his talent into a pair of all-around cowboy titles in 1952 and 1960.

Rodeo Trophy Buckle
R. Schaezlein and Son Silversmiths
San Francisco, California, 1964
NCM—Gift of Dean Oliver, R.234.07

Sponsored by Levi Strauss and Company, this engraved gold-and-silver belt buckle was awarded by the Rodeo Cowboys Association (RCA) to Dean Oliver, the 1964 "World's Grand Champion Cowboy." This buckle design provided the pattern for the huge Schaezlein plates presented by Levi Strauss as "Special Added Awards" to multiple all-around champions such as Casey Tibbs, Jim Shoulders, and Larry Mahan.

Dean Oliver Calf Roping (detail)
Fort Worth, Texas, Southwestern Exposition and Fat Stock Show rodeo, circa 1965
Ferrell Butler, photographer
NCM—Dickinson Research Center
Photographic Study Collection, 1988.9.1532

↑ Rodeo Trophy Buckle
R. Schaezlein and Son Silversmiths
San Francisco, California, 1968
NCM—Gift of Larry Mahan, R.235.05

This enormous belt plate was awarded to Larry Mahan in 1968 for his third consecutive "World's Grand Champion Cowboy" title. Sponsored by Levi Strauss and Company, the solid-silver piece is engraved in a foliate-scroll motif and enhanced with a variety of gold-overlaid elements accented with rubies. Larry Mahan won the Rodeo Cowboys Association (RCA) World's Champion Cowboy title in 1966, 1967, 1968, 1969, 1970, and 1973.

➔ Larry Mahan Bareback-Bronc Riding
Oklahoma City, Oklahoma, National Finals
Rodeo, 1966
Ferrell Butler, photographer
NCM—Dickinson Research Center
Photographic Study Collection, 1988.9.1518

Rodeo Trophy Buckle
Rowell Saddlery Company
Hayward, California, 1969
NCM—Gift of Larry Mahan, R.235.04

This floral-and-scroll-engraved sterling silver buckle with rope border and gold overlay went to "Champion Bronc Rider" Larry Mahan at the Cow Palace Rodeo in San Francisco, California, in 1969. The victory no doubt contributed in part to his all-around-cowboy championship title that year.

Rodeo Trophy Buckle
Gist Silversmiths
Placerville, California, circa 1980
NCM—Gift of Toots Mansfield, 1994.37

The Professional Rodeo Cowboys Association (PRCA) presented this memorial belt buckle, or plate, to calf roper and team roper Toots Mansfield in recognition of his seven world calf-roping championships (1939, 1940, 1941, 1943, 1945, 1948, and 1950). Mansfield's outstanding record remained intact until excelled by Dean Oliver in 1955–69.

Rodeo Trophy Buckle

Gist Silversmiths
Placerville, California, 1987
NCM—Gift of Charmayne James, 1995.21.04

Overlaid with two-tone gold, this sterling silver belt buckle was awarded by Wrangler Western Wear to Charmayne James, the "Champion Barrel Racer" at the 1987 National Finals Rodeo (NFR). During 1986, James ranked as the sport's leading money winner, thus becoming the first female competitor ever to wear the prestigious *No. 1* back-number at the National Finals.

Rodeo Trophy Buckle and Belt

Gist Silversmiths
Placerville, California, 1988
Longhorn Belts
Location unknown, circa 1987
NCM—Gift of Clyde and Elsie Frost in memory of Lane Frost, 2009.23.03 A&B

Sponsored by Circle J Trailers, this sterling silver belt plate features two-tone gold overlay and the National Finals Rodeo (NFR) logo. It went to Lane Frost, "7th Go Round Champion Bull Rider" at the 1988 NFR in Las Vegas, Nevada. The belt has metal-wrapped edges, a sterling silver tip with the gold-overlaid likeness of a bull rider, and the name "LANE" in silver letters. Frost captured the Professional Rodeo Cowboys Association World Champion Bull Rider title in 1987. In the 1988 "Challenge of Champions," he was the first hand ever to ride the infamous bull Red Rock—in four of seven contests.

Rodeo Trophy Buckle
Gist Silversmiths
Placerville, California, 1991
NCM—Gift of Charmayne James, 1995.21.05

Set with rubies and overlaid in two-tone gold, this silver belt buckle was sponsored by the Anheuser Busch Brewing Company and awarded to Charmayne James, champion "Barrel Racer" at the 1991 Dodge City, Kansas, Roundup. By competing in as many sanctioned rodeos as possible from 1984 through 2003, James became the all-time top female money-winner in rodeo history.

Rodeo Trophy Buckle
Wage's Silversmiths
Anaheim, California, 1994
NCM—Gift of Charmayne James, 1995.21.06

Awarded to the champion barrel racer at the California Golden Bear Rodeo in 1994, this gold-overlaid, sterling silver belt plate was won by Charmayne James. Consistent performances from James and her favorite barrel-racing horse, Scamper, brought her an unprecedented—and unequaled—ten consecutive world-barrel-racing championships from 1984 to 1993. She took an eleventh title in 2003.

⬆ **Rodeo Presentation Spurs**
Maker unknown, circa 1885
NCM—Gift of M. F. Peterson, R.256.09 A&B

Presented in 1924 to cowgirl-contender Lorena Trickey by the Hawaiian Ad Club, these spurs were once the property of David Kalakaua, the last king of Hawaii (1874–1891). The spurs feature large eight-point rowels and attached jingle-bobs, characteristics reflecting traditional vaquero influence in Hawaiian ranch culture. Lightly engraved in Mexican style over the heel bands and shanks, they are fitted with heel chains and mounted with border-stamped leathers. Trickey won the ladies' relay race at the Cheyenne Frontier Days rodeo in 1924 and probably received the spurs for that victory.

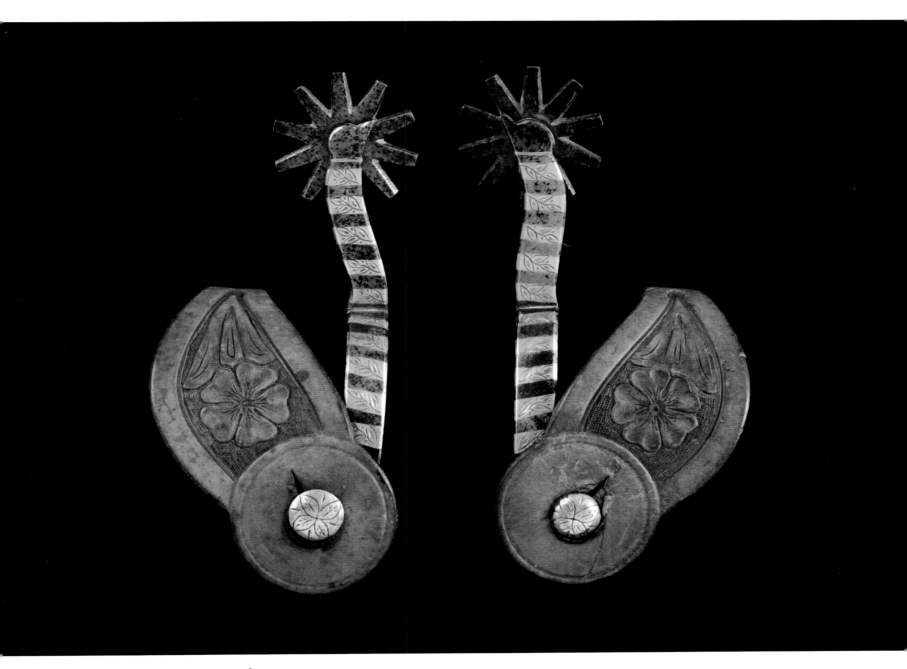

↑ **Rodeo Arena Spurs**
Maker unknown, State Penitentiary
Cañon City, Colorado, circa 1915
NCM—Loan courtesy R. C. Walters, L.1988.02.06 A&B

Worn by widely respected rodeo promoter (and sometime contestant)
Charles Burton "C. B." Irwin, these well-crafted steel spurs feature ten-point
rowels and engraved nickel-silver stripes inlaid on the heel bands and
shanks. The spurs are mounted with fine, hand-floral-tooled leathers from
the F. A. Meanea Saddlery Company of Cheyenne, Wyoming.

←↖
Rodeo Trophy Spurs
Ricardo Metal Manufacturing Company
Denver, Colorado, 1949
NCM—Gift of Buck Rutherford, 1987.32.05 A&B

Donated by the JO Guest Ranch of Pincher
Creek, Alberta, these trophy spurs are half
mounted with engraved silver and gold
overlays and ruby insets and feature slightly
upturned buttons, modest chap guards, and
sixteen-point rowels. They were captured by
Buck Rutherford, the "Champion Brahma Bull
Rider" at the 1949 Calgary Exhibition and
Stampede. He was declared the Rodeo Cowboys
Association all-around-champion cowboy in
1954.

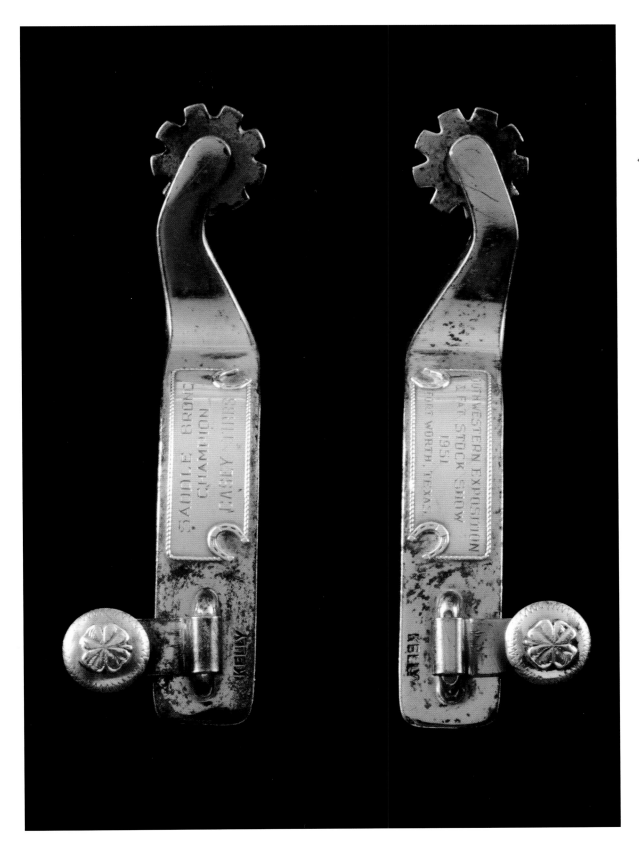

Rodeo Trophy Spurs
Kelly Bit and Spur Company
El Paso, Texas, 1951
NCM—Museum purchase, R.229.05 A&B

These nickel-plated trophy spurs with gold-overlaid presentation plaques went to Casey Tibbs, the "Saddle Bronc Champion" at Fort Worth's Southwestern Exposition and Fat Stock Show rodeo in 1951. Over the course of that year, Tibbs accumulated sufficient points to win both the Rodeo Cowboys Association (RCA) saddle-bronc and bareback-bronc titles, thus riding off with the RCA all-around cowboy title as well.

↑ **Rodeo Presentation Spurs**
Garcia Saddlery and Silversmiths
Salinas, California, circa 1955
NCM—Rodeo Historical Society Purchase, 2007.05.04 A&B

These custom spurs were made and embellished by Less Garcia, who presented
them to prominent rodeo director Everett Colborn. The spurs are full mounted
with foliate-and-floral-engraved sterling silver and feature "EC" monograms in
gold on the heel bands. Sterling silver washers ornament the nine-point rowels,
and the leathers also boast buckles and keepers of engraved sterling silver. Known
as "the King of the Big Time Rodeos," Colborn ran the Madison Square Garden
Championship Rodeo for some twenty years, as well as other major venues
including Phoenix, Fort Worth, San Antonio, Chicago, and Boston.

Rodeo Trophy Spurs
Ricardo Metal Manufacturing Company
Denver, Colorado, 1955
NCM—Museum purchase, R.229.03 A&B

The inner heel bands of these gold-plated, nickel-silver trophy spurs are hand engraved "Bareback Riding Champion / Chicago 1955 / Casey Tibbs." Nineteen fifty-five proved a good year for Tibbs, as he ultimately garnered both the saddle-bronc-riding and all-around-champion cowboy titles.

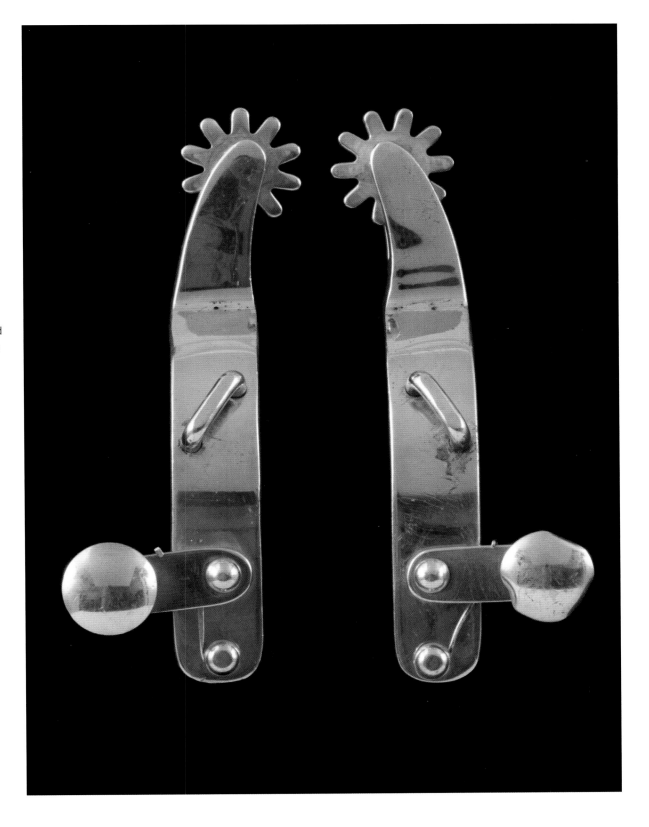

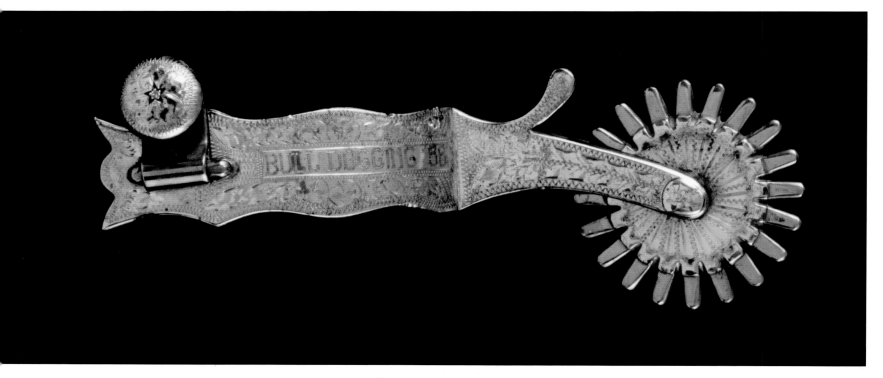

↑ Rodeo Trophy Spur

Kindberg Spurs, location unknown, 1956

NCM—Gift of Mrs. E. A. Spaulding, R.210.17

Half mounted with engraved sterling silver, this single trophy spur with swinging buttons, chap guard, and twenty-point rowel was presented to the great Bill Linderman, winner of the bulldogging event at the Spokane, Washington, rodeo in 1956. Linderman's activity in the arena was slowing at the time, as he applied himself diligently—and most successfully—to the leadership of the Rodeo Cowboys Association.

Rodeo Trophy Spurs
Silver Tip Manufacturing Company
Chico, California, 1956
NCM—Gift of Buck Rutherford,
1987.32.06 A&B

Presented to champion bull rider Buck
Rutherford at the 1956 Pendleton Round-Up,
these trophy spurs feature chrome-plated
steel bodies half mounted with foliate-
scroll-engraved sterling silver on the heel
bands, shanks, and swinging buttons. They
incorporate five-point star rowels and have
canted bars on the bands for auxiliary heel
straps.

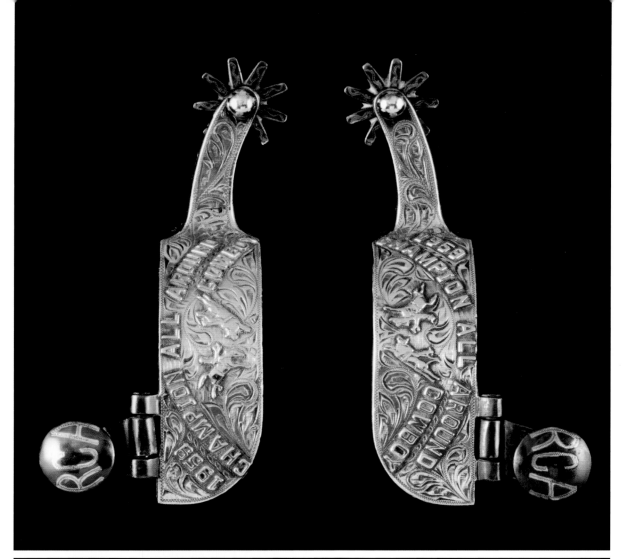

Rodeo Trophy Spurs
Garcia Saddlery and Silversmiths
Salinas, California, 1959
NCM—Loan courtesy Jim Shoulders,
LR.228.26

The indomitable Jim Shoulders won these trophy spurs as the Rodeo Cowboys Association (RCA) "1959 Champion All Around Cowboy" at the first National Finals Rodeo in Dallas, Texas. The spurs are silver- and gold-overlaid and engraved on the outer faces and inlaid with engraved silver foliate scrollwork in a nitre-blued finish on the inner faces. Shoulders also took the bull-riding championship in 1959—the last of his national victories.

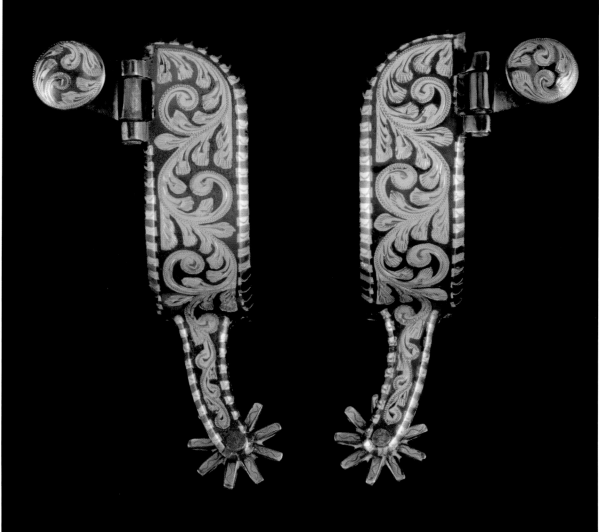

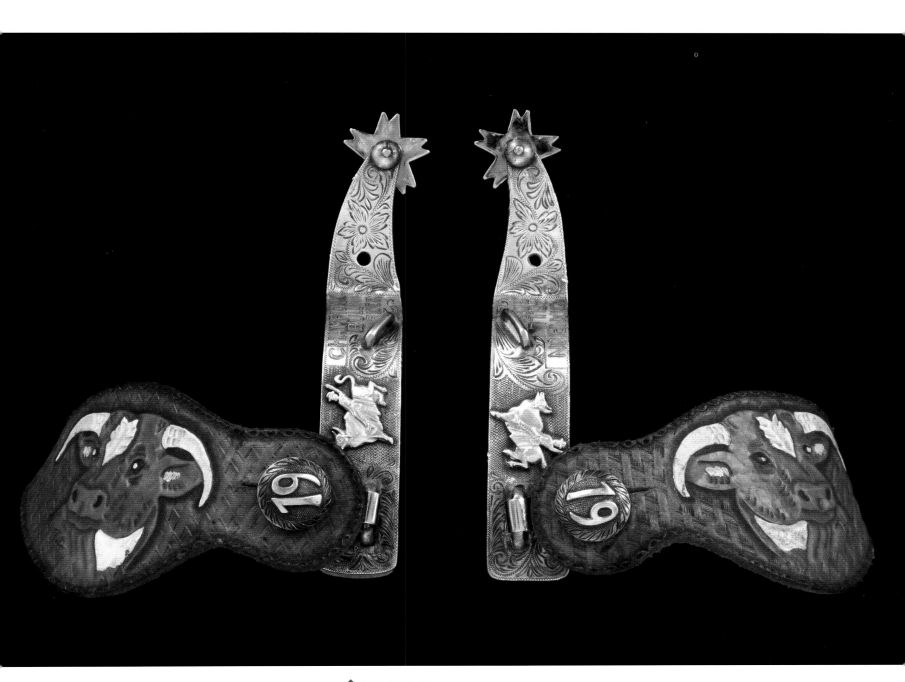

Rodeo Trophy Spurs
Rawhide Spurs
San Diego, California, 1963
NCM—Rodeo Historical Society Purchase, 2009.05.02 A&B

Captured by champion bull rider Bob Robinson at the 1963 Salinas,
California, rodeo, these trophy spurs are of bull-riding pattern with
toothed, five-point star rowels and auxiliary tie-down bars. (Note that
the shanks also are drilled through to take thong or wire tie-downs.) The
bodies are full mounted with engraved silver and boast gold overlays
of bull riders on the outside heel bands and the date (19 and 63) on the
swinging buttons. The spur leathers are basket stamped and feature
carved bull-head motifs.

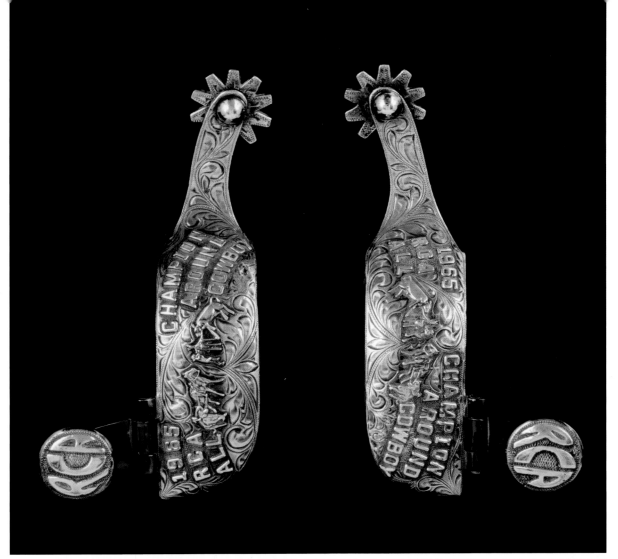

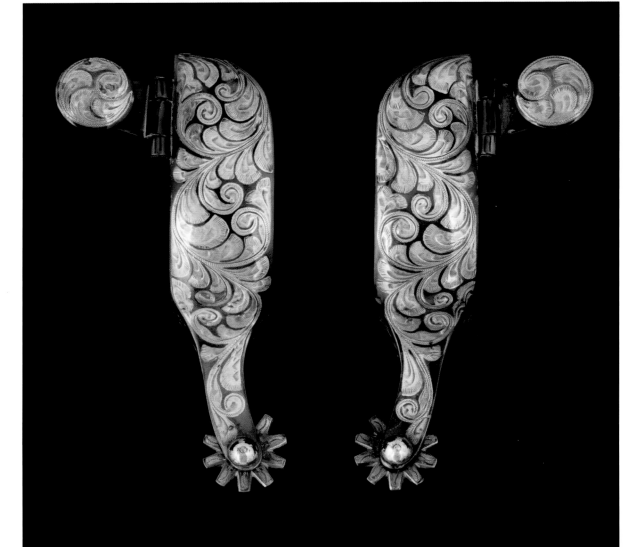

Rodeo Trophy Spurs
Garcia Saddlery and Silversmiths
Salinas, California, 1965
NCM—Gift of Dean Oliver, R.234.03 A&B

These silver- and gold-overlaid, silver-inlaid, and foliate-engraved trophy spurs went to Dean Oliver, the "1965 RCA Champion All Around Cowboy" at the seventh National Finals Rodeo, held in Oklahoma City, Oklahoma. This victory marked the last of Oliver's three consecutive all-around cowboy titles. He would take his final national calf-roping championship in 1969.

Rodeo Trophy Spurs
Garcia Saddlery and Silversmiths
Salinas, California, 1968
NCM—Gift of Larry Mahan, R.235.03 A&B

These silver-inlaid, silver- and gold-overlaid, foliate-engraved, and nitre-blued trophy spurs went to Larry Mahan, "Champion RCA All Around Cowboy [of] 1968" at the tenth National Finals Rodeo. The victory marked the third of five consecutive all-around champion titles for Mahan, and he would take another in 1973.

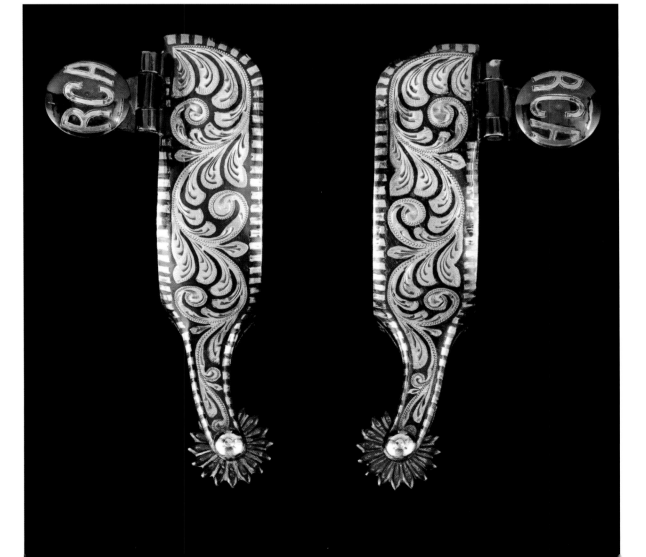

MISS MAMIE FRANCIS AND
NAPOLEON, 4 4"
(DOWBLEHAY)

7 Rodeo Costume

Hats, Shirts, Chaps, Boots, and More

NOT SURPRISINGLY, the distinctive elements of dress adopted by early rodeo contestants drew directly on the cowboy culture from which most of them came. Western hats, chaps, and boots, in particular, identified both the early-twentieth-century range hand and the arena hand as heirs of the same, already romanticized, western cattle culture. These special apparel elements already personified an American type; their adoption and ongoing interpretation in rodeo sport served to perpetuate and broaden their recognition and appeal throughout the twentieth century and to the present.

The western, or "cowboy," hat, incorporating special characteristics favored by the rustic horsemen of the cattle range, has become particularly emblematic of the romantic cowboy persona—and of his arena cousin. Distinguished in relative scale from other headgear, the high crown and wide brim of the cowboy hat served to cool the head and protect the face and neck from prairie sun, rain, and wind. Though these design attributes arose from utilitarian considerations, they resulted in a hat distinctive in form and line and often further distinguished by personal and regional preferences in crown creases and brim rolls. In the early-day rodeo arena, the cowboy hat might also be used to "fan" a bronc or steer to greater exertion or to wave at spectators in a declaration of one's confidence (neither practice is allowed today). Influenced by the Wild West shows, cowboy hats of the large, "ten gallon," size graced rodeo arenas for several decades in the early twentieth century, and these remained popular among cowgirl contenders into the 1940s. Rodeo cowboys, in contrast, began to adopt western hats of more conservative dimensions in the 1930s, and that preference continues today. Both the famed Stetson Hat Company, whose name has long been generic for "western hat," and the Resistol Hat Company have been major sponsors of rodeo prizes and awards over the past century.[1]

As discussed in part 1, female rodeo contenders flaunted an evolving assortment of distinctive and colorful arena apparel from the 1910s onward. The rodeo cowboys, in contrast, usually

← **Miss Mamie Francis and Napoleon, "44"**
Venue unknown, circa 1924
Ralph Russell Doubleday, photographer
NCM—Dickinson Research Center
McCarroll Family Trust Collection,
RC2006.076.228

→ **Early Rodeo Arena Apparel**
Location unknown, circa 1918
Photographer unknown
NCM—Dickinson Research Center
Photographic Study Collection, 06-190.39.08

wore the more-mundane garb typical of working range hands, though some in the first decades of the twentieth century appeared in knit sweaters, jerseys, or rugby-style shirts. A few, such as Paddy Ryan, rode rough stock in a dress shirt, coat, and tie. By the late 1930s, stylish and colorful western-cut shirts had begun to appear among many rodeo cowboys (as among B-western cowboys and crooners as well). With the advent of the middle 1950s, however, long-sleeved white shirts and denim pants had become de rigueur at RCA rodeos, and this outfit would hold sway for a couple of decades. (Levi's jeans reigned supreme at the time, but they soon were all but totally displaced by Wranglers—both firms have been consistent supporters of the sport.) The rise of ready-made western wear influenced the cut and pattern of men's shirts, but most rodeo hands maintained a quite conservative look inside the arena well into the 1960s. Outside the arena, however, rodeo cowboys took on a certain sartorial splendor in distinctive western-cut shirts and suits fashioned by custom tailors such as Rodeo Ben, Nudie Cohn, and Maude McMorries. Arena hands both male and female responded in varying degree to the gaudy, "urban cowboy" look of the 1970s and early 1980s, but a traditional, more conservative taste ultimately reemerged. Today, rodeo competitors enter the arena wearing their Wrangler jeans and western shirts of varying color that are plastered with the symbols and names of the sport's leading commercial sponsors.[2]

↑ Buff Brady, Jr., in Western Costume with Horse
Turk Greenough Rodeo
Fort Riley, Kansas, circa 1946
Ralph Russell Doubleday, photographer
NCM—Dickinson Research Center
R. R. Doubleday Collection, 79.026.2226

Originally adopted from vaqueros to protect a horseman's legs from thorny brush and inclement weather, chaps of two principal patterns appeared among rodeo cowboys in the first decades of the twentieth century. "Woolie" chaps of angora goat hair made the transition from northern range to rodeo arena through the influence of various Wild West shows at the opening of the century. Available in a rainbow of natural and dyed hues, woolies added a dramatic flamboyance to the look and performance of both male and female competitors in the rough-stock events. By the 1910s, however, male rodeo contenders rapidly replaced both the long-serving, narrow-legged "shotgun"-style chaps of the old trail-driving days and the woolie variety with flaring "batwing"-pattern chaps of supple cowhide. These provided even greater flapping motion in the arena, and they could be had with a range of eye-catching ornamentation in the form of vibrant two-tone coloration, custom overlaid or pierced initials or names, and a plethora of flashy nickeled conchas and "spots." Today equally functional and fashionable, rodeo chaps now typically are fastened only down to the knee for greater flapping action in the arena, and many incorporate a shiny Mylar coating to lend an extra glimmer under the lights.

Second only to the western hat as a symbol of the cowboy as a distinctive character type, western-style boots also derived from the functional requirements of the working ranch hand of the later nineteenth century. Initially combining design elements of the British Wellington and the domestic cavalry boot, by 1900 the cowboy variety differed principally in its tall, underslung heels and somewhat narrower toes—both details intended to easily obtain and retain the stirrup. Early on, boot tops, ranging from twelve to fifteen inches in height, featured square throats and vertical welts or rudimentary stitching to maintain their form. Scalloped throats and much more elaborate, decorative stitching soon came to the fore on the uppers, and this fashionable boot pattern dominated in the rodeo arena from the 1910s on. Rodeo cowgirls, especially, proved to be ardent aficionados of such stylish boots in making up their arena ensembles. As noted earlier in discussing the various events, rodeo competition directly influenced the design of the low-heeled "roper" boot popular with calf ropers and steer wrestlers. Otherwise, the western boots worn by male rodeo hands over the past ninety years have generally reflected the broader market: largely unadorned, utilitarian boots for competition and fancier boots outside the arena. Female contenders, in contrast, have tended to favor embellished footwear at all times.[4]

➜ **Champion Bronc Rider Casey Tibbs**
Location unknown, circa 1958
Photographer unknown
NCM—Dickinson Research Center
Photographic Study Collection, 1988.9.834s

Western Hat

Maker unknown, circa 1910
NCM—Grandee Collection, 91.1.0486

The wide-brimmed, tall-crowned western hat has been an important element of cowboy dress since the 1870s. Headgear such as this soft-felt example was commonplace at riding-and-roping matches held by cowboys on the range. Exuberant bronc-riding contestants sometimes swatted, or "fanned," the bronc's head or hindquarters with their hat to elicit greater bucking performance.

Western Hat

Miller Hat Company
Houston, Texas (?), circa 1920
NCM—Grandee Collection, 1991.1.2612

Reflecting the flamboyant character of all Wild West show performers, oversize western headgear became popular at frontier pageants prior to 1910. Such "ten gallon" hats caught the attention of the arena spectators, and they were readily adopted by rodeo hands—many of whom got their start in Wild West productions—as the nascent sport developed.

⬆ **Western Hat**

John B. Stetson Hat Company
Philadelphia, Pennsylvania, circa 1925
NCM—Gift of Jack Maxwell, 1987.19

Made of tan nutria felt, this western souvenir hat carries the autographs of
contestants from rodeo's first golden era in the 1920s. Notable competitors
include Mike Hastings, Mabel Strickland, Chester Byers, Tommy Kirnan,
Fox Hastings, Bob Crosby, and Tad and Buck Lucas.

↑ **Western Hat**

John B. Stetson Hat Company

Philadelphia, Pennsylvania, circa 1925

NCM—Gift of Estelle Gilbert, R.272.07

This black "ten-gallon" hat belonged to steer wrestler Mike Hastings, who was known for his fine and extravagant headgear. The hat boasts an eight-and-one-quarter-inch crown with a three-quarter-inch grosgrain band, and a five-and-one-quarter-inch brim with grosgrain binding.

MIKE HASTINGS BULLDOGGING (© R.R. DOUBLEDAY)

⬆ **Mike Hastings Bulldogging**
Venue unknown, circa 1926
Ralph Russell Doubleday, photographer
NCM—Dickinson Research Center
McCarroll Family Trust Collection, RC2006.076.144

⬆ **Western Hat**

John B. Stetson Hat Company
Philadelphia, Pennsylvania, circa 1925
NCM—Gift of Tad Lucas, R.238.03

Worn by rough-stock and trick rider Tad Lucas, this "ten-gallon" hat is typical of the oversized, yet very attractive, headgear favored by female contenders during rodeo's early decades. Fabricated of finely textured felt, the hat has a seven-inch, creased crown with a wide grosgrain band and a five-inch brim with a grosgrain ribbon binding.

Western Hat

John B. Stetson Hat Company
Philadelphia, Pennsylvania, circa 1925
NCM—Loan courtesy Mrs. Roberta Crosby
Burkstaller, LR.214.42

Worn, soiled, and forever creased, this XXXXX
Stetson was Bob Crosby's lucky talisman in
the arena for more than a decade. Indeed, it
became something of a Crosby trademark, of
which he once remarked, "Someday, to their
surprise, I'm going to wear my Sunday hat and
see if it's the old black felt or the man they're
always cheering." An initial member of the
Cowboys Turtle Association, Crosby displayed
his CTA pin on the hat's crown, where it
remains today.

Western Trophy Hat

John B. Stetson Hat Company
Philadelphia, Pennsylvania, circa 1928
NCM—Gift of W. H. Green, 1990.06

Believed to have been won by champion
calf roper Bob Crosby at the 1928 Cheyenne
Frontier Days rodeo, this gray XXX beaver
Stetson has a six-and-one-half-inch crown
with a cream grosgrain band and a four-inch
brim. Evidently worn outside the arena, the
hat exhibits none of the longtime wear and
grime that lend such character to Crosby's
"lucky black hat" (above).

↑ **Western Hat**
Resistol Hat Company
Garland, Texas, circa 1945
NCM—Gift of Fay Kirkwood, 1989.23.05

This extravagant western hat was worn by noted Fort Worth equestrian and socialite Fay Kirkwood, who produced the first all-girl rodeo at Bonham, Texas, in 1942. Fashioned of tan felt, the hat features a full, six-inch brim and has a ribbon chin tie and red satin lining. The interior is inscribed "Designed by Harry Robuck for Fay Kirkwood."

↑ Western Hat and Band
Donhoy Hatters, California, circa 1955
NCM—Gift of Mr. and Mrs. Glenn Randall, 1989.30.06 & 1989.30.07

Fashioned of brilliant red felt, this hat was worn by equestrian star Lynn Randall as part of an ensemble for arena grand entries and flag ceremonies. The four-and-one-quarter-inch brim is trimmed with rhinestones, while an added band of rhinestones surrounds the four-inch crown. The hat and outfit (shown later in this chapter) are representative of the lavish parade costumes fostered by Gene Autry's rodeo programming and the rise of rodeo queens.

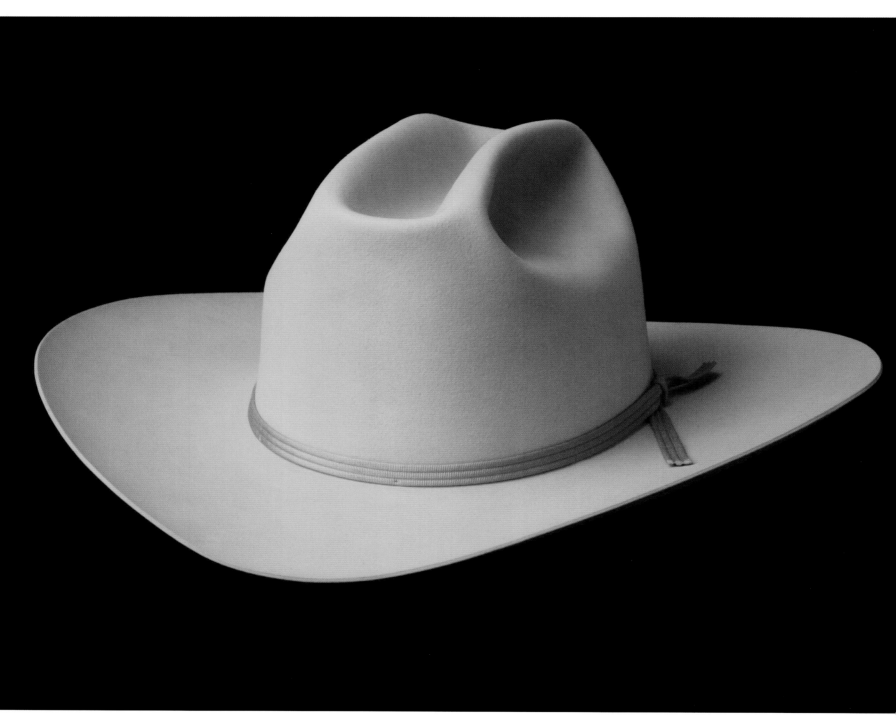

⬆ **Western Hat**
Shudde Brothers Hatters
Houston, Texas, circa 1960
NCM—Gift of Mrs. E. A. Spaulding, R.210.06

Typical western headgear in the early 1960s, this specimen features a six-inch crown with a "cattleman's crease" and a three-and-one-half-inch brim. The dress hat was worn by Bill Linderman while he served as an administrator with the Rodeo Cowboys Association. The "Champ" was killed in an airplane crash in 1965 while on RCA business.

↑ **Western Presentation Hat**
John B. Stetson Hat Company
Philadelphia, Pennsylvania, circa 1965
NCM—Rodeo Historical Society Purchase, 2007.05.05

This stylish cowboy hat, with its custom leather-and-horsehair band, was presented to famed rodeo champion—and clotheshorse—Casey Tibbs by noted western clothier Nudie Cohn of Nudie's Western Wear, Hollywood, California. The interior sweatband is gold-stamped "Made by Nudie Cohn Especially for Casey Tibbs" and "XXXXXX Stetson." A fitted aluminum travel case remains with the headgear.

⬆ **Western Trophy Hat**
Resistol Hat Company
Garland, Texas, 1984
NCM—Gift of Charmayne James, 1995.21.08

This trophy hat, with its five-and-one-half-inch crown and four-inch brim, was awarded to fourteen-year-old Charmayne James as the winner of the 1984 Women's Professional Rodeo Association (WPRA) Rookie of the Year title. She also captured both the WPRA and the National Finals Rodeo Barrel Racing Championships for 1984.

↑ **Western Hat**
Resistol Hat Company
Garland, Texas, circa 1987
NCM—Gift of Clyde and Elsie Frost in memory of Lane Frost, 2009.23.04

This black cowboy hat is fashioned of 20-X beaver felt and adorned with
a custom Hereford-hide band and the signature turkey feather favored
by champion bull rider Lane Frost. He bought the hat from Red's Clothing
Company in Pendleton, Oregon, where he competed and won in 1987 with
a broken collarbone. Frost finished the year winning the Professional Rodeo
Cowboys Association World Bull Riding Champion title at the National Finals
Rodeo—the latter his life-long goal.

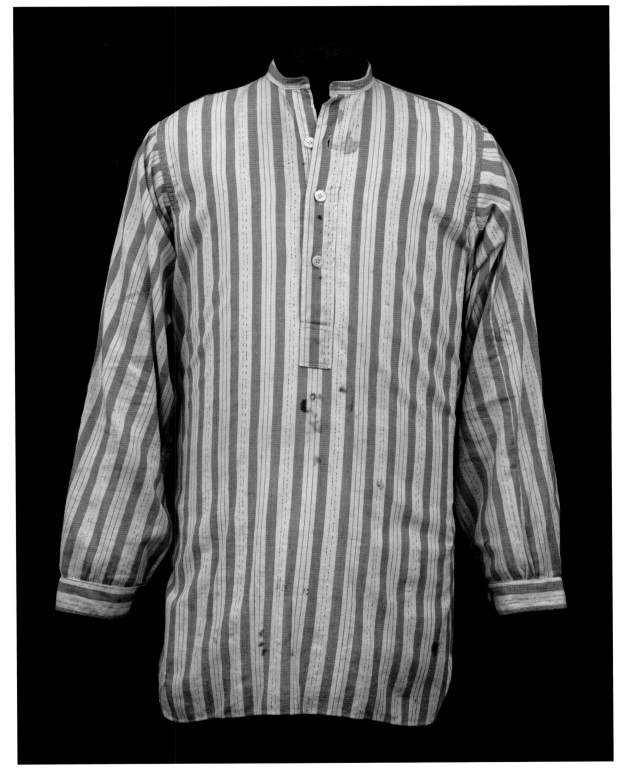

Men's Skin Coat

Cree style, maker unknown, 1890–1900
NCM—Grandee Collection, 1991.1.1761

As displays of western pageantry, Wild West
shows often borrowed or incorporated facets
of American Indian culture. Intended to foster
a frontier image, elaborate garments like this
became classic costume elements among
impresarios and showmen such as "Buffalo
Bill" Cody and "Pawnee Bill" Lillie. Fashioned
of smoked moose hide, the coat features an
unusual shawl-pattern collar with integral
fringing and fine, representational beadwork.

Men's Dress Shirt

Princely Tailors
Location unknown, circa 1900
NCM—Grandee Collection, 1991.1.2846

By the late 1890s, many working cowboys wore store-bought clothing like
this collarless, pullover shirt of striped cotton. Those who participated in early,
informal rodeo contests typically dressed the same until the Wild West shows
introduced a more flamboyant and colorful look to arena apparel.

⬆ **Wrist Cuffs**

Makers unknown, circa 1910
NCM—Gift of Courtenay Barber, Jr., H.10.07

These saddler-made cowboy cuffs are overlaid with fringed panels of colorful,
lazy-stitch beadwork that reflect the craft of a Lakota woman. Early rodeo
contestants, inspired by their Wild West counterparts, often wore such cuffs,
and they remained quite popular with female competitors into the 1920s.

↑ Gauntlet Gloves

Blumenthal Glove Company
New York City, circa 1910
NCM—Gift of Courtenay Barber, Jr., H.10.21

The use of showy gauntlet gloves in Wild West shows helped to create and perpetuate the image of the cowboy as a colorful cavalier. This wide-cuffed pair incorporates fringing, brass studding, and contrasting red embroidery featuring prominent horseshoe motifs. As with wrist cuffs, gauntlets for a time became costume elements in rodeo as well.

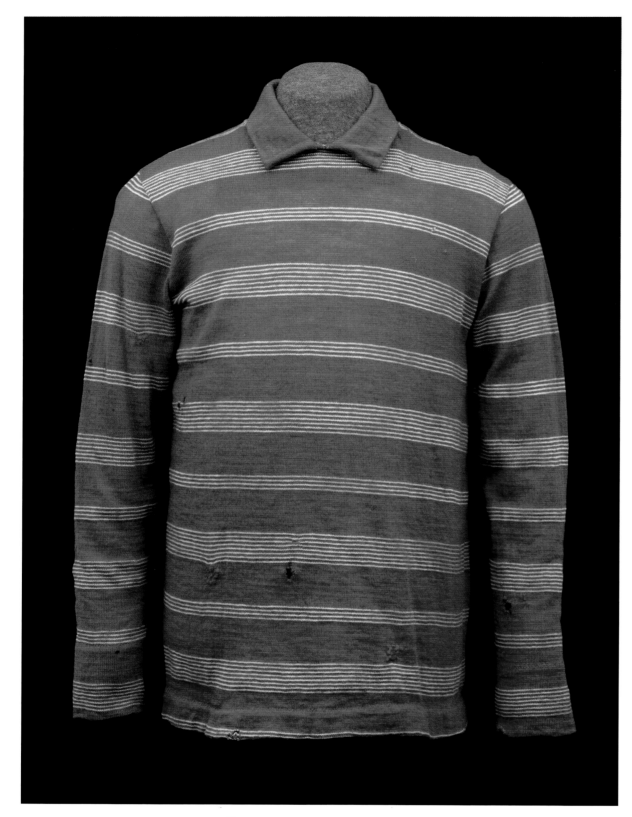

➜ **Ladies' Split Riding Skirt**
Probably Hamley Saddlery Company
Pendleton, Oregon, circa 1915
NCM—Rodeo Historical Society Purchase,
2006.02

A classic costume element among early rodeo
cowgirls, this split riding skirt is typical of
those favored by female bronc riders between
1900 and 1915. (Thereafter, such skirts rapidly
were supplanted, first by bloomers and then
by pants.) Fashioned of tanned, black-dyed
cowhide, the skirt incorporates a buckled
waist, extensive fringing at pockets and
hemline, and contrasting yellow trim featuring
inlaid diamond and tipi motifs.

⬆ **Men's Knit Shirt**
Maker unknown, circa 1915
NCM—Grandee Collection, 1991.1.2844

Between 1900 and 1920, some rodeo contestants abandoned the common
dress shirt of the working cowboy for apparel that was more comfortable and
colorful. Rugby shirts, sweaters, and knit shirts such as this one proved quite
popular among many arena cowboys until western-cut clothing came into
vogue in the mid to late 1930s.

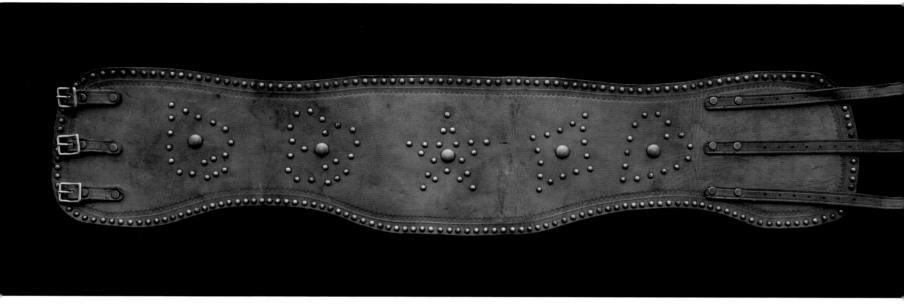

↑ Rodeo Bronc Belt
R. T. Frazier Saddlery Company
Pueblo, Colorado, circa 1915
NCM—Rodeo Historical Society Purchase, 2007.07.02

Sometimes called "kidney" belts, wide leather bronc belts supported the Wild West and rodeo rider's lower back and kidneys during strenuous rough-stock performances. The periphery of this example is border tooled and boasts a tracery of decorative brass "spots," while the body is similarly adorned with "spots" in popular card-suite motifs (spade, club, diamond, and heart) with a star at the center.

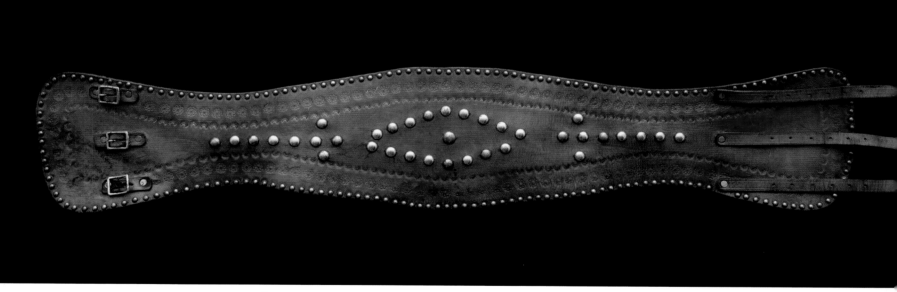

↑ Rodeo Bronc Belt
C. P. Shipley Saddlery Company
Kansas City, Missouri, circa 1915
NCM—Rodeo Historical Society Purchase, 2007.07.01

In addition to their functional attributes, bronc or kidney belts also served as fashionable elements of Wild West and rodeo-arena costume—particularly among cowgirl performers and contenders. This Shipley product is adorned with a multitude of small, nickel-plated brass "spots" around its border, while relatively larger "spots" in arrow and diamond motifs grace the center.

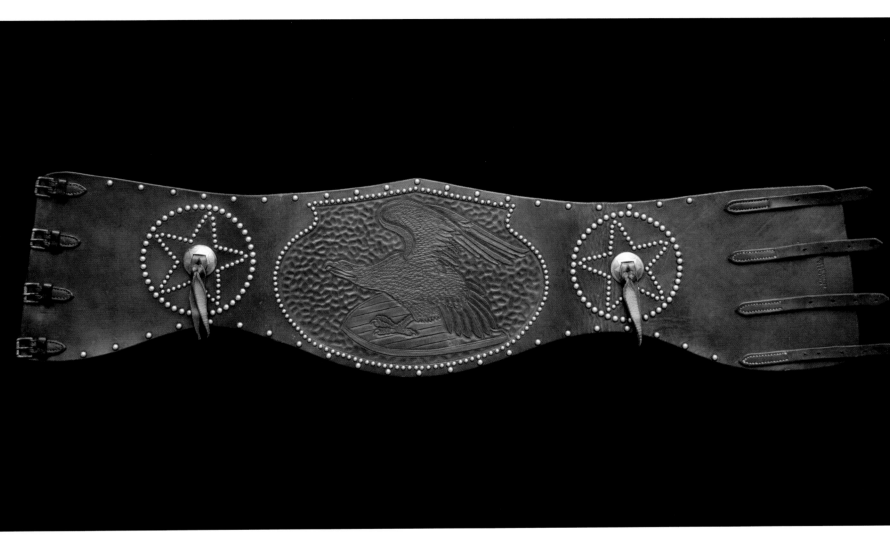

↑ Rodeo Bronc Belt

Hamley Saddlery Company

Pendleton, Oregon, circa 1920

NCM—Rodeo Historical Society Purchase, 2009.05.01

Finely crafted by one of the West's great saddleries, this bronc, or "kidney," belt secures with four sewn billets and diminutive roller buckles. The piece incorporates 380 decorative nickel "spots" that outline the belt periphery, frame the central panel scene, and form the circled, five-pointed stars with their slotted conchas and latigo strings. The central panel is meticulously hand stamped with an American-eagle-and-shield motif—a patriotic icon dating back well into the antebellum era.

Men's Wild West Vest
Maker unknown, circa 1918
NCM—Grandee Collection, 1991.1.1293

Worn by 101 Ranch Wild West performer Tex Cooper, this flashy vest features ornate floral beadwork and elaborate leather trim accented by more than five hundred nickeled "spots" of varying size. While rodeo hands sometimes wore vests outside the arena, few if any sported anything as extravagant as this example.

Men's Western Shirt
Sing Kee Custom Tailoring
San Francisco, California, circa 1936
NCM—Gift of Jane and Pat Holler, 2001.40.01

Produced by one of the earliest tailors of "western-style" clothing, this shirt of navy-blue worsted material features "arrow-smile" pockets and a back yoke line defined with matching cream satin trim. The placket and cuffs secure with unrimmed river-pearl snaps. The garment belonged to competitive calf roper and lifetime cowboy D. C. "Rusty" Holler of Wyoming.

← **Men's Western Shirt**
Maker unknown; marketed by
Edward H. Bohlin
Hollywood, California, circa 1938
NCM—Rodeo Historical Society Purchase,
2007.05.08

Fashioned of lightweight gabardine material,
this early western-cut shirt combines a light
tan yoke and cuffs—set off with cream-
colored whipcord piping—over a burgundy-
colored body. Plain, slant-pattern pockets
adorn the chest, while the placket and cuffs
are closed with unrimmed celluloid snaps.
Bohlin's saddlery and western shop was a
popular stop for traveling rodeo folks on the
West Coast in the 1930s and 1940s.

Men's Western Shirt
Nathan Turk Custom Tailoring
Los Angeles, California, circa 1940
NCM—Gift of Bob Brown, 2001.26.12

By the late 1930s, the western-cut apparel of
several custom tailors was in great demand
among B-western stars, cowboy crooners,
and rodeo contestants. This comparatively
early western-pattern shirt features a
burgundy body with gray yoke and cuff
elements that are highlighted with royal-blue
piping and blue, rimless celluloid snaps on
placket and cuffs.

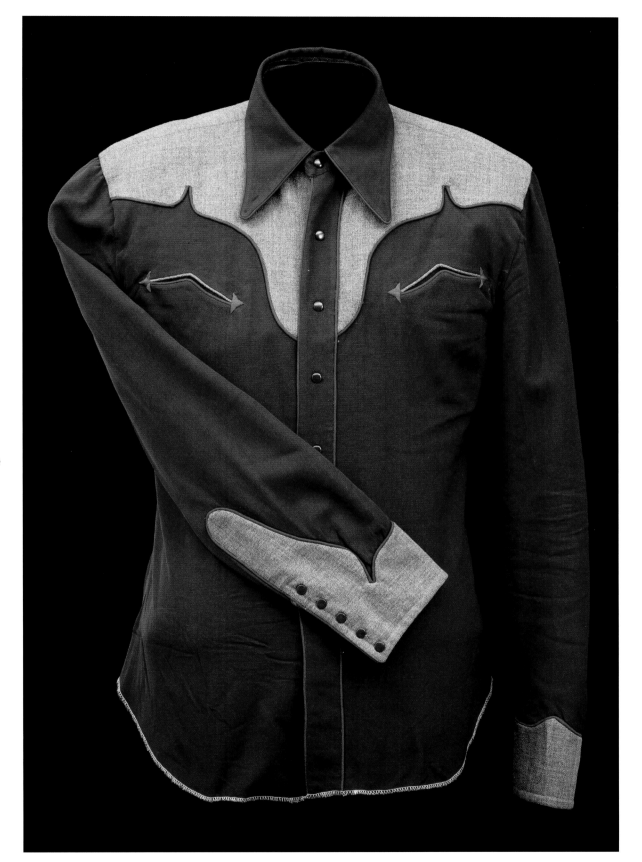

Ladies' Western Shirt

Rodeo Ben (Ben the Rodeo Tailor)
Philadelphia, Pennsylvania, circa 1940
NCM—Gift of Bob Brown, 2001.26.10

Perhaps the most famous of the early "western" clothiers, Rodeo Ben captured much of his rodeo clientele with a temporary showroom and tailor shop at New York City's Belvedere Hotel during the great Madison Square Garden championship rodeos of the 1940s. This handsome shirt features a tan yoke and cuffs over a hunter-green body with "arrow-smile" pockets. Tan, rimless celluloid snaps on the placket contrast with green snaps on the cuffs.

Men's Western Shirt
Nudies Rodeo Tailors
North Hollywood, California, circa 1945
NCM—Gift of Bob Brown, 2001.26.16

Among fashion-conscious rodeo hands, custom tailor Nudie Cohn probably ranked second in popularity to Rodeo Ben. This eye-catching Nudie shirt combines a body of bright green gabardine with mustard-yellow piping defining the collar, yoke, "arrow-smile" pockets, and cuffs. It is finished with brown celluloid snaps on the placket and cuffs.

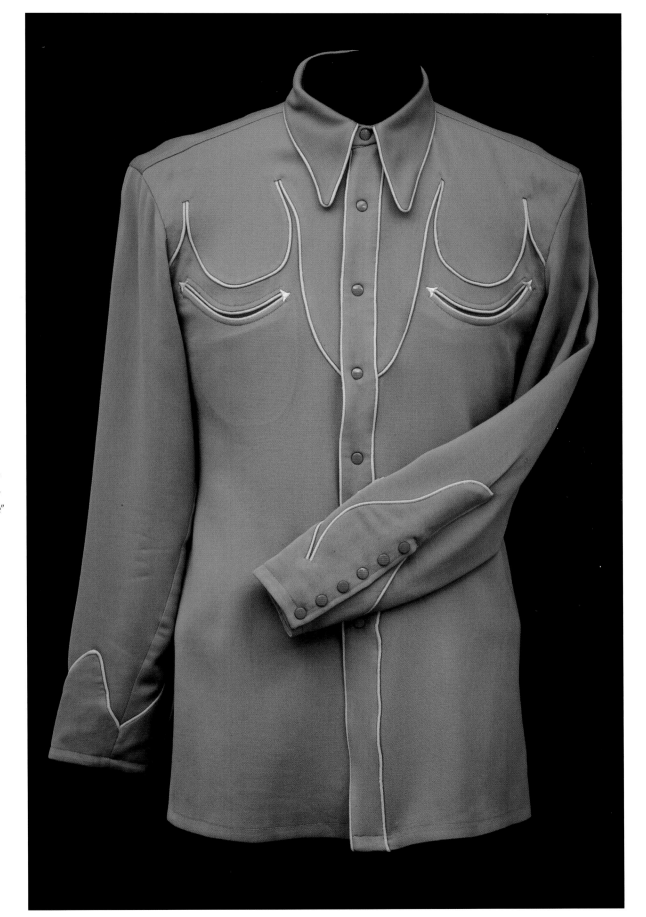

Men's Western Costume

Rodeo Ben (Ben the Rodeo Tailor)
Philadelphia, Pennsylvania, circa 1945
NCM—Gift of Cecil Cornish, 1994.56.07 A&B

Worn by Roman rider Cecil Cornish, this showy western-cut outfit features bright pearl snaps and contrasting piping setting off major design elements of collar, yoke, placket, pockets, cuffs, belt loops, and riding seat. A comparatively small but well-built man, Cornish cut a striking figure in and out of the rodeo arena in tailored ensembles such as this one.

Men's Western Shirt

Rodeo Ben (Ben the Rodeo Tailor)
Philadelphia, Pennsylvania, circa 1945
NCM—Gift of Cecil Cornish, 1994.56.06

Fabricated of bold red gabardine material with cream-colored piping defining the collar, shoulders, "arrow" pockets, and cuffs, this shirt also boasts cream-colored leather fringing at the front- and back-yoke lines. The garment, with matching pants, was part of contract performer Cecil Cornish's rodeo wardrobe.

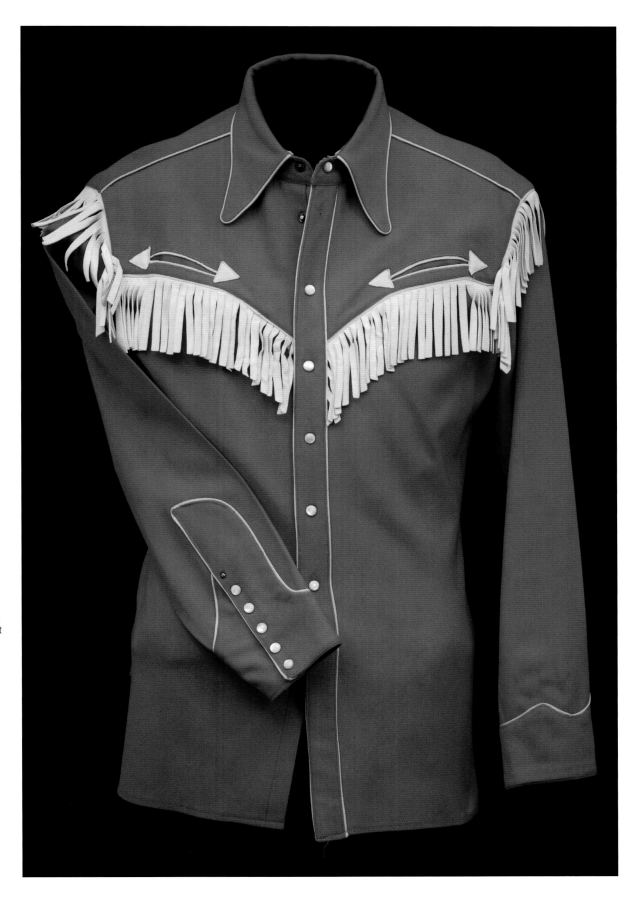

Ladies' Western Jacket

Maker unknown, circa 1945
NCM—Gift of Fay Kirkwood, 1989.23.04

Providing a glamorous look outside the
rodeo arena, this custom-tailored jacket of
soft white deerskin was worn by Fort Worth
horsewoman, rodeo producer, and socialite
Fay Kirkwood. The satin-lined, collarless
design features flamboyant fringing and a
single ornamental fastening at the front using
two silver conchas.

Ladies' Western Shirt

Mrs. Otis Arnold
Hope, Arkansas, 1948
NCM—Gift of Imogene Arnold Cox,
2007.38.05

This western shirt combines a gray-green
gabardine body with a hunter-green yoke and
cuffs and features green pearlized buttons and
floral-and-foliate embroidery. The garment
was home-made for youthful Arkansas barrel
racer Imogene Arnold (Cox) by her mother for
local and state championship competition.
(Matching gabardine pants in collection.)

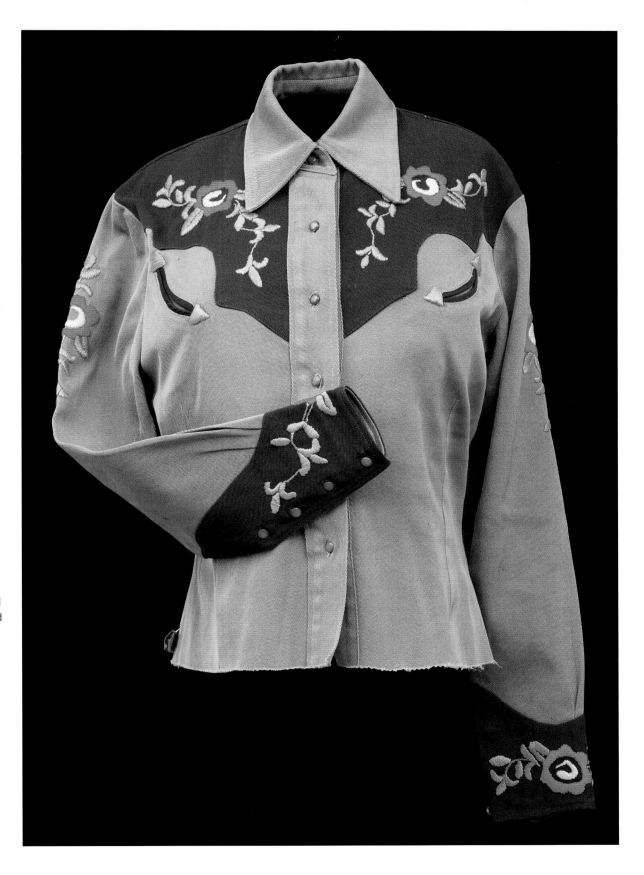

Men's Western Shirt

H Bar C Ranchwear
Los Angeles, California, circa 1950
NCM—Gift of Bill and Betty Price, 1996.25.03

Fashioned of rayon Lustracel, the collar, placket, and flap pockets of this rich burgundy shirt are highlighted with cream piping, while rimless celluloid snaps close the placket and cuffs. The pattern was advertised to prospective rodeo customers in *Hoofs and Horns* magazine in 1949.

Men's Western Shirt

Maker unknown; marketed by McClure's Western Wear
Fort Worth, Texas, circa 1955
NCM—Gift of Cecil Cornish, 1994.56.14

Another shirt from the wardrobe of rodeo performer Cecil Cornish, this flashy red-satin number sports hexagonal pearlized snap closures on the placket, flapped pockets, and cuffs. (Cornish owned a similar shirt in gold satin with river-pearl snaps, also in the museum's collections.)

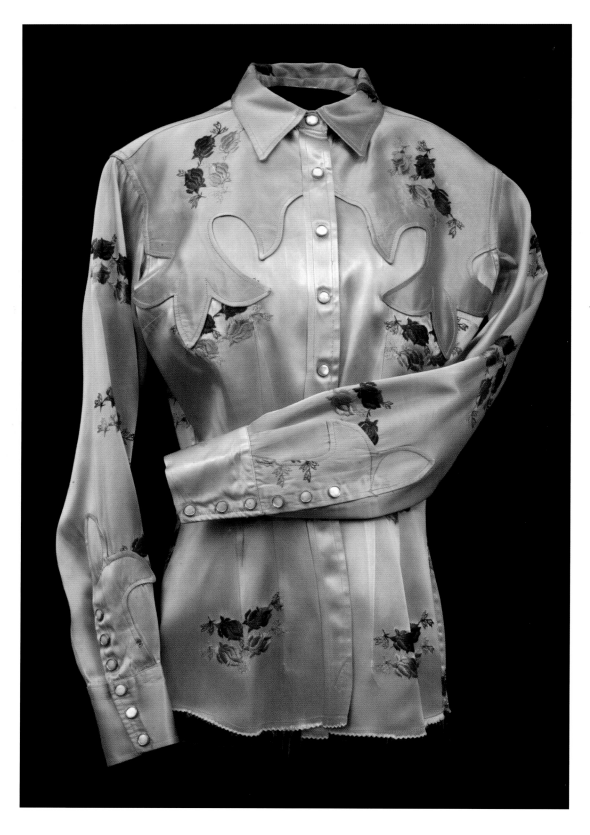

Ladies' Western Shirt
Maude McMorries Custom Tailoring
Doole, Texas, circa 1955
NCM—Gift of Betty Osborne Wilson,
1989.35.02

During the 1950s, Maude McMorries was well
known among Texas and southwestern rodeo
contenders for her stylish western-cut shirts,
outfits, and dress suits. Fashioned of lavender
satin material, this ladies' arena shirt boasts a
fancy scalloped yoke, fine floral embroidery,
and rimmed pearl snap fasteners.

← **Ladies' Rodeo Parade Ensemble**
Maude McMorries Custom Tailoring
Doole, Texas, circa 1955
NCM—Gift of Mr. and Mrs. Glenn Randall,
1989.30.08, 1989.30.09, & 1989.30.10 A&B

Worn by equestrian star Lynn Randall, this
ensemble is representative of the lavish
parade outfits fostered by Gene Autry's rodeo
programming. The western-cut, red-satin shirt
and white pants are joined with a rhinestone-
studded belt with a silver-and-gold plate by
M. L. Leddy and Sons, Fort Worth, Texas. (The
hat and boots associated with this outfit are
illustrated elsewhere in this chapter.)

Men's Western Shirt
Werstein's Custom Tailoring
California, circa 1960
NCM—Gift of Jane and Pat Holler, 2001.40.02

Too elegant for arena contention, this western-pattern shirt combines a very fine wool pinstripe material with meticulous stitchery incorporating front and back yokes, double-snap flap pockets, and rimmed pearl-snap fasteners down the placket and cuffs. Cowman D. C. "Rusty" Holler wore this shirt well after his competitive calf-roping days.

Men's Rodeo Sponsor Shirt
Maker unknown; distributed by Hesston Corporation
Hesston, Kansas, circa 1980
NCM—Loan courtesy ProRodeo Hall of Fame, L.1990.11

A manufacturer of farm equipment, the Hesston Corporation was the underwriting sponsor for the television broadcast of the National Finals Rodeo for more than fifteen years during the 1970s and 1980s. The company established its presence around the rodeo arena with dozens of brown, snap-fastened, bib-front "Hesston Outfit" shirts such as this example.

Ladies' Rodeo Sponsor Shirt
Exquisite Custom Designs
Location unknown, 1985
NCM—Gift of Charmayne James, 1995.21.01

Advertising "Jolly Rancher / Candies from Colorado," this western shirt was worn by eleven-time champion barrel racer Charmayne James during the 1985–86 Winston Rodeo Tour, in which she was the high-money winner. For more than a decade, James ranked as the Women's Professional Rodeo Association's premier athlete and superstar.

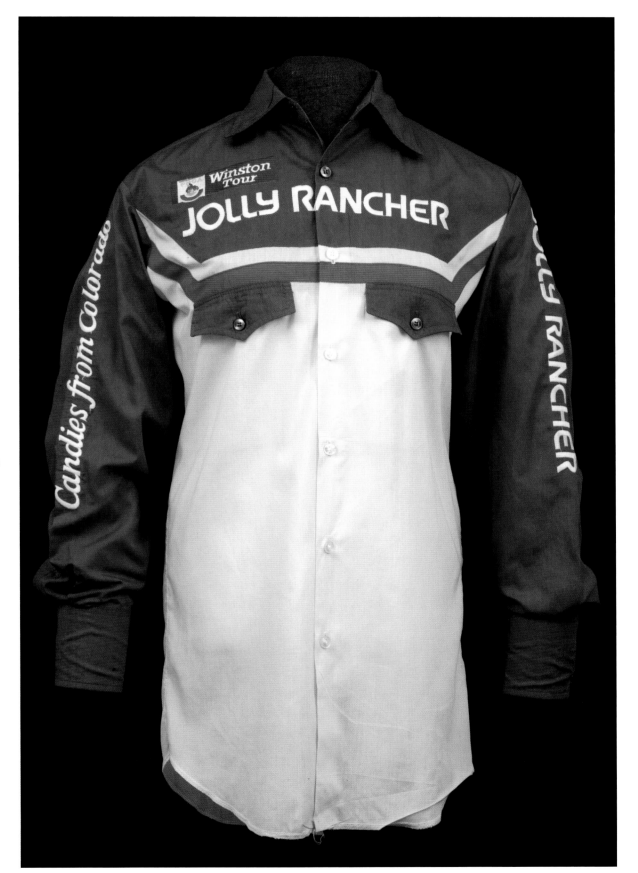

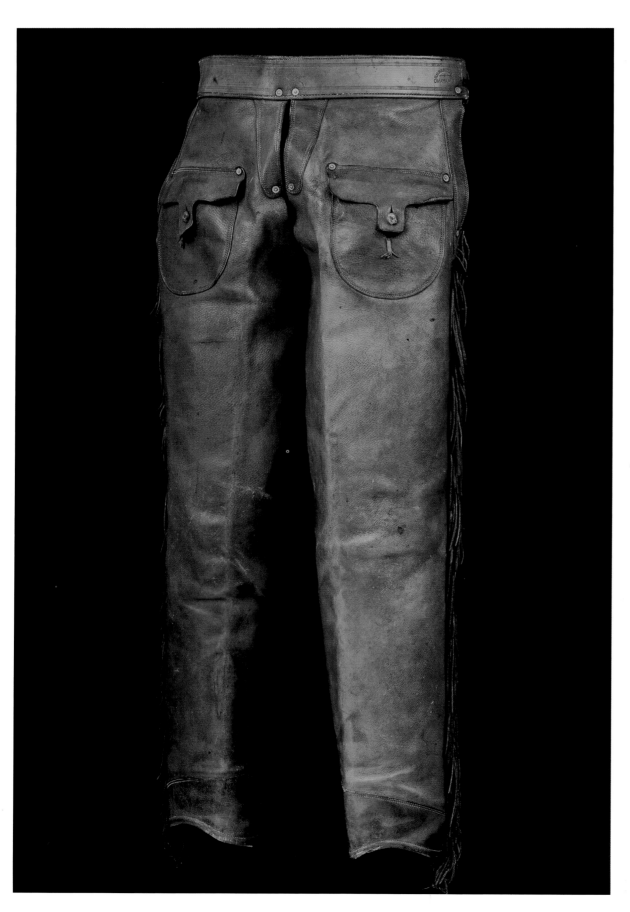

← **Western Chaps**
G. H. and J. S. Collins Saddlery Company
Cheyenne, Wyoming Territory, circa 1880
NCM—Grandee Collection, 1991.1.1263

Designed to protect the rider's legs from thorny brush, leather chaps became a familiar element of cowboy costume. Narrow-legged, "shotgun"-pattern chaps like these appeared at early cowboy tournaments and rodeos throughout the Great Plains and Southwest, but they were supplanted by the more flamboyant "woolie" and "batwing" patterns between 1900 and 1920. This pair features a straight belt, flapped pockets, and decorative fringe down the outer edges of the legs.

→ **Men's Rodeo Chaps**
Al Furstnow Saddlery Company
Miles City, Montana, circa 1910
NCM—Gift of Dan Whitlock, 1982.47.03

These fancy "woolie" chaps incorporate a floral-tooled belt and straight legs covered with angora goat hair in a "salt-and-pepper" pattern. They were worn by Ralph Whitlock, who won a trophy bronc belt as the "Best All Around Cowboy" at the 1916 Glendive, Montana, Frontier Celebration (illustrated in chapter 6).

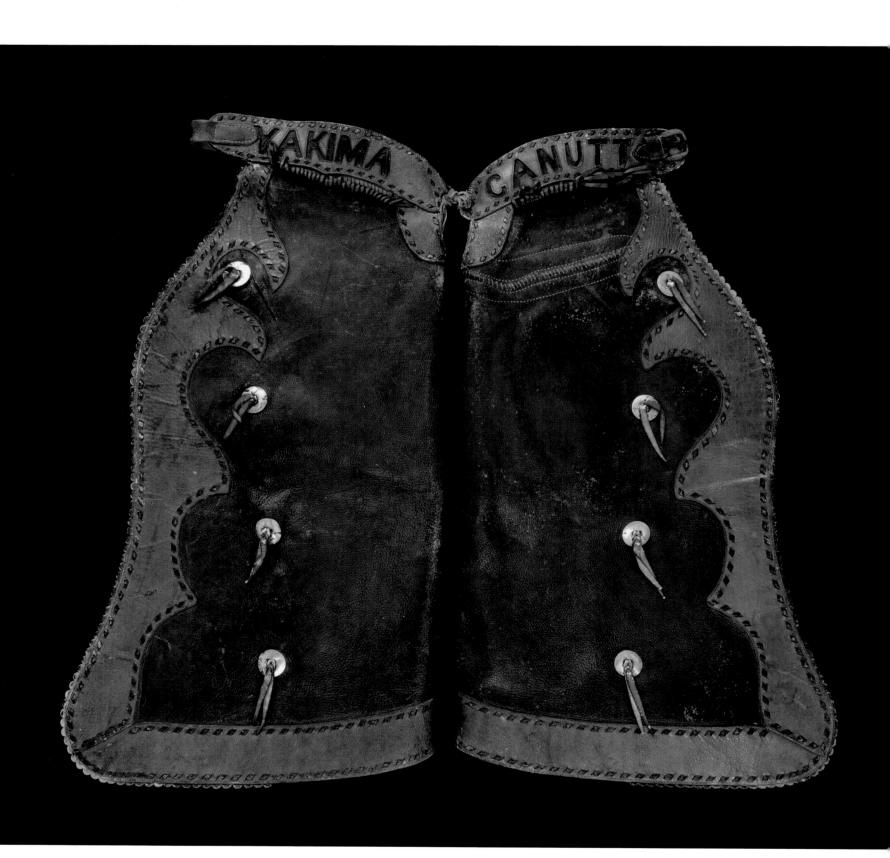

Men's Rodeo Chaps
Maker unknown, circa 1916
NCM—Gift of C. R. Mackey, R.242.03

Appreciated by contestants for their flapping motion in the arena, "batwing"-pattern chaps such as these became widely popular in the 1910s. This custom-made pair belonged to Enos Edward "Yakima" Canutt *(in adjacent photo),* who ranked among rodeo's top hands between 1912 and 1923. He took the all-around championship at the Pendleton, Oregon, Round-Up in 1917, 1919, 1920, and 1923 and was the first to win the Roosevelt Trophy in the latter year. In 1924 Canutt signed with Hollywood, acted in more than forty silent films, and then became a full-time stuntman and stunt coordinator. His stunt-riding credits ranged from *Stagecoach* (1939) to *Cat Ballou* (1965), and he staged the famous chariot race in *Ben Hur* (1959). For his film contributions, Canutt received an Academy Award in 1969.

Yakima Canutt, Ed "Strangler" Lewis, and Frank McCarroll
Colorado Springs, Colorado, Round-Up, 1924
H. H. Garnett, photographer
NCM—Dickinson Research Center
McCarroll Family Trust Collection,
RC2006.076.663

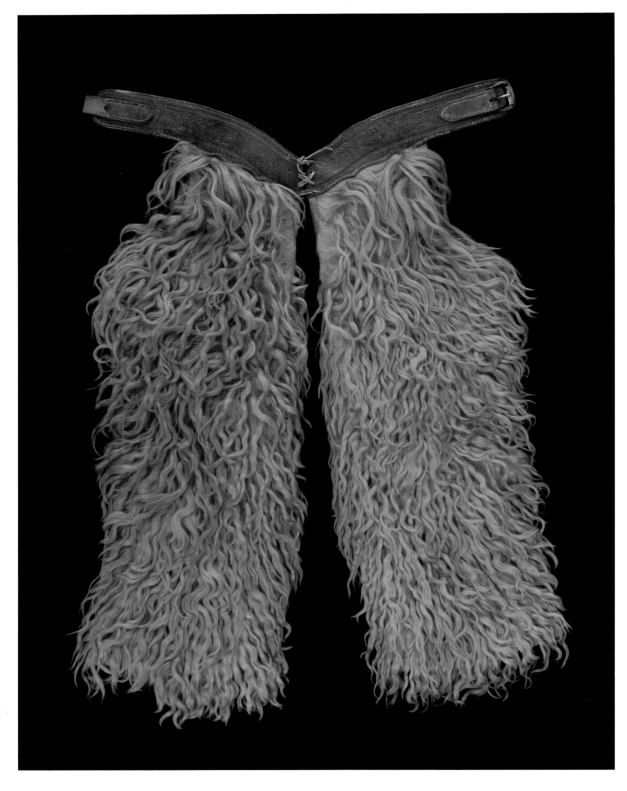

Men's Rodeo Chaps
Maker unknown, circa 1920
NCM—Gift of Louis W. Greger, 1990.04

Fitted with a foliate-tooled belt and dyed a
brilliant orange hue, these "woolie" chaps were
owned by sometime rodeo contestant Shorty
Thompson of Grand County, Colorado. He is
said to have worn them in contests at several
Cheyenne, Wyoming, Frontier Days rodeos
during the early 1920s.

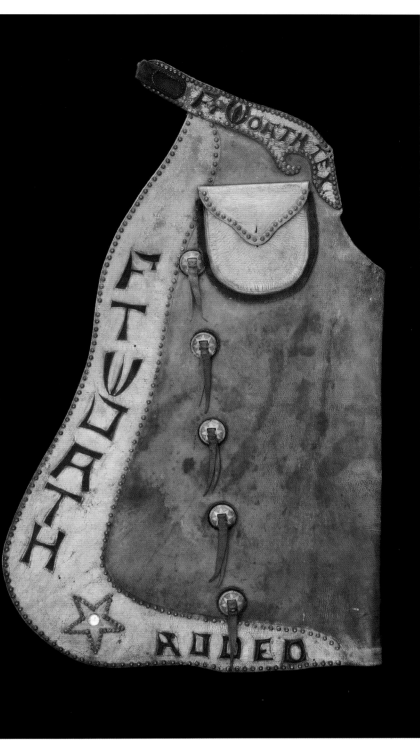

↑ **Men's Rodeo Chaps**
Maker unknown, circa 1920
NCM—Gift of Mrs. Guy Schultz, R.245.07

These extremely wide and flashy "batwing"-pattern chaps incorporate
pierced lettering commemorating the Fort Worth, Texas, Fat Stock Show
rodeo within their yellow borders and feature dual pockets, ten conchas,
and a multitude of decorative brass "spots." They belonged to Guy Shultz,
who performed with the 101 Ranch Real Wild West show and contested as
an all-around hand at many southwestern rodeos. In the adjacent photo,
Shultz models the chaps and an equally flamboyant shirt.

↑ **Wild West and Rodeo Cowboy Guy Shultz**
Fort Worth, Texas
Southwestern Exposition and Fat Stock Show
rodeo, circa 1921
Photographer unknown
NCM—Dickinson Research Center
Aleta Lutz Collection, 2005.123.5

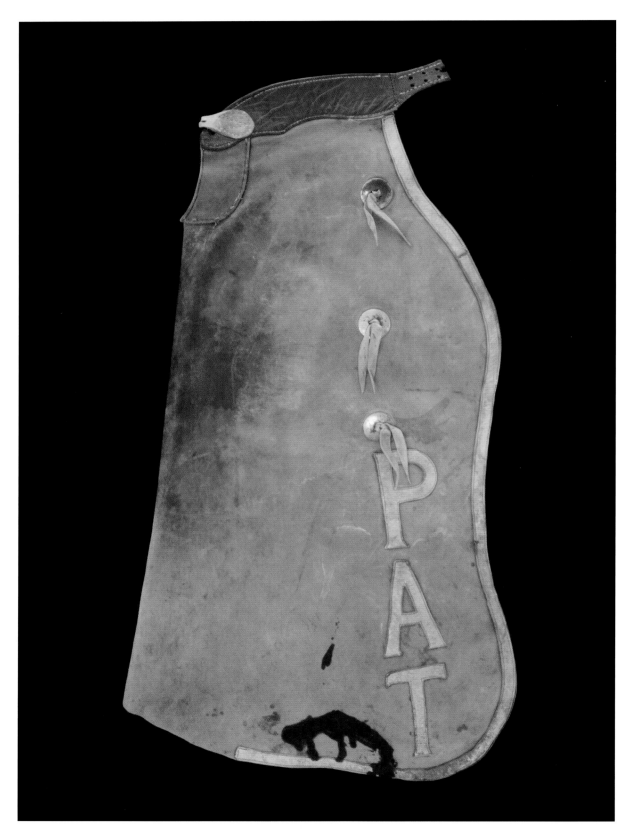

Men's Rodeo Chaps
Maker unknown, circa 1922
NCM—Gift of Ms. Cynthia Olms, 1981.05.02

These well-worn "batwing" chaps belonged to the much-admired, multitalented Paddy Ryan. A champion saddle-bronc rider and consistent winner in most events throughout the 1920s, he claimed the prestigious Roosevelt Trophy in 1924 after winning the all-around titles at both Pendleton, Oregon, and Cheyenne, Wyoming.

Ladies' Rodeo Chaps
Blake Miller Saddlery Company
Cheyenne, Wyoming, 1924
NCM—Gift of Tad Lucas, R.238.05

Tad Lucas wore these white angora "woolie" chaps in bronc-riding competitions for more than a decade. She is credited with introducing and popularizing chaps as a rodeo fashion element among female contenders in the early 1920s. Lucas contested as a top lady bronc rider throughout her career, and she proved equally talented as a relay racer and trick rider.

➜ **Tad Lucas Riding Angel** *(detail)*
Springfield, Missouri, Rodeo, circa 1945
Ralph Russell Doubleday, photographer
NCM—Dickinson Research Center
R. R. Doubleday Collection, 79.026.1634

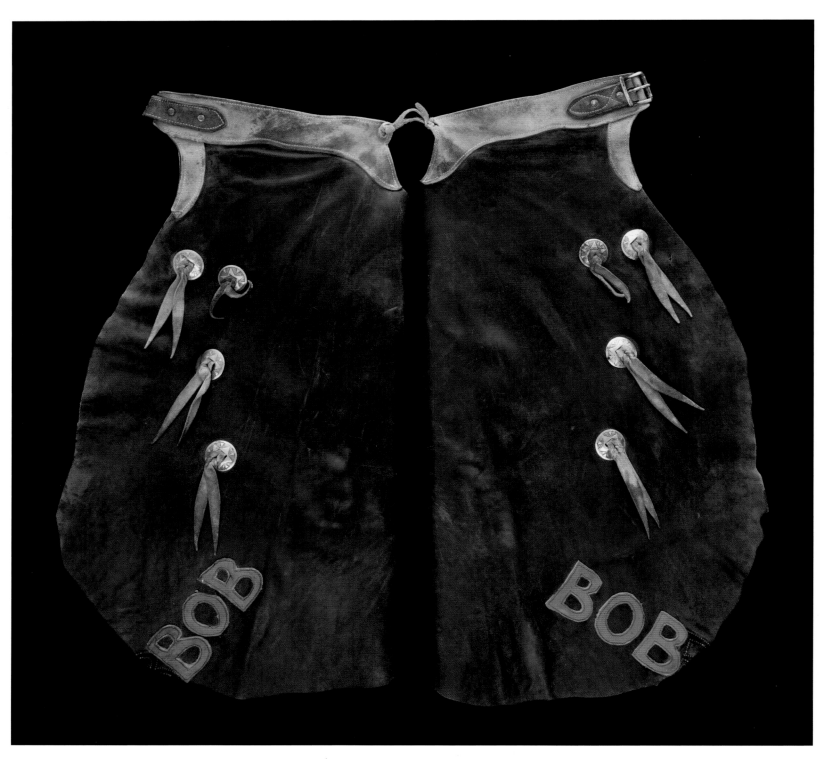

↑ **Men's Rodeo Chaps**
Maker unknown, circa 1925
NCM—Gift of the Bob Askin Family, R.264.02

These relatively broad, multicolored "batwing" chaps were worn by
saddle-bronc rider Bob Askin. During the 1920s and 1930s, Askin took
championship bronc-riding titles at Pendleton, Oregon, and several other
major venues. Fellow rodeo hands admired his poise in riding "unridable"
broncs, among them Midnight, Five Minutes to Midnight, and Hell's Angel.

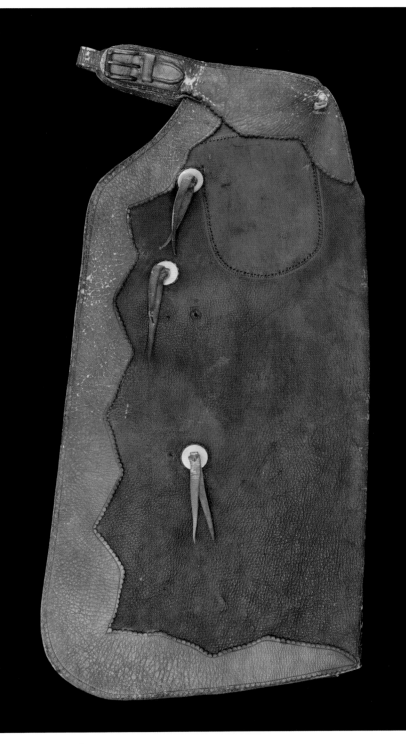

Ladies' Rodeo Chaps

Maker unknown, circa 1930

NCM—Gift of Florence H. Randolph, R.237.23

Finished with nickel-plated conchas and contrasting trim, this pair of "batwing" chaps was a regular part of Florence Randolph's rodeo outfit when saddle-bronc riding. By the late 1920s, most rodeo cowgirls— especially those competing in the rough-stock events—had adopted chaps as both a functional and a fashionable element of their arena attire.

Men's Rodeo Trophy Chaps

N. Porter Saddlery Company

Phoenix, Arizona, 1932

NCM—Gift of Everett Bowman, R.221.03

Rather unusual among rodeo prizes, these chaps are stamped on the belt leather with the inscription "Presented to the Best All-Around Cowboy / Prescott Frontier Days 1932 / by N. Porter Saddle & Harness Co. Phoenix, Arizona." The fancily embellished "batwings" were won—and obviously worn—by Everett Bowman, whose twenty-year career included two all-around championships, plus four in steer wrestling, three in calf roping, and one in steer roping.

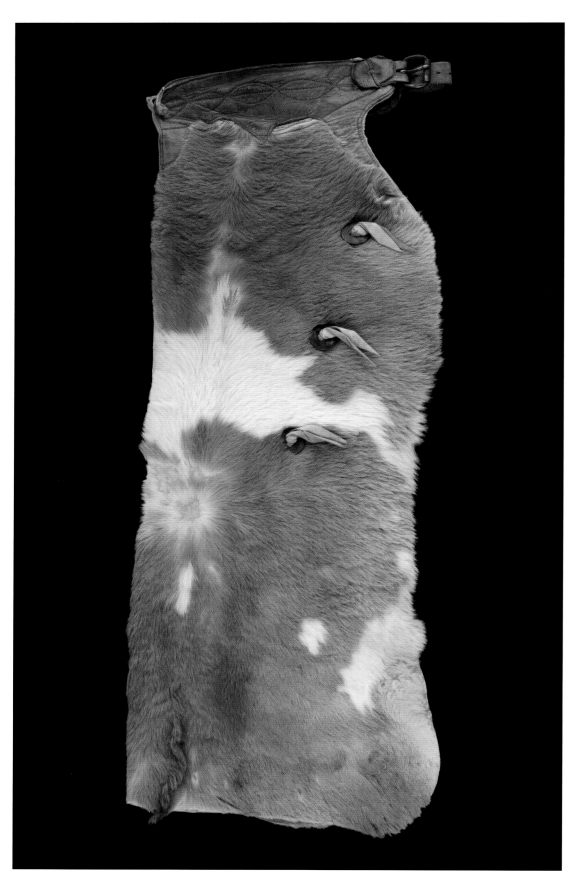

Men's Rodeo Chaps
Maker unknown, circa 1935
NCM—Loan courtesy Frances Fletcher,
LR.215.08

Fashioned from a Hereford cowhide with the hair still on, these "batwing"-pattern chaps belonged to rough-stock rider and steer wrestler George L. "Kid" Fletcher, champion bull rider of the world in 1938. He was recorded as the only contestant ever to make a qualified ride on a peevish Montana mare named Dizzy Bertha and was distinguished in the later 1930s as "the most bowlegged cowboy in America."

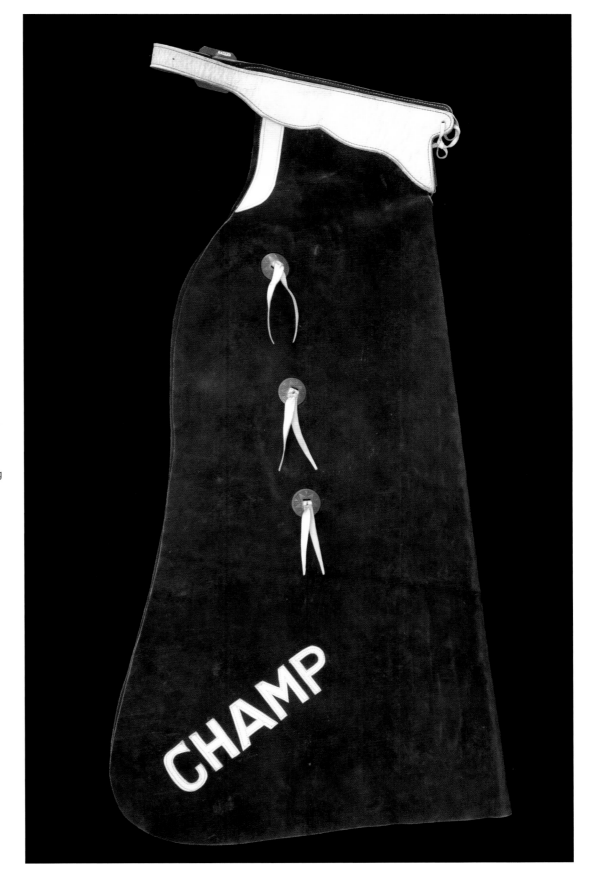

➜ **Men's Rodeo Chaps**
Fred Mueller Saddlery Company
Denver, Colorado, circa 1940
NCM—Gift of Mrs. Vera M. Herder, R.204.05

Finished in contrasting black and white and
adorned with the appellation "Champ," these
"batwing" chaps belonged to bronc rider
Fritz Truan. At the 1939 Madison Square
Garden rodeo, he made a great ride aboard
the notorious Hell's Angel and won the
saddle-bronc championship for the year.
Truan repeated his achievement the following
year and captured the all-around-champion
cowboy title as well.

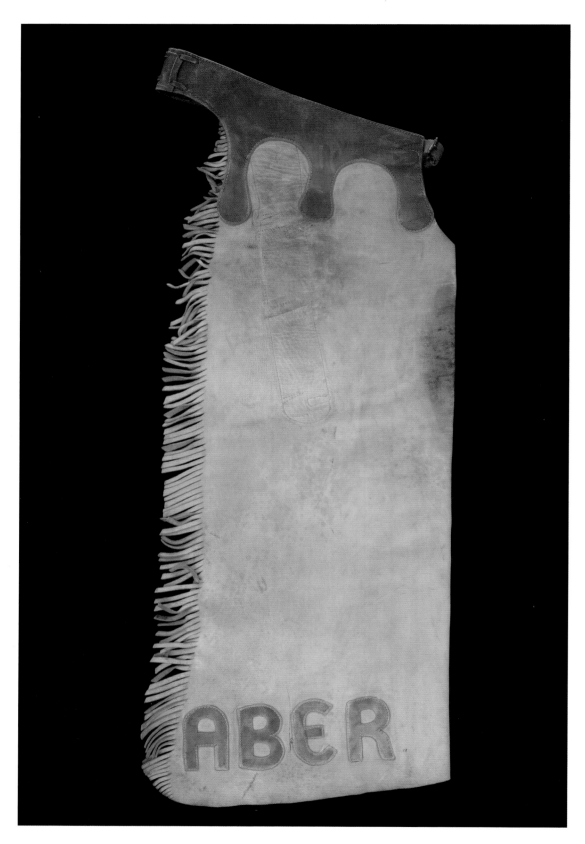

Men's Rodeo Chaps
Maker unknown, circa 1940
NCM—Gift of Mrs. George McElhinney,
R.211.01

Carrying his name in contrasting appliquéd letters, these fringed chaps belonged to Doff Aber, two-time world champion saddle-bronc rider in 1941 and 1942. One of rodeo's great bronc riders, during the late 1930s and early 1940s Aber won on such formidable bucking horses as Five Minutes to Midnight, The Crying Jew, and Goodbye Dan. He was the last hand to make a qualified ride aboard the infamous bronc Hell's Angel.

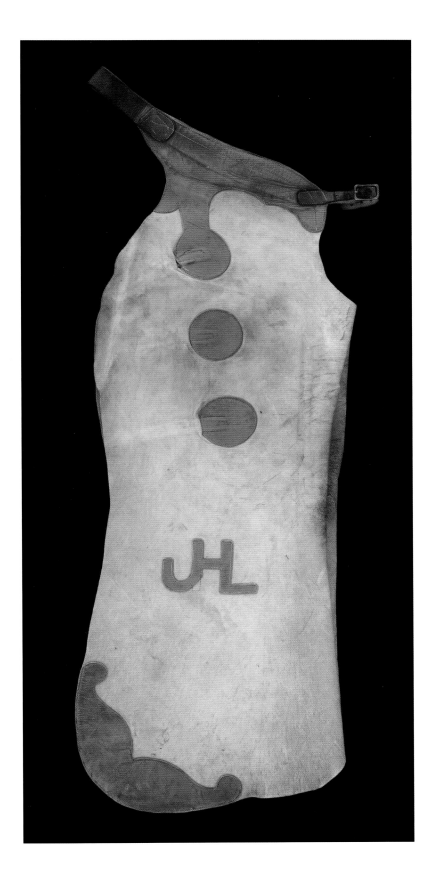

↑ **Bill Linderman on Ham What Am**
Phoenix, Arizona, Rodeo, 1943
DeVere Helfrich, photographer
NCM—Dickinson Research Center
Gene Lamb Collection, 1990.016.113

← **Men's Rodeo Chaps**
Maker unknown, circa 1942
NCM—Gift of Mrs. E. A. Spaulding, R.210.03

Ornamented in red leather trim and carrying his personal brand, these "batwing"-pattern chaps were worn by three-time all-around-champion cowboy Bill Linderman during more than a decade of uncompromising competition. The personalized chaps can be seen in the adjacent image of Linderman as he contests with a saddle bronc named Ham What Am at the Phoenix, Arizona, Rodeo in 1943.

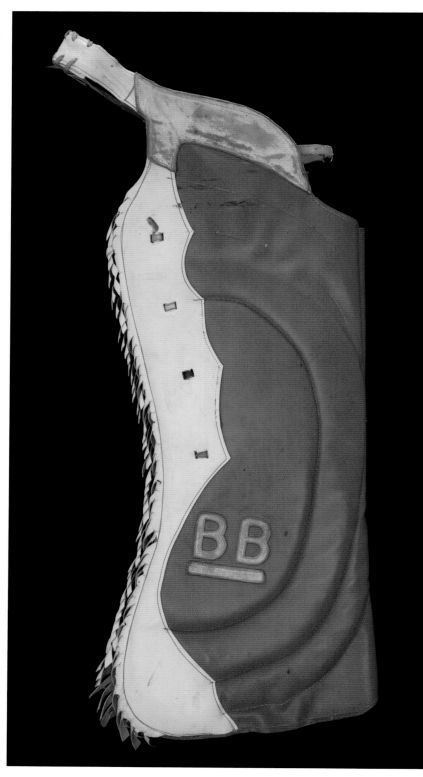

⬆ Men's Rodeo Chaps
Maker unknown, circa 1950
NCM—Loan courtesy Bill Hancock, L.1991.14.01

Well worn and often repaired, these "batwing" chaps with a "Lazy S S" brand were worn by saddle-bronc and bull rider Bill Hancock. Always a contender, in 1952 Hancock won the "Bronc Riding Match of Champions" at Dickinson, North Dakota, defeating leading competitors Casey Tibbs and Deb Copenhaver.

⬆ Men's Rodeo Pick-Up Chaps
Maker unknown, circa 1965
NCM—Gift of John and Mary Villines, 2002.198

Fashioned of red and white vinyl material with leather belt and oversewn brand initials, the legs of these chaps are fully padded to protect against the scrapes and collisions incident to "picking up" bronc riders from their steeds after the arena horn sounds a successful ride.

← **Men's Rodeo Chaps**
Carmen Allen Western Chaps
Stephenville, Texas, circa 1987
NCM—Gift of Clyde and Elsie Frost in memory
of Lane Frost, 2009.23.02

Worn by champion bull rider Lane Frost, these
fancy arena chaps reflect the flamboyance and
quality characteristic of big-business rodeo.
The black cowhide bodies feature pierced,
floral-carved leather overlays at the waist
and thighs (the latter adorned with conchas)
and pearlized or Mylar-covered silver and red
leather overlays along the edges finished out
with silver fringing. Among the top fifteen bull
riders for five consecutive years (1984–88),
Frost won the World Champion Bull Rider title
in 1987. He was killed in the arena by a bull
named Taking Care of Business at the 1989
Cheyenne Frontier Days rodeo.

Ladies' Western Boots and Bronc-Riding Spurs
Hyer Boot Company
Olathe, Kansas, circa 1922
Crockett Bit and Spur Company
Kansas City, Missouri, circa 1925
NCM—Gift of Florence Randolph, R.237.21 A&B and R.237.22 A&B

Displaying fifteen rows of ornamental stitching on their uppers, these diminutive cowgirl boots, with their dainty vamps and underslung heels, were custom made for saddle-bronc rider and trick rider Florence Randolph. The special-order spurs—fitted with nine-point rowels, drop shanks with chap guards, and hand-tooled leathers—feature nickel-silver- and gold-overlaid bands, with stars, crescent moons, and the owner's initials.

Men's Western Boots
Maker unknown, circa 1895
NCM—Grandee Collection, 1991.1.505 A&B

Designed for use on horseback, western-pattern boots—with their comparatively narrow toes, underslung heels, and relatively tall tops—were an important element of the historic cowboy's outfit. Readily adopted by contestants in the arena, today such cowboy boots, in innumerable styles and decorative treatments, are a traditional part of rodeo costume.

Ladies' Bathing Shoes
Maker unknown, circa 1925
NCM—Gift of Tad Lucas, R.238.29 A&B

Worn by Tad Lucas not for bathing but for trick riding, these satin lace-up shoes have thin leather soles applied for greater traction in moving around the horse. Between 1925 and 1933, Lucas captured the trick-riding title at Fort Worth four times, at Cheyenne twice, at Chicago three times, and at Madison Square Garden an unrivaled seven times.

Men's Western Shoe-Boots
Hyer Boot Company
Olathe, Kansas, 1926
NCM—Gift of D. W. Frommer III, 1989.24 A&B

Custom made for sometime rodeo contestant Frank Finch, these lace-up shoe-boots of black calfskin feature narrow box toes, underslung heels, multicolored floral stitchery on the uppers, and the owner's name inlaid at the tops. Such footwear was popular from the 1890s into the 1930s. Custom-boot-maker D. W. Frommer III revived this "packer" style in the 1980s, and the Justin Boot Company has since produced a commercial version known as the lace-up roper.

Ladies' Western Boots and Bronc-Riding Spurs
Hyer Boot Company
Olathe, Kansas, 1928
McChesney Bit and Spur Company
Pauls Valley, Oklahoma, circa 1925
NCM—Gift of Tad Lucas, R.238.07 A&B and R.238.06 A&B

Custom made for rodeo champion Tad Lucas, these diminutive cowgirl boots incorporate floral-inlaid and foliate-stitched uppers with kangaroo vamps over high underslung heels. Half mounted with engraved silver, the spurs have drop shanks with chap guards and twelve-point spoked rowels. For greater stability in the arena, the spurs are secured with auxiliary heel straps and shank tie-downs.

➜ Men's Western Boots and Presentation Spurs
Bohlin Saddlery and Silversmiths
Hollywood, California, circa 1940
NCM—Gift of the Gretchen Elliott Estate, R.271.02 A&B and R.271.01 A&B

Worn by rodeo producer and stock contractor Verne Elliott, these custom-made alligator boots feature floral-carved uppers with silver embellishments and the initials "VE" at the tops. A presentation to Elliott from band leader Paul Whiteman, the Bohlin-made spurs feature cookie-cutter rowels on both the shanks and the chap guards, and engraved silver overlays on the spur bodies with "Verne Elliott" in gold script. The deluxe spur leathers are also from the Bohlin shop.

⬇ Rodeo Stockman and Manager
Vern Elliott
Fort Worth, Texas, Southwestern Exposition
and Fat Stock Show rodeo, 1948
Photographer unknown
NCM—Dickinson Research Center
Photographic Study Collection,
2006-190.39.10

⬆ Ladies' Western Boots
Hyer Boot Company
Olathe, Kansas, circa 1938
NCM—Permanent Collection, R.276.03 A&B

These white calfskin boots, with their box toes and underslung heels, were worn by bronc and trick rider Vaughn Krieg, who won the ladies' bronc-riding championship at Madison Square Garden in 1934. A pioneer in promoting women's rodeo, she organized the Flying V All Cow-Girl Rodeo Company in 1942.

➜ Men's Western Boots

L. White Boot Company
Fort Worth, Texas, circa 1945
NCM—Gift of Cecil Cornish, 1994.56.01 A&B

These custom-made boots belonged to equestrian performer Cecil Cornish. They feature narrow box toes, stitched-in toe bugs on the black calfskin vamps, moderately underslung heels, and uppers inlaid in a varicolored modified butterfly motif. Cornish's trademark was Roman riding and jumping, in which he rode two horses at full gallop, one foot on the back of each mount, taking the team through a ring of fire.

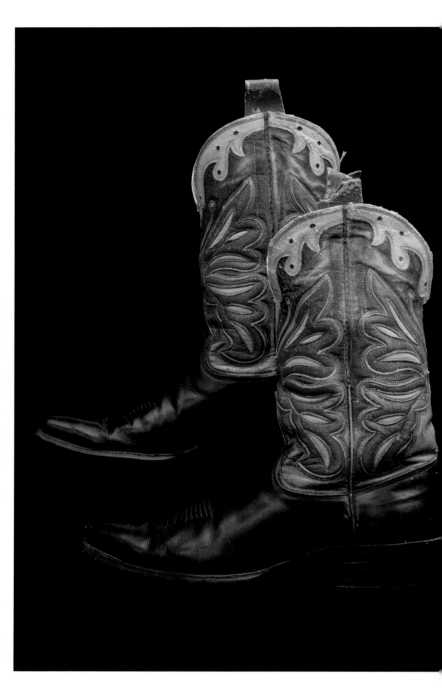

⬆ Trick Riding Boots

Maker unknown, circa 1940
NCM—Gift of Cecil Cornish, 1994.56.04 A&B

Resoled with synthetic rubber for a sure grip around the saddle, these boots were worn by talented trick rider Don Wilcox in the 1940s and 1950s. He headlined for all of the major producers, including Colonel W. T. Johnson, Verne Elliott, Gene Autry, Everett Colborn, Beutler Brothers, and Harry Knight, during a thirty-one-year career.

➜ Men's Western Boots and Arena Spurs

Bootmaker unknown, circa 1950
Crockett Bit and Spur Company
Boulder, Colorado, circa 1945
NCM—Gift of Sam Garrett, 1986.11.11 A&B and 1986.11.12 A&B

Custom made for western performer Sam Garrett, these boots feature calfskin vamps with wing-tipped toes and heels, and colorful butterfly and floral motifs inlaid on the uppers. The spurs are overlaid with engraved silver carrying Garrett's initials. The spur leathers, from the N. Porter Saddlery Company of Phoenix, Arizona, are floral tooled and sport engraved button covers and ranger-style buckles of engraved sterling silver

→ **Ladies' Western Dress Boots**
Justin Boot Company
Fort Worth, Texas, 1954
NCM—Gift of June Ivory, 1989.33.01 A&B

The ultimate in cowgirl footwear, these lavish
boots were custom made by Justin's for rodeo
administrator and entry-parade rider June
Ivory. Incorporating narrow toes and low
walking heels, the boots are fashioned of rich
purple calfskin and embellished with gold
leaf inlay at the tops and unique "raised-rose"
motifs over the vamps and uppers. The boots
were a gift of appreciation from 1954 world
champion cowboy Buck Rutherford.

→ Men's Western Dress Boots
Justin Boot Company
Fort Worth, Texas, circa 1955
NCM—Gift of Mrs. E. A. Spaulding,
R.210.02 A&B

Fashioned of chocolate calfskin, these western
dress boots feature narrow toes and flat
"walking" heels with simply stitched uppers.
They were worn by Bill Linderman during
his years as the president (1951–57) and
secretary-treasurer (1962–65) of the Rodeo
Cowboys Association. Called "The King" on
the circuit, Linderman introduced a new
professionalism to the sport during an era of
rapid growth and fundamental change.

← Ladies' Western Dress / Arena Boots
Nocona Boot Company
Nocona, Texas, circa 1955
NCM—Gift of Mr. and Mrs. Glenn Randall,
1989.30.11

Worn by equestrian star Lynn Randall, these
custom-ordered boots are finished in the
spotted skin of the rare South American
Geoffroy's cat. Such exotic footwear would
have been reserved in the rodeo arena to
entry-parade spectacles and flag ceremonies.
(These boots were part of Randall's parade
ensemble, illustrated earlier in this chapter.)

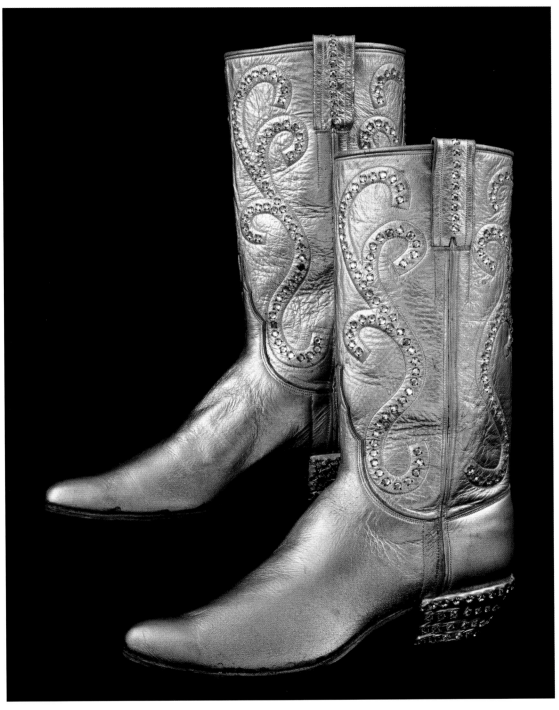

↑ Ladies' Western Arena Boots
Nudie's Rodeo Tailors
North Hollywood, California, circa 1960
NCM—Gift of June Ivory, 1989.33.03 A&B

Fashioned of gold-toned leather with narrow toes, underslung heels,
and rhinestone accents, these boots were worn by June Ivory for riding
in quadrille performances and entry parades throughout the 1960s.
Ivory, however, made her greatest contributions to the cowboy sport in
management and programming, serving as an RCA and PRCA secretary and
timer at rodeos throughout the United States for more than forty years.

→ **Men's Western "Tenniboots"**
Tony Lama Boot Company
El Paso, Texas, circa 1985
NCM—Gift of Brad W. Chill, 2000.14 A&B

Combining tennis shoes with cowboy-boot uppers, this decidedly short-lived craze in western wear won a number of devotees among rodeo's bullfighting clowns. They found that the flat, hard-rubber soles provided good traction in the arena when maneuvering with an outraged Brahma crossbred.

↑ **Men's Western Boots and Spurs**
Tony Lama Boot Company
El Paso, Texas, circa 1965
Spur maker unknown, circa 1960
NCM—Gift of Decie Goodspeed, 1993.19.01 A&B and 1993.19.02 A&B

Featuring simulated elephant hide (actually bullhide) vamps, calfskin uppers, and low walking heels, these well-worn boots belonged to rodeo steer roper Buck Goodspeed. His rather generic, Texas-style spurs feature swinging buttons, slightly dropped shanks, and sharply toothed five-point star rowels. Goodspeed ranked among steer roping's top five contenders from 1945 through 1948. He retired from active competition in 1956.

→ **Men's Western Dress/Arena Boots**
M. L. Leddy and Sons
San Angelo, Texas, circa 1975
NCM—Gift of Toots Mansfield, 1997.13.02 A&B

Well worn by seven-time calf-roping champion Toots Mansfield, these boots feature vamps of exotic anteater skin, low "roping" heels, and calfskin uppers with five rows of flame-pattern stitching. In addition to his many championships, Mansfield operated one of the first rodeo training schools and served as president of the Rodeo Cowboys Association from 1945 to 1951.

8 Rodeo Artwork
From the Fine to the Commercial

FROM HIGH TO LOW, the artistic expression inspired by rodeo may be considered a subgenre of American western art and, more particularly, western cowboy art. Such work derives from the aesthetic tradition of realism; whether created as fine art or made for commercial purposes, it usually embodies the representational and narrative qualities today considered characteristic of western art. Rodeo art finds its origins in the nineteenth- and early-twentieth-century illustration, painting, and sculpture of masters such as Frederic Remington and Charles M. Russell and also in the bold and colorful advertising posters of the ubiquitous Wild West shows that were then popular in America and Europe. Not unlike these principal artistic influences, rodeo artwork focuses heavily on cowboy subject matter, especially on bronc-riding imagery.

Particularly significant among the museum's fine-art holdings relevant to rodeo are the original color drawings created by Charles Simpson at Tex Austin's first London rodeo in 1924. Subsequently published in portfolio as *El Rodeo* in 1925, these include both action tableaus of arena events and field portraits of prominent contestants. Rather less refined are the contestant portraits rendered by esteemed rodeo historian and amateur artist Clifford P. Westermeier in the latter 1940s. Also within the realm of fine art are the superlative rodeo-event bronzes created by western sculptor Robert M. Scriver between 1968 and 1973 for his "Rodeo Series," a sequence of thirty-two bronze castings celebrating the sport. The Scriver bronzes are complemented by the limited-edition etchings of contemporary western artist and sculptor Sandy Scott, whose 1977 "Rodeo Suite" also portrays the sport's principal events. Rounding out the fine art treating rodeo themes are the portraits of all-around champion cowboys originally commissioned by the R. J. Reynolds Tobacco Company and presented to the museum during the 1970s and into the mid-1980s. These principal bodies of work are enriched by a miscellany of rodeo sculptures by artists Harry Jackson, Hollis Williford, Buckeye Blake, Earl Bascom, Jay O'Meilia, Ann Ayres, and Richard Loffler.

The commercial artwork inspired by rodeo appears occasionally in poster format, but it is encountered far more frequently in the cover art of venue programs. Colorful and dynamic, such work presents a range of artistic expression and quality that reflects the broader influences of art and advertising over time. From the early 1920s well into the 1940s, for example, rodeo program covers drew on the earlier chromolithograph-poster tradition of Wild West shows and circuses and on the more contemporary pulp-illustration genre. From the mid-1930s into the 1960s, the often-simplistic, three-to-four-color artwork prevalent in commercial advertising dominated the genre. During the 1970s, several rodeo venues adopted original western illustration for their program covers—a few even appropriated the work of recognized western masters such as W. H. D. Koerner, Philip R. Goodwin, and W. R. Leigh. The use of contemporary western illustrators and artists for rodeo program covers continues today. Though this commercial material, such as the modernist renditions seen on recent National Finals Rodeo program covers, rarely approaches the level of truly fine art, it amply captures the color, drama, and tradition of the sport.

← **Commemorative Rodeo Drawing**
Francis Harden Steele, 1924
Pen and India ink on sheepskin,
60 × 51 inches
NCM—Gift of the McCarroll Family Trust,
2006.08.11

Among the more unusual mediums of rodeo artwork, this finely detailed memorial tribute features a central portrait of Bonnie McCarroll with the Selfridge Trophy, surrounded by smaller portraits of Frank McCarroll and rodeo manager Tex Austin and a varied panoply of vignettes of the couple's arena exploits. The work is titled at bottom: "Bonnie & Frank McCarroll / Champion Bulldogger and International / Champion Ladie [*sic*] Bronk [*sic*] Rider."

Charles Simpson

English illustrator and painter Charles Simpson (1878–1942) trained at Academie Julian in Paris and specialized in oil and watercolor paintings of birds, animals, hunting scenes, and landscapes. He exhibited often at the Royal Academy and at the Paris Salon between 1910 and 1940. His artistic awards included a gold medal at the Panama-Pacific International Exposition in San Francisco in 1914, a silver medal at the Paris Salon in 1923, and a gold medal for sporting art in association with the 1924 Paris Olympics.

In 1924, Simpson attended Tex Austin's First International Rodeo, conducted at London's Wembley Stadium in conjunction with the British Empire Exhibition. Captivated by the activity and color of the western extravaganza, Simpson produced approximately one hundred sketches and crayon drawings of the event and its leading contestants, which he subsequently published as *El Rodeo* in 1925.[1] Through the generosity of Charles M. Bennett, the museum acquired fifty of Simpson's original rodeo works in 1980, a selection of which follow.

➜ **Charles Simpson**
***Vera McGinnis on Horseback,* 1924**
Crayon on paper, 19 × 23 inches
NCM—Gift of Charles M. Bennett, 1980.5.11

➜ **Charles Simpson**
***Tex Austin on Horseback,* 1924**
Signed by the subject; crayon on paper,
19 × 23 inches
NCM—Gift of Charles M. Bennett, 1980.5.16

Vera McGinnis

Charles Simpson

↑ Charles Simpson
***Add P. Day of Medicine Hat,* 1924**
Signed by the subject; crayon on paper,
19 × 23 inches
NCM—Gift of Charles M. Bennett, 1980.5.05

⬅ **Charles Simpson**
Walter P. O'Grote on TNT, **1924**
Crayon and pencil on paper, 19 × 23 inches
NCM—Gift of Charles M. Bennett, 1980.5.13

⬅ **Charles Simpson**
Ruth Roach on Buddy, **1924**
Crayon and pencil on paper, 11 × 15 inches
NCM—Gift of Charles M. Bennett, 1980.5.30

↑ **Charles Simpson**
The Stable Tent—Showing Sea-Chests and Saddlery, 1924
Crayon on paper, 19 × 23 inches
NCM—Gift of Charles M. Bennett, 1980.5.07

⬆ **Charles Simpson**
Getting Ready for the Afternoon Performance, 1924
Crayon on paper, 19 × 23 inches
NCM—Gift of Charles M. Bennett, 1980.5.17

Charles Simpson
War Bonnet, 1924
Crayon and pencil on paper, 11 × 15 inches
NCM—Gift of Charles M. Bennett, 1980.5.41

Charles Simpson
Bronco Busting, 1924
Crayon and pencil on paper, 11 × 15 inches
NCM—Gift of Charles M. Bennett, 1980.5.42

← **Charles Simpson**
*The Wrestler Fails to Throw
an Obstinate Steer*, **1924**
Crayon and pencil on paper, 11 × 15 inches
NCM—Gift of Charles M. Bennett, 1980.5.27

← **Charles Simpson**
Steer Wrestling—Down, **1924**
Crayon and pencil on paper, 11 × 15 inches
NCM—Gift of Charles M. Bennett, 1980.5.24

↑ **Charles Simpson**
Mounting a Bronc from the Chute—
Bonnie McCarroll, **1924**
Opaque watercolor on paper, 22 × 30 inches
NCM—Gift of Charles M. Bennett, 1980.5.01

⬆ **Charles Simpson**
A Mishap—Steer Wrestling, **1924**
Opaque watercolor on paper, 22 × 30 inches
NCM—Gift of Charles M. Bennett, 1980.5.02

➜ **Charles Simpson**
Dorothy Morrell, 1924
Crayon and pencil on paper, 15 × 11 inches
NCM—Gift of Charles M. Bennett, 1980.5.35

⬆ **Charles Simpson**
Ruth Roach, 1924
Crayon and pencil on paper, 15 × 11 inches
NCM—Gift of Charles M. Bennett, 1980.5.44

➜ **Charles Simpson**
Bonnie McCarroll, 1924
Crayon and pencil on paper, 15 × 11 inches
NCM—Gift of Charles M. Bennett, 1980.5.43

Charles Simpson
Tad Barnes [Lucas], **1924**
Crayon and pencil on paper, 15 × 11 inches
NCM—Gift of Charles M. Bennett, 1980.5.22

"Tad" Barnes

Clifford P. Westermeier

Historian Clifford Westermeier (1910–1987) is remembered today as the author of two western classics: *Man, Beast, Dust: The Story of Rodeo* (1947) and *Trailing the Cowboy: His Life and Lore as Told by Frontier Journalists* (1955). His first formal training, however, was in art, at the Pratt Institute in Brooklyn and the New York School of Fine and Applied Arts in Paris, and he subsequently taught the subject at the University of Buffalo. Visiting the West in the mid-1930s, he began depicting the cowboy culture that so entirely captivated him.

In his research for advanced degrees in history at Colorado University during the 1940s, Westermeier became intimately acquainted with rodeo sport, and he sketched and painted many of its events, animals, and leading personalities. Today quite scarce, most of this rodeo artwork resides at the University of Colorado Library in Boulder. The museum, however, retains a few Westermeier portraits of the champion cowboys whom he particularly admired, including rodeo greats Fritz Truan and Doff Aber.[2]

→ **Clifford P. Westermeier**
Doff Aber, circa 1942
Oil on canvas, 25 × 18 inches
NCM—Anonymous gift, 1984.07

→ **Clifford P. Westermeier**
Fritz Truan, circa 1942
Oil on canvas, 25 × 18 inches
NCM—Anonymous gift,
1984.06

Robert M. Scriver

Montana sculptor Bob Scriver (1914–1999) trained in early life as a musician, receiving advanced degrees from VanderCook College of Music in Chicago. Although he pursued a music career into middle age, his experience in taxidermy ultimately sparked an interest in sculpture. Over the ensuing years, Scriver's American Indian, hunting, wildlife, and cowboy bronzes received favorable comparison to the work of western artist Charles M. Russell, and he garnered valued commissions with various museums, businesses, and organizations.

In 1968, the Rodeo Cowboys Association and the National Cowboy Hall of Fame and Western Heritage Center commissioned Scriver to produce a heroic-size bronze statue of rodeo champion Bill Linderman. That work, entitled *The King,* inspired the artist to undertake a sequence of thirty-two bronzes celebrating all of the events and several other facets of the sport. Produced between 1968 and 1973, Scriver's "Rodeo Series" includes many very dynamic works, perhaps most notably *An Honest Try* and *Pay Window.*[3]

→ **Robert M. Scriver**
Pay Window, 1968
Bronze, 28 × 25 × 14 inches
NCM—Museum purchase, 1970.30

This bronze portrays the energy and jarring motion of the bareback-bronc-riding event. The vigorous action of horse and rider are suggested in the strong diagonal lines and the telling arrangement of seemingly off-balance masses.

⬇ **Robert M. Scriver**
Beating the Slack, 1968
Bronze, 22 × 36 × 15 inches
NCM—Museum purchase, 1998.13.03

Beating the Slack captures an impression of the incredible speed and finesse demanded in calf roping. The sculpture portrays the crucial moment as the horse stops and the cowboy dismounts to catch the calf as it hits the end of the catch rope.

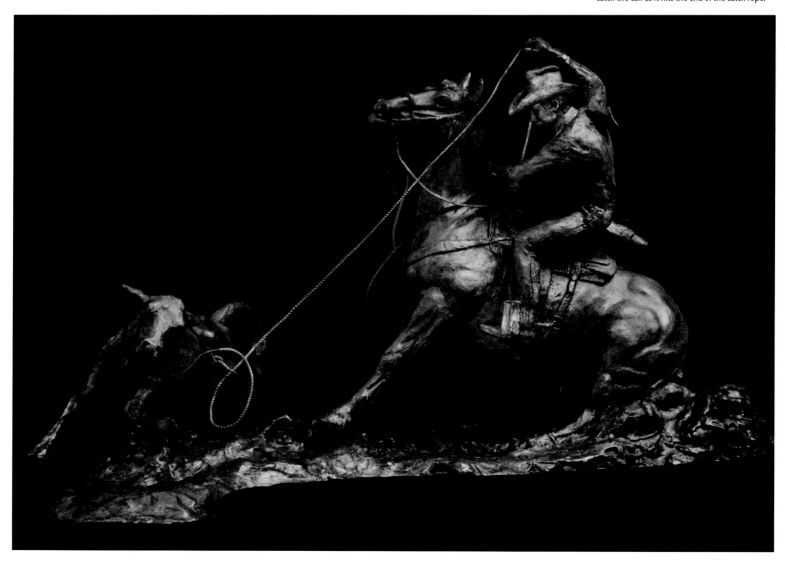

↑ Robert M. Scriver
Twisting His Tail, 1968
Bronze, 11 × 19 × 12 inches
NCM—Museum purchase, 1998.13.04

This work captures the opposing dynamics
of brute force and reckless momentum as
the cowboy slows a 500-pound steer before
wrestling him to the ground. A feeling of
arrested forward motion is created by the
diagonal lines in the legs of cowboy and
steer—as well as by the horizontal line of the
steer's tail.

← Robert M. Scriver
National Finals, 1972
Bronze, 20 × 19 × 14 inches
NCM—Museum purchase, 1998.13.01

One of more than thirty sculptures in the
Rodeo Series, *National Finals* depicts the
classic event of saddle-bronc riding. In its form
and line, the bronze illustrates the essential
rhythm between the horse and rider that
makes for a truly competitive score.

← **Robert M. Scriver**
Steer Jerker, 1972
Bronze, 18 × 42 × 22 inches
NCM—Museum purchase, 1998.13.02

Freezing the dramatic moment when the horse
and rider trip, or "jerk-down," a 600-pound
steer before the tie-down, this bronze captures
the energy and motion of a traditional range
skill and rodeo competition practiced at only a
few venues today.

 Robert M. Scriver
An Honest Try, 1968
Bronze, 31 × 21 × 29 inches
NCM—Museum purchase, 1971.22

An Honest Try depicts the unleashed bucking
power and violent spinning action of a one-
ton Brahma bull as it attempts to unload a
tenacious cowboy. This dynamic bronze is
one of the finest among the more than thirty
pieces in Scriver's Rodeo Series.

← **Robert M. Scriver**
Headin' for Home, 1968
Bronze, 16 × 20 × 13 inches
NCM—Museum purchase, 1998.13.05

Headin' for Home depicts the speed and
coordination that are decisive in the cowgirls'
barrel racing event. The sculpture captures
the crucial moment when horse and rider
negotiate a tight turn around the last barrel
before accelerating down the arena to the
finish line.

⬆ **Robert M. Scriver**
The King, **1968**
Bronze, 90 × 52 × 38 inches
NCM—Permanent Collection, 1973.19

The first sculpture in western artist Bob Scriver's Rodeo Series, this heroic-sized bronze of Bill Linderman was commissioned by the Rodeo Cowboys Association in 1968. *The King* captures not only Linderman's physical likeness but also what he represented—the typical professional rodeo cowboy during the second golden age of the sport. The imposing piece now stands at the entrance of the American Rodeo Gallery at the National Cowboy & Western Heritage Museum.

→ **Robert M. Scriver**
The Champ, 1973
Bronze, 18 × 8 × 7 inches
NCM—Gift of Jim Shoulders, 1998.72.47

The final sculpture in Bob Scriver's Rodeo
Series, *The Champ* immortalizes the character
and athletic prowess of sixteen-time world
champion Jim Shoulders. The piece was
modeled as a companion to the heroic-sized
statue of Bill Linderman, *The King,* but never
cast in heroic scale.

Sandy Scott

Sandy Scott (1943–) took art instruction at the Kansas City Art Institute and began her career as a background animation artist with the motion-picture industry. During the 1970s, she mastered traditional, centuries-old etching and printmaking techniques, creating superb wildlife and sporting scenes and winning awards from the New York Pen and Brush Club, the National Academy of Design, and other prestigious organizations. Scott subsequently turned her talents to sculpting; today, her wildlife bronzes are exhibited at museums throughout the country.

In 1977, Sandy Scott received a commission from the National Cowboy Hall of Fame and Western Heritage Center to execute a series of etchings depicting the principal rodeo events of the time. The resulting "Rodeo Suite," comprising six hand-pulled prints on French hand-laid paper, was produced in a limited edition of one hundred sets. The following year, the "Rodeo Suite" was displayed as part of a forty-piece exhibition of Scott's etchings, making her the first woman and the first etcher to command a dedicated, one-person show at the museum.[4]

➜ **Sandy Scott**
***Saddle Bronc*, 1/100, 1977**
Etching on paper, 14 × 12 inches
NCM—Museum commission, 1984.15.2

⬇ **Sandy Scott**
***Calf Roping*, 1/100, 1977**
Etching on paper, 11 × 15 inches
NCM—Museum commission, 1984.15.1

$\frac{1}{100}$ Saddle Bronc   Sandy Scott

1/100   Bareback Bronc   Sandy Scott

¹/₁₀₀   *Steer Wrestling*   *Sandy Scott*

↑ **Sandy Scott**
***Steer Wrestling,* 1/100, 1977**
Etching on paper, 11 ½ × 15 inches
NCM—Museum commission, 1984.15.6

← **Sandy Scott**
***Bareback Bronc,* 1/100, 1977**
Etching on paper, 14 × 12 inches
NCM—Museum commission, 1984.15.5

$\frac{1}{100}$ *Team Roping*   SS   *Sandy Scott*

⬆ **Sandy Scott**
Team Roping, **1/100, 1977**
Etching on paper, 11 × 15 inches
NCM—Museum commission, 1984.15.4

➜ **Sandy Scott**
Bull Riding, **1/100, 1977**
Etching on paper, 14 × 12 inches
NCM—Museum commission, 1984.15.3

1/100   Bull Riding.   Sandy Scott

R. J. Reynolds Tobacco Company

Commencing in 1971, the R. J. Reynolds Tobacco Company of Winston-Salem, North Carolina, became a prominent commercial sponsor of rodeo—at least partly in response to the ban of tobacco-product advertising on television. In the ensuing years, the firm committed as much as $175,000 in annual cash prizes to the sport through the Winston Championship Awards and the later Winston Rodeo Series program. The company also served rodeo committees and spectators through its contribution of electronic scoreboards at Winston Series venues around the country.

In 1973, the R. J. Reynolds Tobacco Company also commenced underwriting the cost of commissioned portraits of current and several previous all-around champions in its support of the rodeo program at the National Cowboy Hall of Fame and Western Heritage Center. This magnanimous sponsorship brought the museum a dozen works by well-known artists such as William F. Draper (1912–2003), Robert Rishell (1917–1976), Charles Banks Wilson (1918–), and Francis H. Beaugureau (1920–1991), a sampling of which follow.[5]

➜ **Charles Banks Wilson**
Jim Shoulders, 1979
Oil on canvas, 44 × 24 inches
NCM—Gift of R. J. Reynolds Tobacco
Company, 1979.29

↑ **Francis H. Beaugureau**
Casey Tibbs, **1981**
Oil on canvas, 42 × 34 inches
NCM—Gift of R. J. Reynolds Tobacco Company, 1983.46

⬆ **Francis H. Beaugureau**
Dean Oliver, **1978**
Oil on canvas, 36 × 30 inches
NCM—Gift of R. J. Reynolds Tobacco Company,
1978.12

⬆ **Robert Rishell**
Larry Mahan, **1974**
Oil on canvas, 30 × 36 inches
NCM—Gift of R. J. Reynolds Tobacco Company,
1975.18

William F. Draper
Roy Cooper, 1984
Oil on canvas, 44 × 31 inches
NCM—Gift of R. J. Reynolds Tobacco Company,
1984.48

↑ **Philip (Jay) O'Meilia (1927–)**
***Bill Pickett, 1870–1932,* circa 1966**
Bronze, 13 ×26 ×17 inches
NCM—Gift of the 101 Ranch Foundation,
1975.25

Here, the indomitable black cowboy, widely
agreed to have been the originator of the
bulldogging or steer wrestling event in rodeo,
applies some twisting leverage preparatory
to "putting the bite" on a rather substantial
Longhorn steer.

➜ **Earl Bascom (1906–1995)**
***Turk Greenough on Five Minutes
to Midnight,* 1982**
Bronze, 18 ×19 ×10 inches
NCM—Gift of Leslie Bell, 1983.64.01

One-time husband of fan-dancer Sally Rand,
famed bronc buster Thurkel James "Turk"
Greenough became the first American to
capture the so-called Triple Crown of rodeo
in 1936, winning at Cheyenne, Calgary, and
Pendleton. As portrayed here, he successfully
mastered the infamous bronc Five Minutes
to Midnight (on three separate occasions).
Painter and sculptor Earl Bascom, a legitimate
rodeo contender for twenty years, is
remembered as the designer of the Bascom
rigging, the one-handed bareback-bronc
rigging still in use today.

Harry Jackson (1924–)
Two Champs, 1974
Polychrome bronze, 33 ×19 ×16 inches
NCM—Museum purchase, 1998.72.13

Capturing the color and flamboyance of early-day rodeo, this painted sculpture depicts bronc rider Clayton Danks aboard the great bucking horse Steamboat at the Cheyenne Frontier Days rodeo in 1909. Note the presence of a slick-fork saddle, "woolie" chaps, and quirt.

↑ **Hollis Williford (1940–2007)**
Don't Call Me a Cowboy, 1989
Bronze, 21 ×14 ×14 inches
NCM—Gift of Samuel Gordon Jewelers, 1991.03

In form—and title—this bronze of a lady trick roper captures the characteristic grace, skill, and independence of female participants in early rodeo sport. Between 1900 and 1920, many cowgirl competitors moved beyond trick riding and roping to compete in the bronc-riding, steer-roping, steer-riding, and steer-wrestling events.

↑ **Tona "Buckeye" Blake (1946–)**
Fannie Sperry Steele, 1982
Bronze, 25 × 11 × 7 inches
NCM—Museum purchase, 1985.02

This bronze evokes the inherent dignity of Fannie Sperry Steele, one of the early heroines of women's rodeo. She excelled in relay-race riding and bronc riding for nearly two decades, capturing two consecutive bronc-riding championships in 1912 and 1913, at the Calgary and Winnipeg Stampedes, respectively.

Chris Navarro (1956–)
Champion / Lane Frost 1963 to 1989,
1992
Bronze, 17 × 8 × 12 inches
NCM—Bequest of the George Kleier Estate,
2004.102.01

This sculpture commemorates the rodeo
career of 1987 World Bull Riding Champion
Lane Frost (riding Red Rock in 1988). Frost
was killed at the 1989 Cheyenne Frontier Days
rodeo by a bull named Taking Care of Business.
To memorialize the popular champion, 250
of these bronzes were sold to fund a life-size
rendition, unveiled at the Cheyenne Frontier
Days Old West Museum in 1993.

← **Bonnie McCarroll Thrown from Silver**
Pendleton, Oregon, Round-Up, 1915
Walter S. Bowman, photographer
NCM—Dickinson Research Center
McCarroll Family Trust Collection,
RC2006.076.312-17

↓ **Ann Ayres (1951–)**
Bonnie McCarroll / 1915 /
Pendleton Round Up, **2008**
Bronze, 16 × 27 × 12 inches.
NCM—Rodeo Historical Society Purchase,
2008.09

A meticulous reiteration of the famed Walter S. Bowman photograph (*adjacent*), this dynamic and technically difficult bronze depicts bronc rider Bonnie McCarroll thrown from Silver at the 1915 Pendleton, Oregon, Round-Up. For many years, the image was widely—and mistakenly—published as a depiction of McCarroll's notoriously fatal ride at Pendleton in 1929.

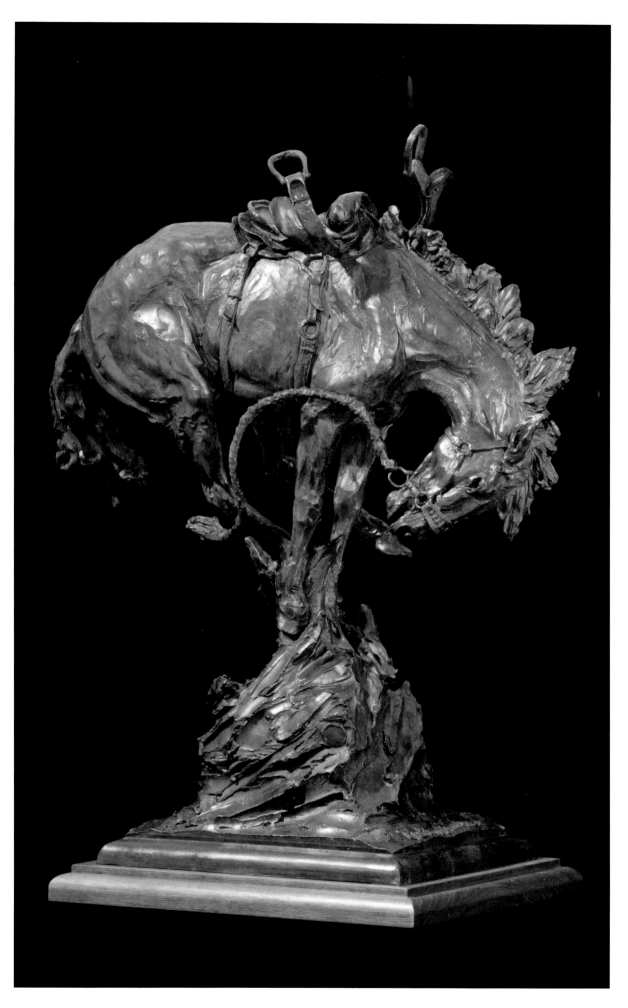

← **Richard Loffler (1956–)**
Makin' Rainbows, **2009**
Bronze, 18 × 13 × 8 inches
NCM—Rodeo Historical Society Purchase,
2009.24

Presenting a nearly complete oval in its
composition, this vibrant sculpture captures
the powerful athleticism and indomitable
spirit of the traditional rodeo bucking bronc.
The potential energy of the animal is evident
in its arched neck and tucked hindquarters—
and in the flying stirrups of the hornless (and
riderless) bronc saddle.

Rodeo Poster Art

The National Cowboy & Western Heritage Museum and its Dickinson Research Center preserve a number of rodeo posters and more than three hundred rodeo programs dating from the 1900s to the present, many of which exhibit dramatic artwork depicting various arena contests. Throughout this subgenre of rodeo illustration, the bronc-buster motif has proven both the earliest and by far the most common. The popularity of the archetypal, bronc-riding figure is encountered first on Denver's Mountain and Plain Festival poster of 1902. Over succeeding decades, other rodeo events also gained artist and illustrator attention. A promotional poster rendered by William "Bill" Gollings (1878–1932) for the 1931 Sheridan, Wyoming, Rodeo, for example, features vignettes of calf-roping and steer-wrestling in addition to a central bronc-riding motif—suggesting that the former contests were gaining in popularity and tradition.

➜ **Rodeo Poster**
The Mountain and Plain Festival Association / World's Championship Broncho Busting Contest / October 7–8 Denver 1902
Chromolithograph after an unknown illustrator
Denver Lithograph Company
Denver, Colorado, 1902
NCM—Dickinson Research Center
Gift of Tom Jacobson, 1983.36

Rodeo Poster
Dewey, Oklahoma / Roundup / July 4–5–6
1923 / Playday for Cowboys
Drawings after Joe DeYong
Quigley Lithograph Company, Kansas City,
Missouri, Dewey Roundup Committee, 1923
NCM—Dickinson Research Center
Joe DeYong Collection, 1980.18

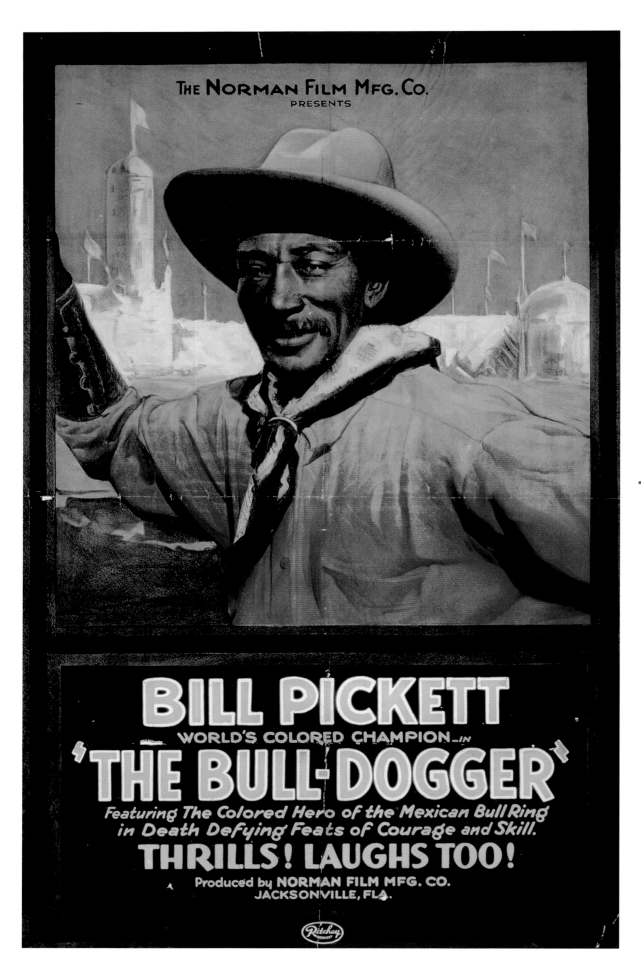

→ **Movie Poster**
Bill Pickett . . . "The Bull-Dogger"
Chromolithograph after an unknown illustrator
Ritchey Lithograph Company
New York City, 1923
NCM—Dickinson Research Center
Gift of Jerry L. Murphy, 1983.23

The originator of rodeo steer wrestling, African American cowboy Bill Pickett gained wide notoriety during the early twentieth century as an arena performer with the Miller Brothers' 101 Ranch Real Wild West show. He also starred in the Norman Film Manufacturing Company's all-black release, *The Bull-Dogger*, a silent movie "proving conclusively that the black cowboy is capable of doing anything the white cowboy does."

Rodeo Poster
Sheridan–Wyo–Rodeo /
July 15–16–17–1931
Chromolithograph after Bill Gollings
Sheridan Rodeo Committee, Sheridan,
Wyoming, 1931
NCM—Dickinson Research Center
Gift of Dave and Joanne Ferren, 2003.122

Rodeo Program Art

Among the Museum's hundreds of rodeo programs, the pervasiveness of the saddle-bronc motif in cover art is most evident in the striking "Let 'Er Buck" image created by Wallace Smith (1887–1937) in 1924 and officially copyrighted by the Pendleton Round-Up in 1925. This image has appeared on Pendleton catalogs ever since—as well as on myriad posters and souvenirs. Still, as with rodeo posters, other events have received attention in rodeo cover art over the years. The drama and danger of Brahma-bull riding, for instance, dominated Fort Worth's 1930 program, while the steer-wrestling event appeared as early as 1934 on the program at Madison Square Garden. Although the depiction of these and other rodeo events has become more common in recent decades, the enduring popularity of the bronc-rider motif still prevails—as it certainly does in the work of contemporary western sculptors as well.[6]

→ **Rodeo Program**
Pendleton / Round-up / Pendleton, Oregon
[1933]
Wallace Smith, illustrator
Pendleton Round-Up Committee, 1933
NCM—Dickinson Research Center, museum
purchase, 2005.171.18

↑ **Rodeo Program**
The Round-Up / Pendleton, Oregon /
September 11, 12, 13 / 1913
Illustrator unknown
Lee Moorhouse, photographer
Pendleton Round-Up Committee, 1913
NCM—Dickinson Research Center, museum
purchase, 2005.001.0882

↑ **Rodeo Program**
Let 'er Buck! / Round-Up / Pendleton,
Oregon [1920]
Illustrator unknown
Pendleton Round-Up Committee, 1920
NCM—Dickinson Research Center, museum
purchase, 2005.001.0746

→ **Rodeo Program**
Pendleton / Round-up / Pendleton, Oregon
[1939]
Wallace Smith, illustrator
Pendleton Round-Up Committee, 1939
NCM—Dickinson Research Center, museum
purchase, 2005.001.0306

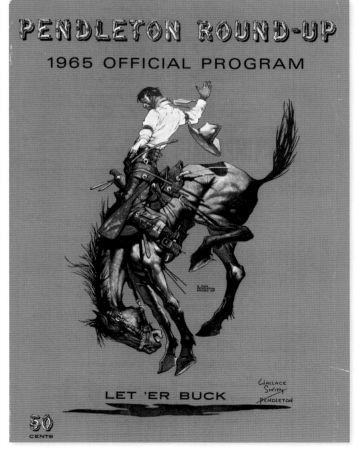

↑ **Rodeo Program**
Chicago / 1926 / Rodeo / Soldiers' [sic] Field /
Grant Park / Aug. 14–22
Illustrator unknown
Chicago Association of Commerce, 1926
NCM—Dickinson Research Center
Willard Porter Collection, 2001.049.02

↑ **Rodeo Program**
Chicago / 1927 / Rodeo / Soldier Field /
Grant Park / Aug. 20–28
Ruth Senfer, illustrator
Chicago Association of Commerce, 1927
NCM—Dickinson Research Center, gift of
Mel Potter, 2002.210

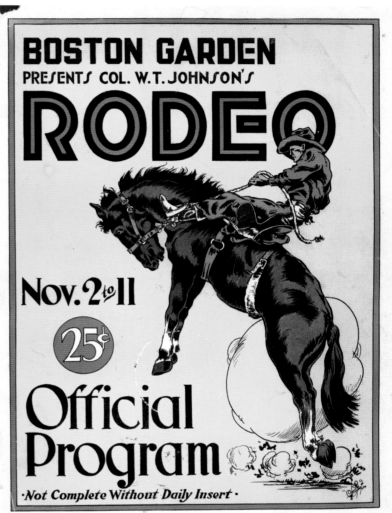

 Rodeo Program
Southwestern / Exposition / and / Fat Stock
Show / Fort Worth, / Texas / 1930
Illustrator unknown
Fort Worth Rodeo Committee, 1930
NCM—Dickinson Research Center
Rodeo Programs Collection, 2006.126.39.10

⬆ **Rodeo Program**
Boston Garden / Presents Col. W. T. Johnson's /
Rodeo / Nov. 2 to 11 [1933]
Les Fouf, illustrator
Colonel W. T. Johnson and Boston Garden, 1933
NCM—Dickinson Research Center
Willard Porter Collection, 2001.049.03

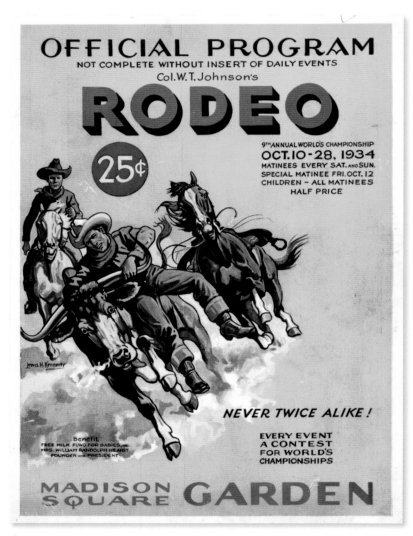

↑ Rodeo Program
Col. W. T. Johnson's / Rodeo / Oct. 10–28,
1934 / Madison Square Garden
Lewis H. Kennerly, illustrator
Colonel W. T. Johnson and Madison Square
Garden, 1934
NCM—Dickinson Research Center, museum
purchase, 2005.171.10

↑ Rodeo Program
Southwestern / Exposition and / Fat Stock
Show / Fort Worth / 1935
E. S. Ingle, illustrator
Fort Worth Rodeo Committee, 1935
NCM—Dickinson Research Center, museum
purchase, 2005.171.22

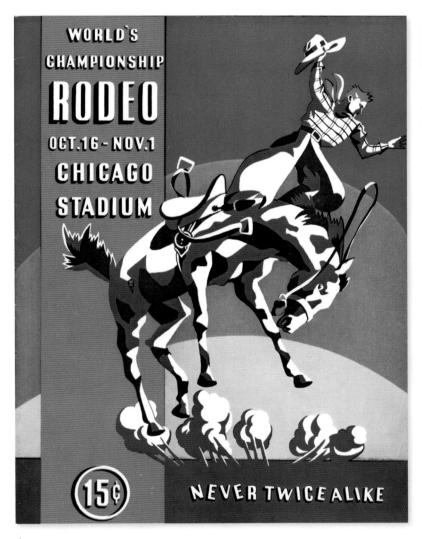

↑ **Rodeo Program**
*World's / Championship / Rodeo / Oct.
16–Nov. 1 / Chicago / Stadium* [1936]
Illustrator unknown
Chicago Association of Commerce, 1936
NCM—Dickinson Research Center, museum
purchase, 2005.171.06

↑ **Rodeo Program**
*Cheyenne / Frontier / Days / 1938 /
Cheyenne, Wyoming*
Illustrator unknown
Frontier Days Rodeo Committee, 1938
NCM—Dickinson Research Center, museum
purchase, 2005.171.23

↑ **Rodeo Program**
National Western / Horse Show / & Rodeo /
Denver 1940
Illustrator unknown
National Western Rodeo Committee, 1940,
NCM—Dickinson Research Center
Rodeo Programs Collection, 2006.126.39.04

↑ **Rodeo Program**
18th Annual / Rodeo / Madison Square
Garden / New York City [1943]
Burris Jenkins, illustrator
Gene Autry and Madison Square Garden, 1943
NCM—Dickinson Research Center, museum
purchase, 2005.171.14

Rodeo Program
*6th Annual / Navy Relief / Rodeo / 7 June
1953 / Camp Pendleton*
Illustrator unknown
Camp Pendleton [California] Rodeo
Committee, 1953
NCM—Dickinson Research Center, museum
purchase, 2005.001.0112

Rodeo Program
*Reno Rodeo / & Livestock Show / July 4th
1956*
Lew Hymers, illustrator
Reno Rodeo Committee, 1956
NCM—Dickinson Research Center, Rodeo
Programs Collection, 2006.126.39.06

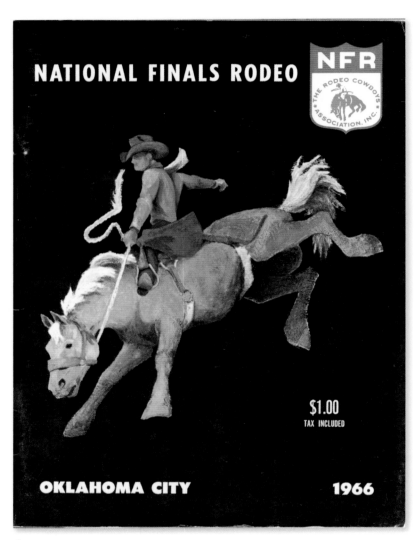

⬆ **Rodeo Program**
National Finals Rodeo / Oklahoma City / 1966
Illustrator unknown
National Finals Rodeo Committee, 1966
NCM—Dickinson Research Center
Rodeo Programs Collection, 2006.126.39.07

⬆ **Rodeo Program**
34th Annual / Pikes Peak / or Bust Rodeo /
August 7–8–9–10 [1974]
"Rock Crusher," after W. H. D. Koerner
Colorado Springs Rodeo Committee, 1974
NCM—Dickinson Research Center
Rodeo Programs Collection, 2006.126.39.02

Rodeo Program
National Western / Stock Show / and Rodeo /
January 11–20, 1979 / Denver
S. L. Humphrey, illustrator
National Western Rodeo Committee, 1979
NCM—Dickinson Research Center, museum
purchase, 2005.171.05

Rodeo Program
41st Annual / Pikes Peak or Bust Rodeo /
August 4, 5, 6, 7, 8, 9, 1981
"When Things Are Quiet," after Philip R. Goodwin
Colorado Springs Rodeo Committee, 1981
NCM—Dickinson Research Center
Rodeo Programs Collection, 2006.126.39.03
(Original painting at the National Cowboy Museum.)

Rodeo Program
Salinas / California Rodeo /
July 19–20–21–22 1984
Greco, illustrator
Salinas Rodeo Committee, 1984
NCM—Dickinson Research Center, museum
purchase, 2004.001.0804

Rodeo Program
Cheyenne / Frontier Days / 1984
Chuck DeHaan, illustrator
Frontier Days Rodeo Committee, 1984
NCM—Dickinson Research Center, museum
purchase, 2005.171.26

Rodeo Program
National Western / Stock Show & Rodeo /
January 9–20, 1985 / Denver
"A Fighting Cyclone," after William Robinson Leigh
National Western Rodeo Committee, 1985
NCM—Dickinson Research Center, museum
purchase, 2004.001.0700

↑ Rodeo Program
Celebrating a Decade of the National Finals
Rodeo in Las Vegas / 36th NFR /
December 2–11, 1994
"Ty Murray," after Haller Buchanan
National Finals Rodeo Committee, 1994
NCM—Dickinson Research Center
Rodeo Programs Collection, 2006.126.39.05

← Rodeo Program
Cheyenne / Frontier Days / 1987
Wayne Baize, illustrator
Frontier Days Rodeo Committee, 1987
NCM—Dickinson Research Center
Rodeo Programs Collection, 2006.126.39.13

RODEO HONOREES, 1955–2009

ORGANIZED IN 1966 under the auspices of the National Cowboy Hall of Fame and Western Heritage Center, the Rodeo Historical Society (RHS) memorializes the prominent contenders and personalities of the sport and aids the museum in collecting and preserving their treasured memorabilia. At this writing, more than five hundred active members belong to the society.

Through 2009, the society has inducted somewhat more than three hundred outstanding rodeo personalities—both living and deceased—into its Rodeo Hall of Fame. This prestigious roster includes all of the all-around champions declared since 1929; most of the great, but often unsung, contenders from 1900 into the 1980s; and many notable rodeo promoters, stock contractors, clowns, trick riders, fancy ropers, arena announcers, secretaries, and administrators.

In addition to these regular inductees, the Rodeo Historical Society annually recognizes a prominent representative of the western character with its prestigious Ben Johnson Memorial Award and celebrates a notable western woman with its distinctive Tad Lucas Memorial Award.

For those interested in more information, or in joining the organization, contact the Rodeo Historical Society at the National Cowboy & Western Heritage Museum.

Rodeo Cowboys and Cowgirls
circa 1958
NCM—Dickinson Research Center
79.026.2645

Ben Johnson and Cowboys
circa 1950
NCM—Dickinson Research Center
81.023.05474

Tad Lucas on Hell Cat
circa 1945
NCM—Dickinson Research Center
79.026.3636

Table 1
Rodeo Historical Society Honorees

Name	Birth–Death	Birthplace	Notes	Induction Date, State
Aber, Doff	1908–1946	Wolf, Wyoming	World saddle-bronc-riding champion, 1941–42; winner at Cheyenne, Calgary, and Pendleton, 1930s–40s	1966, Wyoming
Adams, Leon	1930–	Stuart, Oklahoma	Trick rider and steer wrestler; horse and bull trainer	2004, Oklahoma
Akers, Ira	1933–1974	San Antonio, Texas	Rough-stock competitor; founding member Mesquite, Texas, rodeo	1988, Texas
Akridge, Eddy	1929–	Pampa, Texas	World bareback-bronc-riding champion, 1953–55, 1961	1999, Nevada
Alexander, Joe	1943–	Cora, Wyoming	World bareback-bronc-riding champion, 1971–75	2003, California
Alsbaugh, Walter	1918–1992	Boulder, Colorado	Rodeo producer and stock contractor; PRCA Stock Contractor of the Year, 1986	2009, Colorado
Altizer, Jim Bob	1932–	Del Rio, Texas	World calf-roping champion, 1959; world steer-roping champion, 1967	1995, Texas
Ambler, Jerry	1911–1958	Milburn, Alberta	World saddle-bronc-riding champion, 1946; IRA champion saddle-bronc rider, 1947	1998, Canada
Appleton, Dave	1960–	Clermont, Queensland	World all-around champion cowboy, 1988	1988, Texas
Arnold, Carl	1898–1973	San Angelo, Texas	Champion steer roper at Cheyenne and Pendleton in the 1930s	1985, Arizona
Askin, Bob	1900–1973	Rochester, New York	Saddle-bronc rider, 1912–32; event champion at Pendleton, 1925 and 1927	1978, Montana
Austin, Tex (Van)	1887–1941	Ranch in West Texas	Rodeo promoter and producer; founder Madison Square Garden and Chicago venues	1976, New Mexico
Baldwin, Tillie (Anna Matilda Winger)	1888–1958	Avendale, Norway	Lady trick rider and saddle-bronc rider; first female steer wrestler	2004, Connecticut
Barmby, Bob	1900–1990	Sacramento, California	Livestock contractor	1996, California
Barrett, Hadley	1929–	North Platte, Nebraska	Rodeo announcer; PRCA Announcer of the Year, 1983, 1985, 1989, 2002	2008, Colorado
Beaver, Joe	1965–	Victoria, Texas	World all-around champion cowboy, 1995, 1996, 2000; world calf-roping champion 1985, 1987, 1988, 1992, 1993	1995, Texas
Beeson, Fred	1887–1970	Arkansas City, Kansas	Steer and calf roper, 1910–36; steer-roping champion at Pendleton, 1920	1991, Kansas
Bell, Ray	1899–1996	Dysart, Iowa	Champion saddle-bronc rider at Madison Square Garden, 1923	1986, California
Bennett, Hugh	1905–1994	Knox City, Texas	World steer-wrestling champion, 1932; world steer-roping champion, 1938	1977, Colorado
Berry, Ace	1947–	Bartlesville, Oklahoma	Bareback-bronc rider and team roper	2002, California
Beutler, Elra	1897–1987	Okarche, Oklahoma	Livestock contractor	1982, Oklahoma
Beutler, Lynn	1905–1999	Okarche, Oklahoma	Livestock contractor	1988, Oklahoma
Blackstone, Vick	1912–1987	Medina, Texas	Saddle-bronc rider; all-around competitor, 1930s–40s	1982, Florida
Blancett, Bertha Kaepernik	1883–1979	Cleveland, Ohio	First lady saddle-bronc rider at Cheyenne Frontier Days, 1904	1975, Colorado
Blevins, Earl	1906–1994	Whitetop, Virginia	Steer wrestler	1984, Wyoming
Boen, Ken	1918–	Danville, Illinois	Rodeo clown and horse trainer; steer-wrestling champion at Cheyenne, 1946	1991, Arkansas
Bolen, Berenice Dossey	1913–1974	Ellensburg, Washington	Lady trick rider	1991, Idaho
Bond, Paul	1915–	Seminole, Texas	Bareback-bronc rider, trick rider, and noted bootmaker	1992, Arizona

Name	Birth–Death	Birthplace	Notes	Induction Date, State
Boucher, C. R.	1931–	Livingston, Montana	World steer-wrestling champion, 1964	2001, Montana
Bowman, Everett	1899–1971	Hope, New Mexico	World all-around champion cowboy, 1935, 1937; world-steer wrestling champion, 1930, 1933, 1935, 1938; world calf-roping champion, 1929, 1935, 1937; world steer-roping champion, 1937; first president Cowboys Turtle Association	1955, Arizona
Bowman, John ("Tackhead")	1899–1959	Rogers, Arkansas	World all-around champion cowboy, 1936; world steer-roping champion, 1933, 1936	1955, California
Bowman, Lewis Edward	1886–1961	Brownwood, Texas	Calf roper, steer wrestler, and horse trainer	1962, Colorado
Brady, Buff, Jr.	1918–2004	Butte, Montana	Trick and fancy rider and roper	1992, California
Brazile, Trevor	1967–	Amarillo, Texas	World all-around champion cowboy, 2002–2004, 2006–2009; world tie-down-roping champion, 2007, 2009; world steer-roping champion, 2006–2007	2002, Texas
Brennan, Harry	1880-1934	Sheridan, Wyoming	Prototype saddle-bronc rider; event "world champion" at Cheyenne, 1904	1979, Wyoming
Brooks, Louis	1916–1983	Fletcher, Oklahoma	World all-around champion cowboy, 1943 and 1944; world saddle-bronc-riding champion, 1943 and 1944; world bareback-bronc-riding champion, 1942 and 1944	1955, Oklahoma
Brown, Freckles (Warren Granger)	1921–1987	Wheatland, Wyoming	World bull-riding champion, 1962; first to ride Tornado at the 1967 NFR	1986, Oklahoma
Bruce, Winston	1937–	Stettler, Alberta	World saddle-bronc-riding champion, 1961	2007, Canada
Burk, Clyde	1913–1945	Comanche, Oklahoma	World calf-roping champion, 1936, 1938, 1942, 1944	1966, Oklahoma
Burmister, Hippy (Arthur H.)	1894–1985	Evanston, Illinois	Saddle-bronc rider; western movie extra and double	1995, California
Burrell, Cuff (Cuthbert)	1893–1976	Grangeville, California	Rodeo livestock contractor	1997, California
Buschbom, Jack	1929–	Mobridge, South Dakota	World bareback-bronc-riding champion, 1949, 1959, 1960	1998, Arkansas
Bush, Wanda Harper	1931–	Mason, Texas	Eight-time all-around champion cowgirl in the 1950s; nine-time champion calf roper; seven-time champion ribbon roper; two-time champion barrel racer	2001, Texas
Byers, Chester	1892–1945	Knoxville, Illinois	World champion trick roper, 1916–33; steer roper	1969, Texas
Bynum, James ("Big Jim")	1924–1999	Danville, Alabama	World steer-wrestling champion, 1954, 1958, 1961, 1963	1993, Texas
Caldwell, Lee	1892–1952	Joseph, Oregon	Saddle-bronc rider; all-around cowboy at Pendleton, 1915	1966, Oregon
Camarillo, Jerold	1947–	San Diego, California	World team-roping champion, 1969, 1977; calf roper	2003, California
Camarillo, Leo	1947–	Santa Ynez Valley, California	World all-around champion cowboy, 1975; world team-roping champion, 1972, 1973, 1975, 1983; calf roper and steer wrestler	1975, California
Canutt, Yakima (Enos Edward)	1895–1986	Colfax, Washington	All-around champion cowboy at Pendleton, 1917, 1919, 1920, 1923	1975, Washington
Carney, Paul	1912–1950	Galeton, Colorado	World all-around champion cowboy, 1939; world bareback-bronc-riding champion, 1937 and 1939	1961, Colorado
Carr, Clay	1909–1957	Farmersville, California	World all-around champion cowboy, 1930, 1933; world saddle-bronc-riding champion, 1930; world steer-roping champion, 1930, 1940	1955, California
Carroll, J. Ellison	1862–1942	San Patricio County, Texas	World steer-roping champion, 1904–13; world's record time in 1908	1976, Texas
Carter, Barton David	1894–1991	Pawhuska, Oklahoma	Steer and calf roper, 1914–38	2005, Oklahoma
Chase, Joe, Jr. (Bear Necklace)	1933–2005	Fort Berthold, North Dakota	Saddle-bronc champion at Pendleton, 1961 (the first Native American saddle-bronc title winner at the famed Oregon venue since Jackson Sundown in 1916)	2009, Colorado

Name	Birth–Death	Birthplace	Notes	Induction Date, State
Christensen, Hank	1912–1986	Eugene, Oregon	Rodeo livestock contractor	1988, Oregon
Clancy, Foghorn (Frederick Melton)	1882–1958	Phoenix City, Alabama	Rodeo arena announcer; rodeo historian	1991, Texas
Clark, Bobby	1930–	Seminole, Oklahoma	Rodeo clown and bullfighter	1991, Oklahoma
Clark, Gene	1926–2005	Seminole, Oklahoma	Rodeo clown and bullfighter	1991, Oklahoma
Clennon, Barton	1910–	Aberdeen, South Dakota	Saddle-bronc rider; arena judge	1996, Arizona
Colborn, Ava	1906–1985	Vienna, Illinois	Rodeo producer	1987, Texas
Colborn, Everett E. ("Cobe")	1892–1972	Ranch in Idaho	Rodeo producer	1981, Idaho
Combs, Benny	1931–1977	Checotah, Oklahoma	World steer-wrestling champion, 1955; bareback-bronc rider, bull rider, calf roper	2002, Oklahoma
Combs, Willard	1922–2004	Checotah, Oklahoma	World steer-wrestling champion, 1957; his famed horse, Baby Doll	2002, Oklahoma
Connelly, Edith Happy	1925–1999	Boston, Massachusetts	Trick rider; NFR arena secretary; movie stunt double	2000, Massachusetts
Connelly, Lex	1926–1984	Bryn Mawr, Pennsylvania	Steer wrestler; NFR general manager, 1962–64; NFR arena announcer, 1974	1987, California
Cook, Bob	1932-2001	Lamb County, Texas	Original producer and publisher of ProRodeo	2005, California
Cooper, Felix	1912–1997	Pelican, Louisiana	African American bareback-bronc and bull rider; rodeo clown; first black arena judge	2001, Louisiana
Cooper, Jimmie	1956–	Monument, New Mexico	World all-around champion cowboy, 1981; calf roper and steer wrestler	1981, New Mexico
Cooper, Roy	1955–	Hobbs, New Mexico	World all-around champion cowboy, 1983; world calf-roping champion, 1976, 1980–84; world steer-roping champion, 1983	1983, Oklahoma
Cooper, Tuffy (Clay Tom)	1925–	Lovington, New Mexico	Calf roper, steer roper, team roper; father of Roy Cooper	1998, New Mexico
Copenhaver, Deb	1925–	Wilbur, Washington	World saddle-bronc riding champion, 1955, 1956	1991, Washington
Cornish, Cecil	1909–2003	Waukomis, Oklahoma	Rodeo trick and Roman rider; horse and bull trainer	1991, Oklahoma
Cox, Breezy (Lionel Bert)	1900–1960	Sonora, Texas	Saddle-bronc rider and calf roper; all-around champion cowboy at Calgary, 1926	1982, Arizona
Crosby, Bob ("Wild Horse Bob")	1897–1947	Midland, Texas	Steer roper and calf roper; all-around champion cowboy at both Cheyenne and Pendleton, 1925, 1927, 1928; permanent holder of the famed Roosevelt Trophy	1966, New Mexico
Curtis, Andy (James)	1912–1979	Calumet, Oklahoma	Bronc rider and steer wrestler, Steer-wrestling champion at Chicago, 1938–40	1986, Oklahoma
Curtis, Eddie (Edwin Louis)	1908–1965	El Reno, Oklahoma	Bronc rider, bull rider, steer wrestler; founding member Cowboys Turtle Association	1971, Oklahoma
Davis, Gordon	1919–1997	Redlands, California	Calf roper and steer wrestler; rodeo producer	1994, California
Davis, Sonny	1935–1991	Hobbs, New Mexico	World steer-roping champion, 1964, 1966, 1968; won NFR steer-roping title sixteen times from 1959 to 1980	1993, Texas
Decker, Jo Ramsey	1925–	San Angelo, Texas	NFR arena secretary, 1964, 1966–70	2000, Texas
Decker, Tater ("Spud")	1924–	Roswell, New Mexico	Saddle-bronc rider, steer wrestler, bull rider	1992, Oklahoma
Dightman, Myrtis	1935–	Crockett, Texas	African American bull rider; first black to qualify for the NFR	1997, Texas
Doak, George	1937–	Fort Worth, Texas	Rodeo clown and bullfighter; partner with Junior Meek	2001, Texas
Dollarhide, Ross, Jr.	1921–1977	Burns, Oregon	World steer-wrestling champion, 1953; saddle-bronc rider and calf roper	2003, Arizona
Dossey, Carl	1919–1955	Chandler(?), Arizona	World bareback-bronc-riding champion, 1940	2006, Arizona

Name	Birth–Death	Birthplace	Notes	Induction Date, State
Doubleday, Ralph Russell ("Dub")	1881–1958	Canton, Iowa	First professional rodeo photographer	1988, Iowa
Douthitt, Buff	1924–	Haggerman, New Mexico	Calf roper, steer wrestler, and trick roper	2001, New Mexico
Dunafon, Wayne	1919–2001	Yuma, Colorado	Rodeo contender better remembered as "The Marlboro Man"	2005, Colorado
Duvall, Roy	1942–	Hichita, Oklahoma	World steer-wrestling champion, 1967, 1969, 1972; in 1967 won the event title at Cheyenne, Calgary, and Pendleton	1998, Oklahoma
Elliot, George W.	1900–1981	Indian Territory, Oklahoma	Rodeo arena announcer	2006, Oklahoma
Elliott, Verne	1890–1962	Plateville, Colorado	Rodeo livestock contractor and producer	1973, Colorado
Eskew, Jim (Colonel)	1888–1965	Wilson County, Tennessee	East Coast rodeo producer; founder JE Ranch rodeo	1992, Oklahoma
Eskew, Junior (Jim William, Jr.)	1918–1977	Belfast, Tennessee	World trick-roping champion, 1938–63	1984, Oklahoma
Estes, Bobby	1920–2006	Baird, Texas	Bareback-bronc rider, bull rider, rodeo producer	1991, Texas
Feild, Lewis	1957–	Salt Lake City, Utah	World all-around champion cowboy, 1985–87; world bareback-bronc-riding champion, 1985 and 1986	1985, Utah
Ferguson, Tom	1950–	Tahlequah, Oklahoma	World all-around champion cowboy, 1974–79; world calf-roping champion 1974; world steer-wrestling champion, 1977 and 1978; all-around at Cheyenne and Pendleton, 1976	1974, Oklahoma
Fletcher, George	1890–1971	St. Mary's, Kansas	Early African American competitor; competed in controversial, 1911 Pendleton Round-Up bronc-riding finals with Jackson Sundown and John Spain	2001, Oregon
Fletcher, Kid (George L.)	1914–1957	Competition, Missouri	World bull-riding champion, 1938	1966, Colorado
Fort, Troy C.	1917–1993	Lovington, New Mexico	World calf-roping champion, 1947 and 1949	1986, New Mexico
Frost, Lane	1963–1989	La Junta, Colorado	NFR bull-riding champion, 1986; PRCA world bull-riding champion, 1987	2008, Texas
Fulkerson, Jasbo (Ralph Clayburn)	1904–1949	Midlothian, Texas	Rodeo clown and bullfighter; introduced the reinforced bull barrel to the arena	2001, Texas
Gale, Floyd	1895–1980	Denton County, Texas	Rodeo manager; notably, the Tulsa, Oklahoma, Johnny Lee Wills Stampede	1991, Oklahoma
Gamblin, Amye	1911–1989	Lanham, Texas	Calf roper; first man ever to rope and tie a calf in under 16 seconds	1992, Texas
Gardner, Joe	1877–1921	Sierra Blanca, Texas	Early steer roper, 1904–21; won steer-roping championship at Chicago in 1920	1979, Texas
Garrett, Sam	1892–1989	Mulhall, Oklahoma	Champion trick roper; all-around champion cowboy at Pendleton, 1914; horse trainer	1985, California
Gaudin, D. J. ("Kajun Kidd")	1929–	Baton Rouge, Louisiana	Rodeo clown and bullfighter	1996, Texas
Gay, Don	1953–	Dallas, Texas	PRCA world bull-riding champion, 1974–77, 1979–81, 1984; ProRodeo Hall of Fame inductee, 1979; rodeo producer and television color commentator	2008, Texas
Gibson, Marie ("Ma")	1894–1933	Unknown, Canada	Ladies' bronc-riding champion at Madison Square Garden, 1927 and 1931	2006, Canada
Goodspeed, Buck	1906–1991	Leedy, Oklahoma	Steer roper	1987, Oklahoma
Goodspeed, Jess	1912–1983	Leedy, Oklahoma	Calf roper; event champion at Cheyenne, 1950	1987, Oklahoma
Grammer, Henry	1883–1923	Marlin, Texas	Bronc rider and steer roper, 1903–18; declared world champion steer roper at Guy Weadick's 1916 Sheepshead Bay Stampede	2000, Oklahoma
Greenough, Alice (Orr)	1902–1995	Red Lodge, Montana	Ladies' bronc-riding champion at Boston Garden 1933, 1935, and 1936, and at Madison Square Garden, 1940; taught Dale Evans to ride	1983, Montana

Name	Birth–Death	Birthplace	Notes	Induction Date, State
Greenough, Margie (Henson)	1908–2004	Red Lodge, Montana	Saddle-bronc rider; Hollywood horse wrangler and movie extra	1983, Montana
Greenough, Turk (Thurkel James)	1905–1995	Red Lodge, Montana	Saddle-bronc rider; event champion at Cheyenne, 1933, 1935, 1936	1983, Montana
Griffith, Dick	1913–1984	Canton, Oklahoma	World bull-riding champion, 1939–42	1984, Oklahoma
Groff, Buddy	1925–	Hondo, Texas	Calf roper; runner-up for the RCA champion calf-roping title, 1954 and 1956	2000, Texas
Hadley, Tom	1927–	Lawton, Oklahoma	Calf roper, steer wrestler, rodeo announcer; announced NFR in 1971, 1973, and 1982	2004, Texas
Hancock, Bill	1917–1997	Roswell, New Mexico	Saddle-bronc rider and bull rider; saddle-bronc champion at Cheyenne, 1952	1990, Texas
Hancock, Sonny	1917–1997	Fort Sumner, New Mexico	Saddle-bronc rider, calf roper, steer roper	1997, New Mexico
Harris, Howard, III	1931–	Woodstown, New Jersey	East Coast rodeo promoter	2005, Oklahoma
Hastings, Fox (Eloise)	1882–1948	Unknown, California	Steer wrestler, saddle-bronc rider, trick rider, 1920–40	1987, Texas
Hastings, Mike (Paul Raymond)	1891–1965	Cheyenne, Wyoming	Early steer-wrestling champion; winner at Chicago, 1920 and 1921; at Pendleton, 1922 and 1925; at Cheyenne, 1931; all-around champion cowboy at Pendleton, 1922	1974, Wyoming
Hatley, John	1930–2001	Lometa, Texas	Steer wrestler; event champion at Cheyenne, 1958	2004, New Mexico
Haverty, Del	1928–	Huachuca, Arizona	Multievent competitor in 1950s; IRA all-around champion cowboy, 1951; all-around cowboy at Calgary, 1953, 1959; all-around cowboy at Pendleton, 1954	1996, Nevada
Hefner, Hoyt	1911–1977	Chico, Texas	Rodeo clown and bullfighter	1987, Texas
Helfrich, DeVere	1902–1981	Lamonta, Oregon	Rodeo photographer	1991, Oregon
Hennigh, Duane	1930–	Ashland, Kansas	Multievent competitor in 1960s; all-around cowboy title at Woodward, Oklahoma, 1961–63, 1966–67	2000, Kansas
Henson, Chuck	1931–	Arcadia, Florida	Rodeo clown and bullfighter; 1977 PRCA Rodeo Clown of the Year	2009, Arizona
Holcomb, Homer	1896–1971	Sioux City, Iowa	Rodeo clown and bullfighter	1982, Idaho
Hopkins, Ma (Ethel A.)	1884–1964	St. Joseph, Missouri	Longtime editor of *Hoofs and Horns* magazine; known as "The First Lady of Rodeo"	1999, Arizona
Howard, Duane	1933–	Minnewaukan, North Dakota	Multievent competitor in 1950s; PRCA Pro Judge	2007, North Dakota
Hyland, Mel	1948–	Edmonton, Alberta	World saddle-bronc-riding champion, 1972 and 1976	2006, Canada
Irwin, C. B. (Charles Burton)	1875–1934	Chillicothe, Missouri	Rodeo producer and livestock contractor; steer-roping champion at Cheyenne, 1906	1975, Wyoming
Ivory, Buster	1923–2003	Alturas, California	Saddle-bronc rider; NFR livestock superintendent, 1959–84	1990, Texas
Ivory, June	1932–2004	Pampa, Texas	NFR arena secretary, 1974, 1979	2004, Texas
Ivory, Perry	1905–1983	Dorris, California	Multievent competitor in 1920s; saddle-bronc champion at Salinas, 1929–31	1998, California
Jarrett, Ryan	1983–	Summerville, Georgia	World all-around champion cowboy, 2005	2005, Georgia
Jauregui, Andy (Leandro)	1903–1990	Santa Paula, California	Rodeo livestock contractor; RAA steer-roping champion, 1931; RAA team-roping, 1934	1979, California
Johnson, Ben, Sr.	1896–1952	Harrison, Arkansas	Steer roper; event champion at Cheyenne, 1922, 1923, 1926	1961, Oklahoma
Johnson, Bernis	1932–	Cleburne, Texas	B-J Rodeo stock contractor and producer	2005, Texas
Johnson, Clint	1956–	Spearfish, South Dakota	World saddle-bronc-riding champion, 1980, 1987–89	1999, Texas
Johnson, Sherry Combs	1938–	Addington, Oklahoma	GRA all-around champion cowgirl, 1961; GRA barrel-racing champion, 1962	2005, Oklahoma

Name	Birth–Death	Birthplace	Notes	Induction Date, State
Jones, Cecil	1917–	Menan, Idaho	Rough-stock rider; Rowell Ranch Rodeo coproducer and manager, 1948–69	1997, California
Jones, John W., Sr.	1932–	Fresno, California	World steer-wrestling champion, 1970; NFR steer-wrestling champion, 1965, 1968–69, 1970	2000, California
Justin, John S., Jr.	1917–2001	Fort Worth, Texas	Businessman (Justin Boot Company); founded the Justin Sports Medicine Program in professional rodeo in the early 1980s	2003, Texas
Kesler, Reg	1919–2001	Lethbridge, Alberta	Canadian all-around champion cowboy, 1948, 1951, 1953; noted rodeo stock contractor; Canadian Rodeo Hall of Fame, 1989; recipient of the Order of Canada Medal, 1992	2009, Montana
Kirnan, Tommy	1893–1937	Bayonne, New Jersey	Rodeo trick rider and trick roper, 1920s	1977, New Jersey
Knight, Harry	1907–1989	Quebec City, Quebec	Canadian saddle-bronc-riding champion, 1926 and 1932; rodeo stock contractor	1985, Canada
Knight, Pete	1903–1937	Philadelphia, Pennsylvania	World saddle-bronc-riding champion, 1932, 1933, 1935, 1936; winner of the singular Jack Dempsey "Match of Champions" trophy, Reno Nevada, 1932	1958, Canada
Lambert, Mel	1920–1999	Chiloquin, Oregon	Rodeo arena announcer; known as "the Voice of the California Rodeo"	1998, Oregon
LeDoux, Chris	1948–2005	Biloxi, Mississippi	World bareback-bronc-riding champion, 1976; western/rodeo singer and songwriter	2006, Wyoming
Lefton, Abe	1900–1958	San Francisco, California	Rodeo arena announcer	1990, California
Leuschner, C. O. ("Dogtown Slim")	1913–1996	Waco, Texas	Steer wrestler; rodeo livestock contractor, "The Wild Bunch"	1996, Texas
Lewallen, G. K.	1919–	Van Alstyne, Texas	Rough-stock rider, 1940s–50s	1994, Texas
Like, Jim	1918–2001	Clayton, New Mexico	Saddle-bronc rider and steer wrestler; Walsenburg, Colorado, rodeo named for him	1993, Colorado
Linder, Herman	1907–2001	Darlington, Wisconsin	Canadian all-around champion cowboy, 1931–36, 1938; rodeo stock contractor	1980, Canada
Linderman, Bill	1920–1965	Bridger, Montana	World all-around champion cowboy, 1945, 1950, 1953; world saddle-bronc-riding champion, 1945, 1950; world bareback-bronc-riding champion, 1943; world steer-wrestling champion, 1950; all-around cowboy at Calgary, 1944–48, 1951; widely respected spokesman for rodeo administration and professionalism; known in rodeo circles as "The King"	1955, Montana
Linderman, Bud	1922–1961	Bridger, Montana	World bareback-bronc-riding champion, 1945; all-around champion cowboy at Cheyenne, 1950 and 1951	1987, Montana
Lindsey, John	1906–1974	Goldthwaite, Texas	Rodeo clown and bullfighter	1986, Texas
Logan, Pete	1917–1993	Junction, Illinois	Rodeo arena announcer; movie narrator; NFR announcer, 1959–64, 1967, 1970	1991, Montana
Long, Hughie	1907–1987	Battleford, Saskatchewan	Saddle-bronc rider; later AQHA show judge	1984, Canada
Lowry, Fred	1892–1956	Lenapah, Oklahoma	Steer roper; event champion at Cheyenne, 1916, 1921, 1924, 1925, 1927, 1929; contributed to design of the "low-roping" saddle for rodeo competition	1987, Oklahoma
Lucas, Buck (James E.)	1898–1960	Omaha, Nebraska	Steer wrestler, saddle-bronc rider, trick and Roman rider; rodeo arena judge; co-owner of the Triangle Ranch Rodeo Company; husband of Tad Barnes	2002, Nebraska
Lucas, Tad Barnes (Barbara Inez)	1902–1990	Cody, Nebraska	Lady rough-stock and trick rider; relay racer; all-around champion cowgirl, 1928–30; trick-riding champion at Madison Square Garden, 1926, 1928–31; permanent holder of the Metro Goldwyn Mayer Trophy; competed in the arena longer than any other rodeo cowgirl	1968, Texas

Name	Birth–Death	Birthplace	Notes	Induction Date, State
Lybbert, Chris	1954–	Ephrata, Washington	World all-around champion cowboy, 1982; world champion calf roper, 1986; all-around cowboy at Pendleton, 1976; and at Cheyenne, 1985	1982, California
Lyne, Phil	1947–	San Antonio, Texas	World all-around champion cowboy and world calf-roping champion, 1971–72; world steer-roping champion, 1990; recipient of the Bill Linderman Memorial Award in 1970–72 and 1976; all-around champion cowboy at Pendleton, 1981, 1983	1971, Texas
Maggini, Charles	1894–1982	San Benito County, California	World steer-roping and world team-roping champion, 1929; immortalized in 1982 biographical film *Top Hand*	2003, California
Mahan, Larry	1943–	Salem, Oregon	World all-around champion cowboy, 1966–70, 1973; world bull-riding champion, 1965, 1967; all-around cowboy at Pendleton, 1967; at Prescott, 1973; at Calgary, 1974; called the "cowboy in the gray flannel suit" by *Time* magazine for business acumen in rodeo-related advertising and establishment of name-brand western wear line	1966, Oregon
Mansfield, Toots	1914–1998	Bandera, Texas	World calf-roping champion, 1939–41, 1943, 1945, 1948, 1950; steer-roping champion at Cheyenne, 1948; all-around champion cowboy at Cheyenne, 1947	1981, Texas
May, Harley	1926–2008	Oakdale, California	World steer-wrestling champion, 1952, 1956, 1965; first National Intercollegiate Rodeo Association (NIRA) graduate to enter professional rodeo	1988, California
Mayo, Don	1939–	Grinnell, Iowa	Bareback-bronc rider; rode Osage for a combined score of 194 points at Odessa, Texas, in 1959	2002, Iowa
McCarroll, Bonnie (Mary E. Treadwell)	1897–1929	Boise, Idaho	Lady saddle-bronc rider, steer rider, trick rider; ladies' champion saddle-bronc-rider at Pendleton, 1921 and 1922; Madison Square Garden, 1922; Tex Austin's International Rodeo at Wembley Stadium, London, England, 1924, taking the Lord Selfridge Trophy; died of injuries received bronc riding at Pendleton in 1929; her death contributed to the decline of ladies' roughstock competition	2002, Idaho
McCarroll, Frank	1892–1954	Morris, Minnesota	Steer wrestler; event champion at Pendleton, Cheyenne, Fort Worth, Chicago, and Madison Square Garden in the 1920s; Hollywood bit player, stuntman, and double	2007, Minnesota
McCarty, Eddie	1887–1946	Loveland, Colorado	Dynamic livestock contractor in partnership with Verne Elliott, 1920s and 1930s; multievent competitor with several titles at Cheyenne and Pendleton in 1910s	1970, Wyoming
McClure, Jake	1902–1940	Amarillo, Texas	World calf-roping champion, 1930; nine calf- and steer-roping titles at Pendleton, Cheyenne, and Prescott, 1929–34; known as "the gentleman roper"	1955, New Mexico
McCrorey, Howard	1913–1985	Unknown, Montana	Steer wrestler; event champion at Madison Square Garden, 1940 and 1941; later acted as double for Randolph Scott and Gary Cooper in western films	1984, South Dakota
McEntire, Clark	1927–	Graham, Oklahoma	World steer-roping champion, 1957, 1958, 1961; event titles at Pendleton, 1947, 1957, 1958; at Cheyenne, 1954, 1961; all-around cowboy title at Pendleton, 1947 and 1957; known on the circuit as "Ropentire"	1988, Oklahoma
McEntire, John Wesley	1897–1976	Lula, Oklahoma	World steer-roping champion, 1934; father of Clark	1984, Oklahoma
McGinnis, Vera (Farra)	1892–1990	East Lynn, Missouri	Lady trick rider and relay racer; developed the "flying change" in latter event; "World Champion Cowgirl" at 1924 London rodeo; influential in cowgirl rodeo fashion	1985, California

Name	Birth–Death	Birthplace	Notes	Induction Date, State
McGinty, Rusty	1907–1964	Aspermont, Texas	Steer wrestler; event titles at Madison Square Garden, 1937, and Fort Worth, 1942; a leader in formation of the Cowboys Turtle Association	1995, Texas
McGonagill, Clay	1879–1921	Old Sweet Home, Texas	Steer roper, 1900–1920; event winner at Prescott, 1919; pioneer rodeo figure	1975, New Mexico
McLaughlin, Don	1927–1994	Chester, Pennsylvania	World calf-roping champion, 1951–54, 1957; world steer-roping champion, 1960, 1963, 1970; all-around cowboy at Cheyenne, 1959, 1960; at Pendleton, 1959, 1966	1990, Colorado
McLean, Kenny	1939–2002	Okanagan Falls, British Columbia	World saddle-bronc-riding champion, 1962; Canadian all-around champion cowboy, 1967–69	2005, Canada
McSpadden, Clem	1925–2008	Bushyhead, Oklahoma	Rodeo arena announcer; at NFR, 1960, 1965–66; NFR general manager, 1967–84	1989, Oklahoma
Meek, Junior	1936–2006	Cleburne, Texas	Rodeo clown and bullfighter	2001, Texas
Merchant, Richard	1896–1977	Eddy County, New Mexico	World calf-roping champion, 1932; world steer-roping champion, 1935	1983, Arizona
Merritt, King	1894–1953	Calhoun, Georgia	World steer-roping champion, 1942	1977, Wyoming
Miller, Clyde S.	1898–1974	Waterloo, Iowa	Rodeo producer and trainer of "high-schooled" horses	2002, Iowa
Miller, John J.	1942–	McAllen, Texas	World team-roping champion, 1970, 1971; AQHA rope–horse trainer and judge	2009, Arizona
Mills, George	1912–1980	Palisade, Colorado	World bareback-bronc-riding champion, 1941; rodeo clown and bullfighter	1987, Colorado
Montana, Montie (Owen H. Mickel)	1910–1998	Wolf Point, Montana	Rodeo entertainer and trick roper (lassoed President Eisenhower in 1953)	1989, California
Mortensen, Dan	1968–	Billings, Montana	World all-around champion cowboy, 1997; world saddle-bronc-riding champion, 1993–95, 1997, 1998, 2003	1997, Montana
Mulhall, Lucille	1885–1940	Mulhall, Oklahoma Territory	Protoype rodeo cowgirl and competitive steer roper; President Theodore Roosevelt called her "The Golden Girl of the West"	1975, Oklahoma
Mulkey, Burel	1904–1982	Clyde, Idaho	World all-around champion cowboy, 1938; world saddle-bronc-riding champion, 1937 and 1938	1955, Idaho
Mullens, Johnnie	1884–1978	Granbury, Texas	Early rodeo stock contractor; known as "the bucking horseman"	1975, Arizona
Murray, Leo ("Pick")	1902–1980	Colbert, Oklahoma	Saddle-bronc rider and steer wrestler; won saddle-bronc title at Belle Fourche, South Dakota, seven times between 1930 and 1941	1986, Oklahoma
Murray, Ty	1969–	Phoenix, Arizona	World all-around champion cowboy, 1989–94 and 1998; world bull-riding champion, 1993 and 1998; all-around cowboy at Cheyenne, 1990; at Calgary, 1991	1989, Texas
Nelson, Alvin	1934–	Mobridge, South Dakota	Saddle-bronc-riding champion at Madison Square Garden, 1957	2006, South Dakota
Nesbitt, Don	1907–1988	Old Everetts, South Dakota	World all-around champion cowboy, 1932; rodeo livestock contractor	1955, Arizona
Nesbitt, Pauline	1907–1996	Stanley, Wisconsin	Lady trick rider and saddle-bronc rider	1999, Oklahoma
Nesmith, Tom	1935–1972	Scipio, Oklahoma	World all-around champion cowboy, 1962; world steer-wrestling champion, 1962	1962, Oklahoma
Ohl, Cody	1973–	Rosenberg, Texas	World all-around champion cowboy, 2001; world calf-roping champion, 1997, 1998, and 2001; world tie-down roping champion, 2003 and 2006	2001, Texas
Oliver, Dean	1929–	Dodge City, Kansas	World all-around champion cowboy, 1963–65; world calf-roping champion, 1955, 1958, 1960–64, and 1969; calf-roping champion at Pendleton, 1957, 1971, 1976; at Calgary, 1958, 1964, 1969, 1976; at Cheyenne, 1969, 1974	1963, Idaho

Name	Birth–Death	Birthplace	Notes	Induction Date, State
Oropeza, Vicente	1858–1923	Puebla, Mexico	Early Hispanic trick roper and Wild West showman	1975, Mexico
Parkison, Chuck	1918–1988	Rapid City, South Dakota	Rodeo announcer; Cheyenne Frontier Days, 1962–88; NFR, 1967, 1968, 1977–79, 1981	2008, California
Paul, George	1947–1970	San Miguel Ranch, Mexico	World bull-riding champion, 1968; holds the record of 79 consecutive successful rides	2007, Texas
Pettigrew, Homer	1914–1997	Grady, New Mexico	World all-around champion cowboy, 1941; world steer-wrestling champion, 1940, 1942–45, and 1948; considered by most the finest steer wrestler, or bulldogger, of all time	1955, New Mexico
Pickens, Slim (Louis Lindley, Jr.)	1919–1983	Kingsburg, California	Saddle- and bareback-bronc rider, rodeo clown and bullfighter; character actor in numerous western films	1986, California
Pickett, Bill ("The Dusky Demon")	1870–1932	Austin, Texas	African American cowboy; Wild West performer; originator of the rodeo bulldogging, or steer wrestling, event	1971, Oklahoma
Pickett, Dee	1955–	San Diego, California	World all-around champion cowboy, 1984; world team-roping champion, 1984	1984, Idaho
Plaugher, Wilbur	1922–	Lima, Ohio	Multievent competitor; rodeo clown and bullfighter	2007, California
Porter, Willard H.	1920–1992	Unknown, New Jersey	Rodeo historian and writer	1991, Florida
Potter, Mel	1935–	Wisconsin Rapids, Wisconsin	Calf, steer, and team roper; rodeo producer and livestock contractor	2005, Arizona
Privett, Booger Red (Samuel T.)	1858–1926	Williamson County, Texas	Saddle-bronc rider, 1911–24	1975, Texas
Pruett, Gene	1917–1988	Moscow, Idaho	World saddle-bronc-riding champion, 1948	1980, Idaho
Purdy, Ikua	1873–1945	Mauna Kea, Hawaii	Hawaiian cowboy (great grandson of John Palmer Parker, founder of the famed Parker Ranch); steer-roping champion at Cheyenne Frontier Days, 1908	1999, Hawaii
Ragsdale, Bob	1936–	Harlem, Montana	Calf roper; qualified for the NFR fifteen consecutive times (1961–75)	2003, Montana
Rambo, Gene	1920–1988	San Miguel, California	World all-around champion cowboy, 1946; all-around cowboy at Pendleton, 1944; at Cheyenne, 1948	1955, California
Randall, Glenn	1908–1992	Melbeta, Nebraska	Horse trainer	1989, California
Randolph, Florence Hughes Fenton	1898–1971	Augusta, Georgia	"Princess Mohawk"; champion cowgirl at the 1927 World Series Rodeo, Madison Square Garden; champion trick rider, 1927 and 1933	1968, Oklahoma
Reger, Dixie Lee (Mosley)	1930–	Buffalo, Oklahoma	Charter member Girls Rodeo Association (GRA), 1948; trick rider and trick roper; rodeo clown	2003, Oklahoma
Reynolds, Benny	1936–	Twin Bridges, Montana	World all-around champion cowboy, 1961	1961, Montana
Richardson, Nowata Slim (Ambrose)	1894–1982	Lenapah, Oklahoma	Bronc rider and bulldogger, 1912–32	1981, Oklahoma
Riley, Doyle	1923–1985	Snyder, Texas	Calf roper, horse breeder	1998, Texas
Riley, Lanham	1920–2006	Snyder, Texas	Steer roper and calf roper; champion calf roper at Cheyenne, 1957	1993, Texas
Riley, Mitzi Lucas	1930–	Fort Worth, Texas	Lady trick rider; daughter of renowned cowgirl champion Tad Lucas	1995, Texas
Roach, Ruth Scantlin	1896–1986	Excelsior Springs, Missouri	Lady trick rider and bronc rider; ladies' bronc-riding champion at Madison Square Garden, 1932; proclaimed "The World's Most Beautiful Cowgirl"; competitive debut made at now-said-to-be first indoor rodeo, the 1917 Fort Worth Roundup	1989, Texas
Roberds, Coke T.	1870–1960	West Texas	Famed breeder of "Steel Dust" Quarter Horses	1964, Colorado
Roberts, E. C.	1895–1992	Flint Hills, Kansas	Rodeo producer and livestock contractor	1984, Kansas
Roberts, Gerald	1919–2004	Council Grove, Kansas	World all-around champion cowboy, 1942 and 1948	1955, Kansas

Name	Birth–Death	Birthplace	Notes	Induction Date, State
Roberts, Ken	1918–1975	Council Grove, Kansas	World bull-riding champion, 1943–45; saddle-bronc and all-around champion cowboy at Cheyenne, 1946	1980, Kansas
Robinson, Lee	1891–1927	Haskell County, Texas	Calf roper and steer wrestler; calf-roping champion at Madison Square Garden, 1921 and 1923; all-around cowboy at Prescott, 1922	1967, Texas
Roddy, Jack	1937–	San Francisco, California	World steer-wrestling champion, 1966 and 1968	1997, California
Rollens, Rufus	1891–1972	Claremore, Oklahoma	"World Champion" bronc rider at Calgary, 1913; at Miles City, 1915	1988, Oklahoma
Ross, Gene	1904–1987	Sayre, Oklahoma	World steer-wrestling champion, 1929, 1931, and 1937	1986, Oklahoma
Rowell, Harry	1891–1969	Unknown, England	Rodeo livestock contractor; produced the Rowell Ranch Rodeo for 40 years	1985, California
Rowell, Maggie	1906–1975	Michigan City, Indiana	Helped produce the Rowell Ranch Rodeo	1985, California
Rude, Ike	1894–1985	Mangum, Oklahoma	World steer-roping champion, 1941, 1947, and 1953; all-around champion cowboy at Prescott, 1925; at Pendleton, 1931 and 1936	1974, Oklahoma
Rutherford, Buck (Austin)	1929–1988	Nowata, Oklahoma	World all-around champion cowboy, 1954; all-around cowboy at Cheyenne, 1954	1955, Oklahoma
Ryan, Paddy (John Francis)	1896–1980	Leroy, Minnesota	Bronc rider and steer wrestler, 1916–32; saddle-bronc champion at Cheyenne and Pendleton, 1924 (winner of the Roosevelt Trophy); all-around cowboy at Calgary, 1927, 1928, 1930	1978, Montana
Salinas, Juan	1901–1995	Encinal, Texas	Calf roper, 1936–46; event winner at Prescott, 1938	1991, Texas
Sampson, Charles	1957–	Los Angeles, California	First African American PRCA world bull-riding champion, 1982; Coors Cowboy of the Year, 1986	2008, Colorado
Sawyer, Fern	1917–1995	Yeso, New Mexico	GRA all-around champion cowgirl, 1949; only woman to win the National Cutting Horse world title	1991, New Mexico
Schell, Asbury	1903–1980	Gisela, Arizona	World team-roping champion, 1937, 1939, 1952; calf roper and steer roper	2003, Arizona
Schneider, Frank	1912–1983	Stockton, California	World bull-riding champion, 1933, 1934: world bareback-bronc-riding champion, 1935	1994, California
Schneider, Johnie	1904–1982	Stockton, California	World all-around champion cowboy, 1931; world bull-riding champion, 1929, 1930, 1932	1955, California
Schumacher, Jimmy	1920–2010	Prescott, Arizona	Rodeo clown and barrelman; patented the "walking" barrel for bullfighting in 1954	2002, Arizona
Scudder, Pat	1925–2002	Dewey, Oklahoma	Saddle-bronc rider, steer roper; NFR general manager, 1965–66	2002, Oklahoma
Sewalt, Ronnye	1941–1994	Brownwood, Texas	Calf roper and steer roper, 1960–80	2003, Texas
Sewalt, Royce	1914–1974	Brownsville, Texas	World calf-roping champion, 1946	2007, Texas
Shaw, Everett	1908–1979	Nowata, Oklahoma	World steer-roping champion, 1945, 1946, 1948, 1951, 1959, and 1962; all-around champion cowboy at Pendleton, 1933 and 1948	1980, Oklahoma
Shelton, Dick	1901–1970	Gladewater, Texas	Steer wrestler; event title at Pendleton, 1927, 1928, and 1929	1975, Texas
Shelton, Reine Hafley	1902–1979	Janesville, Wisconsin	Lady saddle-bronc rider and trick rider; ladies' saddle-bronc-riding champion at Madison Square Garden, 1924; trick-riding champion at Fort Worth, 1929, 1930, and 1934	1991, Texas
Sheppard, Chuck	1916–2005	Globe, Arizona	World team-roping champion, 1946; IRA calf-roping champion, 1951	1985, Arizona
Sheppard, Lynn	1926–2009	Globe, Arizona	Calf roper, team roper, steer wrestler	2004, Arizona
Sheppard, Nancy Kelley	1929–	Fort Worth, Texas	Rodeo trick rider and trick roper	1996, Arizona

Name	Birth–Death	Birthplace	Notes	Induction Date, State
Shoulders, Jim	1928–2007	Tulsa, Oklahoma	World all-around champion cowboy, 1949, 1956–59; world bull-riding champion, 1951, 1954–59; world bareback-bronc-riding champion, 1950, 1956–58; all-around cowboy at Cheyenne 1955, 1956, 1963, and 1964; his cumulative record has been challenged but never duplicated in its diversity	1955, Oklahoma
Shultz, Charley	1891–1985	Sun City, Kansas	Rodeo clown famed with his little donkey, Danger	1999, Oklahoma
Slocum, Tex (Lyle Edward Asher)	1902–1963	Armington, Illinois	Saddle bronc rider; later arena judge	2004, Texas
Smith, Bill	1941–	Red Lodge, Montana	World saddle-bronc-riding champion, 1969, 1971, and 1973	2000, Montana
Smith, Dale D.	1928–	Safford, Arizona	World team-roping champion, 1956 and 1957	1995, Arizona
Smith, Dude (Vernon)	1928–	Carrollton, Texas	Rough-stock rider and steer wrestler, 1950–65	2006, Texas
Smith, Velda Tindall	1908–1990	Longview, Texas	Trick rider, relay and barrel racer	2005, Texas
Snyder, Smokey (Albert Edward)	1908–1965	Cripple Creek, Colorado	World bareback-bronc-riding champion, 1932 and 1936; world bull-riding champion, 1931, 1932, 1935–37; bull-riding champion at Cheyenne, 1937, 1939, 1941, and 1944	1977, Canada
Sorensen, Doc	1893–1985	Unknown, Utah	Rodeo producer and livestock contractor	1988, Idaho
Sorrells, Buckshot (Buck)	1913–1977	Patagonia, Arizona	World team-roping champion, 1950	1990, Arizona
Sowder, Thad	1874–1931	Pulaski, Kentucky	The first declared "World's Champion Broncho Rider," at the Festival of Mountain and Plain, Denver, Colorado, 1901	1960, Colorado
Stahl, Jesse	1883–1938	Unknown, Tennessee	African American saddle-bronc rider and steer wrestler	1979, California
Steele, Fannie Sperry	1887–1983	Helena, Montana	Early lady saddle-bronc rider and relay racer; "Woman Saddle-Bronc Riding Champion of the World" in 1912 and 1913	1975, Montana
Steiner, Buck (Thomas Casper)	1899–2001	Cedar Creek, Texas	Rodeo producer and livestock contractor	1993, Texas
Steiner, Tommy	1927–1999	Austin, Texas	Rodeo producer and livestock contractor	1995, Texas
Stillings, Floyd	1904–1995	Atchison, Kansas	Saddle-bronc rider; successfully rode Five Minutes to Midnight five times	1987, California
Stoker, J. W.	1927–	Colorado Springs, Colorado	Trick roper; two-time consecutive PRCA "Entertainer of the Year"	1999, Texas
Strickland, Hugh	1888–1941	Owyhee County, Idaho	Steer roper, calf roper, bronc rider, 1910-1932; all-around cowboy at Pendleton in 1918, 1922, 1924, and 1926	1968, Idaho
Strickland, Mabel DeLong	1897–1976	Wallula, Washington	Lady trick rider and steer roper; all-around champion cowgirl, 1922; at Pendleton in 1922 she roped a steer in 18 seconds flat, almost beating the men's world record at the time; remembered as the sport's "most beloved cowgirl"	1981, Washington
Stroud, Leonard	1893–1961	Monkstown, Texas	Leading rodeo trick rider and trick roper, 1912–28; invented the "Stroud Standout"	1965, Colorado
Sundown, Jackson	1863–1923	Flathead Reservation, Montana	Native American; saddle-bronc champion and all-around cowboy at Pendleton, 1916	1976, Idaho
Taillon, Cy	1907–1980	Cavalier, North Dakota	Rodeo arena announcer; often referred to as "rodeo's Walter Cronkite"; at NFR, 1959–60, 1962–66	1986, Montana
Tallman, Bob	1947–	Winnemucca, Nevada	Rodeo arena announcer; widely regarded as the "Voice of ProRodeo"; At NFR, 1975–76, 1983, 1989–93, 1995–2004	2007, Texas
Taylor, Dan	1923–	Coleman, Texas	Calf roper, 1935–65; PRCA president, 1986–87	2006, Texas
Tegland, Howard	1897–1945	Redding, California	Saddle-bronc rider, 1916–28; event champion at Cheyenne and Pendleton, 1922; at Tex Austin's London rodeo, 1924	1991, South Dakota

Name	Birth–Death	Birthplace	Notes	Induction Date, State
Tescher, Jim	1929–2003	Sentinental Butte, North Dakota	Saddle-bronc rider; event winner at Cheyenne, 1957 and 1965; at NFR, 1959 and 1963	2004, North Dakota
Tescher, Tom	1926–	Sentinental Butte, North Dakota	Saddle-bronc rider and steer wrestler; founded the Bronc Riding Match of Champions	2009, North Dakota
Thode, Earl Ernest	1900–1964	Belvedere, South Dakota	World all-around champion cowboy, 1929; world saddle-bronc-riding champion, 1929 and 1931; saddle bronc winner at Cheyenne, 1927, 1931, 1932, and 1934	1955, South Dakota
Thompson, Claire Belcher	1902–1971	Mansfield, Massachusetts	Bronc rider and trick rider, 1926–52; lady bronc-riding champion, Tex Austin's London Rodeo, 1934; rodeo producer and journalist	2008, Florida
Tibbs, Casey	1929–1990	Fort Pierre, South Dakota	World all-around champion cowboy, 1951, 1955; world saddle-bronc-riding champion, 1949, 1951–54, 1959; world bareback-bronc-riding champion, 1951; all-around champion cowboy at Cheyenne, 1953; at Calgary, 1955	1955, South Dakota
Tierney, Paul	1952–	Kearney, Nebraska	World all-around champion cowboy, 1980; world calf-roping champion, 1979	1980, South Dakota
Todd, Homer	1918–1958	Creek Nation, Oklahoma	Rodeo producer, known as "the Bull Man"	1991, Arkansas
Tompkins, Harry	1927–	Peekskill, New York	World all-around champion cowboy, 1952, 1960; world bull-riding champion, 1948–50, 1952, 1960; world bareback-bronc-riding champion, 1952	1955, Texas
Took, C. E. "Feek"	1909–1968	Redfield, South Dakota	Horse breeder and stock contractor; pioneered the "Born to Buck" breeding program for rodeo broncs, circa 1936	2008, Montana
Trickey, Lorena	1893–1961	Palmer, Oregon	Lady champion saddle-bronc rider and relay racer at Pendleton and Cheyenne, 1919–24; Hollywood movie stunt double	2000, Oregon
Truan, Fritz (Frederick G.)	1916–1945	Seeley, California	World all-around champion cowboy, 1940; world saddle-bronc-riding champion, 1939 and 1940; steer-wrestling and all-around champion cowboy at Pendleton, 1941	1955, California
Truitt, Dick	1904–1980	Rockwall, Texas	World steer-roping champion, 1939; all-around cowboy at Pendleton, 1929 and 1934	1983, Oklahoma
Tucker, Harley	1908–1960	Joseph, Oregon	Rodeo stock contractor	1997, Oregon
Tureman, Sonny	1918–1995	Wenatchee, Washington	World bareback-bronc-riding champion, 1948	2000, Oregon
Vamvoras, Clyde	1948–1985	Lake Charles, Louisiana	World bareback-bronc-riding champion, 1967 and 1968	2007, Louisiana
Veach, C. Monroe	1896–1986	Trenton, Missouri	Saddlemaker and rodeo performer	1993, Missouri
Vold, Harry	1924–	Edmonton, Alberta	Rodeo stock contractor and producer; eleven-time ProRodeo Stock Contractor of the Year	2009, Colorado
Walker, Enoch	1932–1979	Camp Verde, Arizona	World saddle-bronc-riding champion, 1960	1988, Wyoming
Ward, Bill E.	1923–1992	Danville, California	Saddle-bronc rider; RCA and PRCA brand logo is Bill Ward riding Sea Lion	2001, California
Ward, Leonard	1903–1985	Cowlitz County, Washington	World all-around champion cowboy, 1934; world saddle-bronc-riding champion and world bareback-bronc-riding champion, also in 1934	1955, Oregon
Weadick, Guy	1885–1953	Rochester, New York	Rodeo producer and promoter; known as "the father of Canadian rodeo"	1976, Canada
Webster, Shoat (Howard Chouteau)	1925–	Lenapah, Oklahoma	World steer-roping champion, 1949, 1950, 1954, 1955; all-around cowboy at Pendleton, 1949, 1950, 1951, 1952; steer-roping champion at Cheyenne, 1955, 1962, 1963	1990, Oklahoma

Name	Birth–Death	Birthplace	Notes	Induction Date, State
Weeks, Billy	1926–1988	Abilene, Texas	Rough-stock competitor; IRA bareback-riding champion, and all-around cowboy at Cheyenne, 1952; Doff Aber Memorial Trophy winner, 1951	1998, Texas
Weeks, Guy	1932–2007	Fort Worth, Texas	World saddle-bronc-riding champion, 1963; all-around champion cowboy at Calgary, 1958, 1961, and 1962	1992, Texas
Welch, Joe	1906–1991	Lovington, New Mexico	Calf roper and steer roper	1988, New Mexico
Whaley, Slim (William Everett)	1899–1999	Morgan, Texas	Steer-wrestler; trainer-owner of famed bulldogging horse Little Blue	1986, Oklahoma
Wharton, Ray	1920–	Bandera, Texas	World calf-roping champion, 1956	1994, Texas
Whatley, Todd	1920–1966	Rufe, Oklahoma	World all-around champion cowboy, 1947; world steer-wrestling champion, 1947; world bull-riding champion, 1953	1955, Oklahoma
White, Vivian	1913–1999	Enid, Oklahoma	Lady saddle-bronc rider and trick rider; ladies' bronc-riding champion at Madison Square Garden, 1938 and 1941; believed the only woman rider never to have been bucked off in judged competition	1991, Oklahoma
Whiteman, Hub	1910–1977	Clarksville, Texas	World steer-wrestling champion, 1941; steer-wrestling champion at Cheyenne, 1937, 1939, and 1940	1983, Texas
Whiteman, Jim	1914–1978	Clarksville, Texas	Bull rider and steer wrestler, 1937–46	1988, Texas
Whitfield, Fred	1967–	Houston, Texas	First African American world all-around champion cowboy, 1999; world calf-roping (tie-down roping) champion, 1991, 1995, 1996, 1999, 2000, 2002 and 2005	2000, Texas
Wilcox, Don	1914–1984	Arkansas City, Kansas	Rodeo trick rider, 1935–60	1994, Oklahoma
Williams, George	1932–	Amarillo, Texas	Rodeo rough-stock rider; NFR judge; PRCA Board of Directors; saddle maker; rancher	2008, Arizona
Witmer, Nancy Bragg	1926–	Fort Smith, Arkansas	Rodeo trick rider; GRA cutting-horse champion, 1954 and 1955	1999, Kansas
Wood, Marty	1933–	Bowness, Alberta	World saddle-bronc riding champion, 1958, 1964, 1966	2008, Oregon
Worrell, Sonny	1936–	Neodesha, Kansas	Calf roper and steer roper; world steer-roping champion, 1978	1994, Kansas
Yoder, Phil	1898–1941	Torrington, Wyoming	Steer-roping champion at Cheyenne, 1918; saddle-bronc champion at Cheyenne, 1921	1987, Wyoming
Young, Rick	1934–	Tickfaw, Louisiana	Rodeo clown and bullfighter; NFR "Coors Man in the Can," 1991, 1994, 1996, and 1997	2004, Louisiana
Youree, Florence	1933–	Duncan, Oklahoma	All-around champion cowgirl, 1966; instrumental in making ladies' barrel racing an RCA and NFR-sanctioned event; a founder and promoter of the Barrel Futurities of America	2009, Oklahoma
Zumwalt, Oral Harris	1903–1962	Morenci, Arizona	Steer wrestler; rodeo livestock contractor; in 1939 at Palm Springs, California, Zumwalt threw a steer in the fastest official time ever recorded—2.2 seconds without a barrier	1963, Montana

Table 2
Ben Johnson Memorial Award Inductees

Name	Birth–Death	Birthplace	Notes	Induction Date, State
Cooke, A. J. "Jack"	1925–2008	Chicago, Illinois	Rancher; rodeo supporter; civic leader; philanthropist; NC&WHM board of directors	2003, California
Gay, Neal	1926–	Dallas, Texas	Founder of the Mesquite Championship Rodeo, longest running weekly venue in the sport; rodeo clinic instructor; founder and promoter of the M.S. Rodeo fund raiser to fight muscular dystrophy	2009, Texas
Harrington, Don	1925–	Unknown, Missouri	Rodeo announcer; PRCA and RHS director; civic leader involved with youth groups; rancher	2002, Minnesota
Ivory, Buster	1923–2003	Alturus, California	Rodeo bronc rider; NFR livestock superintendent, 1959-1984; PRCA inductee, 1991	1999, Texas
Mahan, Larry	1943–	Salem, Oregon	Eight world champion titles; RHS director; ranch programs for youth; PRCA inductee, 1979	2007, Texas
McSpadden, Clem	1925–2008	Bushyhead, Oklahoma	NFR announcer, 1960, 1965–66; NFR General Manager, 1967–84; NC&WHM board of directors	1998, Oklahoma
Minick, Billy	1939–	Fort Worth, Texas	Livestock contractor and rodeo producer; sponsor of a variety of Texas charitable organizations	2008, Texas
Potter, Mel	1935–	Wisconsin Rapids, Wisconsin	Rancher; rodeo producer and livestock contractor; RHS director; NC&WHM board of directors	2005, Arizona
Rosser, Cotton	1928–	Long Beach, California	Rodeo manager; livestock contractor and stock breeder; high-school rodeo supporter; PRCA inductee, 1995	2006, California
Sheppard, Chuck	1916–2005	Globe, Arizona	Champion team roper, 1946; champion calf roper, 1951; RCA director; NFR judge; rancher	2001, Arizona
Shoulders, Jim	1928–2007	Tulsa, Oklahoma	Sixteen world-champion titles; rodeo instructor and spokesman; youth benefactor; PRCA inductee, 1979	2004, Oklahoma
Smith, Dale D.	1928–	Safford, Arizona	Champion team roper, 1956, 1957; champion calf roper, 1959; as RCA director, brought NFR to Oklahoma City	2000, Arizona

Table 3
Tad Lucas Memorial Award Inductees

Name	Birth–Death	Birthplace	Notes	Induction Date, State
Beals, Imogene Veach	1921–	Trenton, Missouri	Saddle maker; western clothier; rodeo journalist for *Hoofs and Horns* and *Ranchman* magazines	2001, Oklahoma
Blackstone, Faye	1915–	Diller, Nebraska	Rodeo trick rider and barrel racer; rancher. Inducted National Cowgirl Hall of Fame, 1982	1993, Florida
Burson, Polly Drayer Mills	1919–2006	Ontario, Oregon	Rodeo trick rider and relay racer; movie stunt double. Inducted Hollywood Walk of Fame, 1986	1990, Oregon
Camarillo, Sharon	1948–	Los Angeles, California	Rodeo barrel racer and instructor; businesswoman (Rafter C Productions) in barrel racing equipment	1997, California
Dearing, Judy Louise	1935–	Puerto Cabezas, Nicaragua	Horse and cattle raiser; rodeo and horse show supporter; RHS coordinator at NC&WHM	2004, Oklahoma
Decker, Jo	1925–	San Angelo, Texas	Rodeo rider and coordinator (NFR secretary, 1964, 1966–1970); western clothier; RHS inductee, 2000	1999, Oklahoma
Fraser, Geraldine "Jerry"	1930–2008	Big Spring, Texas	Rodeo barrel racer; in later life a skilled saddlemaker and famed leather carver	2006, Texas
Gay, Kay	1938–	Borger, Texas	Producer, Mesquite Championship Rodeo; breeder and trainer of barrel-racing horses	1994, Texas
Gibbs–Munroe, Jimmie	1956–	Clifton, Texas	WPRA all-around champion cowgirl, 1975; WPRA president. WPRA woman of the year, 1990	1996, Texas
Jauregui, Shirley Lucas	1924–	Bartlesville, Oklahoma	Rodeo trick rider; Hollywood stunt double; California Cattle Woman of the Year, 1996; FFA and 4-H supporter	2008, California
Kensinger, Arlene	1930–	Unknown, Wyoming	Rodeo horsewoman and arena manager; Miss Rodeo America board of directors	1995, Wyoming
Kesler, Liz	1926–	Unknown, Texas	Rodeo secretary and timer; promoter of the Justin Cowboy Crisis Fund; founder of the NFR Fashion Show	2009, Montana
Minick, Pamela	1955–	Las Vegas, Nevada	Miss Rodeo America, 1973; WPRA calf-roping champion, 1982; Mesquite Championship Rodeo commentator	1998, Texas
Parks, Mary Elizabeth	1910–1997	Stone, Colorado	Rodeo saddle-bronc rider and barrel racer; inducted National Cowgirl Hall of Fame, 1979	1991, Florida
Pumphrey, Madonna Eskew	1941–	Ardmore, Oklahoma	Rodeo trick roper and rider; in later life a court-appointed special advocate for children	2003, Oklahoma
Serpa, Louise L.	1925–	New York, New York	Rodeo photographer (first PRCA-sanctioned female allowed in arena); Inducted National Cowgirl Hall of Fame, 1999	2002, New York
Shoulders, Sharon	1923–	Bell, California	Rodeo secretary and timer; PRCA rodeo queen judge; cattle breeder; civic and youth supporter	2005, Oklahoma
Taylor, Berva Dawn	1929–	Salmon, Idaho	Rodeo sponsor girl and horsewoman; rodeo secretary for various producers, 1960s–1990s	2007, Texas
Vold, Karen Womack	1939–	Phoenix, Arizona	Rodeo trick rider (The Flying Cimarrons and The Firebirds); inducted National Cowgirl Hall of Fame, 1978	1992, Colorado
Wright, Martha	1951–	Dublin, Texas	Rodeo barrel racer and horse trainer; author, *Barrel Racing: Training the Wright Way*	2000, Texas

NOTES

Introduction to Part I: A Rodeo Overview

1. For thorough treatments of the origin, development, organization, and professionalization of rodeo, see Clifford Westermeier, *Man, Beast, Dust: The Story of Rodeo* (Lincoln: University of Nebraska Press, 1987); and Kristine Fredriksson, *American Rodeo: From Buffalo Bill to Big Business* (College Station: Texas A&M University Press, 1985). For a broad-ranging cultural perspective on the sport, see Michael Allen, *Rodeo Cowboys in the North American Imagination* (Reno: University of Nevada Press, 1998).

Chapter 1
GETTING STARTED: Cowboy Fun from Prairie to Arena

1. For the Spanish-Mexican background of cowboy culture and rodeo, see Mary Lou LeCompte, "The Hispanic Influence on the History of Rodeo, 1823–1932," *Journal of Sport History* 12, no. 1 (Spring 1985): 21–38; and Richard W. Slatta, *Cowboys of the Americas* (New Haven, Conn.: Yale University Press, 1990), 128, 211–13. For a deeper historical and cultural appraisal, see Terry G. Jordan, *North American Cattle-Ranching Frontiers: Origins, Diffusion, and Differentiation* (Albuquerque: University of New Mexico Press, 1993).

2. Quoted in Clifford Westermeier, *Trailing the Cowboy: His Life and Lore as Told by Frontier Journalists* (Caldwell, Idaho: Caxton Printers, 1955), 345.

3. Quoted in Danny Freeman, *World's Oldest Rodeo* (Prescott, Ariz.: Prescott Frontier Days, 1998), 12.

4. For an interesting treatment of the genesis, rapid commercialization, and legal control of such cowboy sport in the Southwest, see John O. Baxter, "Ropers and Rangers: Cowboy Tournaments and Steer Roping Contests in Territorial Arizona," *Journal of Arizona History* 46, no. 4 (Winter 2005): 315–48.

5. Bob Jordan, *Rodeo History and Legends* (Montrose, Colo.: Rodeo Stuff, 1994), 17.

6. Don Rickey, *$10 Horse, $40 Saddle: Cowboy Clothing, Arms, Tools and Horse Gear of the 1880s* (Fort Collins, Colo.: Old Army Press, 1976); Richard C. Rattenbury, "A Century of Western Fashion," *Persimmon Hill* 17, no. 3 (Autumn 1989): 5–15; Laurel Wilson, "American Cowboy Dress: Function to Fashion," *Dress* 28 (2001): 40–52. For a thorough regional treatment, see Tom Lindmier and Steve Mount, *I See By Your Outfit: Historic Cowboy Gear of the Northern Plains* (Glendo, Wyo.: High Plains Press, 1996), 32–93, 111–21.

7. Quoted in Lindmier and Mount, *I See By Your Outfit,* 29.

8. For the history, character, and influence of Wild West shows, see Don Russell, *The Wild West: A History of the Wild West Shows* (Fort Worth, Tex.: Amon Carter Museum of Western Art, 1970).

9. Oropeza files, Rodeo Historical Society Files (hereafter cited as RHSF), Dickinson Research Center, National Cowboy & Western Heritage Museum, Oklahoma City; Willard H. Porter, *Who's Who in Rodeo* (Oklahoma City: Powder River Book Company, 1982), 94–95. See also Frank Dean and Nacho Rodriguez, *Trick and Fancy Roping in the Charro Style* (Las Vegas, Nev.: Wild West Arts Club, 2003), 9–10.

10. Pickett files, RHSF; Porter, *Who's Who,* 96–97. See also Colonel Bailey C. Hanes, *Bill Pickett, Bulldogger: The Biography of a Black Cowboy* (Norman: University of Oklahoma Press, 1977).

11. Allison Fuss Mellis, *Riding Buffalos and Broncos: Rodeo and Native Traditions in the Northern Great Plains* (Norman: University of Oklahoma Press, 2003), 30–35, 162–65; Sundown files, RHSF; Porter, *Who's Who,* 134–35; Peter Iverson, *When Indians Became Cowboys: Native Peoples and Cattle Ranching in the American West* (Norman: University of Oklahoma Press, 1994), 74, 191–99.

12. Quoted in Candace Sherk Savage, *Cowgirls* (Berkeley, Calif.: Ten Speed Press, 1996), 56.

13. Mulhall files, RHSF; Porter, *Who's Who,* 90–91; Mary Lou LeCompte, *Cowgirls of the Rodeo: Pioneer Professional Athletes* (Urbana: University of Illinois Press, 1993), 36–38, 62; "Miss Lucille Mulhall . . . I Am Offering a Genuine Troop of Cowboys and Cowgirls," *The Wild Bunch* 1, no. 3 (May 1915): 16.

14. Blancett files, RHSF; Porter, *Who's Who,* 28–29; LeCompte, *Cowgirls of the Rodeo,* 40–42, 55; Savage, *Cowgirls,* 61–62.

15. Rattenbury, "Century of Western Fashion," 10, 14; Wilson, "American Cowboy Dress," 45–46; Elizabeth Clair Flood and William Manns, *Cowgirls: Women of the Wild West* (Santa Fe, N.Mex.: Zon International Publishing, 1999), 67–81; B. Byron Price, *Fine Art of the West* (New York: Abbeville Press, 2004), 75–78, 83–88.

16. "Guy Weadick Endorses Organization," *The Wild Bunch* 1, no. 8 (November 1915): 8.

17. McGonagill files, RHSF; Porter, *Who's Who,* 84–85; Westermeier, *Man, Beast, Dust,* 45–46.

18. Brennan files, RHSF; Porter, *Who's Who,* 32–33.

19. Hastings files, RHSF; Porter, *Who's Who,* 60–61.

20. For an interesting profile of Steamboat and the bronc riders of his time, see Candy Vyvey Moulton and Flossie Moulton, *Steamboat, Legendary Bucking Horse: His Life and Times, and the Cowboys Who Tried to Tame Him* (Glendo, Wyo.: High Plains Press, 1992).

21. Quoted in Moulton and Moulton, *Steamboat,* 111.

22. "Lucille Mulhall's Fort Worth Round-Up," *The Wild Bunch* 3, no. 2 (April 1917): 1.

23. Irwin files, RHSF; Porter, *Who's Who,* 64–65; Victoria Carlyle Weiland, *100 Years of Rodeo Stock Contracting* (Reno, Nev.: Professional Rodeo Stock Contractors Association, 1997), 168–69.

24. Austin files, RHSF; Porter, *Who's Who,* 20–21; Westermeier, *Man, Beast, Dust,* 332–33; Weiland, *100 Years,* 12, 26.

25. Elliott files, RHSF; Porter, *Who's Who,* 54–55; Westermeier, *Man, Beast, Dust,* 264–66. See also "Verne Elliott," *Hoofs and Horns* 15, no. 6 (December 1945): 14; and Weiland, *100 Years,* 166–67. For a profile of contemporary rodeo stock contracting and livestock, see Lynn Campion, *Rodeo: Behind the Scenes at America's Most Exciting Sport* (Guilford, Conn.: Lyons Press, 2002), 35–53.

26. LeCompte, *Cowgirls of the Rodeo,* 70, 83, 86; Westermeier, *Man, Beast, Dust,* 404–405.

27. Westermeier, *Man, Beast, Dust,* 332–34; LeCompte, *Cowgirls of the Rodeo,* 86; Flood and Manns, *Cowgirls,* 119.

28. Ryan files, RHSF; Porter, *Who's Who,* 114–15.

29. Quoted in Porter, *Who's Who,* 114.

30. Byers files, RHSF; Porter, *Who's Who,* 36–37; Chester Byers, *Roping: Trick and Fancy Rope Spinning* (New York: G. P. Putnam's Sons, 1928), 90–104.

31. Byers, *Roping,* ix.

32. Strickland files, RHSF; Porter, *Who's Who,* 130–31; LeCompte, *Cowgirls of the Rodeo,* 80–83, 86, 88.

Chapter 2
THE MAIN EVENTS: Laying Loops and Staying Aboard

1. "Frontier Days, Walla Walla, WN. September 16, 17, and 18, 1915," *The Wild Bunch* 1, no. 6 (September 1915): 10–11. Interestingly, the use of wild, big-game animals in rodeo competition appears to have climaxed at the 1945 Black Hills Round Up in Belle Fourche, South Dakota. There, four contestants, judged under Brahma-bull-riding rules, bucked out of the chutes on two-year-old buffalo bulls. Sergeant Glen Nutter of the Fort Robinson, Nebraska, Remount Station won the event and was acclaimed the Champion Buffalo Rider of the World—a title that he evidently never had to defend. See Joe Keller, "Buffalo Riding Champion," *Hoofs and Horns* 15, no. 5 (November 1945): 8.

2. For the evolution of the rules and scoring of the principal rodeo events at various early venues, see Jordan, *Rodeo History and Legends,* 69–112. For a thorough treatment of the character, equipment, and conduct of the various contemporary events, see Campion, *Rodeo.* See also Mary S. Robertson, *Rodeo: Standard Guide to the Cowboy Sport* (Berkeley, Calif.: Howell-North, 1961), 12–61; Wayne S. Wooden and Gavin Ehringer, *Rodeo in America: Wranglers, Roughstock, and Paydirt* (Lawrence: University Press of Kansas, 1996), 17–32; and ESPN-ProRodeo, http://www.sports.espn.go.com/prorodeo/news/EventDescriptions. For a colorful pictorial treatment of the judged events, see John Annerino, *Roughstock: The Toughest Events in Rodeo* (New York: Four Walls Eight Windows, 2000).

3. Campion, *Rodeo,* 73–93.

4. Akridge files, RHSF.

5. Campion, *Rodeo,* 193–211.

6. Burk files, RHSF; Willard H. Porter, *13 Flat: Tales of Thirty Famous Rodeo Ropers and Their Great Horses* (New York: A. S. Barnes and Co.; London: Thomas Yoseloff, 1967), 42–45, 48; Porter, *Who's Who,* 34–35; Westermeier, *Man, Beast, Dust,* 223.

7. Mansfield files, RHSF; Porter, *13 Flat,* 79–83; Porter, *Who's Who,* 86–87; Westermeier, *Man, Beast, Dust,* 216; Jordan, *Rodeo History and Legends,* 147–48.

8. Westermeier, *Man, Beast, Dust,* 221–24; Porter, *Who's Who,* 30–31; Porter, *13 Flat,* 82, 207–13; Jordan, *Rodeo History and Legends,* 147–48, 152–54.

9. Jordan, *Rodeo History and Legends,* 38, 76; Westermeier, *Man, Beast, Dust,* 372–73; Wilson, "American Cowboy Dress," 46, 49.

10. Campion, *Rodeo,* 95–114.

11. Knight files, RHSF; Porter, *Who's Who,* 72–73. See also Darrell Knight, *Pete Knight: The Cowboy King* (Calgary, Alta.: Detselig Enterprises, 2004).

12. Quoted in Porter, *Who's Who,* 72–73.

13. Westermeier, *Man, Beast, Dust,* 189–97, 201–205; Wooden and Ehringer, *Rodeo in America,* 118–25; Jordan, *Rodeo History and Legends,* 209–14. For a discussion of rodeo's earlier bucking horses, see Foghorn Clancy, "Famous Bucking Horses," *Hoofs and Horns* 11, no. 1 (July 1941): 5–6.

14. Jim W. McNab to Herman [Linder], January 28, 1970, Midnight files, RHSF.

15. Midnight files, RHSF.

16. Campion, *Rodeo,* 155–72.

17. Pettigrew files, RHSF; Porter, *Who's Who,* 160–61; Westermeier, *Man, Beast, Dust,* 241–42.

18. Quoted in Porter, *Who's Who,* 161.

19. Westermeier, *Man, Beast, Dust,* 239–40; Willard Combs files, RHSF; Fredriksson, *American Rodeo,* 116.

20. Campion, *Rodeo,* 175–91.

21. Schell files, RHSF.

22. Campion, *Rodeo,* 213–26.

23. James files, RHSF; Charmayne James with Cheryl Magoteaux, *Charmayne James on Barrel Racing* (Colorado Springs, Colo.: Western Horseman, 2005), 177–89; ESPN-ProRodeo, http://sports. espn.go.com/news_James_Retires.

24. For background on the protective gear worn in the bull-riding event, see Gail Hughbanks Woerner, *Cowboy Up! The History of Bull Riding* (Austin, Tex.: Eakin Press, 2001), 207–11.

25. Campion, *Rodeo,* 117–37.

26. Snyder files, RHSF; Porter, *Who's Who,* 120–21; Westermeier, *Man, Beast, Dust,* 252–53.

27. Westermeier, *Man, Beast, Dust,* 180–81, 249–50; Wooden and Ehringer, *Rodeo in America,* 118–25; Jordan, *Rodeo History and Legends,* 213–14; Paul Asay, "Building a Better Bull," *ProRodeo Sports News* 44, no. 14 (July 1996): 26–28.

28. Quoted in Dean Krakel, "Requiem to a Bull," *Persimmon Hill* 4, no. 1 (Spring 1974): 31. See also Bob St. John, *On Down the Road: The World of the Rodeo Cowboy* (Englewood Cliffs, N.J.: Prentice-Hall, 1977), 233–35.

29. Tornado files, RHSF; Asay, "Building a Better Bull," 27; Krakel, "Requiem to a Bull," 28–31. For an interesting reflection on "The Ride," see W. K. Stratton, *Chasing the Rodeo* (Orlando, Fla.: Harcourt, 2005), 13–19.

30. Gail Hughbanks Woerner, *Fearless Funnymen: The History of the Rodeo Clown* (Austin, Tex.: Eakin Press, 1993), 73–93; Wooden and Ehringer, *Rodeo in America,* 168–71. See also Jeanne Joy Hartangle-Taylor, *Greasepaint Matadors: The Unsung Heroes of Rodeo* (Loveland, Colo.: Alpine Publications, 1993).

31. Holcomb files, RHSF; Porter, *Who's Who,* 62–63; Westermeier, *Man, Beast, Dust,* 258–59; Woerner, *Fearless Funnymen,* 74–75, 96–99, 160–61.

32. Fulkerson files, RHSF; Woerner, *Fearless Funnymen,* 16–17, 40–42, 89–90, 155–56.

33. Wooden and Ehringer, *Rodeo in America,* 21.

34. Shirley E. Flynn, *Let's Go, Let's Show, Let's Rodeo: The History of Cheyenne Frontier Days* (Cheyenne, Wyo.: Wigwam Publishing Company, 1996), 32, 167. See also Slatta, *Cowboys of the Americas,* 23–24.

35. Crosby files, RHSF; Porter, *Who's Who,* 50–51. See also Thelma Crosby and Eve Ball, *Bob Crosby, World Champion Cowboy* (Clarendon, Tex.: Clarendon Press, 1966).

36. For the history and technique of the roping arts, see Dean and Rodriguez, *Trick and Fancy Roping;* and Byers, *Roping.*

37. Garrett files, RHSF.

38. Stroud files, RHSF; Porter, *Who's Who,* 132–33; Westermeier, *Man, Beast, Dust,* 46–48.

39. Vera McGinnis, *Rodeo Road: My Life as a Pioneer Cowgirl* (New York: Hastings House, 1974), 35.

40. McGinnis files, RHSF; LeCompte, *Cowgirls of the Rodeo,* 55–57, 59, 75, 85–87. See also McGinnis, *Rodeo Road.*

Chapter 3
THE COWGIRL CONTENDERS: Combining Grace and Grit

1. For the best history of women in rodeo sport, see LeCompte, *Cowgirls of the Rodeo.* For a rich pictorial treatment, see Milt Riske, *Those Magnificent Cowgirls: A History of the Rodeo Cowgirl* (Cheyenne: Wyoming Publishing, 1983).

2. Quoted in Sarah Wood-Clark, *Beautiful Daring Western Girls: Women of the Wild West Shows* (Cody, Wyo.: Buffalo Bill Historical Center, 1991), 6.

3. LeCompte, *Cowgirls of the Rodeo,* 49–68.

4. Quoted in Russell, *Wild West,* 79.

5. Quoted in Flood and Manns, *Cowgirls,* 111.

6. LeCompte, *Cowgirls of the Rodeo,* 25–27, 52–53; Savage, *Cowgirls,* 76, 80.

7. Quoted in LeCompte, *Cowgirls of the Rodeo,* 31.

8. Sperry-Steele files, RHSF; Porter, *Who's Who,* 126–27; LeCompte, *Cowgirls of the Rodeo,* 53–55, 59–60; "Fannie Sperry Steele," *Hoofs and Horns* 14, no. 11 (May 1945): 5. For a dramatized account of Sperry Steele's life, see Dee Marvine, *The Lady Rode Bucking Horses: The Story of Fannie Sperry Steele, Woman of the West* (Guilford, Conn.: Globe Pequot Press, 2005).

9. Baldwin files, RHSF; LeCompte, *Cowgirls of the Rodeo,* 46–49, 55, 59, 61–63, 76.

10. Trickey files, RHSF; LeCompte, *Cowgirls of the Rodeo,* 78, 91–92.

11. Roach files, RHSF; LeCompte, *Cowgirls of the Rodeo,* 67, 75, 110, 132.

12. LeCompte, *Cowgirls of the Rodeo,* 70–92.

13. Randolph files, RHSF; Porter, *Who's Who,* 102–103; LeCompte, *Cowgirls of the Rodeo,* 74, 88, 90. See also Foghorn Clancy, "Memory Lane," *Hoofs and Horns* 10, no. 4 (October 1940): 5.

14. Tad Lucas files, RHSF; Porter, *Who's Who,* 78–79; LeCompte, *Cowgirls of the Rodeo,* 77–79, 97–99, 129–32, 169–70.

15. LeCompte, *Cowgirls of the Rodeo,* 99.

16. Rattenbury, "Century of Western Fashion," 14; Flood and Manns, *Cowgirls,* 127–28; LeCompte, *Cowgirls of the Rodeo,* 34–35, 48–49, 61. See also Riske, *Those Magnificent Cowgirls,* 78–84.

17. Flood and Manns, *Cowgirls,* 128.

18. Flood and Manns, *Cowgirls,* 128–129; LeCompte, *Cowgirls of the Rodeo,* 83–85, 90, 103.

19. Quoted in Savage, *Cowgirls,* 75.

20. McCarroll files, RHSF; LeCompte, *Cowgirls of the Rodeo,* 95.

21. LeCompte, *Cowgirls of the Rodeo,* 95–97, 111–14; Westermeier, *Man, Beast, Dust,* 119–20. See also Renee M. Laegreid, *Riding Pretty: Rodeo Royalty in the American West* (Lincoln: University of Nebraska Press, 2006), 176–78; and Guy Weadick, "What Are Rodeos Doing?" *Hoofs and Horns* 7, no. 7 (January 1938): 14.

22. Alice Greenough files, RHSF; LeCompte, *Cowgirls of the Rodeo,* 92, 102, 139.

23. Quoted in LeCompte, *Cowgirls of the Rodeo,* 115.

24. LeCompte, *Cowgirls of the Rodeo,* 114–15, 121–27, 134–38; Laegreid, *Riding Pretty,* 74–82; Savage, *Cowgirls,* 93–94. For a good memoir of a ranch and rodeo cowgirl in this transitional period, see Jane Burnett Smith, *Hobbled Stirrups* (Caldwell, Idaho: Caxton Press, 2006).

25. Foghorn Clancy, "Madison Square Garden Rodeo," *Hoofs and Horns* 15, no. 6 (December 1945): 12.

26. Rattenbury, "Century of Western Fashion," 15; Wilson, "American Cowboy Dress," 47–48. For profiles of rodeo dress in the 1940s and following, see Westermeier, *Man, Beast, Dust,* 137–43; and Steven E. Weil and Daniel De Weese, *Western Shirts: A Classic American Fashion* (Salt Lake City, Utah: Gibbs Smith, 2004).

27. LeCompte, *Cowgirls of the Rodeo,* 129–32, 154–58, 177–78; Laegreid, *Riding Pretty,* 182–95. For the role of cowgirls in contemporary rodeo, see Wooden and Ehringer, *Rodeo in America,* 194–97; and Joan Burbick, *Rodeo Queens and the American Dream* (New York: Public Affairs, 2002).

Chapter 4
COMING OF AGE: Organization, Professionalism, Big Business

1. Tex Austin, "The Contests and the Contestants," *The Wild Bunch* 2, no. 2 (June 1916): 8.

2. Homer Wilson, "Champions," *The Wild Bunch* 1, no. 4 (July 1915): 8.

3. Quoted in Fredriksson, *American Rodeo,* 22.

4. Fredriksson, *American Rodeo,* 21–24; Westermeier, *Man, Beast, Dust,* 183–86.

5. Thode files, RHSF; Porter, *Who's Who,* 142–43.

6. Clyde Lindsey, "I Should Worry," *The Wild Bunch* 1, no. 7 (October 1915): 10.

7. Fletcher Files, RHSF. For a quite imaginary, fictionalized version of the 1911 Pendleton competition between Fletcher, Spain, and Sundown, see Ken Kesey with Ken Babbs, *Last Go Round* (New York: Viking Penguin, 1994).

8. Quoted in Porter, *Who's Who,* 125.

9. Stahl files, RHSF; Porter, *Who's Who,* 124–25.

10. Fay Ward, "Organization," *The Wild Bunch* 1, no. 12 (March 1916): 8, 10. See also Westermeier, *Man, Beast, Dust,* 95–96.

11. Quoted in Fredriksson, *American Rodeo,* 36.

12. Fredriksson, *American Rodeo,* 39–40. See also Gene Pruett, "Cowboys Turtle Association to Big Time Corporation," *Persimmon Hill* 4, no. 1 (Spring 1974): 4–8.

13. "Cowboys Turtle Association," *Hoofs and Horns* 6, no. 7 (December 1936): 24.

14. Westermeier, *Man, Beast, Dust,* 100–103; Fredriksson, *American Rodeo,* 42–43.

15. Westermeier, *Man, Beast, Dust,* 106–20; Fredriksson, *American Rodeo,* 43–50. See also Weadick, "What Are Rodeos Doing?" 14–15; Walt Coburn, "That Five X Beaver Crown," *Hoofs and Horns* 9, no. 9 (March 1940): 3; R. J. Hofmann, "New President Praises Spirit of Co-operation," *RAA News* 5, no. 4 (April 1941) in *Hoofs and Horns* 10, no. 11 (May 1941): 1; and "Rodeo Today," *Hoofs and Horns* 11, no. 1 (July 1941): 3–4.

16. Everett Bowman files, RHSF; Westermeier, *Man, Beast, Dust,* 123–24; Porter, *Who's Who,* 152–53; Jordan, *Rodeo History and Legends,* 143–46. See also "Everett Bowman Resigns," *Hoofs and Horns* 14, no. 11 (May 1945): 14.

17. Fredriksson, *American Rodeo,* 50.

18. Fredriksson, *American Rodeo,* 65–70. See also Bruce Clinton, "Rodeo Conscious," *Hoofs and Horns* 10, no. 8 (February 1941): 13; and "Real Job Lies Ahead for Rodeo Profession; Is Aid in Building Army Morale," *RAA News* 6, no. 3 (March 1942) in *Hoofs and Horns* 11, no. 10 (April 1942): 1.

19. News and Letters, *Hoofs and Horns* 14, no. 8 (February 1945): 8.

20. Ethel Hopkins, This and That, *Hoofs and Horns* 14, no. 12 (June 1945): 2.

21. Truan files, RHSF; Westermeier, *Man, Beast, Dust,* 238; Porter, *Who's Who,* 158–59. See also Eastern News, *Hoofs and Horns* 14, no. 1 (July 1944): 3; and "Sgt. Fritz Truan," *Hoofs and Horns* 14, no. 11 (May 1945): 14.

22. Fredriksson, *American Rodeo,* 80, 83–88.

23. Paul Friggens, "Bronc Bustin' Goes Big Business," *Town Journal* (July 1956): 35–37.

24. Fredriksson, *American Rodeo,* 88–94. For the origin, development, and influence of intercollegiate rodeo, see Sylvia Gann Mahoney, *College Rodeo: From Show to Sport* (College Station: Texas A&M

University Press, 2004); and Elmer Kelton, "N.I.R.A.: The National Intercollegiate Rodeo Association . . . College Rodeo Comes of Age," *Persimmon Hill* 8, no. 1 (Winter 1978): 32–43.

25. Bill Linderman files, RHSF: Porter, *Who's Who,* 76–77; Jordan, *Rodeo History and Legends,* 148–50.

26. Shoulders files, RHSF; Porter, *Who's Who,* 170–71; Jordan, *Rodeo History and Legends,* 130–33.

27. Tompkins files, RHSF; Porter, *Who's Who,* 174–75.

28. Quoted in Fredriksson, *American Rodeo,* 125.

29. Tibbs files, RHSF; Porter, *Who's Who,* 172–73; Jordan, *Rodeo History and Legends,* 129–30. See also Bill Gilbert, "Casey Tibbs . . . Maybe the Best Bronc Rider Ever," *Persimmon Hill* 11, no. 1 (Winter 1981): 22–35.

30. Bynum files, RHSF.

31. May files, RHSF; Jordan, *Rodeo History and Legends,* 65.

32. McLaughlin files, RHSF; Porter, *13 Flat,* 64–68; Jordan, *Rodeo History and Legends,* 158.

33. Oliver files, RHSF; Porter, *13 Flat,* 124–28; Porter, *Who's Who,* 184–85.

34. Fredriksson, *American Rodeo,* 97–102; Jordan, *Rodeo History and Legends,* 191.

35. Dightman and Sampson files, RHSF; Jordan, *Rodeo History and Legends,* 169–73. See also Wooden and Ehringer, *Rodeo in America,* 209–10.

36. Quoted in Jordan, *Rodeo History and Legends,* 175.

37. Whitfield files, RHSF; Jordan, *Rodeo History and Legends,* 175; Wooden and Ehringer, *Rodeo in America,* 211.

38. Fredriksson, *American Rodeo,* 182.

39. Quoted in St. John, *On Down the Road,* 100.

40. Fredriksson, *American Rodeo,* 104–109, 119–20. For a telling look at the character and characters of rodeo as the sport made the transition to a big-business pursuit in the 1970s, see St. John, *On Down the Road.*

41. Quoted in St. John, *On Down the Road,* 63.

42. Mahan files, RHSF; Porter, *Who's Who,* 182–83; Jordan, *Rodeo History and Legends,* 135–36. See also St. John, *On Down the Road,* 45–48, 95; and Stratton, *Chasing the Rodeo,* 7–8.

43. Quoted in St. John, *On Down the Road,* 105.

44. Gay files, RHSF; Jordan, *Rodeo History and Legends,* 138–39; http://www.prorodeohalloffame.com/website/DonGay.

45. Wooden and Ehringer, *Rodeo in America,* 235–36; http://www.prorodeo.org./2006MediaGuide/PRCAPartners/ProRodeoRecords.

46. http://www.prorodeo.org./2006MediaGuide.

47. For the changing character of rodeo over recent decades and perspectives on its future, see Wooden and Ehringer, *Rodeo in America,* 237–38, 255–64; and Stratton, *Chasing the Rodeo,* 291–95.

48. Quoted in St. John, *On Down the Road,* 100.

49. For ranch rodeo, see http://www.wrca.org; and http://www.ranchrodeo.net. For a postmodern perspective on contemporary rodeo, see Michael L. Johnson, *Hunger for the Wild: America's Obsession with the Untamed West* (Lawrence: University Press of Kansas, 2007), 327–32.

Introduction to Part 2: A Collection Portfolio

1. Charles W. Collier, "Rodeo Impressions," *The Recorder,* reprinted in *Hoofs and Horns* 8, no. 4 (October 1938): 18.

Chapter 5
RODEO SADDLERY: Stock, Bronc, Trick, Parade, and Trophy

1. Russel H. Beatie, *Saddles* (Norman: University of Oklahoma Press, 1981), 79–85, 97–99; Lee M. Rice and Glenn R. Vernam, *They Saddled the West* (Cambridge, Md.: Cornell Maritime Press, 1975), 87, 89, 91; Jordan, *Rodeo History and Legends,* 76.

2. Beatie, *Saddles,* 109–10; Rice and Vernam, *They Saddled the West,* 91, 97–99.

3. Frank E. Dean, *Trick and Fancy Riding* (Caldwell, Idaho: Caxton Printers, 1975), 15–17.

4. Price, *Fine Art of the West,* 71–88.

Chapter 6
RODEO HONORS: Trophy Plaques, Cups, Sculptures, Buckles, and Spurs

1. Homer Wilson, Editorial, *The Wild Bunch* 1, no. 3 (May 1915): 6; and "The Stampede," *The Wild Bunch* 1, no. 12 (March 1916): 2.

2. "Star Performer Raises Issue of Lasting Awards," and "1942 R.A.A. Trophy Donors," *RAA News* 6, no. 3 (March 1942) in *Hoofs and Horns* 11, no. 10 (April 1942): 1.

3. Price, *Fine Art of the West,* 206–13. For an extensive pictorial treatment, see David R. Stoecklein, *The Western Buckle: History, Art, Culture, Function* (Ketchum, Idaho: Stoecklein Publishing and Photography, 2003).

Chapter 7
RODEO COSTUME: Hats, Shirts, Chaps, Boots, and More

1. William Manns and Elizabeth Clair Flood, *Cowboys and the Trappings of the Old West* (Santa Fe, N.Mex.: Zon International Publishing, 1997), 20–24; Rattenbury, "Century of Western Fashion," 6, 14; Wilson, "American Cowboy Dress," 45–46; Westermeier, *Man, Beast, Dust,* 141–42. For further information on the genesis of the "cowboy" hat, see Debbie Henderson, *Cowboys and Hatters: Bond Street, Sagebrush, and the Silver Screen* (Yellow Springs, Ohio: Wild Goose Press, 1996).

2. Westermeier, *Man, Beast, Dust,* 137–39; Wilson, "American Cowboy Dress," 47–48; Rattenbury, "Century of Western Fashion," 15.

3. Manns and Flood, *Cowboys,* 65–79; Wilson, "American Cowboy Dress," 40–41, 44–46, 49; Westermeier, *Man, Beast, Dust,* 142–43.

4. Manns and Flood, *Cowboys,* 29–36; Westermeier, *Man, Beast, Dust,* 139–41.

Chapter 8
RODEO ARTWORK: From the Fine to the Commercial

1. AskART, http://www.askart.com/artists/biography/85620; Charles W. Simpson, *El Rodeo: One Hundred Sketches Made in the Arena during the Great International Contest (1924)* (London: John Lane, 1925).

2. Allen, *Rodeo Cowboys,* 110–11, 117.

3. Scriver files, Contemporary Western Artists Files (hereafter cited as CWAF), Dickinson Research Center, National Cowboy & Western Heritage Museum; Bob Scriver, *An Honest Try* (Kansas City, Mo.: Lowell Press, 1975).

4. Scott files, CWAF; M. J. Van Deventer, ed., *Prix de West 2005 Invitational Art Exhibition* (Oklahoma City: National Cowboy & Western Heritage Museum, 2005), 170.

5. For background on the R. J. Reynolds Tobacco Company's sponsorship of professional rodeo, see Fredriksson, *American Rodeo,* 190–94.

6. For insights on the pervasive bronc-riding motif in western and commercial rodeo artwork, see Allen, *Rodeo Cowboys,* 113, 121; and Valona Varnum Crowell, *The Artist and the Bucking Horse* (Taos, N.Mex.: Art of the West, n.d.).

SOURCES

Archival Sources for Biographical Files

Contemporary Western Artists Files (CWAF). Dickinson Research Center, National Cowboy & Western Heritage Museum, Oklahoma City.

Rodeo Historical Society Files (RHSF). Dickinson Research Center, National Cowboy & Western Heritage Museum, Oklahoma City.

Published Works

Allen, Michael. *Rodeo Cowboys in the North American Imagination.* Reno: University of Nevada Press, 1998.

Alter, Judy. *Rodeos: The Greatest Show on Dirt.* New York: Franklin Watts, 1996.

Annerino, John. *Roughstock: The Toughest Events in Rodeo.* New York: Four Walls Eight Windows, 2000.

Asay, Paul. "Building a Better Bull." *ProRodeo Sports News* 44, no. 14 (July 1996): 26–28.

Austin, Tex. "The Contests and the Contestants." *The Wild Bunch* 2, no. 2 (June 1916): 8.

Baxter, John O. "Ropers and Rangers: Cowboy Tournaments and Steer Roping Contests in Territorial Arizona." *Journal of Arizona History* 46, no. 4 (Winter 2005): 315–48.

Beard, Casey. *Tools of the Cowboy Trade: Today's Crafters of Saddles, Bits, Spurs, and Trappings.* Salt Lake City, Utah: Gibbs-Smith Publisher, 1999.

Beard, Tyler. *100 Years of Western Wear.* Salt Lake City, Utah: Gibbs-Smith Publisher, 1993.

Beatie, Russel H. *Saddles.* Norman: University of Oklahoma Press, 1981.

Branch, Douglas. *The Cowboy and His Interpreters.* New York: D. Appleton and Co., 1926.

Bridger, Bobby. *Buffalo Bill and Sitting Bull: Inventing the Wild West.* Austin: University of Texas Press, 2002.

Burbick, Joan. *Rodeo Queens and the American Dream.* New York: Public Affairs, 2002.

Byers, Chester. *Roping: Trick and Fancy Rope Spinning.* New York: G. P. Putnam's Sons, 1928.

California Rodeo Salinas: One Hundred Years of History. Pacific Grove, Calif.: Park Place Press, 2002.

Campion, Lynn. *Rodeo: Behind the Scenes at America's Most Exciting Sport.* Guilford, Conn.: Lyons Press, 2002.

Chesnar, Lynne. *February Fever: Historical Highlights . . . The Houston Livestock Show and Rodeo, 1932–1992.* Houston, Tex.: Houston Livestock Show and Rodeo, 1991.

Clancy, Foghorn (Fred M.). "Famous Bucking Horses." *Hoofs and Horns* 11, no. 1 (July 1941): 5–6.

———. "Madison Square Garden Rodeo," *Hoofs and Horns* 15, no. 6 (December 1945): 12.

———. "Memory Lane." *Hoofs and Horns* 10, no. 4 (October 1940): 5.

———. *My Fifty Years in Rodeo: Living with Cowboys, Horses and Danger.* San Antonio, Tex.: Naylor Company Publishers, 1952.

Clayton, Lawrence, Jim Hoy, and Jerald Underwood. *Vaqueros, Cowboys, and Buckaroos.* Austin: University of Texas Press, 2001.

Clifton, Guy. *Reno Rodeo, a History—The First 80 Years.* Reno, Nev.: Reno Rodeo Foundation, 2000.

Clinton, Bruce. "Rodeo Conscious." *Hoofs and Horns* 10, no. 8 (February 1941): 13.

Coburn, Walt. "That Five X Beaver Crown." *Hoofs and Horns* 9, no. 9 (March 1940): 3.

Collier, Charles W. "Rodeo Impressions." *The Recorder,* reprinted in *Hoofs and Horns* 8, no. 4 (October 1938): 18.

"Cowboys Turtle Association." *Hoofs and Horns* 6, no. 7 (December 1936): 24.

Crosby, Thelma, and Eve Ball. *Bob Crosby, World Champion Cowboy.* Clarendon, Tex.: Clarendon Press, 1966.

Crowell, Valona Varnum. *The Artist and the Bucking Horse.* Taos, N.Mex.: Art of the West, n.d.

Dary, David. *Cowboy Culture: A Saga of Five Centuries.* New York: Alfred A. Knopf, 1981.

Dean, Frank E. *Trick and Fancy Riding.* Caldwell, Idaho: Caxton Printers, 1975.

Dean, Frank, and Nacho Rodriguez. *Trick and Fancy Roping in the Charro Style.* Las Vegas, Nev.: Wild West Arts Club, 2003.

Dempsey, Hugh A. *Tom Three Persons: Legend of an Indian Cowboy.* Saskatoon, Sask.: Purich Publishing, 1997.

Eastern News. *Hoofs and Horns* 14, no. 1 (July 1944): 3.

Ehringer, Gavin. *Rodeo Legends—20 Extraordinary Athletes of America's Sport.* Colorado Springs, Colo.: Western Horseman, 2001.

Englander, Joe. *They Ride the Rodeo: The Men and Women of the American Amateur Rodeo Circuit.* New York: Collier Books, 1979.

"Everett Bowman Resigns." *Hoofs and Horns* 14, no. 11 (May 1945): 14.

"Fannie Sperry Steele." *Hoofs and Horns* 14, no. 11 (May 1945): 5.

Fleming, Steve, and Judi Lakin, eds. *Pikes Peak or Bust Rodeo: The First Fifty Years.* Colorado Springs, Colo.: ProRodeo Hall of Fame and Museum of the American Cowboy, 1990.

Flood, Elizabeth Clair, and William Manns. *Cowgirls: Women of the Wild West.* Santa Fe, N.Mex.: Zon International Publishing, 1999.

Flynn, Shirley E. *Let's Go, Let's Show, Let's Rodeo: The History of Cheyenne Frontier Days.* Cheyenne, Wyo.: Wigwam Publishing Company, 1996.

Fredriksson, Kristine. *American Rodeo: From Buffalo Bill to Big Business.* College Station: Texas A&M University Press, 1985.

Freeman, Danny. *World's Oldest Rodeo.* Prescott, Ariz.: Prescott Frontier Days, 1998.

Friggens, Paul. "Bronc Bustin' Goes Big Business." *Town Journal* (July 1956): 35–37.

"Frontier Days, Walla Walla, WN. September 16, 17, and 18, 1915." *The Wild Bunch* 1, no. 6 (September 1915): 10–11.

Furlong, Charles Wellington. *Let 'Er Buck: A Story of the Passing of the Old West.* New York: G. P. Putnam's Sons and Knickerbocker Press, 1923.

Gilbert, Bill. "Casey Tibbs . . . Maybe the Best Bronc Rider Ever." *Persimmon Hill* 11, no. 1 (Spring 1981): 22–35.

Gray, James H. *A Brand of Its Own: The 100 Year History of the Calgary Exhibition and Stampede.* Saskatoon, Sask.: Western Producer Prairie Books, 1985.

Gray, Robert N. *Mr. Rodeo Himself: Cecil Cornish, His Life and Times.* Waukomis, Okla.: Rodeo Press, 1990.

"Guy Weadick Endorses Organization." *The Wild Bunch* 1, no. 8 (November 1915): 8.

Hall, Douglas Kent. *Let 'Er Buck.* New York: Saturday Review Press, E. P. Dutton and Co., 1973.

Hanes, Colonel Bailey C. *Bill Pickett, Bulldogger: The Biography of a Black Cowboy.* Norman: University of Oklahoma Press, 1977.

Hanesworth, Robert D. *Daddy of 'Em All: The Story of the Cheyenne Frontier Days.* Cheyenne, Wyo.: Flintlock Publishing Company, 1967.

Hartangle-Taylor, Jeanne Joy. *Greasepaint Matadors: The Unsung Heroes of Rodeo.* Loveland, Colo.: Alpine Publications, 1993.

Henderson, Debbie. *Cowboys and Hatters: Bond Street, Sagebrush, and the Silver Screen.* Yellow Springs, Ohio: Wild Goose Press, 1996.

Hinsdale, Harriet. *Born to Rope: The Sam Garrett Story.* Fallbrook, Calif.: Aero Publishers, 1971.

Hofmann, R. J. "New President Praises Spirit of Co-operation." *RAA News* 5, no. 4 (April 1941), in *Hoofs and Horns* 10, no. 11 (May 1941): 1.

Hopkins, Ethel. This and That. *Hoofs and Horns* 14, no. 12 (June 1945): 2.

Howard, Robert West, and Oren Arnold. *Rodeo: Last Frontier of the Old West.* New York: New American Library, 1961.

Hutchins, Dan, and Sebie Hutchins. *Old Cowboy Saddles and Spurs . . . Sixth Annual.* Colorado Springs, Colo.: Hutchins Publishing, 1996.

Iverson, Peter. *When Indians Became Cowboys: Native Peoples and Cattle Ranching in the American West.* Norman: University of Oklahoma Press, 1994.

James, Charmayne, with Cheryl Magoteaux. *Charmayne James on Barrel Racing.* Colorado Springs, Colo.: Western Horseman, 2005.

Johnson, Michael L. *Hunger for the Wild: America's Obsession with the Untamed West.* Lawrence: University Press of Kansas, 2007.

Jordan, Bob. *Rodeo History and Legends.* Montrose, Colo.: Rodeo Stuff, 1994.

Jordan, Teresa. *Cowgirls: Women of the American West.* Lincoln: University of Nebraska Press, 1992.

Jordan, Terry G. *North American Cattle-Ranching Frontiers: Origins, Diffusion, and Differentiation.* Albuquerque: University of New Mexico Press, 1993.

Kahn, Margot. *Horses That Buck: The Story of Champion Bronc Rider Bill Smith.* Norman: University of Oklahoma Press, 2008.

Kauffman, Sandra. *The Cowboy Catalog.* New York: Clarkson N. Potter, 1980.

Kegley, Max. *Rodeo: The Sport of the Cow Country.* New York: Hastings House, 1942.

Keller, Joe. "Buffalo Riding Champion." *Hoofs and Horns* 15, no. 5 (November 1945): 8.

Kelton, Elmer. "N.I.R.A.: The National Intercollegiate Rodeo Association . . . College Rodeo Comes of Age." *Persimmon Hill* 8, no. 1 (Spring 1978): 32–43.

Kennedy, Fred. *Calgary Stampede: The Authentic Story of the Calgary Exhibition and Stampede . . . 1912–1964.* Vancouver, B.C.: West Vancouver Enterprises, 1965.

Kesey, Ken, with Ken Babbs. *Last Go Round.* New York: Viking Penguin, 1994.

Knight, Darrell. *Pete Knight: The Cowboy King.* Calgary, Alta.: Detselig Enterprises, 2004.

Krakel, Dean. "Requiem to a Bull." *Persimmon Hill* 4, no. 1 (Spring 1974): 28–31.

Laegreid, Renee M. *Riding Pretty: Rodeo Royalty in the American West.* Lincoln: University of Nebraska Press, 2006.

Lamb, Gene. *Rodeo Back of the Chutes.* Denver, Colo.: Multi-list, 1986.

Lawrence, Elizabeth Atwood. *Rodeo: An Anthropologist Looks at the Wild and the Tame.* Knoxville: University of Tennessee Press, 1982.

LeCompte, Mary Lou. *Cowgirls of the Rodeo: Pioneer Professional Athletes.* Urbana: University of Illinois Press, 1993.

———. "The Hispanic Influence on the History of Rodeo, 1823–1932." *Journal of Sport History* 12, no. 1 (Spring 1985): 21–38.

Lindmier, Tom, and Steve Mount. *I See By Your Outfit: Historic Cowboy Gear of the Northern Plains.* Glendo, Wyo.: High Plains Press, 1996.

Lindsey, Clyde. "I Should Worry." *The Wild Bunch* 1, no. 7 (October 1915): 10.

Long, Al. *Rodeo Action Photos: Today's Rodeo Cowboys.* Stephenville, Tex.: Rodeo Sports News, 1974.

"Lucille Mulhall's Fort Worth Round-Up." *The Wild Bunch* 3, no. 2 (April 1917): 1.

Mahoney, Sylvia Gann. *College Rodeo: From Show to Sport.* College Station: Texas A&M University Press, 2004.

Manns, William, and Elizabeth Clair Flood. *Cowboys and the Trappings of the Old West.* Santa Fe, N.Mex.: ZON International Publishing, 1997.

Marvine, Dee. *The Lady Rode Bucking Horses: The Story of Fannie Sperry Steele, Woman of the West.* Guilford, Conn.: Globe Pequot Press, 2005.

Mason, Bernard S. *Primitive and Pioneer Sports, or Recreation Today.* New York: A. S. Barnes and Company, 1937.

McGinnis, Vera. *Rodeo Road: My Life as a Pioneer Cowgirl.* New York: Hastings House Publishers, 1974.

McMurtry, Larry. *It's Always We Rambled: An Essay on Rodeo.* New York: Frank Hallman, 1974.

Mellis, Allison Fuss. *Riding Buffalos and Broncos: Rodeo and Native Traditions in the Northern Great Plains.* Norman: University of Oklahoma Press, 2003.

"Miss Lucille Mulhall . . . I Am Offering a Genuine Troop of Cowboys and Cowgirls." *The Wild Bunch* 1, no. 3 (May 1915): 16.

Moulton, Candy Vyvey, and Flossie Moulton. *Steamboat, Legendary Bucking Horse: His Life and Times, and the Cowboys Who Tried to Tame Him.* Glendo, Wyo.: High Plains Press, 1992.

"New Blood for the Rodeo Business: College Students Are Getting Interested." *The Buckboard* 4, no. 7 (January 1949): 22.

"1942 R.A.A. Trophy Donors." *RAA News* 6, no. 3 (March 1942), in *Hoofs and Horns* 11, no. 10 (April 1942): 1.

Norbury, Rosamond. *Behind the Chutes.* Missoula, Mont.: Mountain Press Publishing Company, 1993.

Porter, Willard H. "The American Rodeo: Sport and Spectacle." *American West* 8, no. 4 (July 1971): 40–47, 61–62.

———. *Roping and Riding: Fast Horses and Short Ropes.* New York: A. S. Barnes and Co., 1975.

———. *13 Flat: Tales of Thirty Famous Rodeo Ropers and Their Great Horses.* New York: A. S. Barnes and Co.; London: Thomas Yoseloff, 1967.

———. *Who's Who in Rodeo.* Oklahoma City: Powder River Book Company (National Cowboy Hall of Fame), 1982.

Price, B. Byron. *Fine Art of the West.* New York: Abbeville Press, 2004.

Professional Rodeo Cowboys Association. *Finals: A Complete History of the National Finals Rodeo.* Colorado Springs, Colo.: Professional Rodeo Cowboys Association, 1998.

Pruett, Gene. "Cowboys Turtle Association to Big Time Corporation." *Persimmon Hill* 4, no. 1 (Spring 1974): 4–9.

Rand, Charles E. "Ralph Russell Doubleday: Rodeo's First Professional Photographer." *Persimmon Hill* 27, no. 4 (Winter 1999): 34–41.

Rattenbury, Richard C. "The American Rodeo Gallery." *Persimmon Hill* 27, no. 4 (Winter 1999): 16–24.

———. "A Century of Western Fashion." *Persimmon Hill* 17, no. 3 (Autumn 1989): 5–15.

———. "Rediscovering the Rodeo Memorabilia of Frank and Bonnie McCarroll." *Persimmon Hill* 34, no. 3 (Autumn 2006): 22–25.

"Real Job Lies Ahead for Rodeo Profession; Is Aid in Building Army Morale." *RAA News* 6, no. 3 (March 1942), in *Hoofs and Horns* 11, no. 10 (April 1942): 1.

Reddin, Paul. *Wild West Shows.* Urbana: University of Illinois Press, 1999.

Reynolds, Clay, with Marie-Madeleine Schein. *A Hundred Years of Heroes: A History of the Southwestern Exposition and Livestock Show.* Fort Worth: Texas Christian University Press, 1995.

Rice, Lee M., and Glenn R. Vernam. *They Saddled the West.* Cambridge, Md.: Cornell Maritime Press, 1975.

Rickey, Don. *$10 Horse, $40 Saddle: Cowboy Clothing, Arms, Tools and Horse Gear of the 1880s.* Fort Collins, Colo.: Old Army Press, 1976.

Riley, Glenda, and Richard W. Etulain, eds. *Wild Women of the Old West.* Golden, Colo.: Fulcrum Publishing, 2003.

Ringley, Tom. *Rodeo Time in Sheridan, Wyo.: A History of the Sheridan-Wyo-Rodeo.* Greybull, Wyo.: Pronghorn Press, 2004.

———. *When the Whistle Blows: The Turk Greenough Story.* Greybull, Wyo.: Pronghorn Press, 2008.

Riske, Milt. *Those Magnificent Cowgirls: A History of the Rodeo Cowgirl.* Cheyenne: Wyoming Publishing, 1983.

Riske, Milt, and Joy Riske. *Cheyenne Frontier Days: A Marker from Which to Reckon All Events.* Cheyenne, Wyo.: Cheyenne Corral of Westerners, 1984.

Roach, Joyce Gibson. *The Cowgirls.* Denton: University of North Texas Press, 1990.

Robertson, Mary S. *Rodeo: Standard Guide to the Cowboy Sport.* Berkeley, Calif.: Howell-North, 1961.

"Rodeo Today." *Hoofs and Horns* 11, no. 1 (July 1941): 3–4.

Rupp, Virgil. *Let 'Er Buck: A History of the Pendleton Round-Up.* Pendleton, Ore.: Pendleton Round-Up Association, 1985.

Russell, Don. *The Wild West: A History of the Wild West Shows.* Fort Worth, Tex.: Amon Carter Museum of Western Art, 1970.

Ryan, Jim. *The Rodeo and Hollywood: Rodeo Cowboys on Screen and Western Actors in the Arena.* Jefferson, N.C.: McFarland and Company, 2006.

Sands, Kathleen Mullen. *Charreria Mexicana: An Equestrian Folk Tradition.* Tucson: University of Arizona Press, 1993.

Savage, Candace Sherk. *Cowgirls.* Berkeley, Calif.: Ten Speed Press, 1996.

Savitt, Sam. *Midnight, Champion Bucking Horse.* N.p.: Scholastic Book Service, 1957.

———. *Rodeo: Cowboys, Bulls and Broncos.* Garden City, N.Y.: Doubleday and Co., 1963.

Schnell, Fred. *Rodeo! The Suicide Circuit.* New York: Rand McNally and Company, 1971.

Scriver, Bob. *An Honest Try.* Kansas City, Mo.: Lowell Press, 1975.

Serpa, Louise L., and Larry McMurtry. *Rodeo: No Guts, No Glory.* New York: Aperture, 1994.

"Sgt. Fritz Truan." *Hoofs and Horns* 14, no. 11 (May 1945): 14.

Simpson, Charles W. *El Rodeo: One Hundred Sketches Made in the Arena during the Great International Contest (1924).* London: John Lane, 1925.

Slatta, Richard W. *The Cowboy Encyclopedia.* New York: W.W. Norton and Company, 1996.

———. *Cowboys of the Americas.* New Haven, Conn.: Yale University Press, 1990.

Smith, Jane Burnett. *Hobbled Stirrups.* Caldwell, Idaho: Caxton Press, 2006.

Snyder, Jeffery B. *Stetson Hats and the John B. Stetson Company, 1865–1970.* Atglen, Penn.: Schiffer Publishing, 1997.

"Stampede, The." *The Wild Bunch* 1, no. 12 (March 1916): 2.

Stansbury, Kathryn B. *Lucille Mulhall: Her Family, Her Life, Her Times.* Mulhall, Okla.: privately published, 1985.

"Star Performer Raises Issue of Lasting Awards." *RAA News* 6, no. 3 (March 1942), in *Hoofs and Horns* 11, no. 10 (April 1942): 1.

Stern, Jane, and Michael Stern. *Way Out West.* New York: Harper Collins Publishers, 1993.

Stewart, Paul W., and Wallace Yvonne Ponce. *Black Cowboys.* Broomfield, Colo.: Phillips Publishing, 1986.

St. John, Bob. *On Down the Road: The World of the Rodeo Cowboy.* Englewood Cliffs, N.J.: Prentice-Hall, 1977.

Stoecklein, David R. *The Western Buckle: History, Art, Culture, Function.* Ketchum, Idaho: Stoecklein Publishing and Photography, 2003.

Stratton, W. K. *Chasing the Rodeo.* Orlando, Fla.: Harcourt, 2005.

Taylor, Lonn, and Ingrid Marr. *The American Cowboy.* Washington, D.C.: Library of Congress, 1984.

Tyler, Ronnie C. *The Rodeo of John Addison Stryker.* Austin, Tex.: Encino Press, 1977.

Van Deventer, M. J., ed. *Prix de West 2005 Invitational Art Exhibition.* Oklahoma City: National Cowboy & Western Heritage Museum, 2005.

"Verne Elliott." *Hoofs and Horns* 15, no. 6 (December 1945): 14.

Wallis, Michael. *The Real Wild West: The 101 Ranch and the Creation of the American West.* New York: St. Martin's Press, 1999.

Ward, Fay. "Organization." *The Wild Bunch* 1, no. 12 (March 1916): 8, 10.

Weadick, Guy. "What Are Rodeos Doing?" *Hoofs and Horns* 7, no. 7 (January 1938): 14–15.

Weil, Steven E., and Daniel De Weese. *Western Shirts: A Classic American Fashion.* Salt Lake City, Utah: Gibbs Smith, Publisher, 2004.

Weiland, Victoria Carlyle. *100 Years of Rodeo Stock Contracting.* Reno, Nev.: Professional Rodeo Stock Contractors Association, 1997.

Westermeier, Clifford P. *Man, Beast, Dust: The Story of Rodeo.* Denver, Colo.: World Press, 1947. Reprint, University of Nebraska Press, Bison Book edition, 1987.

———, ed. *Trailing the Cowboy: His Life and Lore as Told by Frontier Journalists.* Caldwell, Idaho: Caxton Printers, 1955.

Whitehead, Lea. "A History of Western Wear Fashion." *Quarter Horse Journal* 41, no. 12 (September 1989): 50–53.

Wilson, Homer. "Champions." *The Wild Bunch* 1, no. 4 (July 1915): 8.

———. Editorial. *The Wild Bunch* 1, no. 3 (May 1915): 6.

Wilson, Laurel. "American Cowboy Dress: Function to Fashion." *Dress* 28 (2001): 40–52.

Wilson, R. L., with Greg Martin. *Buffalo Bill's Wild West: An American Legend.* New York: Random House, 1998.

Woerner, Gail Hughbanks. *A Belly Full of Bedsprings: The History of Bronc Riding.* Austin, Tex.: Eakin Press, 1998.

———. *Cowboy Up! The History of Bull Riding.* Austin, Tex.: Eakin Press, 2001.

———. *Fearless Funnymen: The History of the Rodeo Clown.* Austin, Tex.: Eakin Press, 1993.

Wood-Clark, Sarah. *Beautiful Daring Western Girls: Women of the Wild West Shows.* Cody, Wyo.: Buffalo Bill Historical Center, 1991.

Wooden, Wayne S., and Gavin Ehringer. *Rodeo in America: Wranglers, Roughstock, and Paydirt.* Lawrence: University Press of Kansas, 1996.

INDEX

Pecos, Texas, 6

Pendleton Round-Up (Pendleton, Oregon), 8, 12, 93; Akridge at, 23; Askin at, 294; Baldwin at, 55, 57; Blancett at, 119; Bowman at, 127, 206, 207, 208; and Byers, 18; Canutt at, 289; Crosby at, 45, 123, 172, 202, 207; and discrimination, 10; Fletcher at, 76; Gibson at, 205; Greenough (Turk) at, 128, 352; and Kaepernik, 10; Mansfield at, 27; McCarroll, Bonnie (Treadwell) at, 66, 105, 171, 356; Merritt at, 162; and relay racing, 50; Roach at, 59; rodeo programs of, 362, 363; Rude at, 151; Rutherford at, 241; and Ryan, 18, 292; and saddlery, 97, 99, 105, 116, 127; Stahl at, 76; Strickland (Mabel) at, 19; Tegland at, 160; Trickey at, 58, 120, 163; and trophy saddle, 122, 123; Truan at, 213; and United Cowboys Turtle Association, 78

Pennsylvania rodeos, 17, 59, 60, 110, 153, 163, 183

Peterson, Lorena Trickey. *See* Trickey, Lorena (Peterson)

Peterson, Magnus, 58

Pettigrew, Homer, 33–34, 184, 211, 216, 220

Philadelphia, Pennsylvania, 17, 59, 60, 110, 153, 163, 183

Phoenix, Arizona, 186, 203

Pickett, Bill, 7, 8, 32, 101, 352, 360

Pickett Brothers Bronco Busters and Rough Riders, 8

Pickford, Mary, 58

Pickup man/men, 10, 29, 300

Piggin' string, 25, 26, 43

Pikes Peak or Bust Rodeo (Colorado Springs, Colorado), 370, 371

Plymouth Cordage Company, 25, 43, 47, 147, 207, 214, 215

Plymouth Lariat Trophy, 206

Plymouth Trophy buckle/belt plate, 215

Point-award systems, 81

Poker Chip (horse), 36

Police Gazette, 202

Posters, 317, 358–61

Pow Wow rodeo, 187

Powder Horn (horse), 45

Powder River Saddlery Company, 128, 132–33

Pow-Wow Committee, 184

Pratt Institute, 330

PRCA Champion All Around Cowboy, 140

Prescott, Arizona rodeos, 6–7, 12, 145. *See also* Prescott Frontier Days rodeo (Prescott, Arizona)

Prescott Frontier Days rodeo (Prescott, Arizona), 6, 27, 35, 93, 161, 199, 206, 295

Prince of Wales Challenge Trophy, 30, 60, 189

Princely Tailors, 263

Princess Mohawk's Wild West Hippodrome, 59

Professional Bull Riders (PBR), 92

Professional Rodeo Cowboy Association (PRCA), 93, 140, 193; belt buckle awarded to Mansfield, 231; and Frost, 232, 261; and Gay (Neal), 92; and Ivory, 313; and order of rodeo performances, 22; organization of, 90; and point system, 15, 75

Programs, rodeo, 69, 70, 88, 158, 317, 358, 362–73

Purdy, Ikua, 44

Purse awards, 76, 78, 82, 83, 90, 92, 145

Queen of Sheba, The, 58

R. D. Barnes Saddlery Company, 136

R. J. Reynolds Tobacco Company, 317, 346–52

R. Schaezlein and Son Silversmiths, 147, 204, 205, 212, 221, 223, 226, 229, 230

R. T. Frazier Saddlery Company, 268

Race discrimination, 7, 10, 76

Ragsdale, Bob, 26

Ranch (Sponsor) Girls, 53, 68, 69, 70

Ranch Romances magazine, 59, 147, 179

Ranch Romances trophy, 178–79

Rand, Sally, 352

Randall, Lynn, 257, 283, 312, 313

Randolph, Florence Hughes, 59–60, 66, 67, 106, 163; boots of, 302, 303; chaps of, 295; at Chicago Championship Rodeo, 170; at Chicago World's Fair Rodeo, 179; at Madison Square Garden rodeo, 168, 170; at Southwestern Exposition and Fat Stock Show, 182

Randolph, Floyd, 60

Rawhide Spurs, 243

Real Wild West and Rough Riders of the World show (Tim McCoy), 7

Red Rock (rodeo bull), 40, 232, 355

Red's Clothing Company, 261

Reed and Barton Silver Company, 155

Reins, 29

Relay racing, 45, 50–51, 151; of Barnes (Lucas), 60–61, 293; of Blancett, 119; and female athletes, 53, 55, 62; of Sperry (Fannie), 354; of Strickland (Mabel), 19; of Trickey, 57, 58, 120, 151, 157, 163, 234; trophy cup for, 154, 155

Remington, Frederic, 317

Reno, Nevada, 30, 177, 369

Reserve National Insurance Company of Oklahoma City, 193

Resistol Hat Company, 92, 247, 256, 260, 261

The following photographs appear uncaptioned on the pages noted:

Frontispiece:

[?] Irwin on Light Foot *(detail)*
Venue unknown, 1918
Doubleday-Foster Photo Company, publisher
NCM—Dickinson Research Center
McCarroll Family Trust Collection, RC2006.076.005-1

Endpaper (front) and Part I (pages 2–3):

Panoramic Photograph *(detail)*
Cheyenne Frontier Days Rodeo
Cheyenne, Wyoming, July 1927
Ralph Russell Doubleday, photographer
Loan courtesy Mrs. Roberta Crosby Burkstaller, LR.214.29

Part II (pages 94–95) and Endpaper (back):

Panoramic Photograph *(detail)*
Southwest Exposition and Fat Stock Rodeo
Coliseum, Fort Worth, Texas, March 1930
J. T. Brown, photographer
NCM—Dickinson Research Center, Permanent Collection, 1990.46.05

Part III (pages 374–75):

Cowboys and Cowgirls at the 15th Annual World's Championship Rodeo *(detail)*
Madison Square Garden, New York City
New York, October 9–17, 1940
DeVere Helfrich, photographer
NCM—Dickinson Research Center
DeVere Helfrich Collection, 1981.023.00058A

LONGHORN RESTAUR

SOUTHWEST EXPOSITION AND FAT STOC
COLISEUM. FORT WOR